Legacy of The Lancasters

Martin W. Bowman

Pen & Sword
AVIATION

First published in Great Britain in 2013 by
Pen and Sword Aviation

An imprint of
Pen & Sword Books Ltd
47 Church Street
Barnsley
South Yorkshire
S70 2AS

ISBN 978 1 78303 007 1

A CIP catalogue record for this book is
available from the British Library

Printed and bound in India by Replika Press Pvt. Ltd.

Pen & Sword Books Ltd incorporates the Imprints of Pen & Sword Aviation,
Pen & Sword Family History, Pen & Sword Maritime, Pen & Sword Military,
Pen & Sword Discovery, Wharncliffe Local History, Wharncliffe True Crime,
Wharncliffe Transport, Pen & Sword Select, Pen & Sword Military Classics,
Leo Cooper, The Praetorian Press, Remember When, Seaforth Publishing and
Frontline Publishing

For a complete list of Pen & Sword titles please contact
PEN & SWORD BOOKS LIMITED
47 Church Street, Barnsley, South Yorkshire, S70 2AS, England
E-mail: enquiries@pen-and-sword.co.uk
Website: www.pen-and-sword.co.uk

Contents

Bibliography

At First Sight; A Factual and anecdotal account of No.627 Squadron RAF. Alan B. Webb. 1991.
*Bomber County: A History of the Royal Air Force in Lincolnshire.*Terry Hancock (Midland 2004)
Enemy Coast Ahead. Wing Commander Guy Gibson VC DSO* DFC*
Barnes Wallis' Bombs: Tallboy, Dambuster & Grand Slam. Stephen Flower (Tempus 2002)
Dambuster - A Life of Guy Gibson VC. Susan Ottaway (Pen & Sword).
Never So Young Again. Dan Brennan (George Allen & Unwin Ltd 1943)
A Square Peg. Peter Bone (Privately Published)
Thundering Through the Clear Air: No. 61 (Lincoln Imp) Squadron At War . Derek Brammer
     (Tucann Books 1997).
Not Just Another Milk Run; The Mailly-le-Camp Bomber Raid. Molly Burkett & Geoff Gilbert
     (Barny Books 2004).
Ged Pykeston's History File. RAF Waddington Sentry Magazine.
Legend of the Lancasters. Martin W Bowman (Pen & Sword, 2009).
Flying Into the Flames of Hell. Martin W Bowman (Pen & Sword, 2006).
Pathfinder. W / C Bill Anderson OBE DFC AFC (Jarrolds London 1946).
Gunner's Moon. John Bushby (Futura 1974).
The Bomber Command War Diaries: An Operational reference book 1939-1945. Martin Middlebrook
     and Chris Everitt. (Midland 1985).
*RAF Evaders: The Comprehensive Story of Thousands of Escapers and their Escape Lines, Western
     Europe, 1940-1945.* Oliver Clutton-Brock (Grub Street 2009).
Boots, Bikes & Bombers. Eric Jones (Unpublished manuscript)
A Lancaster Pilot's Impression on Germany. Richard 'Dick' Starkey (Compaid Graphics, Preston
     1999 & 2004).
A Member of the RAF of Indeterminate Race. Cy Grant (Woodfield 2006)
*Over Hell & High Water: My Flying Experiences with Bomber Command & South East Asia
     Command during WW2* . Leslie Parsons (Woodfield Publishing Bognor Regis 2001)
Men With Wings . 'Sandy' Powell (Allan Wingate 1957)
Guns In The Sky: The Air Gunners of World War Two. Chaz Bowyer (J. M. Dent & Sons Ltd 1979)
The Dambuster Who Cracked the Dam: The Story of Melvin 'Dinghy' Young. Arthur G. Thorning
     (Pen & Sword 2008)
The Dambusters. John Sweetman, David Coward and Gary Johnstone (Time Warner 2003)
World War II Fighting Jets. Jeffrey Ethell & Alfred Price (Airlife 1994)
Lancaster At War: 3 . Mike Garbett and Brian Goulding (Ian Allan Ltd 1984).
Round The Clock by Philip Kaplan and Jack Currie (Cassell 1993)
Maximum Effort: The Story of the North Lincolnshire Bombers. Patrick Otter (Archive Publications
     Ltd / Grimsby Evening Telegraph 1990).
Thundering Through The Clear Air: No.61 (Lincoln Imp) Squadron at War. Derek Brammer,
     (TUCANN books 1997).
Flying Into Hell. Mel Rolfe (Grub Street 2001)
Into the Silk. Ian Mackersey (Granada Publishing Ltd 1978)
Chased By The Sun; The Australians in Bomber Command in WWII. Hank Nelson (ABC Books 2002)
Glory Refused: The Memoirs of a teenage rocket pilot of the Third Reich. Joachim Hoehne with
     Randall Holden (2004)
The 'Quiet Life' of a Bomber Pilot. Peter Clowes writing in Wingspan magazine, February 1995
RAF Bomber Command Losses of the Second World War . W R Chorley (Midland)
RAF Bomber Command Losses of the Second World War Volume 9 Roll of Honour 1939-1947. W R
     Chorley (Midland)
Hitler's Jet Plane: the Me 262 story. Mano Ziegler Pilot and Designer (Greenhill 2004)
Air War Diary: An Australian in Bomber Command. David Scholes DFC (Kangaroo Press 1997)
Three Passions and a Lucky Penny; an autobiography. Eric Stephenson (Air Power Development
     Centre 2008)

Author's Introduction

Young or old, nine or ninety, everyone has heard of the Lancaster bomber. Such is the legacy handed down by this aviation icon that although it is not the most numerous aircraft ever built - two are still flying today, one in Britain and another in Canada and many are proudly displayed in museums throughout the world - it is up there with the Spitfire and the Flying Fortress in terms of affection, nostalgia and lasting fame. Statistics indicate that: Total tonnage of HE bombs dropped on primary targets by 6,500 of the 7,366 Lancasters built reached 608,612 in 156,192 sorties. Packed together, the bombs could fill a goods train 345 miles long. Lancasters accounted for two thirds of the total tonnage dropped by the whole of Bomber Command during March 1942 to May 1945. Average of four tons per bomber, equalled 150,000 sorties using a total of 228 million gallons of fuel. Total incendiaries dropped by Lancasters, 51,513,106. - In comparing the bomb tonnage dropped with aircraft lost, Stirling amounted to 41 tons, Halifax to 51 tons, Lancaster to 132 tons. Between February 1942 and May 1945 3,431 Lancasters and approximately 24,000 aircrew failed to return from operations. By March 1945 there were no less than 56 squadrons of Lancasters in front-line service with Bomber Command.

What is rarely mentioned is that the legendary Lancaster has bequeathed to the world, an invaluable heritage beloved of generations of movie-goers, air show enthusiasts, readers of fine literature and historians alike. Exploits such as the famous low-level raid by 617 Squadron on Germany's hydro electric dams on the night of 16/17 May 1943, the nightly raids on Germany and the sinking of the *Tirpitz* in 1945 are all without equal. On 29 October 1944 47 Lancasters (18 from 9 Squadron and 18 from 617 Squadron) attacked the *Tirpitz*, which was moored near the Norwegian port of Tromsø. 32 Lancasters dropped 'Tallboy' bombs on estimated position of the capital ship but no direct hits were scored. On 12 November 30 Lancasters of 9 and 617 Squadrons attacked the *Tirpitz* again and at least two 'Tallboys' hit the ship, which capsized to remain bottom upwards. It has always been a bone of contention between 617 and 9 Squadrons as to whose bombs actually capsized the *Tirpitz* and over the years a piece of metal from the battleship has often been 'removed' from the respective mess of each unit! Today 617 is still a front line squadron (operating the Tornado) long after the demise of nearly all other wartime units. Service rivalry being what it is; in April 1982 when the first eight Tornado GR.Is of 617 'Dam Busters' Squadron arrived at Marham and upstaged the 'Tanker Trash', not to be outdone, the old guard was soon referring to the shiny new upstarts as 'The Dim Bastards'. And, according to the Victor fraternity, MRCA stood for 'Much Refurbished Canberra Aircraft'

The Dam Busters are perhaps the most famous bomber squadron in history. Post war thousands of readers read avidly the exploits of Guy Gibson and his crews and in 1955 thousands more viewed the thrilling spectacle of the Dams' raid unfold on cinema screens. Geoff Mayer in his *Guide to British Cinema* (Greenwood Press 2003) says that Richard Todd, who played the part of Guy Gibson, claimed that

The Dam Busters 'was the best military war picture ever made' and that 'the box office receipts in 1955 provided support' for his 'assertion'. The film was rightly nominated for Best British Film and Best Film from Any Source at the 1956 BAFTA Awards. Mayer added: 'The Dam Busters is a sturdy example of the popular cycle of mid-1950s films that looked back to World War II as a means to celebrate British military achievements and sacrifices during that period.'

To those who wish to denigrate the significance of the raid, the 'Dam Busters' proved that the war in Europe was being prosecuted dramatically well at a time most of President Roosevelt's advisers were committed to targeting Japan first. The raids forced the Nazis to rebuild and fortify the dams and in the process divert 10,000 war workers it could ill-afford to move from other tasks. Luftwaffe aircraft also had to be brought in from other areas to strengthen the defences in the Ruhr dams region, and as for the effect on German morale; it was nothing short of catastrophic.

One of the Dam Busters, Edward C. Johnson DFC, recalled that in 1988 at Derwent Water where 617 practiced shortly before the raid on 16/17 May 1943 - 'practically the whole of Lancashire and Yorkshire came to see us - estimates went up as high as 50,000 people.' Although the dam on the Ladybower Reservoir was completed in 1943 it did not actually hold any water when 617 Squadron were training. During the 50th anniversary of the raid on Wednesday 19 May 1993 the BBMF Lancaster (PA474) memorably crested the parapet of the Derwent Dam and flew between its twin towers. Present were former Dam Buster pilots, Les Munro and Joe McCarthy and Richard Todd and several thousand spectators packed into

Below: Richard Todd and a black Labrador representing Guy Gibson's dog during a break in the filming of *The Dam Busters* in 1954. In the last scene in the film, which involves Wallis and Gibson when the crew losses are known, Gibson says that he 'has letters to write'. Todd was not just acting out his lines. During the war Todd had had to write 'a lot of letters' to bereaved relatives of soldiers under his command. On the eve of D-Day, 6 June 1944, Todd was a 23 year old First Lieutenant in the 7th Light Infantry Battalion, 5th Parachute Brigade.

Above: Eric Coates' who penned the *Dam Busters March* which is as popular today as it was when it made the Top Ten in 1955 and remained there for more than a year.

the length and breadth of the Derwent Valley. PA474 has also flown over Uppingham (Rutland Water) and Abberton near Colchester where the 'Dam Busters' also practiced before the famous dams' raid.

The legend of the Dam Busters lives on. Edward Johnson said in 1993 that 'Among other things it made serious inroads into the English language on a universal scale. If there is a sale in a High Street shop - it must be a 'pricebuster'; if you used to be a 'bobby' in the police force, you must now be a 'crimebuster'; games on TV have now become 'blockbusters'; there are films now called 'Ghostbusters' and even a Black & Decker car vacuum cleaner became a 'dustbuster'. More seriously, one thinks about the comradeship which developed as a result of being a '617 type'.'

The memorable *Dam Busters March* written by composer Eric Coates, which made the Top Ten in 1955 and remained there for more than a year is still popular at functions and events today. It is even played before the start of every football match at Derby County's ground.

Generations of TV viewers continue to watch the 'Dam Busters' and the equally riveting *Appointment In London* - Philip Leacock's feature film about wartime Lancaster squadron, premiered in 1953. Its star, a young Dirk Bogarde, is obviously based on the legendary Leonard Cheshire who flew something like 100 bomber operations, the majority of them on Lancasters.

There is talk of a Dam Busters' 'version two' but nothing will ever match the original. In the meantime we continue to view and attend anything and everything on the Lancaster, whether it is a documentary, repeat showing of the feature films or a news item, such as the BBMF Lancaster sailing serenely over Buckingham Palace accompanied by the Spitfire and Hurricane, or dropping poppies over the Bomber Command Memorial.

In the years immediately following World War Two it became traditional for a Spitfire and Hurricane to lead the Victory Day fly past over London. From this event evolved the idea to form an historic collection of flyable aircraft, initially to commemorate the participation by the RAF in the Battle of Britain and later, to commemorate the RAF's involvement in all the campaigns of WWII. Thus on 11 July 1957 the Historic Aircraft Flight was formed at RAF Biggin Hill, Kent, probably the most famous of all the Battle of Britain stations. The Flight began with three Rolls-Royce Griffon-engined Mk XIX Spitfires and Hurricane LF363, believed to be the last 'Hurri' to enter RAF service. In November 1961 the Flight moved to Norfolk, first to RAF Horsham St. Faith (now Norwich Airport) and then on 1 April 1963, to RAF Coltishall, which had been a 12 Group Station in Fighter Command.

There have been 36 Lancs that famously recorded 100 or more wartime operations and all but one of them was unceremoniously reduced to scrap after the end of hostilities so PA474 has represented several centenarians after more 'humble' beginnings. In 1964 PA474 was painted in a camouflage scheme, though without squadron markings. During this period the Lanc took part in two major feature films - *Operation Crossbow* and *The Guns of Navarone*. PA474 was to have been put on permanent display at RAF Hendon but fortunately a decision was taken to return the bomber to flying condition. The aircraft eventually joined the Flight in November 1973 and it wore the markings of the Lancaster (KM-B) flown by Squadron Leader John Nettleton on 44 Squadron who was awarded the Victoria

Cross for his heroism on the Augsburg raid, 17 April 1942. Following the 1979 season the Lancaster was repainted as ED932 AJ-G of 617 Squadron flown by Wing Commander Guy Gibson DSO* DFC* on the Ruhr dams' raid of 16/17 May 1943.

PA474's next scheme, in 1984, was as SR-D of 101 Squadron, followed in 1988 as PM-M² - better known as Mike Squared, which served on 103 and 576 Squadrons and completed 140 operational sorties, a Bomber Command record. In May 1974 PA474 was christened *City of Lincoln* and city's coat of arms was proudly displayed to the left hand side of aircraft just forward of the cockpit in recognition of the county's strong association with the Lancaster and Bomber Command. At a ceremony at Waddington on 8 May 1975, shortly before the BBMF moved from RAF Coltishall in Norfolk to RAF Coningsby, the City of Lincoln formally adopted PA474. In 1993-94 the size of the nose art of *Still Going Strong!* (better known as Johnnie Walker) applied to the left hand side of the aircraft resulted in the name and coat of arms having to be moved to the right hand side of the aircraft, where it has remained ever since. W4964 WS-J on 9 Squadron flew its 100th operation on 15 September 1944 when 9 and 617 'Dam Busters' Squadrons carried out the first attack on the *Tirpitz* from Russia. After dropping its 12,000lb 'tallboy' bomb, Flight Lieutenant Doug Melrose and his crew returned to Bardney to receive a well-earned crate of whiskey.

From 2000 to 2 October 2006 PA474 flew in the markings and livery of Lancaster III EE176 QR-M *Mickey the Moocher* of 61 Squadron stationed at Skellingthorpe. In 2007 the BBMF Lancaster emerged as *'Phantom of the Rhur'*.

We must never overlook the fact that the Lancaster was forged in war to destroy Britain's enemies but the part it played in winning the peace largely because of the bravery of the crews of Bomber Command is undiminished. Leave them their Glory.

Martin W. Bowman, Norwich 2013.

Acknowledgements

I would like to express my appreciation to my fellow author, friend and colleague, Graham Simons, for getting the book to press ready standard and for his detailed work on the photographs; to Pen & Sword and in particular, Laura Hirst; and Jon Wilkinson, for yet another superb jacket and to the following people and organisations for their immense contributions of stories and photos: 49 Squadron Association; 'Bluey' Arthurs; Ralph Barker; BBMF; Andy Bird; David Bussey; Chris Cannon; Audrey Grealy; Terry Hancock; Johnny Johnson; Eric Jones; Phil King; Terry Millward; Nigel McTeer; Norwich Central Library and the 2nd Air Division Memorial Library, Norwich; Terry Owen; Corriene Simons; Claire Simons; Dick Starkey; Paul Wilson.

Prologue

Never So Young Again

'All set, Broughton?' Kershaw asked.

The Aldis lamp near the Control Tower flashed a green light.

'Sure. What the hell,' said Broughton. 'Sure.'

You depressed the guns, so there was room to get braced and opened the turret doors: if anything happened you would not be caught with the doors jammed. The Aldis lamp near the Control Tower flashed a green light. The engine's roar deepened quickly.

'OK Mack?' Broughton asked. Then, 'all set, you chaps? Here we go.' You felt the engines suddenly accelerated. The fuselage trembled, shook. There was the sensation of moving a little.

Then the aircraft was rushing along between the flare pots. You watched the number of flares increase on both sides until there was a long twin row behind, then you felt the tail rise and you were riding high, looking out between the guns, knowing you weren't airborne yet, still rushing on between the flares. God, why doesn't it lift? Suddenly you were scared. You saw the long diminishing length of the flare path behind, you grabbed the butt end of the guns and got braced. Maybe, nothing would happen. In your mind you saw the burning wreckage on the edge of the field. God, would this aircraft ever come off the ground? Darkness and flares rushed past on both sides.

'Blast!' Broughton panted. 'It won't climb! Hell! Blast!'

The aircraft bumped, rose, touched ground again, rose slightly again.

'Watch it! Watch it!' shouted Kershaw.

'Blast! Oh, blast!' Broughton yelled, panting.

You crouched and got your back braced against the wall of the turret, then you felt the aircraft rise from the ground, heard one of the engines miss, splutter, catch, then miss again, then sinking slowly. 'Oh, God!' one of the wings slowly going down, thinking, terrified. 'Oh, God!' with the darkness rushing past underneath and then Broughton's yelling, 'We're going to prang! Get set! We're going to prang!' Then the shocking, tearing, jouncing impact with the guns and glass perspex vanishing, everything whirling, roaring, faster and faster and blurred rushing streaks of light and then a smashing blow on the head and another on the back and across the shoulders. Then going up and up, bodiless, no feeling; no sight, only darkness and then something tearing at your face, knowing suddenly branches of a tree were clawing at your neck and bare hands and you were still falling, thumping. Oh, God, God, I'm dying, this is it. Then falling ceased and you opened your eyes, or rather you were no longer in a-whirling; rushing darkness. You saw yourself kneeling on the ground. You felt outside your body, kneeling looking over at yourself. You stood up. On the other side of the field, a jagged crest of flame made a roaring crackling sound. Then you heard the ammunition cans exploding. You started to run and fell down. You heard a big explosion, saw a pink flame mushroom suddenly in the middle of the white flame and the white flame expand. There was the steady crackling of the ammunition; and then you were standing again, running. You fell over something in the dark and reached out and felt something dark and lumpy and smelled burning flesh. You rolled it over and saw it was Ed. His flying suit was smoking and charred and in a flash of flame from the burning aircraft you saw his hair was burnt off and part of his face was black. He lay on his back, his eyes open and part of his nose gone.

'Ed!' you yelled and grabbed him by the shoulders, 'Ed!' knowing he was dead. You held him by the shoulders and raised him a little off the ground, as if there were something you might do to help him. His head fell back and his eyes rolled white. He was very dead and you knelt there and looked at the aircraft burning. Then after a long moment thinking started again and you let go of him, stood up and ran toward the aircraft. The grass around it was on fire and you felt the heat from the melting fuselage. God, oh, God, why doesn't the crash wagon come? They're burning to death in there. You saw the flames grow higher, felt the heat, knew you could not get any closer. Where the hell was the crash wagon? You ran across the field, aware of the rain for the first time. Your clothes were soaked, your face was wet and you fell in a ditch and could not get up. You told yourself you were all right, yet you had no desire to move. You lay in the rain and heard the crash wagon go clanging past on the road above. Go on, part of your mind said, get up; go on. You lay perfectly still in the mud and did not care. You felt yourself passing out and tried to hold your eyes open with your fingers. They were burning to death back there in the aircraft. All you had to do was stand up and yell. Somebody would come. You raised your head, opened your mouth on no sound and heard someone hurrying behind you. Turning, somebody put the beam of a flashlight in your eyes. You got to your knees and stood up. They were back there burning to death. You moved, stumbled, someone caught you. You pushed them away.' 'They're burning to death,' you yelled. 'They're—

'Come on, feller. They've had it. The crash wagon's trying to get them out. Are you all right?'

'Get them out.'

'Don't worry. The crash killed them. How'd it happen? Are you sure you are all right?'

'Yes. I'm all right. Can't they get any of them out?'

'No. Come on.'

'Ed's over there.'

'I know. We found him.'

An oxygen bottle exploded. You must have jerked and stopped. 'Come on, Mack,' said a voice. You recognised one of the medical attendants. 'Come on,' said the voice.

'It's all right. Come on, Mack.'

'Maybe they're still alive.'

'Come on, Mack. They've had it.'

Dan Brennan

Chapter 1

A Yank in the RAF

Where are the flyers from Canada's prairies,
From cities and forests, determined to win,
Thumbing their noses at Goering's Luftwaffe
And busily dropping their bombs on Berlin?
Lancasters Audrey Grealy

It was dawn when you left the briefing-room after interrogation. Outside the air was cold and damp. Chill moisture blew in the cold wind off the bare dirt fields as you walked slowly along the road from the sergeants' mess to the Nissen huts. You opened the door of your room and went in. Sitting on the edge of the bed you undressed. Craven was in his bed, the covers pulled over his head. You were exhausted. You heard Craven move and sit up in bed. You looked over at him. He was smiling faintly, sitting up, a grease-stained outline of his oxygen mask still on his face.

'Have a good trip?' he asked. He reached over on to the table near his bed and got a cigarette and his lighter.

'Not bad. Usual stuff, you know. Hot enough.' He put the cigarette in his lips and looked suddenly at me as if to see if I was watching him. I noticed his hand was shaking as he held the flame of the lighter to the end of the cigarette.

'I'm really in the soup!' he said. 'Turned back again.'

'What's the trouble?'

He shrugged his shoulders. 'I don't know. Oil pressure dropped down and I said to hell with it, we'll go back.' He didn't sound too sure about what he was saying. Still, it was none of my business.

'Glad you're back,' he said. 'I suppose you know we lost two crews.' He seemed to be watching you as if he were waiting for you to say something. You couldn't tell what he was getting at. He smoked the cigarette in a hurry and lit another.

'Yes,' I said and got into bed. 'New crews, weren't they? Hell of a place to send fresher crews.'

'You know, Mack - I had a feeling you weren't coming back tonight.'

'They're not going to get me now, brother. Only two trips to go.'

'I know this must sound silly,' he said. 'Look,' he pointed to an old tin candy-box on his table. 'I've just got an itching feeling I'm going to cop it one of these nights. I've got

some letters in there. Wonder if you'd mail them for me. You know, just in case.'

He kept looking as if he wanted to tell me something. You could sense it.

'What's the matter Dickie? Something's really got you.'

'Guess I've lost my nerve.' He looked away.

'Hooey. You just think you have.'

'No. There really wasn't anything wrong with the engine tonight. I just panicked and turned back.'

'You'll be all right.'

'No. I'm finished, I know it.'

'I know how you feel,' you said.

'No,' he said, shaking his head. 'You don't know what it's really like. Each trip I get worse.'

'Have you told the CO?'

'Sure. He thinks I'm trying to pull a fast one. This is the tenth time in twenty-five trips that I've turned back.'

'Don't quit. Can't you just force yourself to go on?'

Craven dinched out his cigarette. There was an abstracted look in his eyes.

'No. I just think up excuses, or take any little thing that comes along and use it for a reason to turn back.'

'You'll come out of it.'

'You've never seen anybody with it bad.'

'Maybe I'm seeing one now?'

'You are, brother. If only we hadn't been shot-up so damn badly on those first trips.'

'That's what started it?' you asked.

'Yes, but I'm hopeless now.'

'What about your crew? What do they think?'

'They think I'm all right.'

'You are up a tree.'

He sat there chewing his lips.

'You know I'm not pulling a fast one, don't you?'

'Sure Dickie, sure. I believe you.'

'You don't just think I'm trying to duck out, do you, Mack?'

'No Dickie. I know how you feel.'

'No, no' he said insistently. 'I know how you feel. But you don't know what it's really like to be so damn scared your legs get paralysed just from thinking about crossing the Dutch coast.'

You could help only yourself in this business. 'Nerves' were a personal matter.

'You don't think I'm just packing in, do you?' he went on, his voice jerky.

'I've got to get some sleep Dickie. You see the MO. He'll fix you up. Everything will be OK.'

I slid under the covers and pulled them over my head to keep my face from getting cold when I was asleep.

'Good night Dickie'. I heard the click of his cigarette-lighter.

'Good night Mack,' he said.

But even under the covers it was still cold in the room, but you did not get up to put on another sweater or Dickie would start talking again. You were too tired for talk. Too tired for anything. Two crews were missing. Ellsworth and Price they had said, in interrogation. At six in the morning still no word from them. Their names scrubbed off the board. What sweethearts, wives, fathers, mothers would get a telegram in what part of the world today? You tried to remember who were in the two crews. You could not even remember their names. Well, none of them were your friends. But did it matter much now even if friends did not come back? You did not think it would. Death now was no more astonishing than catching a train. After a while you went to sleep.

The next morning at crew conference the report came through from Met that the weather was perfect over the Continent and at eleven o'clock that morning in the gunnery office we heard there was a call on, overload petrol tanks, a long trip.

'Say that was rough on old Harris, wasn't it?' Harry said. You were sitting now on the table in the gunnery-room. 'They got a bearing on him about two hundred miles off the coast. Never heard a word after that. He was a cocky son of a bitch. Always figured he'd finish a tour, didn't you?'

'Brother,' you laughed - you thought how lucky you were to be here - many were not after last night, 'never figure on anybody finishing until they've got the thirty trips right in the old log-book,' you said.

'Oh, what the hell,' Harry said. 'We're going to get through. I just have that feeling.'

'You'll need it, brother.'

Harry laughed. 'Goddam' he said, 'I really thought we'd had it last night, for a while. Did you see how close that stuff was bursting? Man, man, I just folded my arms and waited.' He smiled to himself.

You said: 'Hey, Hey, when it starts boomphing along under the fuselage.'

Harry grinned. You laughed. It was fun now to be back and talking about it.

We checked and, harmonised our guns and went back to the warmth of the mess, the *Daily Mirror,* the ceaseless dice and card games, the fire in the hearth holding out the damp cold air. And so after lunch we were again seated around the fire, dozing, talking and listening to the wireless. The bar was open and Harry and you drank two beers, listening to another air gunner playing the piano in one corner of the lounge. After a while you looked at the clock over the doorway. Two o'clock. Two hours until briefing. Where were we going? Overload tanks. A long trip. Where?

'At three o'clock you walked back to your billet, went down to your room and wrote two letters home, changed your shoes and put on two pairs of warm woollen socks and your flying boots and stuck a flashlight in between your socks and boot so that one boot bulged on the outside. Then you slipped your flying sweater on. You felt no apprehension. It was your twenty-ninth trip; an unreal world of fire, smoke, death and fatigue was now almost as ordinary as the old world of going to work in a newspaper office. You sealed the letters; there was nothing in them; only that you were all right and hoped everyone at home was all right. You couldn't think of anything to write. You went out and along the road to the briefing-room, thinking of Diana, wishing you were going to be with her tonight.

And then the room was full of everybody, navigators moving up and down the aisles between the tables, green canvas bags full of maps and instruments heavy against their legs, gunners, pilots, wireless operators, bomb aimers, talking over their white turtle-neck flying sweaters, loose about their throats, each crew getting seated at their table. The door clashed and closed at the back of the room. Just then the wireless operator, gunner and bomb aimer came up and slid in on the benches by the table.

The wing commander, twenty-six years old, a dark-haired young man, took the platform.

'Make it a real prang!' he stood there smiling. 'Special recco' and he tapped his chest, made a funny self-deprecating face and the room roared with laughter.

'I notice the Wingco isn't on tonight,' the bomb aimer said.

'Hell, you can't blame him. If you could pick your targets and scrub yourself when you wanted to, you'd do it,' Fred Maisenbacker a young Canadian gunner with a black moustache and a nice smile, two generations removed from tonight's target said.

'It's hardly fair, though, being exempt from danger when someone else in the same job isn't,' the bomb aimer said.

'This isn't love we're playing at, brother.'

'You're not kidding. But I'll settle for the Victory medal and long-service ribbon,' the bomb aimer grinned.

Now, raising his voice above the murmur of voices, the wing commander spoke to the room: 'You all know the target tonight. I'll give you the latest gen.' He looked slowly round the room and began to smile. 'Gentlemen,' he said, quietly smiling, 'it's low-level tonight.' He stood there grinning. A sighing Phew! went up from the crowded room. The target was Stuttgart! Great God!

The Intelligence Officer, holding a wooden pointer in one hand, a sheaf of papers in the other, came between the tables and stood up on the stage in front of the map. He began to speak on the importance of the target, the last time it was bombed, where the defences were heaviest, where the searchlights were thickest. Sitting there you heard again all the instructions, position of defences, routes, target. All of it entered your mind, while another part of you saw and thought only of Diana.

You looked at the target map of the city between your hands on the table, while in front, on the stage, the bomb leader was giving a few last-minute instructions to the bomb aimers. Pop had been to Berlin before. He would remember it as a long hectic trip because there had been so many variations of course to make, so many new winds to find. Still, you knew he was not worried. He had been through too much to worry. You hoped Craven would be all right. In the old days Craven had been a good pilot. Anybody would have flown with him. But not now, after all those turn-backs and then later just blankly refusing to fly without any apparent reason. Pop had only told Craven to quit out of sympathy, hoping that somehow his sympathy would in some way help to restore Craven's confidence. No one, you felt, had a right to quit unless their nerve was really gone. And you did not believe Craven had ever been like that. You could tell when someone was really finished. Craven, you felt, had quit. Still he might be wrong. Many would like to quit, you thought, many; and we're all scared but we go on. You sat looking at the map of Berlin. You had been scared so many times, but you had gone on. Yes, maybe if Craven got through this one okay a little of his old confidence would return.

The intelligence officer finished.

After that the weather man stood on the stage and with a pointer explained on a tacked-up meteorological map of Europe the weather situation. The room was quiet and everybody looked intently at the wall with the map on it. Everybody was listening carefully and in a few moments the weather man finished and left the stage. The weather is not too bad, you thought. A cold frost over the Dutch coast, but we can climb over it easily.

Maisenbacker caught Craven's eye and grinned. 'Well, here's the ropey lot,' he said and smiling nicely gestured round the table at the others. Craven smiled and nodded hello round the table. 'Hardly a bit of gravy tonight, eh?' Maisenbacker said, with a little laugh.

'It won't be too bad,' Craven said, hoping his voice sounded confident. Mustn't worry, you knew he was thinking.

'Helluva nice spot to come back to Ops on,' Maisenbacker said.

'Oh I don't know' Craven said. 'Lots of worse places. Better than Essen. Besides, it ought to make all the people happy who read the *Daily Mirror*. Really a *Daily Mirror* raid, isn't it?'

'Maybe you'd rather go to Essen instead? Just so you'll be doing some real war work,' Maisenbacker grinned.

'All the same to me,' Craven said. 'I don't give a damn where we go. Long as you get back is what counts.'

' You're not kidding, brother,' Maisenbacker said. He had been shot-up twice out of two trips. In the beginning, before he had seen a target, he had been very keen. Now he was not so keen, you knew, but he was probably more careful.

'Guns OK?' Craven asked.

'Everything jake. Harmonised and tested them this morning,' Maisenbacker said, still smiling his nice easy smile. Craven did not smile back. His gaze returned to the tape on the board.

When briefing was finished, everyone came out and got on their bicycles. And now, when briefing was finished, everyone came out and got on their bicycles. You saw Craven standing alone, looking as if he were remembering being alone like this before and the worry had not started yet. Sometimes it started before briefing. Sometimes after. You never knew when. But Craven might still feel all right. Maybe, you thought, he might go all the way through the trip not worrying. Maybe he was all right again now. But you knew he wasn't sure.

We trooped back to the mess to tea, to news on the wireless, the tireless piano, the patient clock over the door. Harry and you lounged by the fire, waiting for the buses. We sat there saying nothing, looking into the fire. Hell, if anything should happen tonight? Our twenty-ninth trip.

Finally operational tea was finished, the plates of eggs-and-bacon and cups of hot tea and everybody talking and joking or not talking and joking and the bus ride out past the farm-house by the potato-field and the locker-room crowded with everybody pulling their gear out of their lockers. Finally all that was behind and Craven looked confident and happy standing by the aircraft, four-engined, rearing big on clean black tyres on the concrete dispersal point, with the windmill in the field behind silhouetted against a fading western sky.

Now in February it was always dark when we rode along in the bus to flights and so dark by the aircraft we had to use torches to see our way around and under the fuselage. You shone your torch on the perspex of the turret to see if it was clean.

One of the armourers came over.

'Back early in the morning?' he asked.

You rubbed a spot off the perspex and looked at him.

'Yes, about five o'clock.' Yes, you thought, reassuring yourself, five o'clock. What the hell, it's only another raid. You've done plenty. Why worry now?

'Next to your last trip, isn't it?'

You laugh, thinking he might have said 'last.'

He smiled, understanding what you had thought.

'Piece of cake for you lads,' he clapped your back with one hand.

Low-level, you thought. Stuttgart! Hell of a place for low-level. You had seen it before. It wasn't too comfortable a target even from fifteen thousand feet.

'Anybody see the *Mirror* today? See Jane's got clothes on again?' You heard Harry talking and laughing with Pop in the dark.

'Damn' said Pop. 'Missed her today. Oh, well, if she were dressed --.'

You hoped there wouldn't be too many light flak guns. They could play merry hell at the height we were going in.

We stood talking in the still evening air, waiting for the sound of the first aircraft to start up its engines. Craven divided the flying rations and when he came to the bomb aimer, a dark curly-haired boy of nineteen, with an officer's flat hat raked on one side of his head, he stopped. He wanted to make sure of one thing.

'Ever do second dicky?' he asked the bomb aimer.

'Sure,' the bomb aimer said.

'OK. Then right through the gate with the throttles tonight. OK?'

The bomb aimer nodded, not smiling now. He looked serious.

'I'm not taking any chances. Not a hell of a lot of wind to help us off to-night, Full throttle, thirty degree flap. OK?' Craven said.

'Righto' the bomb aimer said.

From across the field came the sound of the first engine starting up.

'OK, let's go,' Craven addressed the crew.

'Cherrio' said one of the ground crew as they passed him. He was under the wing sliding a chock against one wheel.

Then the belly door closed, the black-out curtains on the small side-windows drawn, the compass turned on, ticking over quietly in the darkened fuselage, the navigator, bomb aimer and wireless operator seated in the crash position midway back in the fuselage, the sound of the starboard outer engine spluttering, roaring, catching, missing, catching, filled the intercom wire and the aircraft trembled under the power of the other three engines starting. In the rear turret you switched on the ring sight. Roaring, rising, falling in crescendo, the engines warming strained the aircraft against the wheel chocks.

The aircraft taxied out slowly on to the perimeter path of rolled asphalt that led around the aerodrome to the take-off runway and poking out over the nose, working the throttle slowly on one side to turn the aircraft, you knew what Craven was experiencing, seeing all the remembered familiar features of long ago evenings: the moon over the dark crests of the trees across the drome and dusk changing the world into the kind of soft green lake of light. An aircraft ahead, with its slow blurs of four propellers, braked and, stopped. Craven braked. You felt all the weight of the aircraft lunge forward and stop. You looked at your watch, seven minutes before take-off. And now on the perimeter track, one behind the other, propellers turning slowly, twelve aircraft loomed big in the thickening twilight, waiting to turn on to the runway. In the dark clotting of the people beside the runway a light flashed green and you watched the first aircraft ahead swing big and dark and pause there for a moment and then tail up, sky appearing under the tail, run smoothly forward, faster and faster and then at last only a climbing silhouette of wing against dying sunlight still in the western sky.

Now in your mind you saw all the crew in their positions, knew what they were feeling. Now in your mind you saw Craven looking at his rev and boost gauges, his hands damp inside his gloves and his stomach hollow and empty with fear.

'All set chaps?'

'OK boy, take it away,' said Reg, the bomb aimer.

'OK Craven,' the voices came in from each position.

'There's a green,' Eddie yelled. Engines roared.

Well, here we go, you thought. What will happen tonight? Will we get through? A fighter off the Dutch coast? Flak over the target? A wonky compass? What tonight? You braced yourself in the turret and watched the trees blur that made the skyline in the west. The green light blinked again and was gone. The aircraft bounced, lifted.

'Pop, you got a course?' Craven asked.

Now in your mind you saw the inside of the briefing-room and you were sitting at one of the tables with the crew and that was the map of Dortmund on the table and you were being briefed for your first operation. You would never forget that afternoon, your first, wondering what the night was going to be like and then that night in the dark, looking out between the guns, scared for the first time, seeing flak bursting off the Dutch coast and Pop the navigator asking Craven if he thought the course would go in over the coast in a safe position and then a long pause while Reg, the bomb aimer, said the coast was coming up and then Craven saying, 'Yes, this is it. There's a hell of a big searchlight at Amsterdam. There it is, Amsterdam!' Then: 'Nothing to worry about chaps. Piece of cake. Here we go.'

But it was not a piece of cake, as the saying goes and he flew on the course when he thought it was the right way. But then you were inexperienced and very lucky and they did not get you that night on the coast nor over the target.

It was luck, too, that had saved you on another night taking off for Lorient, the night the undercarriage would not retract with six thousand pounds of bombs and incendiaries in the bomb bays and the aircraft barely cleared the edge of the field, the night Craven wanted to try a landing with the bombs on. He said he could make it and Pop told him he was crazy and would bail out if he did not go out over the North Sea and drop the load.

And at Stuttgart, with the flak so thick you didn't see how it was possible to get through, you wondered if Craven were insane when you saw from the turret that no one had bombed yet and he was going in first. But that was in the beginning, when a searchlight and any small amount of flak appeared dangerous and later at Essen and Berlin you remembered the flak and searchlights at Stuttgart and wondered how you ever could have worried about them.

And that night at Essen the aircraft was held twenty minutes in the searchlights on the third trip there and the flak came up more quickly and with greater accuracy than you had ever seen. And crouching in the turret it did not look as if you could escape. Harry yelling, 'Weave! For F-- sake, weave! The stuff's right behind us'! For F-- sake! Weave!'

You could see the lights glowing all over the fuselage and wings and then Craven's voice, 'Are they gone?'

'For Chrissake, where is it?' And then falling in the darkness, head pressed against the top of the turret and the shocking boompf of the explosions and a panel of glass vanishing miraculously beside your elbow. Essen was always a hell of a place. When you were scheduled to go then: and the trip was scrubbed the crews rejoiced and when it was not scrubbed very few were gay and smiling at briefing. You thought of all the times you had been scared in the past six months and the strange times when you did not worry at all.

You remembered that winter night when Barsolane, a French Canadian rear gunner, had been hit in the back and stomach with flak in one of the first great attacks on Essen as the aircraft he was in went in over the target first and was caught in the searchlights and later, how the pilot told that Barsolane said nothing until they were back over the English coast and his clothes were full of blood and he was almost unconscious over his guns. Yes, you could argue for ever. Yes, his courage had been honourable. But that was the way they worked, the ones who used the words with which to tell lies about the truth. Along with the citation for courage they did not say this man was caught in circumstances beyond his control, the circumstances illustrating only what the mistakes of many can bring one man to do. You would always remember Barsolane and the others. The words honour and glory were nothing to him when they carried him out of the turret and they were still nothing to him when he almost died the next day in bed, with his skin turned yellow and his eyes sunk back into his skull. But maybe you were only thinking this way because you dreaded pain so much and now you were trying to lay the blame on someone for your presence here. No, that was wrong. In the beginning you had joined and fought to escape frustration and boredom and dullness. It was damned strange, you had arrived at the right ends by different means. Now you were fighting to preserve and keep that method of boredom and dullness, as you had once termed the life you had tired of.

You wondered what they were doing back in the newspaper office in Minnesota. At the dance at the Pavilion that night you danced with a WAAF who was home on leave and who, as she said, was trying to enjoy herself. 'Did you like England?' she asked. Yes, you liked England. My God, what were you supposed to say? 'How long have you been over?' she asked. You told her. 'What did you think of English women? Was it very different from America? What part of America were you from?' Minnesota. No, she had never heard of it. It did not matter. How were people different in America? No one could ever explain that. She asked your age. 'What had you done before the war?' 'Had you travelled in England before the war?' she asked. No. 'Well, one ought really to see all of England, then one would understand what England really was'. What the hell, you thought, bored and tired. I'm an American, but no one's going to string together a lot of pretty poetical pictures and make me believe that here now this is America. England was always many things but never any one thing.

You remembered before worry began, before the squadron began to lose, crews.

When it seemed to be impossible for anyone to be missing and it was all a rather pleasant, exciting adventure. But it was no longer an adventure, the night after a low-level attack. And you knew you were a fool ever to expect anything but despair or exhilaration. You remembered afterwards coming in to the interrogation officer, with all the empty tables in the briefing-room and sitting down, drinking hot tea, exhausted and numb, explaining the trip. And how empty the room was and then in the mess at five o'clock in the morning, waiting for the others to come in for breakfast. But they never came back. And when it was light in the morning you knew they were all either dead, prisoners, or in the North Sea.

They were crews you ate and drank and laughed and talked with. And you waited weeks to hear any word of them, expecting each morning in crew conference that a message had arrived from the German Red Cross. But it never arrived and no one ever heard of them again. Deeply regret to inform you that your son, lover, husband, brother, failed to return last night from operations... Gentlemen, our target for tonight is Düsseldorf... New crews will please remain behind for special instructions. And so the days passed.

When you sat in the turret you started thinking. I wish it were all over. I wish this trip were behind us. You heard the engines running. They sounded all right.

'Okay everybody?' Craven called.

'Okay' our voices came back. 'Everything jake.'

Wish this trip were over, you thought. You felt the aircraft roll slowly forward. Wish we were all back in the mess and didn't ever have to go again.

Then we were at the mouth of the runway, waiting now, as we had waited on many nights, for the Aldis lamps to flash a green light. Then the light blinking green in the dark and loneliness and hollowness and fear swept away all feeling; wave on wave of roar, then rushing along again in the dark, swerving, straightening out, then finally the lifting bump into the air.

We climbed over the aerodrome, then turned south; far behind winked the circular lights of the aerodrome. The moon hung naked and high overhead, lighting all the clouds below in a smooth field of white, peaceful as sleep. Here we go again, you thought, resigned, hating it.

And down across England, over the dark land, familiar aerodrome lights winking signals, searchlights already on, awaiting the enemy. How damn tired I am of it all, you thought and cocked your guns. How tired I am of strain and the mere wear and tear of trying to stay alive.

There were lights in the Thames Estuary. Over there is London, down there somewhere, you thought. How wonderful it would be to be there with Diana tonight.

How long since you had been to London on leave. Three months. On leave that spring England was the trains running fast into Southampton and along the tracks the roofless houses and the bombed rubble on the station platform and the sunlight beyond the glassless depot roof with the barrage balloons silver-grey and motionless in the windless blue afternoon. It was that and for the first time the fields of London roof-tops rushing past blurred in the rain beyond the carriage window and you excited and happy and Waterloo Station and the Bond Street whores in their coloured slacks standing in doorways out of the rain, holding their bright parasols and leashed lap-dogs. It was not Westminster Abbey, nor

Parliament, nor the Tower of London, nor all the places you had been taught to see. It was all people's faces and Leicester Square and Tube stations and taxis and pubs up in Chelsea and finally tired and ready for the country. And in the country a great stone house in a valley in Buckinghamshire and an old woman who wore hats and long dresses like Queen Mary and asked polite questions about America, in a long drawing-room with the French windows open and May sunlight on the terrace. It was that and on the table a picture of her son, long dead, among the lost forgotten dead of Flanders.

And you thought of those mornings of going on leave, of the crew walking out, along the road to the bus, everybody gay and a little mad with happiness, suitcases piled in the bus and then the train from Grimsby and Market Rasen steaming plumes of smoke in the winter-afternoon air over the High Street into Lincoln Midland station. 'So long fellows! See you, chaps! Have a good leave!' Tickets in hand; cross over the footbridge to the south side and onward to Newark and London. And a wonderful feeling of relief with the spires of Lincoln Cathedral fading across the afternoon sky and the first beer in London in a pub up the street from King's Cross, the lights bright in a theatre that night and sleeping late in the mornings in a warm room: and worry and cold and fish-and-chips and exhaustion and standing ill the dark in the rain waiting to take off lifted from your life by all the light, weightless hours of looking down Piccadilly or walking in the Park in the mornings knowing the day was all yours.

Yes, you would like to be in London to-night. London with Diana. The things you would do. Where would you go? Riding or walking with her through the traffic up past Hyde Park Corner, cars and buses and taxis honking and rushing past in the twilight. Or maybe in a taxi with Buckingham Palace beyond the driver's cap; sitting close to her, while the Palace came up and then went past on one side and then Sloane Square just as it was getting dark. Then the driver paid and walking through the vacant square along the street to the Antelope pub. And just as you went in, on the stillness of the spring air, the round clear shapes of the barrage balloons beyond the rooftops and then later walking back through Eaton and Grosvenor Squares, the buildings clear in the moonlight.

But those were only some of the places at certain times you would like to have Diana with you. You knew many more places. Chelsea and the Blue Cockatoo; the Strand swarming with people just before dinner. But now you could be in none of those places. You thought of sitting down to warm dinners in fashionable restaurants. That was one of the confusing things about the war. The ones who were fighting ate so badly. Well, perhaps it was only because so many of them were not around long enough even to digest a fashionable meal. Oh, to hell with it. Why die crying?

The world lay below in vague dissolving patterns in the fading light. Then the last winking signal light that masked the edge of England. We were dead on track. How far we have come in experience, you thought. Pop with his navigation, Craven in flying, Harry and me on the guns. How much more confidence we now had. Then you looked ahead and saw the searchlight beams and gun flashes high over the coast of France and forgot all about confidence, feeling once more only your empty hollow stomach) your practised hands now ready on the guns.

We flew on, crossed the coast, joking and talking intermittently; Pop occasionally giving a new course; all our voices as easy and sure as though we were back in the mess.

We saw all the familiar gun flashes and estimated just about where we were, each man picking up an old familiar navigational pin-point here and there.' That's Amsterdam over there,' a voice would say. Or, 'Here comes that old German beacon we picked up for the first time on the way to Munich.'

'There's the coast,' said Reg over the intercom.

'Where are we? Can you get me a pin-point?' Pop asked.

'Anything you bloody want, darling.'

You cocked the guns and leaned back in the turret and thought of Reg. He often said, when everybody was sitting around talking in someone's room, that he had joined only because everybody else had and he didn't want to be left at home and besides he was tired of Toronto. You saw the dark line: of the coast far below and a single light winking on the long dark arm of a headland and then you were out over the sea.

'About five miles south of track,' Reg said. 'But we're all right.'

'Can you see any water?' Pop asked.

'Little. Want a drift reading before it's too dark?'

'Please' Pop told him.

'Hardly any white caps. Very little wind.'

'What's the drift? God damn it!' Pop said. 'Get me a drift!'

You felt the strain closing down on each member of the crew.

It moved there into everybody, into the silence, an invisible emanation, a portent, impalpable as smoke, an emptiness of stomach, a dryness in the mouth, a waiting, looking out into the dark, watching the stars wink and the sky turn darker and then the moon hanging high and naked in a cold, empty and remote world of waiting and hoping.

It was very dark now and the moon had been shining for some time and you saw ahead all over the sky the first small flashes of bursting flak. Just quick, jagged winks of light and then to the left a searchlight beam probing, sabring the darkness and Craven slid the aircraft from side to side and then dived and climbed so as not to lose any height crossing the Dutch coast and the sudden round puffs of flak-smoke burst below with a yellow-red flash in the centre and then you saw the scattered balls of smoke dissolve and thin and drift away in the searchlight beams, for now more beams arched across the sky ahead and then suddenly coming out of nowhere was the thin black shape of a fighter, exhausts glowing, thick-nosed and thin-winged, coming on fast out of the dark side of the sky. You sat tight inside, ready and watching furiously on all sides.

'Get ready to turn starboard!' Harry yelled to Craven.

'There's something coming in!'

'Mack!' Harry called to you. 'Can you see him? I think he's underneath to starboard!'

'I see him. He's not coming in. He doesn't see us.' With the fighter rushing past underneath, your heart

feeling almost stopped with excitement, holding hard to the gun-control handle, watching the shape of the fighter steadily, through the red glow of the ring sight.

'He's going the other way!' Reg called from the nose.

'There he goes!'

Your mouth dry, your stomach empty, you relaxed. You had seen them before. But now this one after you, or at least it appeared he had been going to attack. They always looked dangerous as hell no matter how many times you saw them. Flak did not bother you. Detached, you could watch it bursting. But now you felt shaky and tight inside. You took a deep breath of oxygen. The tension was destroyed. You felt pleasantly drowsy, as if you would like to close your eyes and sleep.

Craven put in the supercharger and crossing the Dutch coast the aircraft climbed steadily. You looked at the guns, they were not freezing up and at the dark side of the sky and the Zuyder Zee passed below in its old familiar shape, the aircraft flew on with Craven weaving it gently from side to side above the depthless dark, seeing now and then below a white night-fighter flare lighting the whole sky, while time passed interminably and then looking out you saw a German beacon flashing, a new one you had never seen before. And ahead the clouds coming up unexpectedly, great motionless piles of cumulus taking light from the moon and a star winking, seeming to move and follow the aircraft until you felt almost certain it was a night fighter with a light on it signalling another; sitting heart pounding watching it, then checking it stationary against the movement of the aircraft; and the star did not really move and then on and on, darkness and stars all around and to the rear the twin dark shapes of the rudders. Then you were passing Bremen to the left, with its flak and searchlights working as a positioning point for Pop and then you were past Bremen and looking ahead in the darkness for the first signs of a single searchlight beam straight up and down, or a cone and an intermittent burst of flak among the beams and the first red flare that would designate the target. Then suddenly ahead there was the first far faint wink of light on the ground and one searchlight beam. Then ten more minutes and the aircraft turned to starboard, Reg calling, 'Seven more minutes to target.'

Craven's voice: 'Right. Can see it now, old man, All set, Reg?'

Reg's voice: 'Give me a wind, will you, Pop?'

Pop gave him a wind.

Reg's voice: 'All set, Craven.'

Seven minutes, you thought. You felt cold and tense, yet confident nothing could happen. I wish it were over, you thought, I wish we were out past the target. You looked ahead at the target, a great bowl of light in the dark sky. Reg began to tell Craven which way to run in so as to avoid the searchlight cones. Then we were in over the fires, swinging and diving, the sky filled with anti-aircraft fire. Craven was singing over the intercom and Reg was calling out instructions. 'Left ... left ....'

Reg said, 'Anybody see any flares yet?' And looking ahead you saw red flares at different heights slowly falling into a cone of searchlights and suddenly in the air among the searchlights more falling flares, like a Fourth of July celebration long ago at home and you knew the pathfinders were in over the target. Then the aircraft turned and made a circle and you knew you were running in directly from the west and then you were diving and in over the barrage, the flak bursting all around so thick it seemed you could not pass between the bursts and then over the fires, really burning now, a monstrous layer of white sparkling glare, as even as cake-frosting and then bombs gone and out of the light into the darkness again and Craven calling jeeringly that the German Home Guard must be working the flak and searchlights to-night and looking back you could see only the great white sparkling round lake of glare, round and as wide as long, the centre of Stuttgart.

Then the upward heave and you heard Reg say, 'Bombs gone! Let's get the hell out of here!' The anti-aircraft fire was bursting just above on both sides, sudden white balls of smoke with a yellow flash in the centre. You swung the turret back and forth, watching directly overhead for circular vapour trails that would mark a night fighter circling high over the target area.

Reg's voice: 'Hold 'er steady, Craven. I'll get another picture.'

The aircraft bounced suddenly and rocked crazily as three black balls of smoke drifted past underneath. It looked too close. Still, with so many aircraft over here, you thought, it's only luck when they hit one. There are too many for them to predict one directly over the target. Anyway, it was a reassuring thought. You went on searching the sky for the fighters.

Then we were beyond the target and looking back you saw, on the rim of lighted area, horizontal lines of tracer, then a sudden glow of fire and the multicoloured burst of flame of an aircraft exploding.

Harry's voice: 'See that guy go down, Mack? There's sloughs of night fighters around. Keep watching, boy.'

Then we saw two twin-engine fighters, with lights in their noses, signalling each other, as they came towards us. They came on flying level toward our tail. As they began to open fire, little winks, of orange light flashing from their wings, we began to climb and dive. In the darkness, the lines of tracer were like long threads of fire.

'Don't fire until they, get in close,' said Harry. Lines of tracer raced past just above the port wing. Then one fighter flew out on to our port beam.

Harry's voice: 'Watch the one on the beam, Mack?'

'OK. OK.' Stomach tight and cold with excitement.

Then you saw the tracer from Harry's turret stream back in a long arc and into the nose of one fighter. Then a pennant of flame jerked suddenly out from the nose of the fighter, then more flame enveloped the wings and it dived suddenly down, through the cloud, an orange glow showing momentarily through the cloud.

'There's one bastard' called Reg.

Then Harry excitedly, 'I got him Mack! I got him!'

'Here comes the one on the beam.' You saw tracer going into our port wing, then part of an engine-cowling whipped past. You held your guns on the fighter, firing steadily. God, why doesn't he go down, you thought; why doesn't he fall? He came steadily firing: You were terribly frightened now, your body covered with sweat, a rotten, dry, copperish taste in your mouth, your stomach tight and cold.

We kept firing and the fighter broke away, diving underneath. We were diving now and then racing along just above the ground. If only the damn moon weren't out, you thought, but there it hung big and naked, all the land and sky drenched in light. Again the fighter attacked, firing, pulling away out of range. Reg called up to say he was hit in the head by something but not to bother because he felt all right. Pop went into the nose with the first-aid kit.

Then suddenly the top of the turret burst off and cold air and splintered glass struck your face. You could see a jab of flame jumping from one of the port engines. You felt faint and tired and continued firing, watching the fighter coming on again winking long curves of tracer. Then suddenly you felt you could no longer hold the gun-control column; you felt too weak and tired even to press the firing button. Oh, God, let it come and all tightness and hollowness seemed suddenly lifted from your body. There was a blinding flash of light in the back of your head and you felt yourself fall backwards and feebly strain to climb out of the turret.

From far away Craven's voice: 'Parachute! Parachute! Bail out!'

If only I could sleep, you thought, just sleep. And another blinding flash of light filled your mind and everything seemed to wilt hazily and beautifully into a kind of pleasant, easy, relaxed dream.

And suddenly to your surprise you were home. There was the house, big and rambling under the leafy coolness of old elms. I'm home, you thought; the war is over, home in my own room again. And you looked out the window of your bedroom into the sunny stillness of the garden. Home, you thought, I'm home. It's all over.

Chapter 2

The Waddington Ghost

As I was walking up the stair
I met a man who wasn't there.
He wasn't there again today.
I wish, I wish he'd stay away.
Hugh Mearns (1875-1965)

'Mrs Murrenbridge and I were fairly accustomed to receive requests for information at our Archive here at Waddington; but one particular supplication, which reached us one sunny October morning, gave Mrs Murrenbridge a puzzled quarter of an hour. A member of the public had written to the station historian asking for information regarding the identity of the 'Waddington Ghost'. After several minutes quizzing herself, sotto voce, about where the facts of this case might be found, Mrs Murrenbridge decided that the best place to look was in the vault underneath the Reading Room.

'You make us both a drink, Ged,' ordered Mrs Murrenbridge. 'I'll have a look downstairs. I'm fairly certain if there is a Waddington Ghost, we'll find him in the 'vault'.

I dutifully brewed up two cups of Earl Grey and waited for what seemed like an eternity for Mrs Murrenbridge to return. I sat patiently in the old chesterfield by the fireplace in the Reading Room drinking my tea - completely contrary to archive regulations about food and drink. Mrs Murrenbridge did not seem to notice, however, when she eventually burst into the Reading Room with a huge album cradled in her arms. The album was thick and black and coated with dust. Its covers were bowed and crinkled; it had been maltreated in its own time. Its spine was missing, or rather it protruded from amongst the leaves like a bulky marker and the album was bandaged about with dirty white tape tied in a neat bow. Mrs Murrenbridge handed me the package and it was immediately clear that this album had been undisturbed for a very long time, perhaps even since it had been laid to rest in the vault. I fetched a checked duster from the cleaning cupboard and wiped away the dust. It was thick, tenacious dust, which blew up into a choking cloud when it was disturbed. I tentatively untied the bindings and the album sprung apart, like a box, disgorging leaf after leaf of faded paper covered with rusty writing. The documents appeared to be notes from a Unit Inquiry into the circumstances surrounding the loss of a Lancaster bomber on 31 October 1942. Towards the back of the album I found a series of captioned photographs of wreckage strewn all over the airfield. The various piles of twisted metal were barely discernible as having once belonged to a Lancaster bomber; however, some of the photographs included buildings in the background that convinced me that the photographs were taken at Waddington.

'I was here when this happened, Ged!' said Mrs Murrenbridge. 'It was the afternoon before a big raid and the boys had been air-testing their Lancasters. I remember the crash well; it was terrible, plumes of black smoke billowing everywhere. I found out later that all the crew had been killed.' Mrs Murrenbridge gingerly turned over a few pages in the album until she came across some pictures of airmen. She read each of the captions through her half-rimmed spectacles until she found what she was looking for. She tapped one of the photographs twice with her index finger. 'That's our man, Ged; Flight Lieutenant Arthur 'Monty' Beaumont. I've heard it said that every year on the anniversary of the crash you can hear a Lancaster circling round the station.'

'What utter nonsense,' I said, sitting back down in the old chesterfield. 'There is no such thing as ghosts! It was probably the Battle of Britain Memorial Flight!' Mrs Murrenbridge looked hurt and I felt a pang of guilt. I tried, awkwardly, to atone for my outburst. 'So, what was the cause?'

'It says here that it was pilot error.'

'Really? Was he a novice pilot then?'

'I don't know.' She scrutinized the album for a moment. 'No! He had completed ten operational sorties flying Hampdens and was three sorties away from completing his first tour on Lancasters!'

I struggled out of the chesterfield and approached the desk. 'Something doesn't sound right here - pilot error? So, this bloke could complete 30-odd missions over enemy territory, but couldn't make a safe landing at his home airfield on a perfectly clear afternoon?' I carried the album back to the chesterfield and sat down with the leaves spread across my lap. 'There is more to this than meets the eye, Mrs M. It's your turn to make the tea, isn't it?'

After a short while Mrs Murrenbridge returned to the Reading Room with two steaming cups of Earl Grey. The excitement of the case had made her quite forget her own rules prohibiting food and drink in the Archive. I poured over the album all afternoon and as darkness began to cloak the airfield Mrs Murrenbridge set a match to the logs and paper she had assembled in the fireplace earlier in the day. We became so engrossed in the album that we completely lost track of the time and when the old Napoleon-clock on the mantelpiece stuck 7 o'clock Mrs Murrenbridge became frantic. 'Good Lord! Is that the time? My husband will be wondering where I've got to. Can you lock up, Ged and leave the keys at the guardroom? Don't disturb the sequence of the leaves until I've finished listing them and let me know of any important discoveries!'

I placed another log on the fire and directed my attention once again to the album. The author of the unit inquiry had based his investigation on the working hypothesis that Monty had stalled the aircraft by lowering the flaps fully with too little airspeed. Eyewitness statements seemed to corroborate this hypothesis, but the engineering content of the inquiry was scant. Air accident investigation was not very well advanced in 1942 and my own engineering training had me convinced that the Inquiry had not examined the technical aspects of the crash at much as it should have. I revisited the wreckage photographs once more and using Mrs Murrenbridge's magnifying glass, I found something that proved in my own mind that this was definitely not a case of pilot error.

Lancaster production at Victory Aircraft in Canada on 28 January 1944. Some 430 B.X Lancasters were built by Victory Aircraft.

Suddenly, the Reading Room window crashed open accompanied by a large gust of wind. The resulting back draft reduced the fire to a pile of glowing embers. The papers from the album were scattered like a flock of pigeons startled by a gunshot and I raced across the room to shut the window. The papers were everywhere and Mrs Murrenbridge's warning not to get the leaves out of sequence was echoing in my ears. I dropped to my knees and began to clear up the mess.

I was still cursing under my breath when a shadow appeared across the floor as if someone was standing next to me. I instantly felt a presence, but I had not heard the door open. My hand was shaking and I suddenly felt a chill - I noticed that the hairs on my arm were stood on end. I slowly turned around to look at the source of the shadow. It was Monty. He was standing over me in his sheepskin flying clothing with a faded yellow life jacket hanging off his shoulder. I could not breathe. I stood up, rather awkwardly and the spectre simply gazed at me totally expressionless I noticed a severe shaking in my left leg and panicked because I could not control it. Monty did nothing to assuage my discomfort: he just stood there staring at me with his piercing blue eyes. He looked so young but there was no youthful spirit in his countenance, only pain and sadness. He removed his leather flying-helmet and spoke softly.

'It can be quite consuming... fear. Don't you think Pykeston?'

He knew my name, I thought to myself, but still I could not relax enough to say anything out loud. The spectre continued the conversation.

'I did not believe in ghosts either... until I became one.' His complexion was pallid and his expression betrayed a sudden anger. My leg was shaking out of control; but I felt a trickle of courage and asked, 'Are you Flight Lieutenant Beaumont... Sir?' 'Monty was what my friends called me. What friends I had: more like family really. How frightfully wretched of me to kill them all.'

'You mean your crew sir?' I replied.

'Yes, the men whose lives I was responsible for.'

'What... er... do you think happened then?'

'I've been asking myself that every year since the crash, Pykeston and the truth is, I just don't know. We were making the approach and the next thing I knew I was standing on the airfield watching my Lancaster burning. It was quite painless really.'

It occurred to me to share my own hypothesis with the ghost. 'Sir, I don't think that it was your fault. I think your aircraft suffered a mechanical failure.'

Monty was not impressed; he became annoyed, 'we had just completed an air test and the aircraft was a honey. How could it have been a mechanical failure?'

'I wish there was some way I could prove it to you, Sir!'

Monty stood up straight and said, 'they're very dangerous things, wishes!' Before he had finished the sentence the scene around me started to spin violently until everything became a blur. When the spinning stopped I found myself in the cockpit of Monty's Lancaster amongst a cacophony of roaring marlins. We were flying towards Waddington in broad daylight at about 1,500 feet - only it wasn't Waddington, as I knew it.

.Lancaster SE-L on 431 'Iroquois' Squadron RCAF at Croft receives a new port outer propeller with the aid of a small mobile crane.

'Now's your chance to prove what kind of engineer you are, Pykeston, D'you think you're up to it?' Monty asked.

Both my legs were shaking now! I was terrified and extremely angry. My unearthly pilot just looked at me and said, 'Tell me what you want me to do Pykeston. I'm in your hands!' Okay then I thought, I'll show you.

I put on a leather helmet that was hanging in front of me, fixed the oxygen mask over my mouth and twisted the switch on the front. 'First we need to shut down the port inner engine and feather the prop.' No time to dwell on my fear, I thought; time to get to work. Waddington was looming into view and I knew I would have to work fast and think back to my trip in the East Kirkby Lancaster. Where was Mike Chatterton when you needed him? With the flight engineer's seat folded away, I stood up in the cockpit and leaned over Monty's right shoulder. I eased one of the throttle levers forward and was relieved to see the port-inner propeller appear out of the blur. I pressed one of the four red buttons on the panel in front of me and watched as the propeller came to a halt. Monty, meanwhile, was twisting the trimming wheels to keep the Lancaster pointing straight ahead. 'Okay, Skipper, I'm going to take you through the landing checks.'

'Ready when you are, Pykeston', said Monty. We joined the circuit downwind of Waddington keeping about a mile to the right of the airstrip at about 1,000 feet. I grabbed the reference cards from their stowage and began calling the checks.

'Flaps 20.'

Monty put down 20 degrees of flap and the airspeed indicator dropped to 160 knots. 'Revs up.' Monty pushed the constant speed propeller controls forward and a loud whine sounded from the remaining three engines.

'Wheels down.'

We were now turning on to the runway and beads of perspiration began to run into my eyes. 'Radiators closed'.

'Okay. Closed.' And then two green lights came on in front of us. 'Wheels locked down,' called Monty seeing this. By now we were pointing straight at the landing strip, which looked all of about 6 feet wide from my position.

'Full flap', I yelled. Monty put the flap lever all the way down, which lifted the nose. He was also frantically twisting the trimming wheels, to balance the Lancaster in the glide. 'Airspeed, Pykeston?' Monty bellowed. 'Speed 130 125 128 130,' I chanted, as we dropped towards the ground. 'Height and speed, now please.' '300, 120.' '200, 120.' '100, 120.' '50, 115.'

'Okay,' jerked Monty; 'throttle back.' I snapped back the remaining three throttle levers while Monty, with both hands on the wheel, pulled off a good landing to the accompaniment of crackling and popping exhaust stubs. The Lancaster eased herself down onto her tail wheel and when we had run about 500 yards, Monty pulled his oxygen mask off his sweating face and grinned. Suddenly an almighty crack was heard from the left-hand side and a split second later the port undercarriage leg collapsed, which rolled the Lancaster towards the left. We veered around anticlockwise and I was bounced all over the cockpit. I eventually landed on top of Monty before the Lancaster came to a halt. Suddenly, it was all deathly quiet. By some miracle, I was unhurt. Monty

Lancaster SE-X on 431 'Iroquois' Squadron RCAF.

Lancaster I R5552 *Muchty Queen* showing a witch riding a bomb which was lettered OF-P on 97 Squadron and later served on 20 MU before going to 166 Squadron at Kirmington as AS-P2. The aircraft was lost with Flight Sergeant Kenneth Bert Renelt and crew on 20/21 December 1943, crashing in Holland on the operation on Frankfurt. All seven crew members were killed.

unstrapped himself and opened the escape hatch in the roof of the cockpit. We both climbed out onto the wing and jumped onto the grass below. I was extremely pleased to be back on the ground. Monty then turned his attention to the large hole in the port wing where the port-inner engine used to be. It had come away from its mountings and fallen in front of the undercarriage leg, which caused the leg to collapse and ruin an otherwise perfect landing. I showed Monty the remnants of the engine mountings and said, 'this is what I saw in the pictures in Mrs Murrenbridge's album. It's a 'classic stress fracture'. These mountings were not up to the job and had I not shut the engine down, it would have crashed into the tail plane when it parted: which would have made the aircraft nose dive into the airstrip. Shutting the engine down stopped it vibrating and bought us the time we needed to get the kite on the ground.'

Monty was rubbing his chin when he turned to me and said, 'how were you so certain that this is what happened?'

'As well as my recognising these fractures, I found the conclusive evidence in a picture of the wrecked tail plane. It had bits of the engine cowling embedded in it!'

'So the engine must have dislodged itself in flight and destroyed the tail plane,' Monty concluded. 'I am indebted to you, Pykeston. Now best you get back to your Archive and sort those leaves out before Mrs Murrenbridge returns.'

Monty smiled a contented grin and then disappeared in a whirlpool of colours. When the spinning stopped I was back in the Archive safe and sound.

Mrs Murrenbridge and I replied to the gentleman who had made the enquiry. We gave him a copy of Monty's picture and then returned the album to the vault. So the identity of the Waddington Ghost was discovered: but strangely enough, no one ever reported hearing Monty's Lancaster circling the station again.'

Chapter 3

Jo Lancaster

Jo Lancaster had on his bedside table a scale model of a Lancaster Bomber. His name was Lancaster, he flew Lancasters and sleeps with a Lancaster!'
**Wing Commander Rex Hayter, CO the Performance Flight
at Boscombe Down.**

'It is said that just before the moment at which the soul departs from a man's body, the pattern of his life is reflected once more before his mind' wrote Wing Commander 'Sandy' Powell in 1957. 'Jo Lancaster was the first man in the world to use the ejection seat to escape from an uncontrollable aeroplane. He did this under such circumstances that he was indeed for a second poised upon the knife-edged division which separates life from death. If at that moment in 1949 his life had been suddenly projected for him in retrospect it would have appeared like this.' In June 1937 Jo Lancaster joined the RAF Volunteer Reserve. At the time he was apprenticed to Armstrong Whitworth Aircraft Ltd at Whitley Aerodrome near Coventry. The firm gave him six weeks leave to go to the aerodrome at Sywell to take his Elementary Flying Training Course. He successfully passed this course while still only eighteen and a half years old and returned to the firm. From then on all his thoughts were of flying and he spent every week-end and half-days flying at Ansty, the nearest reserve aerodrome. One day Jo was showing his prowess at forced landings over this field when the engine passed out just when he opened up to go round again. The Cadet hit the hedge and stood on its nose. Jo scrambled out, highly crestfallen! His instructor arrived, took him back by road and ordered him to 'put down his reasons in writing'. The report did not exactly agree with the circumstances - there was a discrepancy in that part which said 'the engine cut out at 3,000 feet'! The Commanding Officer - 'Poppy Pope' - a famous pilot before and since this incident, said he did not believe a word of the report and proceeded to make an example of Sergeant Lancaster. Two important members of the firm who had been playing golf nearby witnessed the whole incident; one of them tore his own trousers in his anxiety to get to the wreck and the whole thing was reported by telephone to HQ at Ansty. Sergeant Lancaster RAFVR very soon became J. O. Lancaster Esq., but he was at least able to continue his apprenticeship at A.W.A.

It was now April 1938 and Jo's friends were all joining the Volunteer Reserve and Coventry had a 'Town Centre'. Despite the representations of influential friends and an MP to whom Jo had appealed - he even wrote to the Air Minister, Kingsley Wood - and had a reply, it was all to no avail. In May 1939 Jo went for a medical examination and interview in the hope of becoming an Air Navigator, but the Major in charge told him he was just the man for the RAOC. However, no vacancies arose and so he went back to A.W.A. In September 1939 he received a postal order for four shillings together with instructions to report to Budbrooke Barracks, the home of the Royal Warwickshires. With great resource he took this letter to the Chief Petty Officer i/c Royal Navy Recruiting, who said: 'Leave this to me.' A few days later he received official notification: *'Accepted for R.N. Do not report to Budbrooke Barracks.'* This triumph of ambition over bureaucracy was in turn outweighed by a surprise letter from the Air Ministry telling Jo to report to RAF Cardington - he was accepted for training as a pilot. At the time of this activity a patriotic old lady stopped Lancaster in the street and asked why he was not in uniform! On arrival at Cardington Jo found to his horror that in his hastily assembled kit were some A.W.A. blueprints of the then secret Whitley bomber! He managed to hide them until a suitable opportunity arose to return them - there would have been another reverse in his progress had the Orderly Sergeant found them instead.

At last, in July 1940, Jo once again started flying training, on Tiger Moths at Desford, near Leicester. An experienced flying instructor, Flight Lieutenant Hall, soon saw that Lancaster had unusual ability and he encouraged that by giving him much help, advice and extra time to practise aerobatics and low-level flying. This practice proved most valuable at a later date. Towards the end of this course the Battle of Britain was at its height. The Chief Instructor, knowing Jo's ability and intentions, recommended him for fighters and he was posted to No.5 Flying Training School Sealand, near Chester. The aircraft used for operational training units were two-seat low-wing Miles Master monoplanes. One of Jo's fellow pupils was Neville Duke. A big moment in the life of a pupil pilot is his first solo flight in the type of aeroplane he has been learning to fly. Jo Lancaster went off in his Miles

Flight Lieutenant Jo Lancaster on 12 Squadron who usually flew Lancaster W4366, R 'Robert' (behind), pictured astride a 'Cookie' with cans of incendiaries behind, at RAF Wickenby in March 1943.

Master and a hydraulic pipe failed - the one from the pump to the aircraft services. He had to make his first solo landing after lowering both undercarriage and landing flaps with the emergency hand pump. This inconvenience did not bother him nearly so much as the remarks of his instructor who wasted no time in catechising him about taxying in with his flaps down!

One section of the course managed to include night flying on its programme, and when the time came for postings to operational Training Units, the pilots in this section were at once posted to Bomber OTUs. Fate once again diverted Lancaster from his wish to be a fighter pilot, for inevitably he had been in the section which did night flying. The new station was Lossiemouth in Scotland where 20 OTU were training on Wellington twin-engined bombers. The course was intensive, with long cross-country flights, bombing practice and night flying. Night flying instruction was effected by the somewhat brutal method of putting the pupil in the second pilot's seat, the instructor then taking the controls and demonstrating a take-off, circuit and landing. After this the instructor sent his victim off on his own - usually having taken the precaution of dismounting to watch the fun from the first flare!

After passing out successfully Jo Lancaster was given a crew - in it were a Scotsman, a Welshman, two Canadians and a New Zealander, all sergeants. This crew, now operational in all but experience, was posted in May 1941 to 40 Squadron at Alconbury, Huntingdonshire. For the first eight sorties an experienced 'crew skipper' captained the aircraft and so Jo started his operational career as 'second dickie'; they were flying Wellington IC medium bombers. The tour of operations was severe, involving bombing raids on the Ruhr, Stettin, Berlin, and even Turin. These flights were marathons in a Wellington IC, involving great endurance and tenacity over many long hours. In good weather a prey to fighters, in bad weather - itself a test of navigation - and in blind flying they demanded skill, sheer courage and determination. Apart from the leaflet raids in the early part of the war these were the longest trips ever done by Bomber Command up to that time.

One day in the Briefing Room they were warned for an entirely different sort of raid. The German battleships, *Scharnhorst* and *Gneisenau,* were lying at Brest, special antiaircraft defences were strongly entrenched to cover the harbour and many Luftwaffe fighters were stationed at aerodromes nearby. So desperate was the need to destroy or cripple these warships that it was decided to make the raid in daylight. Of thirty aircraft which pressed home their attack on these ships, twenty-six failed to return. Jo Lancaster was lucky to be one of those who did return safely; during the action his rear gunner shot down a Messerschmitt 109 and they saw the pilot bail out. On another occasion they went, in daylight, in search of the German battleship Bismarck after she had engaged and sunk HMS *Hood,* first completing a prolonged reconnaissance over the Bay of Biscay.

By October 1941 Jo Lancaster had completed 31 sorties on 40 Squadron and was therefore rested from ops with a posting to 22 OTU, Wellesbourne Mountford near Coventry and promoted to Pilot Officer. Here he became an instructor on Wellingtons, but took part in two of the '1,000-bomber' raids laid on by the Bomber Command chief, Butch Harris in early 1942. The first of these, to Cologne on 30 May, he flew in a dual-instruction equipped 'tired' Wellington with a scratch crew, returning without undue problems; then flew the same aircraft, XG932, to Essen on the second Operation 'Millennium' two nights later. Learning with more than passing interest that the first Mosquito squadron was forming at Swanton Morley, Jo called upon Wing Commander 'Hughie' Edwards VC the Chief Instructor and asked if he could be posted to the Mosquito Squadron. 'If anyone is going there', said Hughie Edwards, 'it's me!' Another application failed and the result was a posting to 28 OTU Wymeswold, but continued determination resulted in a posting to an operational Lancaster squadron but not before he had made three more operational flights - to St Nazaire, Wilhelmshaven and Hamburg. Jo Lancaster joined 12 Squadron at Binbrook, Lincolnshire operating from the satellite aerodrome at Wickenby. His arrival on 'Shiny Twelve' almost coincided with the squadron's re-equipment from Wellingtons to Avro Lancasters, but his first three sorties on 12 Squadron were flown on Wellingtons; the first was a 'Gardening' (Mining) trip to Hungersund Fiord under a full moon, lasting eight hours. In November the squadron's first Lancaster arrived and conversion training for the crews began immediately. He was one of the first Squadron pilots to fly a Lancaster. So good

Lancaster III LM321 PH-'H-Harry' on 12 Squadron with a knight in shining armour on a charger below the cockpit. This aircraft operated later on 460 and 550 Squadrons and on 100 Squadron at Grimsby, when it was lost with Pilot Officer H. W. L. Skinner's crew on 10/11 June 1944 on the operation on Achères. LM321 crashed near Ste-Laurent-sur-Mer (Calvados) in an area of Normandy secured by the First US Army V Corps. Flying Officer Richard Valentine Carroll, who was from Tramore in County Waterford, left the aircraft clinging to Pilot Officer Skinner but he lost his grip and fell to his death. Three other crewmembers died in the aircraft.

was the Lancaster and so keen the crews that the conversion period occupied little more than two months. Yet with four engines and nearly double the maximum weight of the twin-engined bombers, the Lancaster was a big step for pilots with but a few hundred hours experience. During those weeks Jo Lancaster and his crew spent many hours learning about the various new radio and radar 'black boxes' they would be using on operations, and flew numerous lengthy cross-country training exercises - up to nine hours' duration on occasion - familiarising themselves with Jo's namesake 'kite'.

Jo was now a Flight Lieutenant and Deputy Flight Commander. Actual operations with the Lancaster on 12 Squadron commenced on 3 January 1943 when ten aircraft 'sowed' mines in the La Rochelle area. Shortly after ten aircraft set out for Berlin, and only six returned - a sharp reminder to the crews of the ever-stiffening German defences awaiting them every night. Jo Lancaster's first trip was a mine-laying operation to Hungersund Fiord; the moon was up and the flight took over eight hours. Mine-laying was highly specialised as it demanded expert navigation and map reading as well as the most accurate flying at low altitude during the 'run-up' and 'drop'. By April 1943 the squadron could usually only muster ten Lancasters and crews for operations, but this figure rose to 21 in May and 24 in June, despite casualties amounting to 33 aircraft and crews which failed to return from operations during the first six months of 1943 - the rough equivalent of 130 per cent of the squadron paper establishment. For Jo Lancaster and his crew, usually flying in Lancaster W4366, PH-R 'Robert', it was a period of intense strain; a far cry from the easy-going, near-casual atmosphere of Jo's initial sorties of his first operational tour. In four months he and his crew made twenty-one operational trips, most of them over the Ruhr.

He completed his second tour of operations successfully, now having made 54 operational flights - nearly every one against a heavily defended target in the heart of Germany and he had received the DFC. Once again Jo Lancaster was offered a 'rest' posting, this time as an instructor on Wellingtons, at Harwell. The thought appalled him and he declined, instead taking up a post on 1481 Flight at Binbrook, in command of the Wellington Flight of 1 Group's gunnery training unit. Jo agitated for and succeeded in getting a posting to the Aeroplane and Armament Experimental Establishment at Boscombe Down on Salisbury Plain in October 1943. Among the many trials undertaken by Jo Lancaster was the initial test-drop of Barnes Wallis's 12,000lb DP/HE bomb, more usually called 'Tallboy', which Jo released from a Lancaster at 18,000 feet over a test target precisely. He remained with the A&AEE for two years and then in February 1945 he was posted to the Test Pilots School. A year later Jo was seconded as a test pilot to Boulton & Paul Aircraft at Wolverhampton. But soon he transferred to a similar post with Saunders-Roe of the Isle of Wight where he undertook part of the flying test programme of the jet-propelled SRA.1 fighter flying boat design of huge potential.

Three years of flying for Saunders-Roe came to an end in January 1949 when Jo decided to rejoin Armstrong Whitworth at Baginton where he flew mainly Avro Lincolns and Gloster Meteor night-fighters and also new types of aircraft such as the unorthodox, tail-less 'flying wing' design, the AW52. On 30 May 1949 Jo took off in AW52 TS363 for yet another routine flight in the design's test

Lancasters on a mass 'formation daylight' late in the war.

programme when an asymmetric flutter developed in one wingtip, spreading rapidly across the whole aircraft and shaking the airframe to a pitch threatening to disintegrate it. In the tiny cockpit Jo was literally bounced up, down and sideways in increasing severity until he could no longer focus his vision. Finally, at 5,000 feet, with the air speed indicator building above 300 mph, Jo used his ejection seat to abandon the uncontrollable aircraft - the first man to utilise the Martin-Baker ejection seat 'live' in a real emergency to save his life. Though his parachute opened at 2,000 feet, Jo landed heavily, chipping a shoulder and slightly fracturing his spine, apart from myriad bruises from the battering around the interior of the cockpit. Three months' later Jo Lancaster returned to flying and subsequently survived even more potentially disastrous situations, including having the perspex hood of a 500 mph jet aircraft disintegrate around his head, losing an undercarriage leg on a Meteor during a practice forced landing and having both starboard engines of a Liberator suddenly feather and stop on take-off. To Jo Lancaster these were simply part of a pilot's life - but nothing ever diminished his lifelong love of flying.

Chapter 4

The Dam Busters

On the night of 16/17th May, 1943, 19 aircraft of No 617 Squadron took off to breach a number of important Dams in and around the Ruhr area. There were three primary targets, namely the Mohne, the Eder and the Sorpe Dams, and three alternative targets, the Lister, the Ennepe and the Diemel Dams.

The Squadron trained for six weeks, paying particular attention to map reading and accurate low level bombing.

The attack was divided into three waves, the first wave of 9 aircraft, sub-divided into three sections of three aircraft each, took off at 10-minute intervals, in perfectly clear weather, and with a full moon to assist them. They were detailed for the Mohne and the Eder Dams, in that order of priority. The second wave, consisting of five aircraft, took off to attack the Sorpe Dam, taking a different route, but timed to cross the enemy coast at the same time as, though at different points from, the leading section of the first wave. The third wave, consisting of the remaining five aircraft, formed an air bomb reserve and took off three hours later, each detailed for one of the alternate targets, and all detailed to be prepared to attack the Mohne or Eder Dams in the absence of any direct orders in the air to carry on to the alternative targets.

Wing Commander Gibson, en route to the target leading the first section of the first wave, met about 12 searchlights, and some concentrated light flak at the lakes 10 miles NE of Haltern, which was reported to Group by W/T and passed by Group to all the other aircraft. On arrival at a point 10 miles from the Mohne Dam, the formation went over to R/T control, and each individual attack was controlled by W/Cdr Gibson. There were between seven and ten light flak guns around the target, believed to be mainly 20mm. One or two were located on the Dam itself, and there were two positions on the N bank of the lake on each side of the Dam. W/Cdr Gibson attacked first and dropped his load accurately. Four other aircraft then attacked under his control, one of which was seen to be hit by light flak during its run up, and overshot with its load. The Dam was seen to breach on the fifth attack and this was reported to 5 Group by W/T. The remaining four aircraft were then diverted to the Eder Dam. One of these however had been shot down on the way to the target and only three attacked. One load was seen to overshoot, and this Dam was seen to breach after two successful attacks. This fact was also reported by W/T to Group Headquarters.

Of the five aircraft detailed to attack the Sorpe Dam, two returned early, one is known to have attacked, and two are missing without trace. A sixth aircraft from the mobile reserve was also detailed by W/T to attack the target, and did so successfully. The two aircraft attacking both reported that the crest of the Dam was seen to crumble for some considerable distance.

Two of the remaining four aircraft of the mobile reserve were detailed to attack the Sorpe Dam, one attacked successfully and one is missing and it is believed did not attack. The fourth attack was detailed by W/T to attack the Lister Dam and acknowledged the order. There is no further trace of him, and it is not known if he attacked it. The fifth aircraft successfully attacked the Dam at Enneppe.

The most important consequence of this operation is that the Ruhr industries will be deprived of a great deal of their industrial water for the coming summer. The immediate of the floods from the two Dams breached was to cause devastation and disruption throughout the valley of the Ruhr as far as Duisburg and serious flooding below the Eder Dam at Kassel and other places down the Weser Valley.

617 Squadron Operations Record Book (ORB)

War finally came to Fritzlar in a most unusual fashion on the night of 17 May 1943. Fritzlar lies in a low lying valley not too far distant from the Eder dam, which holds back the Eder basin. Joachim Hoehne, a 15-year old Hitler Youth, whose father was a Oberstleutnant (lieutenant colonel) in KG 54, had been to the dam many times and had always thought it a magnificent structure, but he had never thought of it as anything that could cause him any harm. His father's house, a three-storey sandstone villa on the edge of the airfield, nine miles from the Eder dam, was a far bigger house than young Joachim had ever dreamed of. His bedroom was on the third floor, his sisters rooms were on the second floor, along with his parents' room. Joachim lay there awake in his room late that night, the last person still stirring in the whole house. He liked to read and spent many late evenings lying in bed after the day was over.

'As I lay there, I became aware of an unsettling distant roar. The noise was strange and distant at first, but it was definitely got my attention. Somehow, instinctively, all I could think of was that the dam had broken - nothing else could make such a noise. I sprang from my bed and ran through the house banging on doors and yelling to wake up my sisters, my mother and my grandmother. As they hastily gathered themselves together downstairs pulling on robes and gowns, they didn't need me to tell them why I was so excited; by this time the roaring noise was much louder and could be clearly heard by all. We all agreed quickly that the dam had broken and knew we were hearing an on-rushing torrent of water. There was a moment's indecision and then I suggested we get atop the main hangar, as it was the tallest building on the field. Everyone agreed and we ran out of the house toward the hangar as the noise increased even more. People were running everywhere; each with their own ideas of what was happening and what to do about it. By the time we reached the hangar, water was already swirling around our feet and flowed rapidly across the field; it was ice cold and instilled absolute panic in everyone.

'We reached a long metal ladder which led up the side of the hangar to the roof and others were already climbing up. Being the man of the family, I hurriedly ushered my sisters up the ladder first, followed by my mother and grandmother, but they didn't need much pushing; they couldn't get up that ladder fast enough! For a moment, as I clung to the ladder, I was convinced I would drown before they would get out of the way and make room for me. By the time I started climbing the ladder, the water was literally up to my neck and roaring past like a raging river. There were screams everywhere, which could be heard over the roaring water. I raced up the ladder behind my mother and I think only a few others managed to get up the ladder after me, as the water was too deep and moving too rapidly for anyone else to reach it. The ladies were helped off the ladder on the roof by some of the French workers who were already up there and then we settled down, watching in the inky darkness at one of the most surreal things I would ever see. As far as the eye could see, water was cascading through the base and across the fields nearby. The forests surrounding the base swayed wildly as though a huge wind was buffeting them. The whole landscape swirled and churned below us, consuming everything in its path. We could see others atop the roofs of houses, on other buildings, and some terrified souls screamed hanging out the windows of their homes. It was an utterly helpless feeling. The women wept, the men were too stunned to speak. I shivered, soaked to my bones, and couldn't understand how such a thing could've happened. We spent the entire night atop the sprawling hangar roof anxiously awaiting daylight and help.'

Two months' earlier, on 17 March a letter from Bomber Command Headquarters was received at 5 Group Headquarters which said that a weapon, a special mine, had been produced which was codenamed 'Upkeep' and which it was intended to use against a large dam in Germany. The water level in the dam was then rising but after the beginning of June would again be too low for the projected operation; the attack was accordingly to be carried out in the moon period of May. A new squadron, the letter continued, was to be formed and equipped with Lancasters modified to carry the new weapon. Twenty-three such Lancasters would be built and twenty supplied to the new squadron, the remaining three being kept for various trials. Training for the operation, which was to be known as Operation 'Chastise' was to begin as soon as possible so ten unmodified Lancasters were immediately transferred to Scampton in Lincolnshire where 'Squadron X' began to form on 21 March. Twenty-four year old Wing Commander Guy Penrose Gibson DSO* DFC* was chosen to command the new squadron, soon to be known as '617'. Its formation was so secret that at 5 Group Headquarters at St. Vincent's, a house in Grantham, only the AOC, Air Chief Marshal Sir Ralph Cochrane, and the Senior Air Staff Officer, Air Commodore Harry V. Satterly, knew anything about Operation 'Chastise'. Gibson himself knew nothing of the target 617 Squadron were to attack or the nature of the weapon they were to use. Pilot Officer H. Watson was appointed armament officer and Pilot Officer C. C. Caple engineering officer. Scampton's station commander was 31-year old Group Captain J. N. H. 'Charles' Whitworth DSO DFC who was born in Buenos Aires and he would work closely with Gibson.

Seven air crews had reported to Group Headquarters on 24 March, seven on 25 March and a further seven would report on various dates before the end of March. Of the 133 men who would crew the Lancasters on the secret operation only twenty of them were decorated. Gibson selected many but not all of these personally. He chose 27-year old Squadron Leader Henry Melvin 'Dinghy' Young DFC* who came from 57 Squadron at Scampton, as his 'A' Flight Commander. Young, whose father was a solicitor and a second lieutenant in the Queen's Royal West Surrey Regiment and his mother, Fannie Forrester Young, formerly Rowan, an American from a socially prominent Los Angeles family, was born in Belgravia, London on 20 May 1915. Educated in England and in California and Connecticut, he attended Trinity College, Oxford where he studied law and was an Oxford rowing Blue. The first of his ditchings which earned him his nickname was in a Whitley in October 1940. His flight

Wing Commander Gibson VC in a more relaxed pose.

commander on 102 Squadron was Squadron Leader O. A. Morris:

'We were attached to Coastal Command for a while in September and October 1940, hunting for U-boats and protecting convoys, operating out of tents at Prestwick with packing cases for furniture. It was not a popular posting. We had no training for a maritime role and no instructions about what we were supposed to be doing. Our Whitleys were not suited to the job either. For a start they wouldn't take the standard depth charge so had to be modified, and we soon found out that low flying over the sea made the engines liable to fail. One chap who could certainly vouch for that was Flying Officer Young, who was well out in the Atlantic when his engines stopped. After a considerable time in the little dinghy they issued you with, the crew were picked up by an American destroyer, one crossing the ocean on the lend/lease scheme. Anyway, it had a photographer on board from *Life* magazine and this was just the ticket for him, and a well illustrated feature subsequently appeared. It happened on 7 October and they had been in that little dinghy for 22 hours before Town Class destroyer HMS *St Mary*, ex-US Navy, picked them up.'

'Dinghy' Young was rescued again in November following a raid on Turin. In May 1941 'Dinghy' Young was awarded the DFC and a bar followed in September 1942 when he completed a tour on 104 Squadron. The following summer he married his 33-year old American fiancée, Priscilla Lawson, a graduate of Brearley School, New York and Bryn Mawr College. Young has been described as, 'a large, calm man' and 'a very efficient organizer'. 'His favourite trick was to swallow a pint of beer without drawing breath.' By mid 1943 he had completed 65 ops.

The 'B' Flight Commander on 617 was 21-year old Squadron Leader Henry Eric Maudslay DFC who came from 50 Squadron. Originally from the Cotswold village of Broadway in Worcestershire, he was an accomplished middle-distance runner and former Captain of Boats at Eton. He was well-liked and was considered a 'real gentleman' and 'quiet, kind, purposeful - nothing was too much trouble.'

Gibson rang 1654 Heavy Conversion Unit to speak to 'Mick' Martin. He had met the Australian with a 'wild glint in his eyes and a monstrous moustache that ended raggedly out by his ears' at Buckingham Palace when Gibson received his DSO and Martin the first of his DFC's. Harold Brownlow Morgan Martin, born at Edgecliff, New South Wales on 27 February 1918 had been pronounced unfit to fly because of asthma but he worked his passage to Britain, where he obtained a medical degree at Edinburgh University before joining the RAF in 1940. Martin trained as a fighter pilot but saw no action because he was posted to the north so he applied for a transfer to bombers. Commissioned in 1941, 'Mick' Martin served on 455 Squadron RAAF, was transferred to 50 Squadron, with whom he flew a further 23 operations and was then taken off operational flying and awarded the DFC. He was probably the RAF's greatest exponent of low-level bombing.

At Skellingthorpe, another Australian pilot on 50 Squadron and the crew of 'N-Nan' were told that they were being posted to Scampton. Twenty-year-old Pilot Officer Leslie Gordon Knight RAAF was a trainee accountant from a small Outback town. His crew was composed of a rich mix of RAF and Dominion airmen. Sergeant Ray Grayston, a Surrey-born apprentice engineer when he was called up in December 1939 was the flight engineer. He says. 'The two gunners, Sergeant Frederick 'Doc' Sutherland and Sergeant Harry O'Brien were Canadians. The wireless operator, Flight Sergeant Bob Kellow was another

A beaming Guy Gibson flanked by David Maltby (left) and Mick Martin (right).

Australian. Flying Officers Harold Hobday navigator and Edward 'Johnny' Johnson, bomb aimer, were English.'

'Johnny' Johnson adds: 'The pilot, two gunners, the wireless operator, the flight engineer, were all non-commissioned and were pre-21 or just, years old. The navigator and I were commissioned and pretty ancient at over thirty years and married with children.'

Grayston had serviced Lancasters before volunteering to join 50 Squadron as a flight engineer in 1942. 'When the other lads found out, they told me I must be crazy. We were losing about 50 aircraft a night at that time. You certainly felt a bit jelly-like in the legs for the first few ops, but once you got over that, you would have volunteered to go every night. It was amazing really; you just got hyped up on it. As you saw the target area ahead, glowing on fire and with all the flak flying up, you wondered how the hell you were going to get through it. That's when you began to think, 'My God...' Over the Ruhr in particular, they put up a box barrage, just firing the guns, endlessly, endlessly, hoping to hit something. At first you'd imagine that it would be impossible to fly through

Wing Commander Guy Gibson VC (right) presents Pilot Officer Les Knight RAAF to the King during the Royal visit to 617 Squadron at Scampton on 27 May 1943. During the Dams raid 10 days earlier, Knight's Lancaster had formed part of the first wave of nine aircraft briefed to attack the Möhne Dam. In the event, the dam was breached before he had a chance to bomb and so he was ordered to fly on to the Eder Dam. His was the third and last mine to be successfully exploded against this target, after which it too was breached. For his part in the operation, Knight was awarded the DSO. On 15/16 September he was killed during another low-level operation by the squadron, this time against the Dortmund-Ems Canal at Ladbergen.

this tenor and get out the other side. But when you did, it gave you an exhilaration on the back end of the journey - so you thought, well, I want to keep doing that. And at the start of the next op, you never once considered that you were going to die. No, you never reckoned on that. I think that for most people, who flew on operations, the excitement became a sort of drug. I rode high-speed motorbikes before I joined the RAF and it was thrilling. Flying ops was that sort of atmosphere. You never knew when you could be shot, so it was wise to have somebody to take over in an emergency. Even though I was the flight engineer Les would let me fly the plane to get used to the controls. I did quite a few hours flying. Les Knight was remarkably quiet. He didn't smoke or drink, didn't go out with women, couldn't drive a car or even ride a bike. But he could fly a Lancaster! He was a brilliant pilot, even in the worst predicaments. I never heard him issue a harsh word, apart from telling us to shut up because we were all talking at the same time on the radio telegraphy. As a crew, we were close but we didn't live in each other's pockets. On the ground we didn't socialize at all.'

On 26 March ground crew member 20-year old Harold Roddis was posted to Scampton. 'I had hardly put my foot inside the main gate when I was put on a charge for dirty boots and buttons, scruffy uniform and long hair; what a welcome! For two years I had a clean record or 'got away' with it. Anyhow, I was not the only one as quite a number of the ground crews had also been charged. Nothing ever came of these charges and we later learned that Gibson had in fact torn them up and threw them in the waste paper basket. He also tore a strip off the Station Police presenting the charges and told them that his ground crews were to be left alone and that they had better things to do than 'Jankers'.

Ray Grayston recalled that 'Gibson was a straight talking, no bullshit sort of bloke. He wouldn't ask you to do anything he had not first done himself. Later, because we were flying so intensively we were scruffy, with un-pressed suits and tarnished buttons and when the Station CO saw us, all hell was let loose. He read us the riot act and told us to parade for a punishment march. Gibson told him, 'In that case, I'll be leading them.' That shut him up! Gibson made it clear we were there to do a job, not to play silly buggers.'

'After completing my arrival chit, collecting my blankets and getting a billet' continues Roddis, 'a message came over the tannoy that all ground crews were to report the following morning to 'A' Flight hangar. We hadn't been there very long when a camouflaged car drew in and out of it came a very young looking wing commander with a row of ribbons, he jumped onto the bonnet and introduced himself and then went on to tell us about the aircrews. He then turned his attention to the ground crews and he wasn't so complimentary about us. He then went on to inform us that our DISCIP Flight Sergeant would be 'Chiefy' Powell who would look after us, but he would demand and get 100% effort and dedication from us with no excuses for kites that were not airworthy when he wanted them. He then went on to talk about security and that letters would be censured and anyone, highest to lowest, disclosing information about the Squadron would be in very serious trouble.'

'Security was intense' recalls Vera Baker, a WAAF. 'Even our mail was censored and not a word seeped out. When the squadron was formed and the new Squadron Commander came into the Ops Room I recognised Gibson from his first tour of operations when he was a Pilot Officer. I was rather surprised that he had survived when so many had not. No one knew the reason for the presence of this squadron when there were already two operational squadrons on the station. One of the very few people who knew from the beginning all that there was to know about the proposed operation was a WAAF Intelligence officer, the only woman on the team involved with planning. She attended every briefing, but never gave the slightest indication of her knowledge. Even on the night of the raid, when she was pressed by another officer to tell her what was going on, she wouldn't say anything other than 'If it comes off, it's going to shorten the war!' And then she left the Ops room.'

'I had noticed when I arrived at the hangar' continues Harold Roddis, 'dozens of engine trestles, these were very heavy and cumbersome, used mainly by the engine mechanics when doing their D.I's [Daily Inspections]. Gibson told us that we would be formed into flights immediately and that these engine trestles would be removed by us to the dispersal points straightaway. I was very relieved to be on 'A' flight which was only approximately 200 yards or so from the hangar.

Wing Commander Guy Gibson and personnel making a fuss of 'Nigger' who is wearing a Victoria Cross' on his collar.

The flight sergeant in charge of 'A' flight was Chiefy Smith, a small tubby man with a black moustache. Along with two engine mechanics, I was allocated 'H for Harry', the pilot being Pilot Officer Geoff Rice.'

The 23-year old Mancunian, a hosiery mechanic in peacetime who had maintained knitting machines in Hinckley, had come from 57 Squadron (reluctantly). Two other pilots and their crews - Sergeant Lovell and 23-year old Flight Lieutenant Bill Astell DFC – were also from 57 Squadron at Scampton. By 24 April the number of crews was reduced to twenty-one and Lovell's returned to 57 Squadron and were replaced by that of Sergeant William G. Divall, 21, from Thornton Heath, Surrey, though they would be prevented from flying the operation through sickness. Flight Lieutenant Harold Sydney Wilson, 28-years old, who came from Tottenham in North London and crew also would miss out. Both crews were killed later, on 15/16 September on the disastrous trip to Ladbergen which claimed many of the Dam Busters. Flight Sergeant Lanchester and crew had opted to leave 617 Squadron, as Guy Gibson wanted to replace the navigator.

Flying Officer Joseph Charles 'Big Joe' McCarthy DFC RCAF, a burly 23-year-old, 6-foot 3-inch Irish-American from New York City, had just beaten the odds by completing his first tour on 97 Squadron at Woodhall Spa, on 11 March 1943. A few days later he received a telephone call from. Gibson told him, 'I'm forming a new squadron. I can't tell you much about it except to say that we may only be doing one trip. I'd like you and your crew to join us.' All but one of Joe McCarthy's crew of six eventually decided to follow their aircraft captain to Squadron 'X'. Sergeant George L. Johnson his bomb aimer, almost did not make it, as he was due to get married on 3 April and his bride to be had warned him that if he was not there on that date then he needn't 'bother to come at all.' McCarthy with his customary directness; told Gibson that they had finished their tour and were entitled to leave. They got four days leave and Johnson made it to the church on time.

From 97 Squadron also came Flight Lieutenant David J. H. Maltby DFC and Flight Lieutenant J. L. 'Les' Munro RNZAF. Maltby, born at Hastings in 1920, had trained as a mining engineer before the war and he had joined the RAFVR in 1940, earning the DFC on 106 Squadron on Hampdens. He was 'large and thoughtful, a fine pilot.' Les Munro was described as 'a most charming fellow with an excellent operational record'. Pilot Officer Warner Ottley DFC, born in 1923 in Battersea and growing up in Herne Bay, had joined the RAF in 1941 and trained in England and Canada before serving on 83 and 207 Squadrons. Flight Lieutenant Robert N. G. Barlow DFC RAAF, 32, originally from St. Kilda, Victoria, who had joined the RAAF in 1941, arrived from 61 Squadron at Syerston. Sergeant Cyril T. Anderson and 22-year old Flight Sergeant William Clifford Townsend DFM were from 49 Squadron. 'Bill' Townsend had joined the Army in 1941 but soon transferred to the RAF. From 467 Squadron RAAF at Bottesford in Leicestershire came Pilot Officer Vernon W. Byers RCAF, who at 32 was older than most Lancaster captains and his crew. Born in Star City, Saskatchewan he had joined the RCAF in 1941, training in Manitoba before coming to England and joining 467 Squadron RAAF in February 1943. Recently commissioned, he had flown three ops since he and his crew had joined the

The Derwent Dam and reservoir in Derbyshire's Peak District which was used for practice by 617 Squadron prior to the raids on the Ruhr Dams. (Author)

Australian Squadron seven weeks earlier.

Many of the crews who arrived at the aerodrome on 30 March had completed fewer than ten operations. Twenty-six year old Sergeant Dudley Heal, Flight Sergeant Ken Brown RCAF's navigator, had flown seven on 44 Squadron. In 1939 he was an Assistant Preventative Officer in the (then) Waterguard Branch of HM Customs and Excise at Southampton Docks. Steve Oancia the bomb aimer mentioned the fact that he 'did not recall volunteering for this transfer'. Basil Feneron had also protested. On Flight Lieutenant David John Shannon DFC RAAF's crew on 106 Squadron only the navigator had agreed to go with his skipper to Scampton after they were posted to the Pathfinders. Dave Shannon was a 21-year-old from South Australia who did not look 'any more than sixteen, so he was growing a large moustache to look older'. Some short while after his 18th birthday in 1940 he and his 'great chum' Batty Marks, had presented themselves at the Royal Australian Navy's recruitment office for volunteers in Adelaide. When they were told that they could expect a long wait before being called up for training, Shannon walked around the corner and signed on with the RAAF to train as aircrew. Shannon graduated as a pilot in single- and twin-engined aircraft and was shipped off to England. After OTU Kinloss Shannon was posted to 106 Squadron, where Wing Commander Guy Gibson had recently been appointed to command, completing 36 operations. Flight Sergeant Len J. Sumpter, who became Shannon's bomb aimer, was a former Grenadier guardsman. 'Tougher than a prize fighter' he had completed thirteen operations since volunteering for air crew. From Gibson's old squadron too came Flight Lieutenant John Vere 'Hoppy' Hopgood DFC* and Flight Sergeant Lewis Johnstone Burpee DFM RCAF, 25, known as 'John', recently married and from Ottawa, Ontario. He received his commission shortly after joining 617. Hopgood, 21, who came from Seaford in Sussex, has been described as 'English, fair and good looking except for a long front tooth that stuck out at an angle'. It was he who had taken Gibson up to familiarize him with the Lancaster.

'Then came the morning' recalls Dudley Heal, 'when we were all called to the Briefing Room. Our new CO, Wing Commander Gibson DSO* DFC* called us to order to tell us that the squadron had been formed to attack a particular target; the identity of which could not be revealed to anyone until briefing for the operation took place. Security would be at maximum and anyone caught talking about the squadron outside Scampton would be severely disciplined. We would be training for an unidentified period by night and at low level. With that we were dismissed.

'During the next six weeks there were few days when we were not flying. At first it was just low level, say 200 feet above ground. As time wore on more and more flying was over water, the sea, rivers, or canals by day and then gradually by night. Tinted screens were affixed to the perspex around the cockpit in the daytime to simulate night flying. We practiced flying over Derwent Water and attacking the dam with a newly designed bombsight that looked just like a dam, strangely enough. Of course, we all laughed at the idea that we might be going to attack a dam - we all knew that the *Tirpitz* was the target. All this time 57 Squadron at Scampton were steadily plugging over

Germany at night and no doubt suffering the same percentage of casualties as the rest of Bomber Command. I don't think they thought much of 617 (as we now were). While we were doing all this low-level flying, one incident comes to mind. We were flying along a canal and Steve called out, 'Bridge ahead'. Ken, of course, could see it and there was some discussion as to the size and height of it, ending with Ken saying, 'Let's find out', whereupon he put the nose down and flew under it! I still remember those feelings as we were momentarily enclosed on four sides. I did not enter that in my log.'

617 Squadron also practiced over the reservoirs at Uppingham (Eyebrook) near Corby and Abberton near Colchester and Bala Lake in Wales. Ray Grayston recalled: 'You'd never get a licence to fly that low anywhere in any air force under any conditions. It was forbidden. The other two squadrons on the base took an intense dislike to us because we were allowed to violate all the rules of flying. Locals on the ground who had us flying at rooftop height over their homes obviously hated it, but we thoroughly enjoyed it…'

On 27 March Bill Astell flew over to his native Peak District to make a low-level daylight over the waters of the narrow Derwent Dam. Bill's home was Spire Hollins, a rambling country house on a wooded hillside at Combs near Chapel-en-le-Frith in Derbyshire. His father was the chairman of a Manchester textile company and Bill spent most of his teenage years at a public school in Berkshire. A spell in Germany at Leipzig University and climbing in the Dolomites was followed by a short period working for his father at the company's mill in Staffordshire. When, on the night of 28 March, Wing Commander Guy Gibson did the same as Astell he nearly flew his Lancaster into the stone towers. On 6 May a flight of six Lancasters made several dummy night attacks on the Derwent

Pilot Officer Les Knight RAAF and his crew. L-R: Flying Officer H. S. Hobday RAFVR; Flying Officer Edward Johnson RAFVR; Sergeant Fred Sutherland RCAF; Les Knight; Pilot Officer Bob Kellow RAAF; Sergeant Ray Grayston RAFVR, Sergeant Harry O'Brien RCAF.

Approaching Abberton Reservoir South-South-East of Colchester, one of several stretches of water that was used in practice flights prior to the Dams Raid. During the night of 14/15 May the 19 Lancasters flew their last practice exercise before Operation 'Chastise'. Gibson wrote in his log book: 'Full dress rehearsal on Uppingham Lake and Colchester Reservoir. Completely successful.' (Author)

Dam, much to the consternation of villagers in the valley below. Nonetheless it brought joy to young lads like Edwin Marsh, a 17-year-old telegram delivery boy, who recalled: 'I was making deliveries when I heard a tremendous roar. To my amazement, three Lancasters were following each other down the valley. It seemed as if their wing-tips were almost touching the sides. They were no more than 50 feet above the road at the bottom of the valley and as I looked down below me I could look into the cockpits and see the faces of the aircrew. People who saw them knew something special must be on, but never in our wildest dreams could we guess what it would be.'

Eight year old Alf Steadman remembered: 'We saw the Lancasters swoop so low over the dam that the turbulence from their propellers sent ripples across the water. It wasn't until the news got out about the raid that we realised that we had witnessed history in the making.'

'617 Squadron were a special band of men to whom the usual restrictions did not seem to apply' recalls Vera Baker, a WAAF. 'Each watchkeeper suffered a tirade of complaints from farmers whose cows had gone off milk, or hens off lay because of the low-level flying and all we could do was apologise.'

Flight Lieutenant Les Munro RNZAF was one who had two close calls during training, which could well have had disastrous results. 'The first one was when flying down the North Sea at low level at night in rather hazy conditions when all of a sudden there appeared immediately ahead of us a convoy of ships. I quickly requested the wireless operator to fire off the colours of the day. In the light cast by the flares I could see a number of barrage balloons attached to the various ships by cables. I immediately pulled back on the control column and with the good fortune of 'Lady Luck' went shooting up through the balloons and cables and cleared the convoy without hitting either. The convoy remained silent with the ships giving off a ghostlike appearance.

'The second one was when flying across the Fen country southwest of the Wash. A seagull was a bit slow in avoiding the monster intruding over its habitat and hit the front screen to my left of dead centre, smashed a hole in the screen and came through the cockpit like a cannon ball between the flight engineer and myself. Hit the curtain shielding the navigator's compartment and ended up as a rather messy lump of flesh and feathers on the cockpit floor. Again luck was on my side! If it had hit the screen only a matter of about 18 inches to the left it would have hit my head and face with disastrous results. At the height at which I was flying maybe one crashed aircraft and no survivors!'

'The days and weeks were filled with endless flying, both day and night' recalls Harold Roddis. 'And from the amount of debris we removed from the rad's quite a lot of this flying was at low level. I quite enjoyed this period, the weather was good and on the bonus side there were no flak holes to be patched up. The DI's were straight forward, check air pressure, check aileron, rudder and elevator controls, check hydraulic tank, check undercarriage, legs and tyres and clean all perspex to cockpit and turrets. Later on electricians came along and fitted spotlights and yellow screens were fitted to the cockpit to simulate night flying. About the beginning of May I was out on dispersal when I saw for the first time the new aircraft arriving. They looked as though a great chunk had been taken from the underside and someone suggested that it looked like a Lanc that had had an abortion and thereafter they became known to the ground crews as 'Abortions'. They looked even worse on the ground. The neat lines of the Lanc completely destroyed. It could not, however, have affected the performance as training went on continuously.

'On 13 May' recalls Dudley Heal 'the first of the bombs for our operation arrived. It looked like an outside garden roller and would be slung beneath the aircraft, the bomb doors having been removed and replaced by special fittings.'

'Rather than spheres, the mines were cylindrical' says Ray Grayston 'and were made to spin in reverse before being dropped, so that they would skim over the tops of torpedo booms. They were massive great things that made us wonder how the hell we were supposed to fly with them. We knew the operation was something out of the ordinary, but there was no mention of dams or bouncing bombs. The only test run, using dummy concrete mines, took place off Reculver, Kent with mixed results. The Lanc didn't like the thing hanging underneath it, stuck right out in the slipstream. It interfered too much with the aerodynamics. So on our run with a dummy mine, we thought we were flying at 30 to 50 feet but were actually below that and the splash badly damaged our machine. The tailplane and back end looked like a sardine can where the water had hit it. It was so simple you could make it with a pencil and a piece of string, but it worked a treat.'

To achieve the right altitude, two Aldis lamps fitted to the fuselage were played on to the water until they met in a figure of eight at precisely 60 feet. Judging the distance from the target proved equally simple, by making use of the twin towers which flanked both the Möhne and Eder dams. A triangular wooden 'sight' was made with a peephole at the apex and nails at the other two ends. The bomb aimer would peer through the peephole and when the nails lined up with the towers, release his mine.

Dr. Barnes Wallis, who in 1942 overcame design obstacles to produce a 'bouncing bomb' that would destroy German dams in the Ruhr heartland. The bombs were actually mines with a 6,600lb explosive charge, dropped in such a way to skip along the surface of the water, slide down the dam face to a depth of 30 feet and then explode alongside the dam wall.

Sergeant Leonard Sumpter recalled: 'When we first saw the experiments with bouncing bombs - well, we thought it was marvellous. It's hard to think, when you first see it, that when about five tons of metal hits the water, whether its spinning in a backwards direction at about 450 revs a minute will make any difference to it. You'd think, 'Well, it'll just go straight in - straight down.' But it didn't. It just hit the water - and up she came, and did about three bounces to the beach. It was an impressive sight - mine did four bounces to the beach. That's why I got chewed off. I dropped it too soon, and it would have hardly reached the dam wall. The idea was to bounce it up to the dam wall, and it was spinning against the wall and sticking to the wall by its spinning, until it got to the depth where the hydrostatic fuse exploded.'

'Security at Scampton' continues Dudley Heal 'reached a high point over the next 48 hours. There was no chance of a trip into Lincoln. In the early afternoon of 15 May the Tannoy came to life: 'All pilots, navigators and bomb aimers of 617 Squadron report to the briefing-room immediately.' The great moment had arrived and we were to spend the next four or five hours learning all about the Ruhr dams, listening to Wing Commander Gibson and to Dr. Barnes Wallis, inventor of the bomb we would use. We studied models of the dams as well as the route we were to follow. Every known concentration of anti-aircraft fire would be noted as well as every possible landmark. No effort was spared to equip us for this 'op. We were dismissed, with the injunction that we were to tell nobody, not even our crewmates what the targets were. Preparations continued on 16th and then all the aircrew were called for briefing. We learned that we would form part of the third, reserve wave to take off, would set course for the Möhne Dam but be ready to receive fresh orders en route.'

Chapter 5

Après Moi Le Deluge

'In the early hours of this morning a force of Lancasters of Bomber Command led by Wing Commander G. P Gibson DSO* DFC* attacked with mines the dams of the Ruhr Basin. Eight of the Lancasters are missing…'
BBC Home Service 17 May 1943

'On 16 May' recalls Harold Roddis 'we reported to the dispersal as normal, took the covers off the engines, cockpit and turrets and went about our usual procedure of carrying out the daily inspection with not the slightest idea that this was to be the day! Later the armourers came with this 'dustbin' shaped object which they secured to the cut-out portion below the fuselage, even then I could not believe it was a bomb and it was only later when we noticed the crew buses dropping at each dispersal point the aircrews, fully kitted out for operations, that we realised that an 'Op' was on.'

'That Sunday' continues Grayston 'I had breakfast and saw the officers go off to their briefing. We had been quarantined for six weeks, having no contact with civilians, no access to telephones and being unable to write letters. I'd been married for less than a year, but I couldn't tell my wife what I was up to. So speculation was rife. Some of us thought the targets were submarine and torpedo boat pens. It was a great surprise when we found out where we were going. We had to hug the ground so the Germans couldn't vector us with their radar otherwise they would have picked us off like flies.'

Les Munro recalls. 'The day of the Dams raid had arrived and for the majority of the crews the first indication of the target was when entering the briefing room and viewing the tapes on the wall.' Nineteen crews spent the next four or five hours learning all about the Ruhr dams, listening to Wing Commander Gibson and to Barnes Wallis and studying models of the dams. Les Munro adds. 'The actual target did not give much cause for concern but the fact that the route to the targets led through the heavily defended area of the Ruhr did.' Every known concentration of anti-aircraft fire was noted as well as every possible landmark.

A brass rubbing of 617 Squadron's crest in St Clement Danes London, with the motto *'Après Moi Le Deluge'* - *After Me, The Flood*

Before take off the crews went through a variety of rituals. 'Dinghy' Young tidied his room, several played cards, rolled dice and or dozed, many wrote letters home and Doug Webb, Townsend's front gunner took a bath, 'determined to die clean'. As the crews went out to their waiting Lancasters, Basil Feneron, Brown's flight engineer, tried to lift the Upkeep bomb attached to the underside of the Lancaster. Warrant Officer Abram A. Garshowitz RCAF, Astell's Canadian wireless operator, chalked on their 'Upkeep', 'Never has so much been expected of so few.' Hoppy Hopgood said to Shannon just before takeoff. 'I think this is going to be a tough one Dave and I don't think I'm coming back.' Hopgood's bomb aimer Flight Sergeant James W. Fraser DFM RCAF had completed a tour on 50 Squadron and he had married his fiancée Doris on 29 April. The rear gunner, Pilot Officer Tony Burcher DFM RAAF who was from New South Wales, had been 'boot-faced' about starting a second tour. He had hoped to be posted home as he wanted to fight the Japs who had killed his brother at Kokoda Trail. Burcher's mother in Vaucluse often sent him Comfort Fund parcels and always enclosed a jar of malted milk tablets which he built up in a store in his drawer in his quarters. He never took them on any trip but while walking down to the flight with Brian Goodale the wireless operator on Shannon's crew, something prompted him to go back and pick a jar of the malted milk tablets and put them on the inside pocket of his battle dress. 'I don't know why; it was a premonition' Burcher said. 'Later they were quite useful.'

Joe McCarthy, commander of the second wave assigned to attack the Sorpe dam and his crew climbed into 'Q for Queenie'. A bouncing bomb attack would be ineffective against this target because an earthen wall surrounded the dam's concrete core so McCarthy would have to make a conventional bomb drop. However, during the pre-flight check 'Q for Queenie' was found to have a coolant leak in the starboard outer engine and the aircraft had to go unserviceable. Then only reserve Lancaster was ED825 AJ-T which had been flown from Boscombe Down that afternoon by a ferry pilot. Although 'T-Tommy' was bombed up there had been no time to fit a VHF radio or Aldis lamps. McCarthy and his crew jumped out of 'Q-Queenie', the big American snagging his parachute on a hook in the process and finally they got all moveable equipment out of the aircraft and rushed over to 'T-Tommy'. There they found that the compass deviation card vital for accurately flying the carefully charted route was not in the cockpit. The chances of flying the Lancaster at low level (between 75- and 120-feet) through the myriad of flak emplacements and around night fighter bases, which lay between them and their target, were zero without it. Joe McCarthy climbed down from the cockpit for the second time that evening and with his 'Irish Temper' near boiling point, jumped into a truck and headed for the hangar where he ran into Flight Sergeant G. E. 'Chiefy' Powell, 617's Senior NCO. After a very short, expletive-filled, one-sided conversation, Powell took off at the double to the squadron's instrument section. He was unsure of what exactly he was looking for but he managed somehow to locate a blank card. He thrust another parachute into the impatient pilot's lap and McCarthy headed off to the hard stand where the compass was swung with 'Upkeep;' in position. He finally got airborne at 2201, thirty-four minutes behind his section. By the time 'T-Tommy' reached Vlieland, at 2313, McCarthy had reduced the deficit to 21½ minutes. He received a 'hot reception from the natives' when 'T-Tommy' crossed the coastline. 'They knew the track we were coming in on, so their guns were pretty well trained when they heard my motors. But, thank God, there were two large sand dunes right on the coast which I sank in between.'

'The crews were tense' recalls Harold Roddis. 'They always made time to have a chat and a joke with us but when the time came they climbed the steps into the kite whilst we climbed on to the top of the main wheels, plugged the starter battery in and at a signal from the pilot primed and started starboard inner and outer, then ducked under the fuselage and repeated this with the port inner and outer engines. We then unplugged the starter battery, pulled it to the edge of the dispersal and waited until the pilot and crew had carried out their checks and the flight engineer

The Eder Dam before the attack. (IWM)

had checked oil pressures etc. After they were satisfied that everything was OK Rice signalled 'Chocks Away'. We moved to the rear of the engines, grabbed the chock ropes, pulled these to the edge of the dispersal and gave the all clear sign to the pilot. 'H-Harry' then taxied from dispersal on to the perimeter track and that was the last I saw of that kite.'

On the night of the raid Vera Baker had been visiting friends in Lincoln before going on duty. 'When I entered the Ops room it was obvious that this was the night when all speculation would be at an end and all questions answered. By the chance of the roster I was the watchkeeper on duty that night and the only WAAF NCO present. The aircraft took off; even at this stage security was intense and I was taken to task very severely by the 5 Group Controller for not being able to give details of the squadron's destination, purpose or the estimated time of arrival at the English coast on return. When I couldn't answer his questions, he said ominously 'Very well, on your head be it!'

The nineteen Lancasters were to fly across the North Sea at 150 feet, then across occupied Holland at 100 feet and into Germany at 'naught feet'. Lancasters took off in three waves. The first nine aircraft were to target the Möhne and then carry on to the Eder Dam followed by other targets as directed

Guy Gibson's Lancaster III ED932/AJ-G showing the Upkeep mine mounted between the pair of side-swing callipers and the belt drive to the weapon. The belt drive was attached to the hydraulic motor in the forward end of the bomb bay by which means the mine was back-spun before release. The mine was filled with a high explosive called Torpex and fitted with a hydrostatic fuse.

by wireless from 5 Group Headquarters. The second wave of five was to act as a diversionary force and to attack the Sorpe and the final five were detailed as back-up aircraft with alternative targets at Achwelm, Ennepe and Diemi dams if they were not needed in the main attacks. The first wave would fly in three sections of three aircraft about ten minutes apart.

Wing Commander Guy Gibson wrote: 'The moon was full; everywhere its pleasant, watery haze spread over the peaceful English countryside, rendering it colourless. But there is not much colour in Lincolnshire, anyway. The city of Lincoln was silent - that city which so many bomber boys know so well, a city full of homely people - people who have got so used to the Air Force that they have begun almost to forget them. Lincoln with its great cathedral sticking up on a hill, a landmark for miles around. Little villages in the flat Fenland slept peacefully. Here nice simple folk live in their bastions on the East Anglian coast. The last farmer had long since gone to bed; the fire in the village pub had died down to an ember; the bar, which a few hours ago was full of noisy chattering people, was silent. There were no enemy aircraft about and the scene was peaceful. In fact, this sort of scene might not have changed for a hundred years or so. But this night was different - at least different for 133 men: 133 young fliers and I was one of those men. This was the big thing. This was it.

'We were flying not very high, about 100 feet, and not very far apart. I suppose to a layman it was a wonderful sight, these great powerful Lancasters in formation, flown by boys who knew their job. Below us, and also practically beside us, at 200 miles an hour flashed past trees, fields, church spires and England.

'We were off on a journey for which we had long waited, a journey that had been carefully planned, carefully trained for, a journey for which was going to do a lot of good if it succeeded; and everything had been worked out so that it should succeed. We were off to the Dams.'

After crossing the north-west coast of The Wash about five miles north-east of Boston, the Lancasters' route was across Norfolk past East Dereham and Wymondham near Norwich to Bungay in Suffolk and on to Southwold before heading out across the North Sea to Holland to the Möhne. The second wave would fly a different route to confuse enemy defences, to the Sorpe dam. This route was slightly further via the Friesians Islands so the second wave actually took off first. The third wave of five Lancasters was to set off later and act as a mobile reserve to be used against such dams as were still unbroken. Flight Sergeant Ken Brown's crew were on one of the last five Lancasters ('F for Freddie') as Dudley Heal recalls.

'Soon after 21 hours we watched the first wave of nine aircraft take off in formations of three. This was most unusual for bombers. They lumbered over the grass (Scampton had no runways) with their bombs slung beneath the aircraft and gathered speed slowly to clear the perimeter fence with little to spare. We silently wished them 'God-speed'. The second wave had taken off a little earlier as they would follow a different route, rather longer, to distract the defences. We now had something like two hours to wait. I think most of us wrote a letter, just in case, collected our equipment and went down to dispersal to get organized in the aircraft and to chat to our ground crew. They had spent so many hours making sure that all was done that could he done to ensure that everything would work perfectly.

We expressed our appreciation for their efforts. It was twenty past midnight when we, in our turn, lumbered across the airfield and climbed slowly into the air, as did the other members of the third wave. We set course according to the expected wind and headed for the coast. We would be in touch with base and had code words with which to signal to base the result of any attack we made. We flew as low as possible over the North Sea, 100 feet and less, to avoid attracting the attention of the enemy radar. At the Dutch coast we were a little off track so I made some adjustments. Steve kept me informed of any landmarks and I realised after a while that we had this tendency to drift off to starboard, so from then on I added or subtracted five degrees whenever the planned route called for a change of course. I was lucky that I had three pairs of eyes up front to report anything of interest to me - and other matters such as the loss of one Lancaster over Holland and another near the notorious Hamm marshalling yards. I was glad that we also had two pairs of eyes, which could see behind, should fighters appear. Our mid-upper gunner, incidentally, was off sick and Dave Allatson from a reserve crew, took his place. Both he and Grant, the rear gunner, used their guns to good effect during this 'op'.'

'We took off into a full moon - almost daylight' said Tony Burcher. 'It was a lovely night after a beautiful, balmy day. I was a little concerned about the fact that we were going to fly very low but we'd had all those practice flights over England. We didn't see any fighter aircraft at all. I was looking out more for guns to shoot up. I shot some searchlights out just before we got to the target. I think that was some help to us. It was discussed that whoever went in to the target first might get them by surprise but the second blokes they would certainly be waiting for and we knew that.'

'N for Nan' took off at 0959 into a clear sky' continues Ray Grayston. 'There was no chit-chat. When you're bombed up and you're going out on a raid you're on the alert from the time you take off until you get back, if you get back. On this mission, the height we were flying at made us even more watchful. We were all on the lookout the whole time for churches, pylons, hills and tall trees. It was hair-raising stuff. We were flying in threes and were only half a wingspan apart. We couldn't use the radio, so we had to keep in sight of each other to be able to communicate by lights. There was a lot of flak; though most of it went into the sky above where the Germans expected us to be. We also lost one out of our three on the way in. One minute 'B for Baker' piloted by 'Bill' Astell DFC was on our starboard side and the next moment he'd gone. Just like that, gone. I believe he flew into an obstruction. Now that's how close you were to sudden death. Whatever the hell he hit ripped the mine off his machine and killed them all.'

Astell's Lancaster was fired on by flak guns at Dorsten and was probably hit by shells after delaying when the others turned at a pinpoint. Two lines of tracer came up and Astell's gunners returned fire but 'B-Baker' hit high-tension cables and crashed in flames near Marbeck, 3 miles SSE of Borken, Germany. There were no survivors.

Pilot Officer Geoff Rice flew so low that his Lancaster hit the sea before crossing the enemy coast and he lost its bomb. Rice aborted and flew back on two engines. 'W-William' flown by Flight Lieutenant Les Munro RNZAF, part of the Northern Wave of five aircraft with the Sorpe as their target, was also forced to abort as he recalls. 'Our route was to fly due East across the North Sea and cross the Dutch coast at the coast of Vlieland. When flying down the Waddenzee side of the sand dunes of the coast my aircraft was hit by a single light shell, which severed the intercom and electrical systems. Without instrumentation at low level it was impossible to carry on and I made the decision to return to base with my Upkeep still on board.' The remaining Lancasters swung up the Rhine and arrived over the Ruhr and the first target, the Möhne Dam. As Gibson flew over a hill he saw the lake and then the dam itself. In the moonlight it looked 'squat and heavy and unconquerable…grey and solid as though it were part of the countryside itself and just as unmoveable'. 'We'd never practiced anything like it' Ray Grayston continues.

'When we saw the location, we thought it was near impossible. The Germans were so certain no aircraft could attack it that they had not defended it with anti-aircraft batteries, which was the good news. The bad news was that the dam wall was at the head of a narrow, crooked reservoir in a steep, wooded valley with a sharp hill at either end and a peninsula jutting out in the middle. We would have to fly over a castle 1,000 feet above the reservoir, drop down like a stone, fly above the water at no more than 60 feet, hop over the peninsula, drop down again and release our mine. Then climb like fury to miss the hill at the far end.'

Forty-seven year old auxiliary policeman Wilhelm Strotkamp, captain of a pleasure boat on the Möhne Lake, was on duty guarding the 6,000-kilowatt powerhouse below the Möhne dam. Towards midnight, while doing his rounds, he heard air-raid sirens in the distance. At first he took little notice, as air-raid warnings were not uncommon in the Ruhr in 1943. Then he realized that something was wrong; the RAF did not normally venture over the Ruhr on nights with a full moon but there was one tonight and the water in the lake was at its highest. Fear showed in the eyes of Wilhelm Strotkamp and his fear was soon confirmed when

Lancaster III ED825/G ('Guard') 'T-Tommy' on 617 Squadron which was used at A&AEE Boscombe Down for handling trials of the fully loaded bomber and was flown by Flight Lieutenant Joe McCarthy on the Dam's raid after his original aircraft (ED923 'Q-Queenie') went unserviceable. He made ten runs against the Sorpe before returning safely to Scampton. ED825 was one of five aircraft lost on SOE operations from Tempsford to Northern France on 10/11 December 1943 when Gordon Herbert Weeden RCAF and crew on 617 Squadron were killed. ED923 was lost with Flying Officer Robert Bertram Douglas Palmer's crew on 97 Squadron on 8/9 July 1943 on the operation on Cologne.

he heard the Lancasters' engines, not droning past overhead, but swarming around the distant end of the lake; and one was getting nearer. He finished his round of the powerhouse as fast as he could, opened the entrance to the turbine room and shouted a warning to the engineer on duty. At that moment the gun on one of the towers opened fire and Strotkamp ran for cover in a cavity in the dam's wall. Then the guns on both towers began non-stop firing. The noise of aircraft engines was now very loud and one thundered right over him, just missing the dam's parapet so that the whole valley appeared to vibrate to the roar of its engines. It was Gibson's Lancaster. A huge explosion tore at Strotkamp's lungs and masses of water spilled over the top of the dam. Drenched to the skin, he began to run as he had never run before until he reached the north side of the valley, hundreds of yards away. He stopped breathless behind a tree half way up the slope and turned to gaze as though hypnotized at the enormous dam wall. The dam was still intact.

Gibson had sent his mine bouncing three times towards the concrete wall but it sank and exploded sending up a column of water. When the lake settled he saw that the dam had not been breached. The 'Upkeep' mine had probably stopped and sunk just short of the dam, possibly having hit and broken the anti-torpedo nets thus clearing the way for the following mines. Mick Martin 'watched the whole 'process'. 'The Wing Commander's load was placed just right and a spout of water went up 300 feet into the air.'

Next it was the turn of 'M-Mother' flown by Flight Lieutenant 'Hoppy' Hopgood to brave the return fire from the two towers on top of the dam. 'They just put up a wall of fire which we had to fly through' said Tony Burcher 'and this was what got us. We were actually hit about twenty minutes before we got to the target. Hoppy was wounded when he got a shell burst in the cockpit. We never heard anything from the front gunner from then on.[1] I got some pieces of shrapnel in my stomach and lower leg but they were only scratches really; they just drew blood. Then 'Hoppy' said on intercom, 'Right, right do you think? Do you think we should go on? I intend to go on because we've only got a few miles to go. We've come this far. There's no good taking this thing back with us. I can handle the aircraft okay. So any objection? We said 'okay, just go on.' The engineer[2] who was sitting on the rumble seat beside the pilot said to 'Hoppy'; 'What about your face? It's bleeding. 'Hoppy' said, 'Just hold a handkerchief over it. The final run in seemed an eternity to me.'

Dave Shannon watched as 'M-Mother' attracted tremendous flak and he saw Hopgood's starboard wing catch fire. 'I think his bomb-aimer must have been hit, because the bomb was released late and bounced over the wall' Shannon said.

'When one of the port engines got hit', continues Burcher, 'Hoppy' didn't feather it; we had a glycol leak and we lost a lot of power but he kept it going. At that time I felt a terrific shuddering in the aircraft. I saw flames hooting past my turret. I had the turret on the beam waiting until I was within range. Suddenly my turret stopped; it was one of the port engines that actually drove the hydraulics to it. Next minute I heard 'Christ, the engine's on fire' 'Hoppy' said: 'Feather it, press the extinguisher' but the flames got even worse so he said, 'Right prepare to abandon aircraft'. The soon he said, 'Right, everybody, get out'. I cranked the turret back. Normally this would take time but it was the fastest wound turret you ever saw. I got back into the aircraft, put my parachute on and unplugged my helmet but I plugged in again and said on intercom 'I'm abandoning aircraft. 'Hoppy' said, 'For Christ's sake, get out.'

Burcher opened the door and then saw John Minchin, the 27-year old wireless operator from Bedford coming along on his hands and knees and dragging his leg. 'He was terrible; he was in a hell of a state. I didn't know what to do but he was dragging his parachute with him. I took it from him and put it on. I was near the rear step and he wasn't moving so I thought 'there's only one thing to do - throw him out'. I grabbed the D-ring on his parachute and threw him out.

'I don't know if 'Hoppy' realized it or not but we were in a steep climbing turn to starboard. The two port engines were shot out so he was turning into the two good engines but we only had a very light fuel load on because we only going to the Ruhr. Normally a Lanc would have about 2,000 gallons on; I think we had about 1,200 and of course we'd got rid of our four and a half ton bomb, so we were pretty light. He just couldn't get any more height and the other crews reckoned it was about 300 feet when our aircraft blew up. With the billowing white silk in his arms Burcher was blown out as the Lancaster exploded. 'I hit the top of the tail fin apparently and broke my back. The next thing I knew I was being jerked in the air and seemed to hit the ground at the same time. Normally, a parachute jump landing is the equivalent of a twelve foot fall. I was told later by doctors that if I had had taken that impact of a twelve foot jump it would have snapped my spine completely. The jerk of the parachute and a combination of other things saved my life. I got that little bit of extra time by throwing Minchen out; I landed in the middle of a recently ploughed field which cushioned my fall and it was in a little bit of a valley so that must have given me a bit of extra height and if 'Hoppy' had gone straight ahead I'd have landed in the flood waters so I would probably have drowned.'

The bomb aimer, Flight Sergeant James Fraser had also survived, having pulled the ripcord inside the aircraft when he had realised that he stood no chance if he made a normal parachute jump. The trees below 'looked awful damned close' and 'the tail wheel whizzed by his ear'. He saw 'M-Mother' crash before he touched the ground in seconds. Fraser 'landed on the ground and he walked away without a scratch. It was probably the lowest free fall in history. Fraser, who was a woodsman from Nanaimo in British Columbia, evaded for about ten days before he was captured and sent to PoW camp. Burcher did not see Fraser again but learned later on that after the war he took his own life. 'Another irony is that Freddy Tees [the front gunner and only survivor on Ottley's crew, which was lost en route to the Lister dam and suffered flash burns] also took his life after the war.'

Minchen did not survive the descent and Hopgood and the three other crewmembers were killed when the Lancaster exploded.

'M-Mother' was shot out of the sky by 23-year old Gefreiter Karl Schutte manning the 20mm gun on the North Tower. There were six 20mm guns positioned on the Möhne Dam, two of which were put out of action by bomb blast. One gun on the dam wall and the three near Günne continued throughout the remainder of the attack, putting up sporadic resistance against

Lancaster III ED817/G ('Guard') 'C-Charlie' on 617 Squadron which was used to carry out drop tests of the 9,150lb 'Upkeep' mine at Reculver before the weapon was finally cleared for use.

other aircraft even after the dam had been breached.

Alfred Lengherd, an anti-aircraft gunner at the Möhne dam spent his days and nights on duty reading, playing cards and chatting to his comrades. He lived only 20 miles away in Dortmund. 'On the moonlit night of 16 May I was at my gun post inside one of the towers on the dam. A bomber came straight towards me at zero feet; there seemed to be no space between the bomber and the water. There were two spotlights shining from the bomber onto the surface, which I could not understand. The night was so bright I could read my newspaper, so why did they need spotlights? Then I saw it coming towards the dam, something that looked like a big ball, skipping across the water. It jumped over the anti-torpedo nets, hit the wall and sank. A few moments later, the dam shook. I also was shaking. I had never seen such daring nor anything like the rolling mine that hopped over the water so easily.

'We were now busy returning fire. More bombers had come and their gunfire was greater than ours. They shot the roof right off our tower. I could see flashes from our guns hidden in the hills. The sky was alight with tracer and fragments of stone were flying everywhere. One bomber was hit by our guns. We knew he was in trouble and watched him crash 20 or 30 kilometres away. Then the raid was over, but we could still hear the drone of the bombers.'[3]

Next it was the turn of the Australian with the 'wild glint in his eyes and a monstrous moustache that ended raggedly out by his ears'. Mick Martin recalled: 'There was still no sign of a breach. I went in and we caused a huge explosion up against the dam.' But still the dam held. The mine had probably hit the water slightly off level and thus did not bounce straight and it had veered off to the left and exploded near the southern shore of the lake. Gibson flew just ahead of Martin and to his right to distract the German defences and told his own gunners to fire back. 'P-Popsie' was hit but not badly damaged. The fourth and fifth hits on the dam by 'Dinghy' Young and David Maltby finally breached the dam at 0056 hours. Martin, who flew alongside Young to draw some of the flak, adds, 'The dam at last broke. I saw the first jet very clear in the moonlight. I should say that the breach was about fifty yards wide.'

Shannon, who had been called in by Gibson was just starting the run and Gibson was flying down one side and Martin was flying down the other side, when there was a tremendous explosion. There were excited yells over the R/T, 'It's gone! It's gone!' The whole wall had collapsed and the water had started spewing out down the valley. It poured out of the lake, taking everything in front of it. After a few minutes, it was just an avalanche of mud and water rushing down the hill. Gibson rapidly said to me, 'L-Love - steer off the run. Stand by. I think it's gone!' Then he came back and said, 'Yes, it has gone!'

Alfred Lengherd wrote: 'We heard this noise, like a giant tree being split in half. There was 160,000,000 cubic metres of water pressed against the dam and out came the water. Incredible was the sound and spectacular the effect. The valley was soon flooded and we saw the power station with its seven transformers had gone.'

Gibson, who was now flying on the far side of the dam to distract the gunners, wrote: 'Nearly all the flak had now stopped and the other boys came down from the hills to have a closer look to see what had been done. There was no doubt about it at all. The Möhne Dam had been breached and the gunners on top of the dam, except for one man, had all run for their lives towards the safety of solid ground. This remaining gunner was a brave man but one of the boys quickly extinguished his flak with a burst of well-aimed tracer. Now all was quiet, except for the roar of the water, which steamed and hissed its way from its 150 feet head. Then we began to shout and scream and act like madmen over the R/T, for this was a tremendous sight, a sight, which probably no man will ever see again. Quickly I told Hutch to tap out the message, 'Nigger' to my station and when this was handed to the Air Officer Commanding there was (I heard afterwards) great excitement in the operations room. The scientist jumped up and danced around the room.

'Then I looked again at the dam and at the water, while all around me the boys were doing the same. It was the most amazing sight. The whole valley was beginning to fill with fog from the steam of the gushing water. Down in the foggy valley we saw cars speeding along the roads in front of this great wave of water, which was chasing them and going faster than they could ever hope to go. I saw their headlights burning and I saw water overtake them, wave by wave and then the colour of the headlights underneath the water changing from light blue to green, from green to dark purple, until there was no longer anything except the water bouncing down in great waves. The floods raced on, carrying with them as they went - viaducts, railways, bridges and everything that stood in their path. Three miles beyond the dam the remains of Hoppy's aircraft were still burning gently, a dull red glow on the ground. Hoppy had been avenged.'

Tony Burcher heard the two other bombs go off. 'After that I didn't hear any more and then I heard the aircraft going away so I wasn't too sure whether it was successful. I crawled across the field towards a culvert on the other side going under a road. I thought that my back was only sprained. I did not think that it was broken and I thought 'I'll just hold up here 'till it gets better. I thought I could hear a train. I don't know whether I was delirious or not because I had lost some blood and I had been pretty badly knocked about. We were always told that to get out of Germany one of the best things would be to get on a freight train going west to either France or Holland. I shouldn't imagine there was a train running with the flood waters but I had that set in my mind.'

Gibson, Maudslay, Shannon and Knight meanwhile, flew on to the Dam Busters' next target, the Eder Dam, the largest masonry dam in Germany at 1,310 feet wide, 138 feet high, 119 feet thick at the base and 20 feet thick at the top. The Eder Dam was not defended by guns but as Shannon said, 'The Eder was a bugger of a job' lying in very difficult terrain along a valley and very hard to find. Shannon only found the dam after Gibson fired a Very light over it. Gibson called Astell but there was no reply and then ordered Shannon to make his attack in 'L-Love'. 'I tried, I think, four times to get down, dropping down - and each time I was not satisfied with the run that I'd made and told Len Sumpter not to release. To get out of this predicament, we had to immediately pull on full throttle and do a steep climbing turn to the right with a 9,000lb bomb revolving at 500 rpm to avoid a vast rock face that was up in front.' Then Gibson told him to take a 'breather' and 'Z for Zebra' piloted by Squadron Leader Henry E. Maudslay DFC went in. Ray Grayston recalls. 'Maudslay made his run and it was a disaster. His mine bounced over the dam wall and exploded in the valley below. [The 'Upkeep' demolished the ashlar parapets, part of the roadway and pavement on the crown]. Gibson called him up to ask him if he was all right and all he said was, 'I think so' and those were the last words we heard from him. We think he flew on for a while before crashing or being shot down.[4]

Then Gibson told Shannon to have another go. 'I had another dummy run. Then I got what I thought was an excellent run-down and we released the mine - as far as we could tell, there was a small breach made on the port side... but there was no significant sign there.' (Shannon's 'Upkeep' had exploded in the area of the steps at the right-hand end of the dam and cracked the wall). Grayston recalled that 'It was way off centre. So then it was us; the last of the main wave of nine aircraft. I suppose we were lucky really. We did one dummy run and got it pretty well right. So we circled and came in again at about 800 feet. As flight engineer, I was responsible for the air speed. I'd tumbled to the fact that if I chopped my engines right back and let them idle, she would glide down to 60 feet. That's what I did - with my fingers crossed that they'd open up again. At 60 feet I slammed the throttles forward and they did. The machine took a few moments to level off and seconds later we released the mine. Immediately afterwards we went into a blistering climb, with engines hammering up through the emergency gauge to get enough power to get out the other end. As we banked, we looked back and, by God, we'd been spot on, absolutely spot on. A huge column of water had been thrown up to about 1,000 feet. We had hit bang in the middle of the dam and had blown a hole straight through it. The bottom came out, then the top fell away and that was it. There was great excitement among the crew about our success. We were all on a high for a few minutes. Gibson called up and said simply, 'OK, fellas; that's your job done. No hanging about, you know. Make your way home' that was easier said than done and they were out to get us. And they did get a few.'

Gibson described the breach 'as if a gigantic hand had pushed a hole through cardboard'. Banking below him, Les Knight reported a 'torrent of water causing a tidal wave almost 30 feet high'. Dave Shannon, who had guided Knight on the radio telephone called: 'Good show Dig'. Homeward bound Knight found himself well off track in the area of Zutphen and Harderwijk His rear gunner Sergeant H. E. 'Harry' O'Brien recalled: 'We were flying very low during the return journey; at the Dutch coast the terrain rose under us. Les pulled up, over and down. On the sea side of this rise and invisible to Les was a large cement block many feet high. This block passed under our tail not three feet lower. As the rear gunner, I was the only one to see it.' Knight landed safely back at Scampton at 04.20.

The crew of 'N for Nan' watched in awe as car headlights in the path of the water turned from bright white to murky green to nothing. The two Hemforth power stations next to the dam were put out of action and two more close by. Melvin Young's nickname 'Dinghy' was transmitted back to 5 Group Operations Room at Grantham where Air Chief Marshal Arthur 'Bomber' Harris, Barnes Wallis and others were waiting for news. On hearing the code word, Wallis, who until then had been morose, punched the air with both fists. Harris turned to him and said: 'Wallis, I didn't believe a word you said when you first came to see me. But now you could sell me a pink elephant!' Another story, probably apocryphal, was that Harris needed to ring Sir Charles Portal, Chief of the Air Staff, who was at that moment in Washington DC visiting President Roosevelt. The AOC picked up the telephone and said to the WAAF switchboard operator who controlled calls out of the 5 Group HQ, 'Get me the

The Eder Dam showing the Transformer Station and the Engine House.

White House' 'Yes sir' replied the WAAF and put Harris through to the White House Hotel in Grantham, which was popular with 5 Group officers!

The Lancasters flown by Ken Brown and Joe McCarthy headed for the 226 feet high Sorpe dam. Dudley Heal says. 'Some time before we were due to reach the Möhne Dam 'Hewie' Hewstone the WOp, reported that both it and the Eder had been breached and we were to aim for the Sorpe. We changed course, much encouraged by this news. Barnes Wallis' bomb was designed to be released by an aircraft heading over water towards a dam, the bomb then bouncing over water (like a pebble skimmed over the sea from the shore), hitting the dam and sinking to 20 feet, when it was set to explode. It had been realised quite late in the day that this was effective if the dam was built of concrete but no good for an earth dam, as the Sorpe was. Our instructions, therefore, were to fly over and along the line of the dam at 60 feet, releasing the bomb as near the centre of the dam as we could.'

Arriving over the valley at fifteen minutes after midnight, Joe McCarthy initiated a diving attack on the dam nestled at the bottom of two steep hills. As the Lancaster circled over Langscheid, McCarthy exploded; 'Jeez! How do we get down there?' He decided that he must go round the church steeple of the village to line up his run. Coming over the top of one hill, using full flaps to keep the speed of his 30-ton Lancaster under control, the American dived down the slope toward the 765-yard long dam. To escape, he had to apply full power to his four Packard-built Rolls-Royce Merlins and climb at a steep angle up the side of the second hill. And if that wasn't difficult enough, a thick mist was filling the valley as he arrived. The blinding moonlight turned the mist into a writhing phosphorescent pall, which made it extremely difficult to judge the bomber's height above the lake. On the third attempt to locate the target, McCarthy almost flew 'T for Tommy' into the water. It was not until the tenth

Water pours through the breach in the Eder Dam at a rate of 1.8 million gallons per second.

run that bomb-aimer, Sergeant George 'Johnny' Johnson, was satisfied and released the bomb from a height of just 90-feet. The weapon exploded squarely on top of the parapet, damaging and crumbling for more than 50-yards the crown of the earthen wall.

Shortly thereafter Flight Sergeant Ken Brown attacked the dam. His trip was quite eventful. Even before he reached the Sorpe his gunners shot up three trains en route. They were fired on by flak and hit in the fuselage but suffered no serious damage to the aircraft. Dudley Heal recalls.

'We found the Sorpe Dam with no trouble and could see it quite clearly at the northern end of the Sorpe River. The ground rose steeply on each side, heavily wooded, with a church steeple on our line of approach, all, except the river and dam swathed in mist. The only good point appeared to be that there were no defences. After two or three abortive runs, Ken decided to try the Wigsley 'gambit' of dropping flares along the approach route. We could see that the top of the dam was already damaged.' [Brown made eight runs on the Sorpe but he was still not happy about dropping his mine. On the ninth he dropped incendiaries on the banks of the lake to try to identify the Sorpe dam through the swirling mist. On the eleventh run they saw the dam and Brown's mine was released. The mine exploded on impact, as it was dropped while flying across the dam and not dropped towards it in the planned method, without it bouncing off the surface of the water. The explosion caused a crumbling of 300 feet the crest of the dam wall]. Eventually avoiding the steeple, dropping the bomb at 60 feet and pulling up sharply over the wooded hill we saw our bomb go off, causing an enormous water spout and an extension of the damage already done.' (The Germans, unsure of the dam's integrity, were forced to drain off over 50% of the reservoir's capacity until the structure could be inspected and repaired).

'After a good look at it we set course for base, 'Hewie' transmitting 'Goner', indicating that we had attacked but not breached the dam. Our homeward track took us near the Möhne Dam and we stared in awe at the breach through which the Möhne River was rushing down the valley. After that the journey back was uneventful until we approached the Dutch coast and could see the sea ahead. Then, without warning we were caught and held by searchlights and blasted by gunfire. Even in my curtained compartment those searchlights blinded me so how Ken and Basil coped I shall never know. Ken even put the nose down although we were already flying as low as seemed possible and we flew on. Then we were over the sea and I could see shells whizzing over our heads and hitting the water. The searchlights lost their effect and Ken handed over the controls to Basil, while he and I examined the holes in the fuselage. The starboard side of the aircraft at just above head height was riddled. I think there is little doubt that had we remained at the same height, or even attempted to climb, it would have been disastrous. (We learned later that Squadron Leader Young had gone down earlier at this same spot.) Back at Scampton we were the last aircraft but one to touch down. Flight Sergeant Townsend landed about half-an-hour later, having attacked the Ennepe Dam but, like us, failed to breach it.'

Townsend was ordered to attack the Ennepe Dam on the Schelme River. He made three runs on the dam before his bomb aimer, Sergeant Charles Franklin

DFM, was satisfied. Their bomb was released, bounced once and exploded thirty seconds after release. On leaving the target much opposition was encountered but by great determination on his part, plus the navigational skill by Pilot Officer Cecil Howard from Western Australia, 'O-Orange' made it safely back, landing at 6.15 am. Most of the latter part of the homeward trip was flown in broad daylight.

The 'last resort' targets, the Lister (Schweim) and Dieml dams were not attacked. However, the damage inflicted in the first two attacks proved the operation's success. The surge of water from the Möhne and Eder dams knocked out power stations and damaged factories and cut water, gas and electricity supplies. Ray Grayston concludes. 'There was great excitement among the crew about our success. We were all on a high for a few minutes. Gibson called up and said simply 'OK fellas, that's your job done. No hanging about, you know. Make your way home.' That was easier said than done, of course, because the Germans had woken up to what we'd done and they were out to get us. And they did get a few'.

Apart from Warner Ottley's Lancaster, those piloted by Byers, Burpee and Barlow, who hit high tension cables on the outward flight at Haldern, 2½ miles ENE of Rees, were also lost. Byers Lancaster fell victim to 10.5cm heavy flak on the heavily defended island of Texel and crashed into the Waddenzee. Barlow's 'Upkeep' mine did not explode and was recovered for examination by the Germans. Young's Lancaster was hit by gunners at Castricum-aan-Zee at 0258 who claimed a 'Halifax' shot down after it had crossed the Dutch coast. Between 25 and 27 May seven bodies were washed up along 15 miles of shoreline near Bergen-aan-Zee.

'N for Nan' did make it back, though not without incident. Ray Grayston said. 'We were picked up by searchlights and machine guns and it was so bad that we thought, 'This is it'. We were so low that the searchlights were beaming straight into the cockpit and blinding Les, who couldn't see a thing. But luckily our Brownings were loaded with 100 per cent tracer bullets and when 'Doc' Sutherland opened up from the front turret; it was like two streams of liquid lightning. Then Harry O'Brien in the rear turret opened up with four Brownings. With all these streams of lightning flying at them, the Germans panicked and ran away from their guns. So we got away with it. If they had stood by their guns, we'd have been shot down for sure. We landed back at Scampton at 4.20 in the morning and went straight into debriefing. All the nobs and senior officers, as well as Barnes Wallis, were there waiting to talk to the pilots, but they didn't have much to say to us. The senior officers didn't mix with the fry. We got egg and chips in our mess, with rum and coffee. But all we really wanted to do was get into our sacks and go to sleep for a few hours. We had been in the air for almost six-and-a-half hours.'

Dudley Heal recalled: 'The importance with which the powers-that-be regarded this operation is demonstrated by the fact that Air Chief Marshal Harris, Head of Bomber Command, attended the de-briefing of the returning crews, as did Barnes Wallis and the Station Commander, Group Captain Whitworth. I don't think any of us went to bed that night.' The euphoria became more muted when news of the losses came in. Of the 133 men who flew on the raid, 53 men were killed and three were captured on the eight Lancasters that were lost. 'I suppose we had become hardened to loss' recalled Dave Shannon. 'We could shrug it off. We had to; otherwise we could never have flown again. We were debriefed, then we all went back to the Mess and opened the bar and started drinking. The beer started flowing till late in the morning when we struggled off to bed, and slept for a few hours.'

'We will never forget the training we learned on bomber stations' recalls Vera Baker. 'We bore the sorrow of talking, laughing and dancing with boys one evening when next morning they were gone. To sit in the mess, eating our meals, looking at the faces of young men from many countries of the world, knowing they could die in the course of their next operation; it was something we as young girls never imagined and yet in the WAAF we bore it all - the work, responsibility and understanding the pain of others. I remember one night, when neither of the squadrons was flying and there were only two WAAF flying control operators on duty. There was a Mayday call from the only survivor on board a US Flying Fortress returning very late from a raid over Germany...the mid-upper gunner, slightly wounded but all the other members of the crew were either dead or too badly wounded to fly the aircraft. He was calling for help or guidance, but the frequency on which he was transmitting was not the same as ours. Although we tried everything, we couldn't get through. I called the nearest US station but they couldn't hear him; we put on the lights of our flarepath but that was no use if he couldn't land, so we had to sit and listen to his lonely voice fading away into the distance...'

Hans Werner Konig - Head of the Association of Ruhr Reservoirs recalled: 'I came from Halve five hours after the raid. There was a slight fog over the valley. I did not see any water in the reservoir. I stopped the car and saw that there was no water. I realised that something terrible must have happened. Shortly after five 'o clock I came to the barrage wall and saw the extent of the destruction: there was a big hole in the wall and large amounts of water were flowing into the valley. Nothing was left of the large power station building, only a large water-covered area, big rocks, torn torpedo nets - a picture of terrible destruction which I will never forget.' As many as 1,300 civilians, including about 500 Ukrainian women slave labourers, died.

'By morning' recalled Joachim Hoehne, 'the waters had subsided a great deal but the base was still very much flooded. As the sun rose, more and more people began moving about the field seeking to find lost loved ones and looking to salvage their personal belongings. Gradually, all of us on the hangar climbed down the ladder, satisfied that the water had spread itself out and wouldn't be rising again; the entire valley was flooded. I reached the ground before the rest of my family and dashed to our house, sloshing through the water the whole way but now immune to the cold; my curiosity regarding how much damage had been done to our house was more consuming than the cold biting at my ankles and calves. In many places, the water still stood knee-deep. The entire first floor of our house was a shambles, wrecked by the rushing water which had blasted through that night. Water still stood in the house, making clean up impossible. I ran up the stairs to find the second floor less damaged, but the water had reached this height at some point because things were pushed about in a very crazy fashion.

'Finally remembering my vegetable garden, I ran downstairs and outside to see if anything would remain of all my hard work. I'd worked on the garden quite a bit the day before and assumed the worst as I ran into the back yard, but I was certainly not prepared for what I found. Instead of simply finding my ruined garden, I stood gazing down at the cold blue body of Margaret Fennel. Margaret was jokingly known around the base as my girlfriend, even though she was only ten-years-old. The daughter of farmer Fennel, she and I had played together countless times. She helped me tend my garden and look after my animals; she was a wonderful friend, almost a sister to me. She lay there, eyes frozen and lifeless, drowned in my flooded vegetable garden. This was the first time I came face-to-face with the spectre of death. It was a devastating moment. Why this little girl? Why did this innocent little girl have to die? My mind struggled to process what had occurred; why was my little friend dead in my back yard? I don't know how long I lingered there with her, but my mother eventually led me into the house and her father came for her body. All over the base, similar scenes were being acted out. A good number of men, women, and children had failed to reach safety before the flood claimed them. There were funerals for weeks following, as bodies were found sometimes quite far from where they had disappeared, having been swept into the forests that terrible night.

'Within the day, we learned that the dam hadn't broken, the RAF had bombed it. For the RAF, it was considered a major triumph. The pilots and crews were heroes. In the years following the war, the 'dam busters' became somewhat legendary figures, but I regret I never saw any glory in the act and I doubt the crews themselves did either. I realize that innocents always suffer in times of war and that soldiers of all nationalities can only obey the orders they are given, so I bear no animosity today toward those who performed the bombing; I'm certain they derived no pleasure from the raid. Just as our bombers of KG 54 had carried out raids which certainly caused the deaths of innocent civilians, the Lancasters of the RAF had brought unintended death and destruction to my home. In the spring of 1943, however, this was more outrage than a boy of fourteen could contain. The savagery of it was beyond comprehension. Margaret Fennel was dead - the RAF had killed her. It was as simple as that. I had nightmares for weeks afterwards and am still haunted by the image of that morning.'

At 0730 hours on the morning of 17 May a Spitfire PR.IX on 542 Squadron flown by Flying Officer Jerry Fray left Benson to be over the dams at first photographic light. Fray recalled:

'Visibility was exceptional. When I was about 150 miles from the Möhne Dam, I could see the industrial haze over the Ruhr area and what appeared to be cloud to the east. On flying closer I saw that what had seemed to be cloud was the sun shining on the flood waters. I was flying at 30,000 feet and I looked down into the valley, which had seemed so peaceful three days before, but now it was a wide torrent with the sun shining on it. Twenty-five miles from the Ruhr the whole valley of the river was inundated, with only patches of high ground and church steeples, which I had seen as part of the pattern of the

The Möhne Dam before the attack. (IWM)

landscape a few days before showing above the flood waters. The even flow was broken as it rushed past these obstacles. As I came nearer the dam I could see that the water was about a mile wide. I was overcome by the immensity of it and when I realized what had happened I just wondered if the powers that be realized just how much damage had been done.

'The Ruhr was covered with haze and when I broke clear of this, I began my photography, moving up towards the dam. It was easy to pinpoint because the breach showed up and I could see the water rushing through. The control house at the foot of the dam, which I had seen two days before, had already disappeared. The level of the water above the dam had fallen, leaving huge tracts of dark brown mud around the edges. This was eight hours after the

The Möhne Dam after the attack. (IWM)

bombing. The upper reaches of the lake were completely dry, except for a small portion where the sluice gates had been closed.

'I then flew on to the Eder dam. The floods were easy to see. The long winding lake above the Eder dam was almost drained and as a landmark it was no longer there. If it hadn't been for the flood-water breaking out of the breach in the dam it would have been difficult to find the lake. The water flowed through the narrow valley and from 30,000 feet I could see the course of the original stream. It stretched eastwards and northwards to Kassel. On my second run over the Eder dam I saw two aircraft coming from the north-east so I decided that it was time for me to come home.'[5]

After about three days in the culvert in the field Tony Burcher's delirium had worsened and he now had unwelcome guests. 'There were a lot of rats in this culvert. I think they might have been attracted by the blood or the dried blood on my hands. They were becoming a bit of a nuisance so I thought I'd try somewhere else and I was crawling across the road when a Hitler Youth pushing a bicycle came along and of course that was it. He spoke English - most well-educated German kids did. He looked at my airman's jacket and said 'Where the hell did you come from?' I said 'Up there.' He said 'What aeroplane were you in? I said 'Tiger Moth'. Well, even the kids in Germany knew that Tiger Moths didn't fly over Germany and I got a kicking for that. He realized that when he kicked me that I wasn't in a very good state so he desisted. Soon after that a policeman came by, also wheeling a bicycle. They put some fence posts between their two bikes and put me on it and took me to the village police station. I was put on a flat board with no mattress. That evening I asked for a drink of water. The policeman looked at me incredulously. He said 'Vasser? I said 'Ja, vasser.' Finally a leutnant who spoke English came. He said, 'You want Vasser and your mob has just blown up our bloody supply!' It was then that I realized that the raid was successful!'

It was only long after the war that Burcher learned how successful it had been. In Singapore he met a British Army officer who had been in the Ruhr with the Army of Occupation and he met his counterpart, a German engineer, who told him that though considerable damage had been done they had rebuilt the dam 'pretty quickly' but the power house that 'some fool' had bombed took

Devastation caused to the Möhne dam and the surrounding area.

The Sorpe Dam after the attack. (IWM)

many months to repair because replacement dynamos were not available. Burcher, who did not know that their bomb had overshot until after the war when he read Guy Gibson's book, *Enemy Coast Ahead*, felt much better at hearing this news.

'In hospital I filled in a Red Cross form with my name, number, rank and next of kin and that was my then fiancée Joan, a WAAF. She was actually notified before my mother in Vaucluse, who received word after six weeks. I was given the best hospital treatment and if it wasn't for the doctor I would never have walked again. I was put in a concrete cast. One day the doctor came in and said, 'Right, get up and walk.' I said 'Oh don't be bloody silly; I can't walk.' He just goaded me into it. He said, 'You're a coward like the rest of the British'. I hung onto him and walked along the ward and a few days later I walked out of the hospital. When my back was X-rayed at Eastbourne in England after the end of the war I found out that he had got the perfect articulation. My spine was cracked and it was just resting slightly on the spinal cord. That was why I was slightly paralyzed but when he set it, he'd got it away from the spinal cord and when I got feeling back in my leg I discovered then that I had a broken knee-cap.'

During his subsequent interrogation Burcher realized that his captors were unsure that he had been on the Dams' raid three days' earlier. To make him talk they put the heat on - literally. 'They'd raise the heat to about 40 degrees' and then they'd drop it to sub-zero so that one moment you were sweating like a pig and the next you're freezing and this was done for some time. Of course you complained and they said, 'Well okay; tell us what we want to know.' After a while a major who spoke English perfectly with an Australian accent said 'G'day sport, how are you? He handed me a fag out of a pack of Australian 'Turf' cigarettes and said 'I understand you're from Vaucluse?' I said 'yes'. 'Oh' he said, 'I'm from Waverley myself'. I said, 'Well, what are you doing with this bloody mob then?' He said 'Well, I'm a German national. I was recalled by the German authorities just before the outbreak of war to fight for the Fatherland. 'Incidentally', he added, 'we should be both be fighting against the common enemy; the Bolsheviks. We shouldn't be fighting each other.' He tried to soft soap me so I clamped up straight away. And I said 'Well, you're a bloody traitor as far as I'm concerned; get out!' He concentrated on me for a couple of days, trying to talk about cricket, about football; anything but he gave up after a while.

'There must have been a guiding hand. I was sent to Stalag Luft III and not an NCO camp.'

In England meanwhile, the returning Dam Buster crews were all given a week's leave. Dudley Heal recalls 'Halfway through the week I was sitting at the tea table with my parents and my brother, Les, (my other brother, Don, being at sea) when the doorbell rang. Being nearest, I got up and answered it. It was a telegram for me from Scampton. Back in the living room I held it up and said, 'I hope that isn't a recall from leave.' I opened it, everybody watching me apprehensively and read it aloud. It said, 'Heartiest congratulations on award of the Distinguished Flying Medal. Wingco.' We were all speechless. Then my father, who was Secretary of the British Legion Club in Gosport, said, 'We're all going down to the Club tonight', which we did. Back at Scampton after the leave I found that Steve had also received the DFM while Ken had been awarded the CGM (Conspicuous Gallantry Medal). Basically, awards had been given to pilots, navigators and bomb aimers who had reached and attacked their targets accurately, whether or riot they had been breached. Where other members of the crews, gunners for example, had distinguished themselves in some way they could also have been decorated. The matter of rank was always a problem in this connection. Commissioned pilots had received the DSO, a most prestigious decoration, as Ken knew. Non-commissioned pilots received the CGM, which few people had heard of at the time. Similarly, if I had been commissioned I would have received the DFC. I think that Ken, who was a Canadian, was miffed about this class distinction although he did realize that he had received one of the rarest 'gongs' of all. For my part I could not have been more thrilled if I had been awarded the Victoria Cross.'

The raid received maximum publicity. Scampton was honoured by a visit from Their Majesties the King and Queen and the decorations were presented by the Queen, (the King being in Africa), at a Special Investiture on 22 June. In

The Möhne in full flood.

the message he sent to the crews, congratulating them on their brilliant work, Air Chief Marshal Harris said:

'Please convey to all concerned my warmest congratulations on the brilliantly successful execution of last night's operations. To the aircrews I would say that their keenness and thoroughness in training and their skill and determination in pressing home their attacks will forever be an inspiration to the Royal Air Force. In this memorable operation they have won a major victory in the Battle of the Ruhr, the effects of which will last until the Boche is swept away in the flood of final disaster.' Congratulations came from the War Cabinet. They were addressed to Sir Arthur Harris by the Secretary of State for Air, who wrote: 'The War Cabinet have instructed me to convey to you and to all who shared in the preparation and execution Sunday night's operations - particularly to Wing Commander Gibson and his squadron - their congratulations on the great success achieved. This attack, pressed home in the face strong resistance, is a testimony alike to the tactical resource and energy of those who planned it, to the gallantry and determination of the aircrews and to the excellence British design and workmanship. The War Cabinet has noted with satisfaction the damage done to German war power.'

It was, as Wallis said, 'the most amazing feat the RAF ever had or ever could perform'. The massive Möhne, Eder or Sorpe dams served the industrial Ruhr Basin and more than a dozen hydroelectric power plants relied on their waters. So did foundries, steel works, chemical plants and other factories fuelling Germany's war effort. Dr. Rohland, Head of the main committee for the iron-producing industry in Albert Speer's Ministry for Armaments Production, said that 'The actual loss of production achieved was in no case proportional to the destruction'. Speer said: 'The first serious threat to production came after the attack when the pumping stations were flooded and chocked with mud and the water supply to the mining and blast furnaces was stopped.' He went on to say that if the Sorpe dam had been destroyed instead of the Eder dam, production in the Ruhr would have suffered more. The loss of electric power to the Ruhr as a result of the raid was negligible because hydro-electric power represented only a small percentage of supply needs. Most of Germany's electricity came from coal-fired generating stations and the Ruhr, in common with other parts of Germany, was fed on a grid system. Speer admitted that 'what was the harm to us was the water for the coking plants for gas which was a key to our industrial processes in the Ruhr and water for the cooling processes in steel production and other industry. We needed a lot of water and the Ruhr wells could not possibly supply sufficient water. If the Sorpe could have been breached as well it would have been a complete disaster. But it was a disaster for us anyway. It was urgent to rebuild the dams to be able to conserve the water in the lakes again when the rainfall would be coming in October, November and December and great priority was given to this.' Speer's greatest fear was that the RAF would bomb the reconstruction work from high level 'and so prevent us storing again the water so urgently needed.'[6]

Winston Churchill had authorized the operation and he used it as a coup to seek greater support from the USA. At the time, most of President Roosevelt's advisers were committed to targeting Japan first. The 'Dam Busters' proved that the war in Europe was being prosecuted dramatically well. Two days after the operation, Churchill was given a standing ovation at the 'Trident' Conference with Roosevelt in Washington. Gibson, who already had two DSOs and two DFCs was awarded the VC for leading the 'Dam Busters' and many of the officers got DFCs and DSOs. Brown was awarded the CGM. Joe McCarthy, David Maltby, Mick Martin, Dave Shannon and Les Knight were awarded the DSO. Ray Grayston adds. 'The officers got their invitations to Buckingham Palace. We thought we'd get something sooner or later, but it

The Möhne dam undergoing repairs.

never happened. The senior officers celebrated for weeks as they visited various messes around the country. Les Knight acted as taxi pilot most of the time because he didn't drink.'

On 18 May Reich Minister Dr. Joseph Goebbels wrote in his diary: 'Last night seriously damaged our side in the air war. The raid by British bombers on our dams was very successful. The Führer is extremely impatient and angry at the inadequate preparations made by the Luftwaffe.' Joachim Hoehne visited the Eder Dam with his camera several days after the raid and took some photos of the giant hole in the dam, which had finally ceased pouring water into the valley. 'This was more of my cavalier attitude, as we had been clearly told by the local political authorities to stay away and we were not to photograph any of the destruction or speak of this to anyone. According to Herr Goebbels' propaganda administration, the bombing of the dam didn't result in any major damage. I became very disillusioned by this attitude and I'm certain this was the first time I realized that all the news coming from Berlin was suspect. I hid my photos of the broken dam in my room for safekeeping. Goebbels could go to hell as far as I was concerned. I wasn't going to forget about that night.' Soon after, at one of the Hitler Youth meetings, Joachim and his school friends were informed that since they were now fifteen, they were needed as Luftwaffenhelfer ('Luftwaffe Auxiliaries', equivalent of the British Air Training Corps) to help man flak batteries within the Reich. In all, 75,000 students from secondary schools were drafted into the Luftwaffe Flak arm from February 1943 onwards, manning the heavy batteries.

Harold Roddis concludes: 'The ground crews were given three days leave and along with one of the engine mechanics called Jack Staveley hitched home to Sheffield. I remember my parents being surprised when I turned up and although the news of the raid had been headlined in the press, I still did not tell them that I was a member of the Squadron that had carried it out and it was not until the war was over that I disclosed this fact. When I returned to camp, I was given Gibson's kite 'G for George' to look after. One day whilst cleaning up inside, Gibson brought his wife in to show her round. He told her who I was and what my job was and I then left and waited outside. About the end of May the King and Queen visited the Squadron, met the aircrews and spent the day with them. We quickly received replacement Lancs and new aircrews. Then followed further weeks of training and it was during this period that someone composed the Squadron Song of which I only remember one verse:

> *Now the Möhne and Eder Dams were standing in the Ruhr,*
> *but 617 Squadron they bombed them to the floor.*
> *They gave us three days holiday, they said 'that's quite enough',*
> *but since the operation, we've been treaty bloody rough.*
> *Chorus: Come and join us, come and join us, come and join our Happy Band.*

'After the training was completed 617 were back on ops again and one I recall was to Italy. As they had insufficient fuel to do the round trip, they flew on to North Africa to re-fuel. Whilst there the aircrews took the opportunity to obtain amongst other items, crates of oranges. On their return we, the ground crew, were given one crate to share between us. My share was about 15-20 oranges. I hadn't seen an orange since before the war and I ate the lot in about two days. This I found was an extremely stupid thing to do as they worked as an efficient laxative, so I was never without the *Daily Mirror* and it wasn't for the news it contained!'

Guy Gibson with Roy Chadwick, Chief Designer of the Lancaster at the awards ceremony at Buckingham Palace on 22 June 1943. Chadwick received his award of the CBE at the same ceremony. Born in Farnworth near Bolton in 1893, Chadwick began work in the drawing office in 1911 and in 1936 he designed the Manchester twin-engined bomber to specification P13/36. When by mid-1940 he knew that the bomber would not prove successful he instructed his design staff to convert the Type 679 to a four-engined bomber using either Rolls-Royce Merlins or Bristol Hercules radials and the Lancaster was born. Chadwick was killed on 23 August 1947 in the crash of the Avro Tudor II during a test flight.

Late on the afternoon of 17 May a messenger cycled to Spire Hollins in Combs with an ominous telegram from the Air Ministry. 'We deeply regret...' Bill Astell and all his crew were killed.

Of the nineteen crews that took off for the Dams' raid, only six survived for more than six months. Twenty-two veterans of the raid were killed on ops later, many of them on two operations to the Dortmund-Ems Canal at Ladbergen in September 1943 with even bigger delayed-fuse mines than 'Upkeep'. The first raid on the night of 14/15 September was aborted and Squadron Leader David Maltby DSO DFC and crew were killed on the way home when his mine detonated. With little sleep, eight of the crews were ordered back into the air the next night to try again. 'We didn't think it was a very good idea,' says Ray Grayston, now promoted to Pilot Officer. 'And we were right. The new CO[7] took us across the Dutch coast and over an industrial area with no shortage of anti-aircraft batteries. Bang, bang, bang and all of his fuel tanks were hit. There was a mile of burning fuel flying out behind him and we were panicking to get out of the way before his mine went off. We just made it clear of him as he dropped out of the sky.'

South Australian Flying Officer Frederick Michael 'Spam' Spafford DFC DFM RAAF, Flight Lieutenants Torger Harlo 'Terry' Taerum DFC RCAF and Robert E. G. Hutchison DFC* and Flying Officer George A. Deering DFC RCAF on Guy Gibson's crew were KIA along with Squadron Leader Holden.

'At the target area' continues Grayston 'there was fog and we couldn't even see the ground. We circled at low level and saw a couple of guys fly into the deck. Then we did too. We clipped the top of a wood, had two engines ripped off and had part of a tree sticking out of the starboard wing. We knew we weren't going to last long. Les Knight tried to get us back up to a height where we had a chance of survival if we jumped. He got it to 1,500 feet and ordered

617 Squadron increasingly carried ever more powerful weapons including the 8,000lb HC (High Capacity) bomb (two 4,000lb Cookie bombs joined together) and on the night of 8/9 June 1944 the first 12,000lb 'Tallboy' earthquake bombs (pictured) were used on the raid on a railway tunnel near Saumur. Each 'Tallboy' required a team of four to prepare and bolt together the bomb, which resembled three 4,000lb 'Cookies', and an annular 250lb tail unit and took 2 hours 15 minutes with a further 35 minutes for loading.

us to bail out. But the aircraft was keeling over and Les needed me to help him struggle with the controls. Everyone grabbed their parachutes and dived out... and that left just me and Les. He had his leg stretched out rigid on the rudder bar and he couldn't move because if he let go, the machine was going to just fall over.

'So Les said, 'OK, I'll do what I can. Away you go.'

'I jumped out at about 800 feet and the chute opened. The Lanc flew straight into a tree, caught fire and Les was killed.'

Flight Lieutenant Les Knight DSO RAAF was later Mentioned In Dispatches for holding his Lancaster steady so that all his crew could bail out. Ray

On 21 March 1945 the Arbergen railway bridge over the River Weser was attacked by 20 Lancasters on 617 Squadron who dropped 'Ten Ton Bombs' on the structure and damaged two piers of the bridge. One Lancaster was lost. In the photograph is Lancaster Mk.I Special PB996/YZ-C minus nose or dorsal turret, flown by Squadron Leader C. C. Calder.

Lancaster B.I (Special) PB995 with a dorsal turret which was operated briefly by AAE&E on 22,000lb Deep Penetration bomb trials in July 1945 before going to 617 Squadron.

Grayston roamed the Dutch countryside for a couple of days and was given sanctuary in a village until a search party of German troops sent him on the run again. He was captured and ended the war in the infamous Stalag Luft III. 'But being an officer gave me better conditions,' says Ray 'so I've got Guy Gibson to thank for that.' Harry O'Brien was also captured.

Harold Hobday recalled: 'We managed to ditch our bomb and climb up, but because of the damaged tail, the aircraft kept wanting to go around in circles. Eventually it got worse and worse and the pilot couldn't hold it, so he told us to bail out. The crew in the front bailed out, but the people in the back, who were shovelling ammunition out to lighten the load, didn't hear the 'bail out' order. They sensed Les was coming down, and called over the blower, 'Are you ditching, Les?' and Les said, 'Jump out quickly.' He tried to land the aircraft in a field, but it hit a tree and he was killed - but the other two got out. Naturally we didn't find each other. I landed in a tree, clambered down and started walking. 'I found someone who could speak English. I was given some clothes and told to shave off my moustache, as Dutchmen don't have them. The underground movement looked after me in a wood for a month, then eventually they fixed up that I should go up to Rotterdam, stay with somebody there, and get used to mixing with Germans. Then I was met by a fellow who took me down to Paris on the train, which was very overcrowded. This was done on purpose, of course. We had to go through the customs where the Germans were on the Holland/Belgium border, and also on the Franco/Belgian border, which was a little hair-raising, because there were two Gestapo people at each place. I had to hand my papers in. I'd got forged papers in which I was supposed to be a deaf and dumb Dutchman working on an airfield in the South of France. Sounds a little bit of a tall story. The Germans were just about to ask me a question and then said, 'Well, go through' and I didn't have any trouble.'

Of the other crew members of 'N for Nan', 'Doc' Sutherland, Bob Kellow and 'Johnny' Johnson split up and individually trekked across occupied Europe to Gibraltar. In December 1943 they and Harold Hobday burst into the Officers' Mess at Woodhall Spa wearing French berets. What Ray Grayston did not know until after the war was that he was one of the lucky ones. Out of the eight Lancasters on the canal raid, only three returned.

On 20/21 December 1943 Flight Lieutenant Geoff Rice DFC failed to return when he was shot down southwest of Charleroi by Hauptmann Kurt Fladrich, Staffelkapitän, 9./NJG4 at Juvincourt flying a Bf 110G-4. Rice was thrown clear as his Lancaster exploded. His crew was killed. All had flown the famous dams' raid with Rice who had aborted after hitting the sea on the outward flight, ripping off the 'Upkeep' mine. Despite a broken wrist, Rice managed to evade capture for six months until April 1944 by which time the Belgian Resistance had moved him to Brussels.

Flight Lieutenant Richard Algernon Dacre Trevor-Roper DFC DFM, with his Oxford accent and Billingsgate vocabulary, had been a sergeant gunner at Swinderby before he was commissioned and became Guy Gibson's tail gunner on the Dams raid. Trevor-Roper was killed on the night of 30/31 March 1944.

Guy Gibson was sent to America as an air attaché but he begged the Air Ministry to allow him to return to operations. At Woodhall Spa Gibson persuaded the CO of 627 Squadron to let him fly a Mosquito, against his better judgement, for the operation to Rheydt on the night of 19/20 September 1944 when he was to act as Controller for the raid. While returning over Walcheren (according to Anton de Bruyn, a night watchman at the local sugar factory in Steenbergen, who witnessed the incident) both engines of Gibson's Mosquito cut. The aircraft crashed near the sea wall at Steenbergen, killing the Dam Buster and his navigator 23-year old Squadron Leader James Brown Warwick DFC, an Irishman and veteran of two tours. Both men are buried at Bergen-op-Zoom. The most likely theory for the incident is that the fuel transfer cocks were not operated in the correct sequence and the engines ran out of fuel.

On 10 November 1943 Wing Commander Geoffrey Leonard Cheshire DSO** DFC took command of 617 Squadron. Les Munro recalls. 'Leonard quickly gained my respect both as a man and a leader. It was not long following his arrival that a renewed sense of purpose and reason for being developed in the Squadron. In conjunction with Micky Martin, Cheshire introduced low level marking of targets by the Squadron with the result that 617 became highly efficient in destroying individual targets. The cosmopolitan make-up the Squadron was exemplified when it was restructured into three flights with Cheshire an Englishman as CO and three originals, McCarthy an American, Shannon an Australian and myself a New Zealander, as flight commanders. It later became known as the Cheshire era and I have always felt a great deal of satisfaction and pride in being part of that period.'

'It was only a month after D-Day that Cheshire, Shannon, McCarthy and I were taken off operations and so ended my operational career and my service on 617 Squadron. I have always maintained that the international and cosmopolitan make up of 617 was one of its strengths with its English majority strongly supported by men from the Commonwealth - Canada, Australia, Rhodesia and New Zealand and even two from the USA. In post war years that cosmopolitan make up resulted in a strong worldwide Association with all members fiercely loyal to 617 Squadron's history and their ties thereto.'

The 617 Dam Buster Squadron Memorial at Woodhall Spa, Lincolnshire by K. Buckingham.

Footnotes for Chapter 5

1   Pilot Officer George Henry Ford Goodwin Gregory DFM.

2   Canadian, Sergeant Charles Brennan.

3   A week later Karl Schutte, who commanded the flak detachment, was decorated with the Iron Cross (Second Class).

4   He did. Badly damaged over the Möhne by the detonation of his own 'Upkeep' weapon and hit by flak fired by 16 year old Hitler Youth Hans Durveld on the return flight, Maudslay crashed at Netterden, 1¾ miles east of Emmerich, one mile inside the German border. There were no survivors.

5   *Above All Unseen: The Royal Air Force's Photographic Reconnaissance Units 1939-1945* by Edward Leaf (PSL 1997).

6   Interview with Albert Speer quoted in *'Bomber' Harris: The Authorised Biography* by Dudley Saward (Cassell Ltd 1984)

7   Squadron Leader Holden DSO DFC* MiD.

Chapter 6

A Member of the RAF of Indeterminate Race

Cy Grant

Sergeant Percy Gabriel Montgomery placed his tankard on the mantelpiece over the fire of the Golden Lion, his left breast pocket surmounted with the newly stitched half-wing of an Air Gunner. And because the missionary strain had won only a Pyrrhic victory over the deeper and blacker roots of the Montgomery family, the gunner's nickname was now firmly fixed. He liked it. George, who was the black man's Observer, said, 'Why if it isn't Persil himself!' They drank various toasts, including 'Death to the slave-traders!' This caused the blonde barmaid with the blue parting to change her mind about the port and lemon offered her by the Food Control officer in the corner and have a brandy instead., remarking that thank Christ her bloody mother didn't know the company a decent girl was expected to serve in a good-class bar.

Colour Bar, The Fire Was Bright by Leslie Kark, 1943

I was born in the little village of Beterverwagting in Demerara in British Guiana (now Guyana), an independent and impoverished republic on the northeast coast of South America and part of the British Commonwealth. I grew up in the sleepy village for the first eleven years of my life and then in New Amsterdam, the capital of Berbice. By the outbreak of World War II in 1939 the RAF had changed its mind about the recruitment of 'men of colour' into its privileged ranks and by 1941 it was even prepared to recruit them as aircrew!

I qualified as navigator and astronomical navigator on 5 February 1943 and was told that I was being recommended for a commission. This news was extremely welcome and in some way compensated for my disappointment in not continuing my training to be a pilot. The Commanding Officer, no doubt aware of the RAF's previous policies about recruiting 'men of colour', said he was taking an unprecedented step in making the recommendation, but that it was fully deserved and that he would take full responsibility for the decision and that should I encounter any difficulties in future that I should not hesitate to get in touch with him.

In March I was posted to No 30 Operations Training Unit at Hixon, Staffordshire. Here I teamed up with my Captain, Flying Officer Alton Langille, a French Canadian who chose me to be his navigator as he was to choose all the other crew members - because we were the best at our respective trades among the new batch of air crew. They were three Englishmen, Pilot Officer Don Towers, radio-telegrapher, Pilot Officer Charles Reynolds, bomb aimer and Flight Sergeant Geoffrey Wallis, mid-upper gunner.

Our last flight at this unit, in which we trained on Wellingtons, ended in a crash landing on Greenham Common in the early hours of the morning of 5 May 1943 after a training flight across the English Channel to drop leaflets on Nantes. No one was hurt. We had an engine failure on the way back and we were warned by the pilot that we would have to make a crash landing. I do not recall that there was any great panic. We all had great trust in Al. We landed with the nose of the Wellington up against the trunk of a very large tree and crawled out, completely unscathed, in the early morning of May 6th.

That same day we were picked up by another Wellington and flown to a Conversion Unit to train on the Lancaster Bomber. The Lancaster was to prove the most successful bomber during the ensuing months and indeed for the duration of the war. Pilots loved flying them and the navigator's station was well equipped with navigational aids. Here we acquired our last two crew members: Pilot Officer Joseph Addison, tail gunner, from Canada and Sergeant Ronald Hollywood, flight engineer, from England. They were the only members of the crew who did not survive the war.

Less than two weeks later, on 19 June, we were ready for ops as members of 103 Squadron, stationed at Elsham Wolds in Lincolnshire, situated south of Hull, on the other side of the Humber. The aerodrome had been built on land that had once been a farm, after which it took its name.

This was the time of the massive bomber raids on Germany, known as 'the Battle of the Ruhr', which started in March 1943 and lasted until July. The objective was the 'progressive destruction and dislocation of the German military industrial and economic system' as well as the hoped-for demoralizing effect on the German people. After just one 6½-hour cross-country flight by night on 19 June, thus clocking up a total of one hundred and sixty three hours flying time, half of which were by night, we went on our first bombing raid to Mulheim on 22 June 1943.

As navigator one was kept continuously occupied. You did not see much of what was going on below. It may have been completely different for my pilot, having to fly the Lanc through all that flak, or for the gunners looking out for fighters, or indeed for all the other members of the crew. For myself, my sense of responsibility for getting us there and back was paramount, and that may be why the obvious dangers of the situation did not seem to get to me. In the Lancaster, the navigator's position, just behind the pilot, was screened off so that no light could escape to betray our aircraft's position to enemy night-fighters. In any event, whenever I had a peek, and that was only when we were over the target, I was only too happy to get back to my station to work out a course that would get us away from the scene; away from the noise of the battle, the flares, the searchlights, the inferno below and the unnerving jolting of the aircraft whilst we were over the target.

Two nights later we took part in another raid, this time on Wuppertal. It was a surreal repeat of the first flight. I don't think aircrew were fully conscious of the havoc and destruction they were causing. All they were thinking was 'drop those bombs on the target and get out of there'.

Warfare denudes you of your humanity. Yes, I had sought adventure, an escape from a dull future in a British colony, but reflecting on it afterwards, I feel no sense of pride.

In a sense I am grateful that we were destined to complete no further operations over enemy territory. Our next flight would be our last. The very next night, Friday, 25 June 1943, one of the shortest nights of the summer, 473 bombers from Bomber Command of the RAF (twin- and four-engine) attacked, among other places, Bochum and Gelsenkirchen in the Ruhr. A total of 24 Lancaster bombers from our Squadron were incorporated into the operations. Our Lancaster, W4827, was one of them.

At 22.42 hours the first of 24 planes of 103 Squadron took off for a rendezvous near Harwich on the East Coast of England. There we joined a large stream of bombers, which set out across the North Sea in the direction of the Ruhr. The excitement was intense.

I was to learn after the war that of the 24 planes from 103 Squadron, four had to return early to base. The remaining 20 proceeded towards the target. Our aircraft was trailing slightly behind the main force of bombers when we arrived over the already blazing target.

Even amidst the deafening drone of scores of other aircraft, the muffled explosions below, the glow of the target area, the flak, the sweeping searchlights and the sudden bumps as the aircraft rode the frenzied skies; I never questioned what I was doing there. I cannot remember feeling particularly frightened; the thought of imminent death did not cross my mind. It was as though we were in another state of consciousness, emotionally switched off yet our minds functioning clearly as we got on with the things we each had to do.

The navigator's station was immediately aft of the pilot's position, with a small table on the

Cy Grant in RAF uniform with his observer brevet.

Sergeant Leslie Francis 'Darky' Gilkes, a gunner on 9 Squadron, who was from Siparia, Trinidad, was KIA on the night of 2/3 August 1943 on the raid on Hamburg when Lancaster III ED493 WS-A was shot down and crashed off Bergen aan Zee. Twenty-one year old Sergeant David MacKenzie of Helmsdale and all seven members of his crew were killed. On Gilkes' left is Canadian, Sergeant Jack Dickenson who would return home safely to his homeland.

port side of the cabin on which sat the chief navigational aid - the Gee radio navigation system.

On arriving over the target, we dropped our bombs from a height of between 19 and 20,000 feet. Shortly after doing so we were hit by flak, which penetrated the bomb hold, leaving the fuselage on the other side, but without causing any further damage. A minute earlier and we would have had it!

We headed for home at an altitude of 21,000 feet, still trailing a bit behind the main stream of bombers. Shortly afterwards, over Holland, the tail gunner, Pilot Officer Joe Addison, shouted over the intercom that a German fighter was closing in from underneath us. The German fired a long volley and a jet of tracer spat out towards us. Addison, from his tail turret, returned fire immediately. During the exchange the fighter climbed a little and veered off to the right. This manoeuvre brought him into the field of fire of the mid-upper gunner, Sergeant Geoffrey Wallis, who immediately opened fire.

Everything was happening very fast. All hell had broken loose. Flying Officer Alton Langille pushed the nose of the heavy plane into a dive... In a moment the world was turned upside down. With the sound of the vicious cannon-fire from our attacker and of our two gunners returning his fire, AI, took evasive action. Then, surprisingly, as suddenly as it all began, everything was normal again. The German fighter was nowhere to be seen. Our gunners must have shot it down!

'Great work, guys!' the Canadian accent of the skipper betrayed both the strain we were all under and the relief.

He levelled out, the plane behaved normally and no serious damage had been observed. Wallis was missing one of the covers of his ammunition boxes next to him, shot away during the attack. But none of us had been hit. With our spirits high again, we were soon lulled into a false sense of security...

The pilot checked our position with me. Despite the evasive action I had a good idea of where we were. The attack had occurred shortly after we were over Holland on route to our base at Elsham Wolds. We should be somewhere south of Amsterdam, near the small town of Haarlem. In half an hour we would be back.

But once again our peace of mind was to be short-lived.

This time it was the mid-upper gunner's voice over the intercom that shattered our complacency.

'Starboard outer afire, Skipper!'

So we'd been hit after all! But the fire was only a small one and we never thought for a moment that we would not make it back to base. We dived steeply, in an effort to smother the flames, but when we levelled out they had spread to the dingy stored below the starboard wing. However, we dared not jettison it for fear that the slip-stream would take it onto the tail-plane.

Then one of the wheels of the undercarriage fell away in a flaming circle...

Now, we were up against it! Without our dingy we could not ditch in the sea in the event of the plane breaking up before we could cross the channel; and even if she did last that long we'd have to face a crash landing in England and who knew where we might be forced to set down!

The situation was tense and worsening as each moment went by. By the time we reached the coast, we were a flaming comet over the Dutch sky. Both wings were afire now and I gave the shortest course to the English coast.

Unfortunately, we were flying into a headwind of about 80 miles an hour at 20,000 feet.

Undaunted, we unanimously decided to risk getting across the Channel rather than turn back and bailout over enemy-occupied territory. But it was becoming extremely difficult for Al to control the aircraft and he sensed that we would not make it across the channel. He decided to turn back over land.

No sooner had he got her round than he was forced to make another decision.

'Well, guys, this is it. Bail out and good luck! Get to it! '

Our nose had gone down again and there was no other option. I moved forward towards the hatch in the bomb-aimer's compartment...

I had never contemplated being in this situation. We had been instructed in the use of parachutes but never had to practise leaving an aeroplane by one. When I went forward I found that the bomb aimer and engineer, who should have already left in that order, were still fighting to free the hatch-door, which was situated underneath the bomb-aimer's cushion in the nose of the plane.'

Al, seeing me go forward, left his controls and came after me. The four of us were soon piled one on top the other, tossed from side to side in the cramped space of the nose of the plane. Though not comprehending why we were unable to escape the now fiercely burning plane, I do not recall any sense of fear or panic. We seemed locked in a timeless moment of inertia when suddenly, with a deafening blast which lit up everything, our craft blew up and disintegrated, freeing us from each other - a free-fall into Eternity. On reflection I realise that the whole sequence lasted for less than 30 seconds.

I found myself swallowed up by the silent stretches of space ... My chute opened readily and I felt a sudden jerk and the strain of the harness on my shoulders as the wind snatched at the canopy, buffeting and tugging at it so that I swayed violently from side to side.

Except for the rush of the wind I was now in an unreal world of mist and utter silence. It was quite light up there above the clouds, which stretched like a white ethereal sea below. To add to the unreality, it seemed as if I was suspended in the air, for at first I experienced no sensation of falling.

The canopy of my parachute spread above me like a sinister shadow and I felt as if I were being borne swiftly aloft in the claws of a gigantic eagle.

I became aware of distant searchlights and the glow of a fire far below me. Our aircraft?

It still seemed that I was drifting aimlessly, with only the sound of the wind swelling the silk of the chute above me. Then came the sudden rush of a shadow coming towards me at immense speed. It was the ground reaching up to gather me.

Instinctively, I grabbed for the release knob on my harness, turned it and slapped it hard. The next thing I knew I was running on firm ground with ghostly, billowing folds of silk collapsing all about me.

Amazingly, I had made a perfect landing. I wriggled out of the harness, my heart throbbing loudly. A glance at my watch showed that it was 2.38am. This was June 26, one of the shortest nights of the year. It was already quite light and I could see that I had landed in an open field. The countryside was flat, with canals everywhere, reminiscent of the country districts of Guyana. I recalled that Guyana had been a Dutch colony before the British acquired it.

It was deadly quiet except for the barking of dogs in the far distance. The Germans were obviously searching for us. I knew I had to get away... fast.

'Head South,' that's what they had instructed us to do if ever we found ourselves in this predicament. 'Travel by night.'

We had been given maps of the continent printed on silk handkerchiefs and a few other aids in case we did have to bail out. We were to head south and contact the British Consul in Spain, who would make speedy arrangements to get us back to England and back onto operations.

How I looked forward to that!

Then I remembered that I had to hide my parachute. It must not fall into the hands of the Germans. I started folding it up as I retraced my steps.

To my horror, and then relief, I found that I had landed just a few feet from the side of a huge ditch, a dyke, I supposed. What a baptism I had missed! In my bewildered state it might have proved fatal.

The soil by the bank was soft, but I do not think I made too good a job of hiding my chute. I was in a hurry and it was bulky. I recalled seeing them being packed, neat and compact.

Was I imagining it, or was the sound of men and dogs getting closer? I decided that would have to do.

For a while longer I stopped to gather my thoughts. And so it was that I found myself standing like Ruth among the alien corn (or was it oats?). I estimated that

'Hitler's Haunters' air and ground crew on P-Peter on 428 'Ghost' Squadron RCAF with bombs for the 2,000th sortie.

that I should be somewhere in the region of the small town of Haarlem - I could not have missed that name on my navigator's map.'

Trust me to land near a place where the colour of my skin would not matter! Definitely a good omen. But I also knew that I would be well within the coastal defences, where the Germans would be highly concentrated.

Yes, I'd better get on with it, head southeast, away from the coast. The Germans would be picking up our trails by now...

I wondered what had happened to the other members of the crew; had they survived the blast? Would I link up with one or more of them?

I walked, ran and trotted, but my legs and lungs were giving out with the stress of the situation. I prayed that the plane had crashed north or west of where I had landed, for I presumed that the Germans would commence their search for us from that point outwards. It would have been ironic if in trying to evade them I was, in fact, running straight into their arms.

The sounds seemed to be getting dimmer. I came suddenly to the edge of a field I had entered. A road bordered the field. Could I risk crossing it? It was already getting light and I knew that I could not move about during the daytime. Then I heard the sound of a motor approaching and a vehicle of some sort went by - Germans, I figured, hot on our trails!

That settled it. I was already very tired, even though I had not travelled very far. I would not be attempting to travel until I had got some rest and grub. For the time the fields of what I thought of as oats were high enough to provide good cover.

This part of the country was very open. There were only isolated farmhouses in small clusters with a main road separating them. I considered whether it was time to strip off my badges of rank and trade, but decided against this. After all, there was no way I could pass as a Dutchman in the event of being caught. I opened my survival kit and distributed its contents into the pockets of my uniform. My plan was to spy out the land from my hideout behind the tall oats, to rest during part of the day and, when an opportunity presented itself, to try to contact a friendly Dutchman.

I watched the sleepy Dutch village awaken. I wondered if they were aware of what had been taking place over their heads whilst they slept, if they were indeed able to sleep with all the activity above and below. I was to learn many years later that an engine from our Lancaster (W4827) had fallen through the roof of a nearby farmhouse, killing the wife of a farmer.

As it grew lighter, a sense of déjà vu suddenly overwhelmed me. Had I been here before? I was to get this feeling later on when I was in a prisoner-of-war camp. But now it could have been because of the familiarity of the Dutch countryside. It reminded me of the country districts of Guyana, low-lying and flat, with canals everywhere. The village in which I was born was probably laid out by Dutch colonists before the British acquired it - it even had a Dutch name, Beterverwagting. Later I grew up in a town called New Amsterdam, which I left in order to come to England to join the Royal Air Force.

Here there were the same early morning sounds - a cock crowing, in the distance a man shouting, the bark of a dog, the sound of a pail clattering to the ground - simple every day sounds that made it hard to believe that only a few hours ago an air-battle had taken place overhead or that a war was in progress.

Then I heard the sound of something moving along the main road. I peered from behind the shafts of oats. It was my first sight of the enemy; a German soldier, cycling along the road, whistling, blissfully unaware that I was lying only about 10 yards away.

It was a long and frustrating day. It started to rain mid-morning and I got soaked, thus making it impossible to grab some sleep. I was already cold and cramped, lying on the damp earth. Then, as suddenly as it had begun, it stopped raining, only to start again about an hour later.

I was wet, miserable and hungry, but I dared not come out into the open, there were too many people milling about. I thought I should first approach someone who was alone to ask for help. I needed some grub and to know my exact position and where the Germans were stationed; I also needed somewhere to stay overnight - a barn would be ideal - there were certainly many around.

By mid-afternoon my spirits were very low. The day seemed terribly long. It was, after all, the 26 June.

Still no sign of any members of my crew. Had they survived? The thought kept recurring. Would it be easy for me to pass as a field labourer? Definitely not. I realised that I would have to move by night unless befriended by a Dutchman.

Crawling on my hands and knees, I had explored the area on three sides of the field. I was leaving a long muddy trail behind me and I was covered in mud. The road adjoining the field ran north-east to south-west. I would have to cross it at some time. To the east were a few small houses and a large barn within fifty yards of the ditch adjacent to where I hid. To the southwest and about 500 yards away was a huge solitary building. It was from that direction that the soldier on the bicycle had come and I suspected this very big house might be full of Germans.

Early in the evening the workers were coming home and things were settling down at last, although it was still bright.

Looking about me, I was suddenly aware of the opportunity I had been waiting for. He was alone in a plot of land adjacent to mine and well away from the main road. I crawled on my stomach towards him. When I was near enough I made small pellets of mud and threw them at him. The expression on his face as these started to drop about him was a poem of bewilderment. He looked upwards, caught himself and then looked about him.

Then he saw me. He must have recognised me for an airman immediately, for he beckoned to me to move further way from the road and proceeded to do likewise himself. In a minute or so, he signalled to me to jump the six-foot ditch that separated us.

I threw myself at the other bank and clambered up to the man. He thrust a shovel towards me and immediately I knew I was in safe hands. From the road we'd just be two workers. He spoke no English, but showed me where I was on the silken escape map I held out to him. I was not far from where I expected to be; south-east of Haarlem, in a place near Nieuw-Vennep.

I intimated that I was famished and he nodded and led me to the big barn behind the nearest farmhouse. Suddenly I was the centre of attraction for a group of farm people and their children. A shot-down airman would always arouse people's curiosity, but there was something else here. I had encountered a similar kind of curiosity in parts of England where the natives had never seen someone of my colour close-up.

It wasn't going to be easy for me to escape ... But these Dutch country folk were warm and helpful, particularly the farmer's wife, who was young, about my own age and very pretty. She took me to the cottage and attended to the wound I had sustained to the side of my head. Then she made me a hot meal, so when the interpreter arrived my spirits had risen considerably. He was a small, nondescript man in an ill-fitting pin-stripe suit. His English was fairly good and he was able to translate all the questions the villagers put to me. They were anxious to know when the invasion would begin. They seemed to think it was long overdue.

'How long before it will commence?' they asked of me, as if I was the War Office.

I thought I should give them some hope so I replied; 'Soon now ... it will not be long before your country will be yours again.'

That seemed to cheer them up; they turned excitedly to each other. My plight was forgotten by all except myself and probably the interpreter, for he soon broke the bad news.

I had asked him to find out from the farmer whether he would permit me to sleep in the loft of the barn that night and the following day, as I was too tired to attempt to move that night. It was only then I was told that if the Germans did not already know of my presence at the farm, the chances were that they were certain to find out.

I had been seen by too many people, any of whom might be a quisling.

He told me that if they did not hand me over, the farmer and his wife would be shot. I caught the look in the eyes of my benefactors. They were obviously distressed by the grim choices that faced them.

This came as a great blow. I pleaded that I simply had to get away, that surely everyone there could be trusted. I looked about me, they all seemed so concerned for me, but I also detected concern for their own safety. The interpreter told me of cases where people had been shot in the past for helping Royal Air Force personnel.

Nevertheless, I found it very hard to resign myself to literally giving myself up and asked the interpreter to help me find another way out, but all he said was that it was 'quite impossible under the circumstances'.

My frustration was complete. I knew that he had no choice in the matter. The sudden arrival of a Dutch policeman settled it. I was not aware that he had been sent for, but suddenly he was there, a large, amiable man who beckoned me to follow him outside.

There was nothing else to do. Turning to thank the farmer and his wife for their kindness, I followed him out. He motioned to me to occupy the pillion seat of his motorcycle and soon we were speeding along a very lonely country road.

Sitting there behind this friendly policeman, I did not quite grasp the fact that he was about to hand me over to the Germans. His manner was so warm and comforting that I entertained the irrational hope that he was helping me to escape in some way. But at the same time I was feeling emotionally drained and apprehensive. I was still in a state of shock from the events of the past 20 hours and was becoming resigned to my fate.

Then I became aware of the huge revolver protruding from its holster by his side. It seemed to be inviting me to grab it. It would have been very easy. Perhaps my friendly policemen was inviting me to do just that? All sorts of thoughts were going through my mind then. Was I up to it? I was not a very tough individual and I did not know how to ride a motorcycle. Even if I could, would it not be too conspicuous a way of getting about?

My speculations were short-lived. At that moment, he turned his head towards me, smiling, and said something that I did not understand. It could have been, 'I wouldn't try that if I were you ...' His nonchalance was off-putting. He must have known it would have been easy to disarm him.

Soon we were passing houses and the road was no longer deserted. We were entering a beautiful and quaint little Dutch village. I would not have expected the policeman to take me to his home, but this is exactly what he did. His wife made tea, and a teacher who spoke English and lived nearby by was called over. The daughter of the house put on a pretty frock. They were the essence of hospitality.

I gathered that I was to be called for by the Germans. They were very sorry about that. Meanwhile they went out of their way to be pleasant and to ask again about the Invasion. They kept a short-wave radio upstairs and fetched it to show me. They listened to the BBC every night.

It was still light when the Germans arrived to fetch me. There was a screech of brakes, a big Ford V8 pulled up and two gefreiters entered the house. They were matter-of- fact and abrupt. They exchanged hardly a word with the policeman. I was frisked and led out to the car. Soon we were driving along the same country road I had come along behind the policeman, but this time in the opposite direction.

We arrived back at the farmhouse from where I had been fetched and one of the soldiers got out. The farmer and his wife came out, as if expecting this, and stood before their front door. The soldier unceremoniously pulled out his revolver and started shouting at the two people who had befriended me. I felt terrible. Was he going to shoot them then and there? The man and his wife started speaking together. They were violently denying something. I do not know the German word for parachute, but it suddenly occurred to me that perhaps that was what the soldier wanted. The parachute was made of silk and would be very valuable, I thought.

To my relief the soldier put away his gun and soon we were off again, but for a brief second my eyes had caught those of the young wife who had been so concerned for me and I knew that she would have run the same risk all over again if need be.

And thus my captivity began...'

Two of the crew were killed and Cy and the rest became prisoners of war. *A Member of the RAF of Indeterminate Race* is the translation of a sardonic caption that appeared under Cy's photograph in a German newspaper shortly after his capture. For Cy it was a timely reminder of what he was fighting for. What followed was an uncomfortable two-year period as a prisoner of war, spent mostly at Stalag III, Sagan. As the war neared its end, he and his comrades faced a succession of fatiguing route marches in freezing conditions intended to delay their liberation by the advancing Allied armies. They were eventually freed by the Americans in 1945.

Chapter 7

Kiwi

Where are the kiwis who left all the sunshine
For bleak windy airfields and fenland and dyke,
Playing wild Mess games like high cockalorum,
And knocking the Hell out of Hitler's Third Reich?
Lancasters Audrey Grealy

James Bayntun Starky was born at Gisborne, New Zealand on 10 November 1916. His father was a sheep-farmer, a pioneer of 'backwoods farming'. His father before him had emigrated from Spy Park, Wiltshire and bought land in New Zealand. In 1939, at the outbreak of war, Jim Starky was twenty-one; his younger brother, Pilot Officer David Starky, was already in the Royal Air Force. He flew Fairey Battles on 53 Squadron in the Advanced Air Striking Force in France. Later, when flying a Blenheim, he was shot down in the North Sea. His elder brother was a gunner in the Desert Army with the 4th Field Artillery of the 2nd New Zealand Force, under General Freyberg VC. He served in Crete, Greece and again in the Desert. One fortnight before he was due to return home he was killed by a stray bullet. The younger brother in his letters used to tell Jim what a fine thing it was to be in the RAF, but the elder brother did not, in the same way, recommend the army. And so Jim Starky decided to join the RAF. Sergeant Pilot Starky gained his wings, had a week's leave and embarked on SS *Aorangi* and sailed to Vancouver via Fiji, where the young pilots sampled 'Kava', a much stronger drink than they were expecting, but they could not swim in Suva Bay owing to the sharks. From Vancouver they went on the railroads and rolled along for five days and five nights before reaching Halifax, Nova Scotia; the Negro steward on the train earned a lot of good will by calling all the air-crew 'Boss'. From Canada they sailed across the Atlantic in the MV *Georgic,* a merchant vessel which was later sunk in the Mediterranean and then salvaged. Lashed to the foredeck was a batch of Lockheed Hudson bombers on delivery to Coastal Command. The crossing was a rough one and the *Georgic* zigzagged to present a less easy target for Hitler's submarines. After North Atlantic gales the Mersey was swathed in fog and the *Georgic* threaded her way through the balloon boats. The first proof that this was England was a buoy which they passed; clearly painted on its side were the words *'The George Formby'.* And then they saw the great Liver Building with its strange birds. The deck-hands wasted no time in telling these young airmen that the birds only bowed when a virgin walked by! This reference to Lime Street, a famous Liverpool thoroughfare, was perhaps not entirely groundless! And then three Spitfires flew over in formation and every New Zealander felt a tingling of excitement and of pride. At any time throughout the war to every Allied serviceman, the Spitfire was a synonym - it was the sword with which Saint George would defeat the dragon. Jim Starky felt the thrill of this moment and never forgot it.

Lancasters on 75 Squadron RNZAF at their dispersals at Mepal in Cambridgeshire.

Sergeant Pilot Starky had to decide which Command he should apply to join - the candidate's choice was no sure guarantee as to where he would go - but Jim Starky chose Bomber Command and there he went. With 149 Squadron, Starky went as second pilot, with an experienced Australian as captain of aircraft and did five bomber operations over the Ruhr. He then took his own crew and a Wellington IC 'D-for-Donald' - an identification letter which he managed to stick to through all his bomber operations.

At the end of 1942, Warrant Officer Starky was promoted to Pilot Officer and posted to 115 Squadron operating Lancaster IIs. The Lancaster II was powered by four air-cooled Bristol Hercules engines and was more powerful than the standard and brilliant Merlin-powered version. The squadron was based at East Wretham, Norfolk. The targets ranged from Berlin and Hamburg to the Ruhr. It was with 115 Squadron that Starky was to have some of the toughest trips ever survived by an aircraft of Bomber Command.

Soon after his arrival on 115 Squadron, Starky was awarded the DFC. The DSO was to follow it and was awarded after the second of two of the most remarkable flights ever made over Germany. On the first, Starky, now a Flight Commander, was turning his Lancaster II for his run up on to the target. They were flying at 1,400 feet. There was an appalling crash and the whole aircraft shook with the impact. Another Lancaster then appeared in front of them and blew up. It had struck off over six feet of Starky's starboard wing. It was quite impossible to identify this particular Lancaster, but it was flying as though there were fighters on its tail and flying in a way which Starky himself had advised his pilots not to fly. Violent evasive action completely upset the crew and gave the rear gunner an impossible task. Gentle weaving prevented the fighter from getting a steady bead on the bomber but gave its defensive gunners a fair chance of shooting down the fighter. But the immediate awareness in Starky's mind when he had recovered from the first shock of the collision was that to keep the Lancaster level - he had full left aileron on the control wheel had to be held hard over. His second thought was concerning the 4,000lb bomb suspended in the under part of the Lancaster's fuselage. At reduced speed he flew straight on towards the target and there dropped the great bomb. Miraculously all four Hercules engines went on running as smoothly as ever and they were able to turn and set course for home. They reached the island of Texel without incident but still, of course, with full left aileron countering the loss of lift on the severely cropped starboard wing. Over Tezel, a strongly defended area, Starky, by force of habit, took evasive action. His left elbow, already low down due to the position of the control wheel, hit something with a resounding crack when making an attempt to apply opposite aileron. He was thus harshly made aware of the need to keep the controls full over to avoid doing a complete roll towards the damaged wing! This produced another shock. At the moment his elbow struck there was a torrent of German on the R/T, for his elbow had pressed the buttons on the radio switch-box and the circuit engaged happened to pick up the comments of a German ground controller below. The landing was not the least of the difficulties, as extra speed was clearly necessary for fear of stalling the crippled wing. Lining up on the flare-path must be exactly right as it would have been courting disaster to make any but the most gentle manoeuvre on the approach. Suffice it to say a safe approach and landing was made and no additional damage of any sort was done to the aeroplane.

More operations followed, punctuated by short rest periods and leaves. A flight to the secret German Experimental Station at Peenemünde where the 'V' weapons were developed stands out in his memory. 115 Squadron went in strength. They flew at low level all the way up the North Sea to the north of Sylt, over the Baltic Islands and on to their target, the military barracks. Starky flew over Denmark at 50 feet. When crossing a lake at no more than 50 feet on his altimeter - as low as he dare fly, Starky was horrified to see a Stirling pass directly underneath him! There were many burning wrecks all the way to the target. The attack was made in brilliant moonlight. It took the Germans by surprise and defences were weak by comparison with what Hamburg, the Ruhr or Berlin could offer. 115 Squadron scored seven direct hits upon the targets they had been allocated. The trip took most of them over eight hours.

As examples of determination and resourcefulness there can be few in the history of operational flying which exceeds Starky's 47th and final operational sortie on the night of 5/6 September 1943. (The remainder of the crew had about twenty sorties each to their credit). The target was Milan. All tanks were full as Milan was about the limiting range for a Lancaster II. But it was not to be Milan; they were called to the 'ops' room and rebriefed. The new target was Mannheim. Weather was about perfect for a bomber operation with plenty of cloud and not too much moon. Starky took Lancaster DS682/Y off at 20.11 hours.

The outward flight was uneventful until twenty miles short of the target, as they approached ETA (estimated time of arrival). The weather was clear and the aircraft was flying at 19,500 feet. It appeared that they had drifted a little to the left of the main stream but the searchlight belt had suddenly 'coned' them. Starky found himself 3,000 feet lower, flying level with what had been an orderly array of searchlights going from side to side. The control column was flailing backwards and forwards. At this moment a stream of tracer flew at them from right ahead - so quickly did it come that there was no time to take any sort of evasive action. Over the intercom someone said: 'We have been attacked.' Then Johnny Willis, the rear gunner said: 'Port rudder-port rudder.' Then he spoke again: 'Weave, weave!' He was a magnificent little man from Limehouse with incredible courage. He had again got a Ju 88 into his sights. By holding his fire until he could almost see the pilot he poured a burst into it and it was despatched a fraction of a second before it could have delivered a

Lancaster HK551 A4-E on 115 Squadron at Witchford in 1944.

lethal burst of cannon shell. It was doubtless this night fighter which had caused the earlier destruction with a head-on attack. In that attack it had pierced the main spar with seven cannon shells. More shells had passed through the perspex forming the top of the windscreen just above the heads of the first and second pilots. The second pilot had his scalp furrowed by a bullet and his elbow blown off by another; he collapsed on to the cockpit floor. The flight engineer had a bullet in his shoulder and was incapacitated after a paroxysm from which Sergeant Tugwell the mid-upper gunner had to release him by a smart blow on the head with his torch. Later he came round. Next this same gunner went forward to help the second pilot. The cockpit filled with smoke and Tugwell saw that there was a fire under the instrument panel. It was the pipe line to an oil pressure gauge and mercifully it went out. There was just one favourable fact at that moment; all four engines were running but, passing through the fuselage, one of the cannon shells had released the dinghy, which blanked off the elevator control. The Lancaster went into a violent spiral - the central column rocking violently. Being unable to regain control Starky gave the order to abandon by parachute. Tugwell called out that Johnny Willis was stuck in his turret and Starky made a desperate effort to regain control. And then, like the quiet after a hurricane, the pitching and lurching ceased, the elevator snatching subsided and the stick became a little easier, due to the dinghy which had become jammed in the tail unit blowing free, but it took the starboard half of the elevator with it.

Starky cancelled the instructions to bail out but the wireless operator and navigator had gone. Flying Officer Ernie Beer, the bomb aimer, had attempted to jump from the front exit, but had been unable to jettison the escape hatch. When he was finally half-way out of the aircraft, he heard Starky say: 'Hold on!' as he had the aircraft under control and he changed his mind! Both the wireless operator and navigator landed safely and were soon picked up by the Germans.

Starky then attempted to take stock. He found that wireless operator and navigator had jumped by parachute; that his engineer was wounded in the shoulder and the second pilot wounded in the arm and head. Johnny Willis was now manning the mid-upper turret, while Tugwell and Ernie Beer attended to the wounded. Starky considered returning via Switzerland, ordering his crew to bail out over neutral territory and flying back home solo, but decided instead to risk returning alone and out of the bomber stream. The Lancaster had set out with considerably more fuel than it needed for the trip; but for this it would have had no chance of reaching England, for the cannon shell had knocked the main tank out of the starboard wing. This soon caused the starboard engines to stop! Fortunately, the flight engineer came round and saw fuel warning lights flashing and switched to inner tanks. Not aware of this Starky had not throttled back these engines and with a renewed supply of fuel they restarted at three-quarter throttle with a roar and the Lancaster 'yawed', causing another alarm throughout the aircraft! All intercom had been wrecked, so there was no means of one crew member letting the next know what had happened, but the rear gunner was not to be beaten by a technical fault of this sort. He gave instructions for evasive action to the flight engineer who struck the pilot on the appropriate shoulder when it was necessary to weave. They were now still not far from Mannheim, upon which the 4,000lb bomb was dropped.

Starky then attempted the most difficult task of bringing his badly damaged aircraft back to base without the assistance of a wireless operator or navigator. He set an approachable course for base and carried on this for over thirty minutes. By this time the bomb aimer had gone back to do the navigation, but as the navigator's log had gone he had no plan to work on. However, Beer produced an air plot and gave Starky an amended course for base. The pilot always carried a simple get-you-home plan with courses to steer after correction for wind and it was this scrap of paper which enabled him to fly and navigate the stricken Lancaster back to England. Spared by night fighters on the return trip, ground defences gave them no peace. On their way across France they were repeatedly fired at by AA batteries and as his intercom had

Lancaster II DS652 KO-B on 115 Squadron at East Wretham which crashed near Udem in Holland on 12/13 June 1943 on the raid on Bochum. Flight Sergeant Ian Richard Victor Ruff RNZAF and his crew were killed.

Lancaster III ED413 DX-M on 57 Squadron returned from Oberhausen in the early hours of 15 June 1943 with Sergeant Reginald Frank Haynes dead in his rear turret. ED413 later served on 630 and 207 Squadrons (as EM-P, pictured) and finally, 1651 CU before being SOC on 27 January 1945.

now gone, Starky was compelled to take evasive action only from the judgment of the gun flashes. On one occasion Ernie Beer had to go through to tell him that shells were bursting dangerously near the tail.

The mid-upper gunner manned the wireless set and succeeded in getting acknowledgment to a laborious SOS. The bomb aimer tried unsuccessfully to work 'Gee'. Eventually the Channel was reached and as they drew near the coast Starky and bomb aimer flashed SOS on their lights. As they crossed the Sussex coast an immediate green Aldis signal from Ford was received. Starky recognised three lead-in searchlights indicating Tangmere, a fighter station. Two Mosquitoes on patrol formated on the Lancaster and radioed Ford to receive it and to lay on every possible help. Starky approached at 160 mph and reduced to 140 mph near the boundary - about 30 mph more than normal. At 01.50 hours he landed safely at Ford with the navigator and wireless operator missing and two more of the crew wounded. The Lancaster was met by an ambulance and the doctor gave the second pilot a blood transfusion where he lay. Every part of the Lancaster was damaged. The starboard elevator was almost completely shot away, the wings and fuselage were riddled and even the tyres were grazed in many places. All members of the crew received immediate decoration. Squadron Leader Starky received an immediate award of the Distinguished Service Order.

His second tour completed, Starky had the usual posting to a training school, in this case to RAF Waterbeach, where they were converting pilots from Stirlings to Lancasters and later to Methwold, Suffolk. A rather gloomy twelve months passed and then in January 1945, Starky found himself on the Empire Test Pilots' School Course at Boscombe Down. Early in 1946 Starky was repatriated to his native New Zealand and demobilised. Six years before, he had sailed for England; a sergeant pilot with barely a hundred hours flying. Now he was returning, a Squadron Leader with great operational experience, wide knowledge of aeroplanes, a test pilot in the making, a graduate of the ETPS and with a DSO and DFC to boot. He went back to his father's farm, but only for a few months, for on 15 April 1946 the RNZAF Contingent sailed for England on SS *Maunganui* to take part in the Victory Parade.

Chapter 8

The Seven Year Twitch

Eric Jones

There are many different grades of fear
From simple fright to scared-severe
And each can cause the bowls to itch
This, regular airmen call 'Ring-Twitch'.
The twitch, too, has its much or slight
According to degree of fright;
You really know its dicey flying
If your ring's like an egg that's frying.
Jasper Miles

'On 22 June 1943 I had completed 88 hours on Wellingtons with a total flying time of 419 hours and I collected yet another average assessment. No. 1661 Lancaster Conversion Unit Winthorpe was not very far up the road from my old airfield at Ossington and only a short distance from the city of Nottingham and the town of Newark. It was here, at last, I was to meet up with the four-engined Lancaster bomber. Conversion onto the Lancaster was a comparatively short course lasting only approximately four weeks and in that time I had to learn everything about the plane because my life and the lives of my crew depended on it. In this present day one might be forgiven for thinking the Memorial Flight Lancaster small fry against a modern 747 Jumbo jet but when I first saw a Lancaster bomber I thought it massive and wondered with trepidation how I would ever manage to fly it. The blow was somewhat softened by first being introduced to the Manchester, a twin-engined aircraft which, with two huge and unreliable Vulture engines was not an operational success and was given a training role. Someone thought of replacing the two Vultures with four Merlins and the Lancaster was born. We have Roy Chadwick to thank for the design and A. V. Roe (Avro) for constructing it. Over 7,000 Lancasters were built and largely by women factory workers and to create the Lancaster they had to piece together 80,000 individual pieces. They did the job well - many a Lancaster still stayed in the air when all the known aeronautical laws said it should have crashed into the ground.

'We did a few hours on the Manchester and I was fascinated by the propellers on those huge Vulture engines. They seemed to rotate so slowly I could see the individual blades. Fortunately they kept turning for me until we were transferred onto the 'Lanc'.

My crew of five was now inadequate to man the Lancaster so it was here that the engineer and the mid upper gunner joined the crew. Ron Harris the engineer was even younger than I. His training lasted about twelve months and he was just nineteen when he joined the crew. 'Jock' Brown was a wee Scot and he was to man the two Browning machine guns in the mid upper turret. If I ever knew his real Christian name I have forgotten. Jock was at least ten years older than I. He rarely joined in our social activities but he, like Ron, slotted into the crew very well and, although a bit of a loner, he was to prove an invaluable asset in the air. Ron's task was to care of and nurse the engines, monitor the petrol supply from the various petrol tanks, take stock of all the pressures etc. and would be constantly at my right hand side at all times in the air. He was the youngest member of the crew and I was second youngest and at first it sounded a little odd when they referred to me as 'Skipper'.

After completing 34 hours on the Lancaster the 'powers that be' must have considered the crew ready for operations so we were duly posted to an operational squadron. But before we arrived at that squadron I would like to mention how readily I settled down to flying the 'Lanc'. Big she was, but she handled beautifully and although we were not flying with a full load I could sense the power of those four Merlins and felt confident that they would handle all that was demanded of them. As on the Wellington, asymmetric flying was practised again and again, feathering first one engine and then, on the Lancaster, two engines. The 'Lanc' held height quite satisfactorily on two engines when unloaded and many a pilot having lost an engine on the way into the target was able to press on and deliver his bombs before turning for home.

Either the pilot's seat or the rudder pedals adjusted to accommodate my long legs. I can't remember which but I did fit quite comfortably into the 'Lanc' which was just as well as our longest trips were to take over nine hours. Whilst on the question of comfort there was a tube suitably placed between my legs which did cater for half of nature's requirements. If a direct result of using this device was to create a block of ice which fell on some German's head - who cares.

Whilst I was at Winthorpe my fiancée Sylvia presented me with a pair of rabbit fur lined gloves. Hitch hiking into Nottingham from the main entrance, I secured a lift in a Rolls Royce (there were a few around even in wartime) but on leaving the car I left my gloves behind. I went back to the guard room for quite a few days in the hope that the Rolls owner had dropped the gloves off. Somewhere there was a Rolls driver with a pair of gloves to match his car. When I got that Rolls Royce lift into Nottingham I would almost certainly have been with one or more crew members and we would almost certainly have been on our way to savour the Nottingham pubs and maybe take in a dance as well. It's funny how an Englishman always uses public houses to direct someone who is lost. Turn left at this pub and turn right at that pub. When I think of Nottingham I'm very much afraid that I always think of the Flying Horse, the Black Horse and the Hole in the Wall.

At this time asthma did not cause me any undue problems although it had returned when I came back to England from Canada. I always kept a supply of tablets to hand, so they, along with Potter's Asthma cigarettes and Potter's powder, must have done the trick. All through the war (and after) I was a heavy smoker, smoking up to forty cigarettes a day and this coupled with a considerable intake of beer whenever the opportunity arose must have convinced the crew that the asthma was not a problem and could easily be contained. It could, except for one situation. Throughout our stay on an operational station we slept in Nissen huts on iron-framed beds with those three biscuit mattresses I mentioned much earlier. The huts were heated with coke fired stoves, two to each hut and they could be a problem. In a strong wind coke fumes would be blown back into the hut and in spite of all the remedies

The famous Saracen's Head (Snake-pit) in Lincoln.

that smell could keep me wheezing all night.

I did not consider myself to be a great letter writer and indeed letters to my parents were few and far between. This lack of consideration I later regretted and as I had only a limited letter writing capability all my endeavours in this direction were centred on Sylvia.

So it was to Fiskerton, home of 49 Squadron with the motto *Cave Canem* (Beware the dog) that our Course from Winthorpe journeyed. 'The small village of Fiskerton lies in the heart of the Lincolnshire fens about four miles due east from the city of Lincoln. The countryside, as flat as a pancake right up to the suburbs of Lincoln, was ideal flying country. In fact, the only small hillock in sight was in the centre of the Royal Air Force's main runway on the airfield constructed to accommodate a squadron of Lancasters in Bomber Command's ever enlarging force. Arguably, Fiskerton's only claim to fame was due to the very close proximity of RAF Fiskerton and one must hesitate a moment to sympathise with the inhabitants of a quiet rural village who were suddenly in the middle of a welter of building activity followed by a mass influx of 2,000 odd young service men and women. Fiskerton wasn't the only village to suffer in this way; airfields were springing up all over Lincolnshire to join those peace-time aerodromes already in existence. Some airfields came under the command of 5 Group, one of Bomber Command's most prestigious Groups. Fiskerton was one of these.

We now knew that we had finally arrived at the cutting edge of the war with Germany and that every time an operation was 'laid on' we would crew one of a maximum of eighteen participating Lancasters. We also knew that on most operations perhaps one, two or even more aircraft would fail to return. We would have to complete 30 operations before our tour was completed. From the moment of arrival at Fiskerton and for some weeks to come we thought our chances of survival rather slim, but it was a fact that the odds against us were accepted as a matter of course and that somehow these would be overcome and our crew would always return. Living was very much on a day to day basis and our main objective was to survive each 'op' and catch that crew bus into Lincoln on the next non-operational night.

But we were not pitched into battle straight away - it was standard routine for each 'sprog' crew to do a 'Bullseye'. This exercise entailed stooging over a number of English cities at night to give their searchlight crews a bit of practice and also to get us used to being 'coned' in a pyramid of searchlights. We did not do too much evasive action so we did spend a considerable amount of time in the dazzling glare of these lights.

With that trip behind us the next step was the '2nd Dickie' operation. This involved the sprog pilot, in this case me and not his crew, flying with an experienced crew on a real live operation. On 22 August 1943 I went to Leverkusen in the Ruhr with Flight Sergeant Kirton and very little happened. There was complete cloud cover (10/10ths) very little 'flak' (anti-aircraft fire) and no fighters. We probably bombed by the Wanganui method (named after a small town in New Zealand) which involved marker flares being dropped on parachutes and ignited above the clouds. The flares, dropped by the Pathfinder Force, indicated the point of release for the Bomb aimers.

Squadron Leader Day, our Flight Commander must have considered this operation a poor example of the real thing so the next night I was detailed for another '2nd Dickie'. In the meantime the crew were left kicking their heels on the base awaiting their first baptism of fire. Sometimes the aircraft carrying the '2nd Dickie' would be shot down and there were such cases on 49. Then the waiting crew would sometimes wait around for weeks for a spare pilot or fill in their time making up other crews to full strength.

My skipper for this second '2nd Dickie' trip was Flight Lieutenant Munro, a New Zealander with the Distinguished Flying Cross displayed on his chest. Although I felt a little minnow in the presence of such austere company (remember I was still only a sergeant pilot) I also thought, as I looked at him, 'This is experience and I am going to come back from this trip'. On entering the Briefing room the first thing I noticed was the large map at the far end of the room and on it the route markers pointed straight to Berlin. The weather forecast was a clear sky over the target with no cloud. 'The Big City' on a clear night on only my second op. Every time Berlin was the target (and this was not to be until a few months had elapsed) my heart used to skip a beat, such was the impact of that major target.

As a matter of interest Flight Lieutenant Munro gets a mention for this particular operation in Martin Middlebrook's *'The Berlin Raids'*. The date was August 23rd and Middlebrook assumes that this Berlin raid was the commencement of the Battle of Berlin. On page 35 he writes that Munro's aircraft was airborne before any other Bomber Command planes on that night. Probably to do an air test before setting course. So, one of my very few doubtful claims to fame was the fact that I was in the very first Lancaster to get airborne in the Battle of Berlin.

The weather men turned out to be correct and the skies were clear over Berlin. The trip I had made the previous night bore no comparison to this one. The 'flak', the marker flares on the ground, the fires, the bombs bursting, the searchlights and the fighter flares all contributing to a scene I had never thought possible. As we left the target area I reflected with amazement on our survival and thought of the remainder of the tour which I had to complete with my crew. I returned to barrage of questions from the crew. 'Well, what was it like', 'was the flak heavy', 'did you see any fighters' etc, etc. How could I adequately describe the scene over the target? They would have to wait and see for themselves.

I kept no diary of events and recorded no details in my log book so these are all memories mostly conjured up by looking at the destinations in my logbook.

Most crews usually carried some form of good luck talisman, these objects presented by one's girl friend or wife. Sylvia had been to a West End show before our tour commenced and had acquired two rag doll Lupino Lane's. One of these was to be our Good Luck talisman. I didn't know what odd bits and pieces the rest of the crew carried but after a number of ops they always ensured I had Lupino stuffed down the front of my flying gear. I still have-one of these to this day. It was necessary for Ken, my navigator, to complete his tour with another crew (he had missed a few of our operations due to illness). This he did successfully with Lupino carried in his green canvas navigator's bag. But Lupino did not reappear after Ken finished, so then there was one, the one I still have. He has a scorched hole in his chest which I would like to say was a war wound but unfortunately it is just a cigarette burn caused by one of those countless cigarettes we used to plough through every day.

The other item I carried other than official flying requisites was sheaf knife pushed down my right flying boot. Some carried revolvers they had been able to obtain illicitly but these were very much in the minority. I don't really know why I carried a knife but I suspect it was more for self-preservation rather than self-protection.

Before proceeding on a raid every flying crew member had to hand in all his personal belongings which were retained until his return. Also escape kits were issued containing minimal iron rations and escape map etc, Mae Wests (floatation jackets) and also parachutes were collected and all crew members ensured that his whistle was attached to the lapel of his battledress. These would be of use for identifying position in the event of being shot down in the 'drink' (sea). All this in addition to the normal flying gear - silk underwear, including those long pants, long woollen frock 'airmen for the use of, silk, woollen and leather gloves, one pair on top of the other, battledress and any other extra bits of clothing supplied by yours truly and which in my case included a silk scarf. The Mae Wests went on top of this lot and on top of the Mae Wests a parachute harness. The parachute was carried separately and each member of the crew was responsible for stowing his own in a convenient place on board the aircraft.

Although the memories of many incidents and events come crowding in, the difficulty is pinpointing them with a specific raid. But this was not the case with our first operation as a full 'rookie' crew.

Prior to a raid the navigator, bomb aimer and wireless operator all had separate briefings then all the crew would join up for the main briefing in the

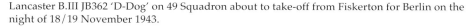

Lancaster B.III JB362 'D-Dog' on 49 Squadron about to take-off from Fiskerton for Berlin on the night of 18/19 November 1943.

special Nissen hut set aside for this purpose. This was the procedure adopted for our first operation and was normal for all operations throughout the Command. That large map at the end of the Briefing Room told us that our target was to be a city deep into the heart of Germany - Nuremburg. The proceedings commenced with the arrival of the Station Commander, Group Captain Windell. Wing Commander Adams, Squadron Commander, called all those present to attention and the CO took his seat. We had already heard rumours that the CO had been known to sit in his quarters and shoot out his windows with his service revolver. A story confirmed later to be absolutely true. Maybe he was one of those Commanders who felt some stress at watching us young chaps go out to do battle or maybe he was just drunk. Then we had all the specialist officers. They told us of the weather en route (to the accompaniment of low hisses), the petrol load and bomb load we were carrying, which wave of aircraft we would be in (there were usually three) and the time on target. Also the defences we were likely to encounter and all the other information deemed to be necessary for the trip. The emergency runways available at Manston and Marham - they were 3,000 yards long instead of the usual 2,000 - and the single searchlight on the coast at Mablethorpe maintained under all conditions as a guiding beacon for those in distress.

Then a good luck message from the CO and a message sent in from our Commander-in-Chief, Bomber Harris 'Go out there and give those Germans hell' or something like that. There was not a single aircrew member who would not have followed Bomber Harris - into hell and back had the occasion arisen, such was his immense popularity. He seemed to make all the hazards we were facing worth all the risks and he always believed and made us believe that what we were doing could end the war without the necessity of invading Europe. That he was proved wrong in the long run was no fault of his - but there I am wandering off the beaten track. Bomber Harris is a different story and I have recorded my thoughts about this man elsewhere.

We left the Briefing Room to while away the hours until take off time. During this time no-one was allowed off the station. With everyone on the station keyed up for the off a 'scrub' or cancellation went down like a lead balloon. It meant that the whole procedure would have to be gone through the next night and maybe the next night. And for us, no trips being deducted from tour requirements. It is appropriate to mention here that operations were never laid on during the full moon period. Too much light meant too many losses. But we weren't idle during these moon lay-offs - the time was always filled in with training flights.

Little Audrey was our crew bus driver throughout our tour. Audrey would not have won any beauty contests but she had a heart of gold and we all loved her. After the ground crew that flagged us into dispersal after an op, she was the first person to greet us. As time went by she was to remain our driver and was to wait patiently for our return at all hours of the night and in all kinds of weather. We would not have swapped her for any other driver on the station. Our lucky mascot but taking second place to Lupino. Later, when Fiskerton's damaged runways were being repaired we continued to operate from Dunholme Lodge, just a few miles away and it was Audrey who ferried us backwards and forwards.

So it was Audrey who transported the crew out to Lancaster 'G-George' for our first operation - destination Nuremburg. I walked round the aircraft carrying out the laid down external check. Ron, our engineer chatted to the ground crew to ensure everything was OK from his angle and then the crew prepared to board. We had heard from some of the old hands that it was good luck to pee on the tail wheel before boarding the plane. It was a good idea anyway thinking of those long hours ahead. So we all queued up to carry out this ritual having previously ensured that there was sufficient content to carry out this task. A ritual to be repeated on all our trips and I suspect, by most other crews. Entering the aircraft, Peto turned left towards the rear gun turret (housing four Browning machine guns) and Jock, the mid upper, only had a few steps to reach his two gun turret but the rest of crew had to clamber over the notorious centre spar, something I would have great difficulty in doing today.

As take off time approached engines were started up, intercom checked with each member of the crew and all the necessary cockpit checks made, many of these with Ron who would be at my right hand side at all times. Finally, a signal to the waiting ground crew to pull away the wheel chocks; a last thumbs up to them and we start to roll. The ground crew would remain on duty until 'their' aircraft returned, hopefully with a minimum of damage or none at all. It was always their aircraft and we were only its custodians for a few hours, but of course we thought differently. So we took our place in the queue of eighteen or so Lancasters making their way slowly to the take off point. Slowly, because the perimeter tracks were narrow and our undercarriage wide. One Lanc dropping a wheel into the soft earth at the side of the track could abort the trip for everyone behind. At this time, loaded with maximum petrol and bomb load the aircraft weighed over 30 tons.

Our turn for take-off eventually arrives by way of a green Aldis lamp flashed from the small black and white chequered hut at the end of the runway and we slowly move out onto the 2,000 yard runway lowering 20° of flap to give added lift to the wings for take-off. With the pitch of the propellers in fully fine I line up the Lanc on the runway, apply the brakes, come to a stop and test all the engines at 0lb boost. I mustn't hesitate too long, the planes behind me will all be anxiously awaiting their turn so, to vigorous waves from the small knot of station personnel who always turned up for ops take-offs, I slowly ease the four throttles forward. The Lanc starts to swing, it always does and I check it by correction on the throttles. As the tail comes off the ground and I have rudder control I move all the throttles to fully open, I then leave the throttles to Ron whose hand has been following closely behind mine and I concentrate on the take off. The throttles fully open give 18lb boost, which was in excess of the recommended setting for the Merlin engines. We can only hold this throttle setting for three minutes. Ron shouts out the airspeed, I have no time to look at the instruments, 60, 70, 80 and at about 110 mph I feel the plane wanting to leave the 'deck'. How different this was to the lightly loaded Lanc, the end of the runway looming ever nearer until suddenly we are airborne. I reach down and select the undercarriage lever to the 'up' position and immediately I gain a few more miles per hour. Nothing like your zooming jet take-offs of modern days, we are still only a few feet into the air as we roar over the edge of the airfield and if an engine fails now we have had it. The speed is now 145 mph and if an engine fails now we might just make it. The three minutes are up and I throttle back to a powered climb at 9lbs boost. At about 300 feet I start to ease off that 20° of flap, if I do it too quickly I will sink back into the ground. So we slowly, very slowly, climb away until I reach a safe height where I can throttle back to a normal climb at 7lbs boost and 2,650 revs per minute.

As our tour progressed I became more and more aware that any fear or apprehension I may have had on the ground about pending operations over Germany seemed to disappear as soon as I was airborne and settled on course. As skipper of the aircraft my concern was not to show any loss of face in front of my crew and to prove to them above all things that I was sufficiently competent to take them through a full tour of operations and I have no doubts that they were all thinking along the same lines. We had already spent many hours in the air and on the ground together, then it was training and now it was for real and each one of us were unaware how the other would react now that we were involved, irrevocably, in the real thing.

It was customary to obtain at least 10,000 feet (oxygen height) over England before setting course for the continent and one of the more usual points from which the Group set course was Fakenham in Norfolk. It could still be half light at this time and we would be able to see Lancasters amassing all around us. Halifaxes from 4 Group and other bombers from other Groups would be carrying out a similar exercise in other parts of the country. As soon as darkness fell one felt all alone, suspended in the night sky with only the occasional glimpse of another Lanc to reassure that there were others heading towards the enemy coast.

From the outset of the operation strict radio silence was maintained, hence the use of the Aldis Lamp for permission to take off and although Pat, our wireless operator kept a continuous watch for a possible recall etc, he was unable to send any messages. As our tour progressed, Ken, our navigator might be asked to send back new wind speeds and directions he may have assessed. These were given to Pat. He would send them back to base and they would be redirected back to main force aircraft. This may have happened once or twice at the end of our tour when Ken's reliability would have been proven. Pat also had the capability of transmitting the roar from our engines into the frequencies used between German night fighters. This was code-named 'Tinsel'.

As our Lanc was now heading out over the North Sea gradually gaining height it might be an appropriate time to briefly mention some of the radio equipment and navigational aids we had at our disposal. Pat, of course, had his high powered transmitter/receiver, also there was IFF (identification friend or foe) which, some thought, the German fighters could home onto. At my left hand side was TR 1196 with which I could communicate with the crew, with my home base from a shortish range and with other aircraft. There was another device with the code name of 'Monica'. A red light on my instrument panel meant enemy planes in the vicinity of our aircraft, but unfortunately, this device was not always serviceable. 'Gee' was a navigational system which extended as far as the Ruhr, by the use of intersecting radio beams it was possible to place ones aircraft within a few miles of its actual position. 'Oboe' which came later had a much longer range but unfortunately, both these were susceptible to jamming by the enemy. A new device and we were one of the first squadrons to use it, was H$_2$S. A large radar reflector housed in a bulge on the underside of the Lanc projected beams to the ground and the return reflections were transmitted to a screen in the navigators department. This piece of equipment was ideal for picking up coast lines and large towns (reflection of waves from roofs etc.) and when it was working it was a great asset. Unfortunately Ken would often come up with the words the damn thing has packed up again. Also, on a clear star-lit night Ken could use Astro. This meant flying straight and level for some considerable time in order for Ken to align his sextant on a suitable star. Pilots flying over Germany just did not like to fly more than a few minutes straight and level, it could be lethal. By using Astro navigation Ken reckoned he could place his within 8-10 miles of our actual position. Useful in an emergency, 'Darky' was the emergency call to base if it could not be found in 'duff weather conditions. They would respond with a QDM, a course to steer which should take the lost pilot over his own base.

'Rear gunner to Skipper, permission to test guns.'

'OK rear gunner, go ahead but take a good look round first. This goes for you mid upper and you bomb aimer'. Guns were always tested at height over the North Sea and as one bullet in every five was a tracer shell it was possible to see the line of fire as the bullets streamed away from the aircraft.

I mentioned earlier that emotional moment in the Briefing Room when the target for the night is first disclosed. This is only matched when a dim coastline is sighted ahead. Enemy country and this would be my crew's first experience of crossing over a coast into hostile country. 'Skipper to crew, enemy coast ahead; keep a good look out'. Sometimes, on future operations we would have the misfortune to be fired at by coastal batteries, or even by 'flak' trains which

Eric Jones who flew a tour on 49 Squadron at RAF Fiskerton. (Eric Jones)

had been positioned across our track, but this time, on our first operation we had a clear run in over the coast.

Occasional coloured route markers of a predetermined colour, dropped ahead of the main force by specialised aircraft from the Pathfinder Force, marked our route across Germany. But these were infrequent; it was not advisable to show the enemy our final destination. Often when flying in poor weather they were not visible and one would fly on into the darkness assailed by doubts as to whether the aircraft had wandered off course or were still maintaining our position in the main stream? A reassuring 'OK Skipper, we are on course' from Ken would work wonders and I would settle down to flying an accurate course at a consistent speed whilst maintaining operational height. Although the Lancaster was equipped with Automatic 'pilot' (George) few pilots used it over Germany. A constant searching weave on course was favoured to enable the crew to keep a constant watch on all segments of the sky. Not an easy task, staring out into the blackness for hours on end. The imagination could play funny tricks at times and many an imaginary fighter would be sighted during the months to come.

The planning chiefs at Bomber Command devised all kinds of ploys to try and deceive the enemy, some of which worked and some didn't. Dog legged routes with considerable alterations of course coupled with diversionary raids by smaller groups of bombers in an attempt to divert fighter strength away from the main force were some of the methods used. Frequently, the route would be seen by the enemy to be going anywhere except the target then a sharp 90° turn to port or starboard with a short run into the aiming point, with luck, would still have the enemy guessing. Even if this ploy was successful, they still knew we would have to return home and used to set up their ambushes accordingly.

Unlike my '2nd Dickie' to Berlin which was a successful raid with much damage being caused (but with the highest losses Bomber Command had experienced to date) the records show that the Nuremburg raid was not a success. The main target was not hit, many bombs falling in open country and on the south eastern suburbs of the city. Apparently the Pathfinder Force marking the target had difficulty with their H_2S sets and also there was a 'creep back' by the bombing of the Main Force which was not corrected in spite of repeated radio requests from the Master Bomber. Apparently these instructions were only received by quarter of the force due to poor reception over the target. The Master Bomber was the only skipper allowed to break radio silence. They were brave men, few in number and - would fly at low level amongst the falling bombs and the lighter 'flak' with the use of their radio providing an additional hazard in the shape of enemy aircraft homing onto their radio signals.

Although I will relate many operational memories I find it difficult to relate them to individual raids; nevertheless I do have a lasting memory of this, our first operation, something a 'rookie' crew could have done without.

Searchlights operated in groups and they took their lead from a radar controlled searchlight. This was always an intensely blue light and if the radar beam picked up an aircraft the blue light would lock onto its prey and immediately other searchlights would follow suit. On this occasion we were the prey over Nuremburg. It's difficult to describe the intensity of that light. All sense of direction went and it was impossible to see the instrument panel and I knew I had to get out of that cone quickly before the guns were also targeted onto us. But the lights hung on like leeches in spite of violent twists and turns to try to escape their clutches. At one stage I remember dust and papers flying around the cockpit. At this point we must have had negative gravity. But we did escape that cone and on checking up with the crew found that they were 'shaken and stirred' but intact. I must admit I did have visions of them banging around inside the aircraft. Although we must have finally completed our bombing run I do not recall it but we might have been forgiven if our bombing effort was one of those which 'crept back'. On the return journey there was another 'incident' worthy of a mention. At least I hope it was on this trip when we were so inexperienced. I contacted Ken on the intercom and told him we were over the North Sea and that I would start to descend. The records state that it was a very dark night and inexperienced me, after hours of flying on instruments, thought we must have reached the North Sea. Ken replied 'Hold your height Skipper we are still over enemy territory'. An argument ensued, the only one we ever had in the air, but I did hold my height and he was correct and we were still over Holland. To maintain height over enemy territory was of paramount importance, to lose height too soon brought the aircraft into the range of even more weaponry. In the future it was to be either consultation with or taking instructions from Ken when it came to the navigation of the aircraft. My job, so far as he was concerned, was to steer an accurate course no matter what (even though we weaved from side to side) and to maintain a consistent altitude. Only once did Ken come from behind his curtain and that was because he expressed a wish to look at Berlin on a clear night at the height of a raid. His words were something like 'Oh my God' and he never looked out again except, that is, from the little Astro dome to take the occasional sextant reading.

Ken, like other members of the crew, was excellent at his allotted task. It was common knowledge that should you stray further than ten miles either side of the given track you could find yourself on your own with all the enemy radar equipment directed just on your one aircraft.

If this situation did arise the chances of survival might have been improved by 'Window' being pushed out of the aircraft. This was issued to every aircraft on ops and was not unlike the paper used in making Christmas paper chains, except that this had one silvery side. Each piece reflected a dot onto the enemy radar screens and, delivered in bulk, gave the illusion of many attacking aircraft. The use of this secret weapon was held back until the German raids on England diminished. It was thought that the Germans would use the same idea on us. First used on Hamburg, many months before our tour, it was a great success and caused havoc amongst the defences.

I would regularly call each member of the crew to see if they were OK and remind them to keep a keen look out for enemy fighters or our own aircraft, the risk of collision being ever present. On one occasion I only got a slurred response from Ken and when asking him for a course to steer only received a loud laugh. After a time the truth dawned on me, his oxygen tube must have become disconnected. This was the case and it was soon remedied but oxygen lack had this very inebriating effect. Good job I checked the position at that moment, we may not have had a capable navigator take us home. This incident provided yet another step up the ladder of experience and it also got me thinking about a course of action I should take should we lose Ken at any time. On a clear night I would keep the North Star in a certain position on my starboard side and by doing this I couldn't hope to get back to base but at least I would probably reach a point where Pat could get a radio bearing back home. Or at the worst I would at least arrive at the English coast. But it was a known fact that pilots with their aircraft badly shot up had done just this only to find that winds had kept blowing them to the south and off course and they had flown the full length of the English Channel and out into the Atlantic never to be heard of again.

On the Nuremburg raid, as on most other raids into Germany, three types of aircraft were used; the Stirling, Halifax I and Lancasters I, II and III. The Wellington was last used on ops in the autumn of 1943. Of these three aircraft types the Lancaster was the most powerful, carrying the largest bomb load. It was capable of flying at least 8,000 feet higher than the Stirling and 2-3,000 feet above the Halifaxes. As I said before, height was imperative so we had a distinct advantage over the other two types. We always thought we were a good deal safer than those flying below. This could have been wishful thinking as the losses on the Nuremburg raid were equally distributed amongst all three types. Eleven Lancasters were lost out of a total of 33 aircraft, or 4.9% of the total force. We were to learn later that losses over 5% were unsustainable and if losses continued at this rate the strength of Bomber Command would slowly ebb away.

During our next few operations we were to hear of a new type of Halifax becoming operational. The Halifax III had Hercules radial engines to replace the previous in line engines and what was even more disconcerting - she could operate at the same height as the Lanc, but still not with the same bomb load.

But the 'rookie crew' had survived their first sortie over Germany and

Eric Jones and his crew on 49 Squadron at RF Fiskerton. (Eric Jones)

confidence had probably increased by .01% and the pattern of visits into Lincoln, operating whenever the moon and weather and sleeping permitted, was beginning to take shape.

We were still all Sergeants at this stage, all sharing the same Mess and Nissen hut sleeping quarters. Remember it was the winter of 1943 and a bad winter it was. This sometimes gave rise to harrowing flying experiences. I sometimes thought the list of hazards we had to encounter were topped by the weather with fighters running a close second and 'flak' taking the third slot, although this sequence could easily be reversed on a clear night.

At some time in the early stages of our tour I got the crew together and told them of my plan for climbing as high as possible to release our bomb load and then continuing to climb out of the target area. In reaching this decision I knew that most pilots, on releasing their bombs, dived to build up speed in order to clear the target area as quickly as possible. I thought, rightly or wrongly, that adopting this procedure carried them into the more intense 'flak' at lower levels end also deeper into the fighter belt. I assumed that the enemy would think this the natural thing to do and that the last thing a pilot would wish to do would be to prolong his stay over the target area. Well, we survived a tour of operations and who's to know; maybe this plan could have been a major contribution.

The crew agreed to this plan of action and we stuck to it except on operations of a specific nature such as mine laying ('Gardening') or flying under the enemy radar belt.

One cold night and the colder the night the more powerful our engines, I reached 29,000 feet, climbing out of the target area. 49 Squadron Association pilots have since ridiculed this story, saying it was impossible for a Lanc to fly that high even without a bomb load and half empty petrol tanks. But I distinctly remember that night, particularly the manner in which the plane wallowed in the thin rarefied air, way beyond the design ceiling of the Lancaster.

Air crew 'in the know' said that if a crew survived the first five operations the chances of survival considerably increased. So we went to Nuremburg, Mönchengladbach in the Ruhr, Hanover, Mannheim and Hanover again and our first five ops were completed. On these raids 154 aircraft went missing including many of our squadron comrades. We didn't know it at the time but by completing the five trips this could mean that we may be the one out of every three crews who would complete a tour.

It was an unwritten law on an operational squadron not to become too friendly with other crews. Yes, we knew quite a few of them because we had trained with them. Hodgkinson and Brunt both come to mind but both were to go missing before reaching the middle of their tour. Sergeant Brunt was spread across the two centre pages of the *Daily Mirror*, giving the thumbs up from his cockpit window as he taxied out. I thought he went missing that night but I am now told he went a few nights later.

One member of the crew always carried a pack of cards and our game, our only game was solo whist. I used to keep a running list of the debts and gains and we used to play 1d, 2d, 3d, 4d & 6d for solo, mazairs, bundle, mazairs ouvert and bundle declared, if ever we found ourselves at a loose end out would come the cards and solo would be played.

Not all the crew would go to Lincoln on every off duty night and therefore the nucleus of the pleasure seekers was usually navigator Ken, wireless operator Pat and myself. I must admit we did get through a lot of beer and fags on those Lincoln nights. My favourite tipple was bottled brown ale but for sheer drinking ability Pat had us all licked to a frazzle. I often think back to those days and wonder how we were able to be ready to operate the next night. But we were and able to fly on trips up to nine hours long with most of that time constantly on guard and watching the night sky for fear of attack.

In the Sergeants' Mess there was always a bowl of Cod Liver Oil capsules and a bowl of caffeine tablets and we were expected to dip in and take a supply of each before each op. I recall taking the caffeine tablets but only in a limited way, we might have to operate the next night and sleep is only delayed by caffeine.

We were well aware that we differed from the Navy and the Army as we were able to return to normal civvy street activities wherever released from station duties. Our colleagues in the other services were on duty 24 hours of every day, but I sometimes wondered who were the better off. They were not so likely to be caught off guard but as each 24 hours of our squadron life brought such massive contrasts perhaps we could be. In a pub, drinking amongst civilians, it was difficult not to think of where one might be the next night. Almost certainly over a German city with all hell let loose and then when over that German city thinking, if one had the time, of that pint of beer in the friendly atmosphere of a British pub on the following night.

It was not 'all hell let loose' all the time. Sometimes it was possible to fly out over Germany and remain in a quiet part of the sky for most of the operation. Just a mile or so away I could sometimes see other raiding aircraft coned in searchlights with flak bursting all around and I would be grateful it wasn't us but when would our turn come? Perhaps it had over Nuremburg, but was it too much to hope that this would be the only time? It was difficult not to stare transfixed at these scenes, waiting for the inevitable to happen, but a call over the intercom 'Keep a sharp look out for enemy aircraft' would get the crew concentrating once again on searching the night sky.

Earlier, when at briefing, we had been told that, if we saw a massive explosion in the sky far greater than a flak burst, it was a 'Scarecrow', a device put up by the Germans to demoralise us. We saw many of them during our tour. After the war the Germans said there was no such animal - that what we were witnessing were other aircraft exploding in mid air.

Whatever the outward journey might have been like, it was never quiet over the target area. If we were in the first wave of aircraft we would be suspended in the night sky approaching a target of which there was no sign. Ken would be reassuring me that we were on track and that time over the target would be, say, 20 minutes from now. There would be no sign of other aircraft and elements of doubt would creep into one's mind. 'Have we got it right or are we way off track' then suddenly, ahead, the first of Pathfinders' target indicators (TI) would start to go down and the flak barrage would open up. The colours of these TI's were predetermined and would not be confused with the dummy ones the Germans sometimes used. Our height would be around 22,000 feet and as we approached the target area I would intensify my weaving of the aircraft. The first bombs would start to go down followed by high powered photo flashes which enabled photographs of the aiming point to be taken. As we approached the target the extent of the flak barrage became more evident and I wondered how we could possibly get through it in one piece. Sometimes, if the Germans had got it right and guessed our destination fighters would be amassing in the area and this would become increasingly evident as they dropped flares to further illuminate the scene and silhouette the bombers against the glare beneath. Slowly the pot would be coming to the boil, with the German fighters often operating amongst their own flak. Steve would now be at his bombsight Mark XIV having left his front gun turret would call me over intercom 'Target sighted Skipper, keep her straight and level' and then 'Left, left a little, OK hold her there' and we were into the worst moment of the raid - straight and level over the target area - time drags for this period and then 'Bombs gone Skipper' and a few more moments for the photo flash to explode and hopefully give us a good target picture. Then left hand down to select the bomb bay lever into the closed position, then stick back, more power on and the bomb-free Lanc climbs, initially, like a lift, carrying out our prearranged plan.

So it was if one was in the first wave. In later waves, when the Germans were fully awake, the scene was even more devastating and it was this kind of scenario that Ken looked out on when he said 'never again'. Fires would have started on the ground and smoke would have started to billow upwards, incendiaries would be carpeting the target area and twinkling amongst the bomb bursts. Also the Germans might have lit decoy fires on the outskirts of the city in an attempt to divert the bombing. Additional, different colour TI's would be going down in order to concentrate the bombing on a different part of the city.

And in the air, well, in all possibility the flak barrage would have increased as more personnel manned the guns, bombers would be twisting and turning to get out of the clutches of searchlights and if German fighters were operating in the target area individual combats would be clearly visible. For the whole period in the target area we awaited the shell burst which would blow us to pieces or the burst of machine gun which would rip right through us. Such thoughts I tried to put out of my mind and get on with the job of getting the aircraft and crew safely back to base.

Raids, such as these, on a clear night, used the Parramatta system of marking the target. Parramatta was the code name given to the method by D. C. T. Bennett the founder of the Pathfinder Force and it was the name of a small town in South West Australia. Wanganui was the name given to bombing a cloud covered target and was the name of a small town in New Zealand. In cloud conditions the target was located by Pathfinders using H_2S and then flares would be dropped on parachutes set to ignite above the clouds and so indicate the target to the incoming Main Force.

One night, when we were doing our first raid on Berlin as a crew, Steve, when approaching the city on his bombing run said 'Sorry Skipper, dummy run, go round again' and I put the Lanc into a 3600 turn to come round onto the same heading. Well, we nearly finished our tour there and then and I might add, some other poor devil's as well. When I had gone through 1800 and facing the oncoming stream I was left in no doubt where the rest of the stream was.

Lancs were visible all round and on a reciprocal heading. How we escaped a collision I will never know. It was like driving up a motorway the wrong way. Flying to the target one rarely saw another bomber unless they were being attacked by a fighter or coned by searchlights. To find the stream, fly on a reciprocal course. I said to Steve 'Don't you ever ask me to go round again. You make sure you line up correctly and we drop 'em first time'. We did and that was the first and last time we went round again.

We knew that to go LMF was to be secretly wafted away from the Squadron and never be seen again. LMF meant Lack of Moral Fibre which in plain language meant refusal to flyover enemy territory. It would not do for those in Command to make these events known, they wanted us to think it never happened and at the time this was so. I never did know of anyone going LMF. Since the war ended I have read that LMF aircrew were reduced in rank and given some menial task. All air crew were volunteers so no LMF's were court-martialled for this offence although I stand to be corrected on this point. The crew's first raid on Berlin was our twelfth sortie over Germany and after Steve's call for a 'dummy run' over the target and turning to set course for home we hoped that no further problems lay ahead. Our wish was not granted. As the homeward trip progressed Ken started to calculate very high winds. At first he thought he had got it all wrong but eventually established that we were running into a 100 mph headwind and it was cutting our ground speed back to a comparative snail pace, I doubt if we were moving over the ground any quicker than 120 mph. This situation had Ron doing rapid petrol calculations and as the homeward journey progressed it was obvious we were not going to make base and we might not even make England. Our luck lasted out and we crossed the coastline but it meant getting down onto the 'deck' as quickly as possible and this turned out to be an American base in Norfolk. That night the main Bomber Force was scattered all over Eastern England, obviously seriously disrupting any operational plans for the following night. Our American hosts, delighted at having a Lancaster in their midst feted us with a cracking meal and excellent overnight accommodation (for what was left of the night). When we flew out the following morning we noticed that our night flying rations had been stolen from our Lanc, we suspected by American ground crew as some kind of souvenir. So who cared? They had looked after us so well.

We usually polished off the remains of any flying rations as we were dropping off height over the North Sea on the way back to base. Also, contrary to rules the smokers used to light up for a much needed smoke. This time, because we were watching those petrol gauges so closely, we forgot to eat the rations.

On every return there was always one hazard we had to watch out for when approaching the English coast - British convoys plying the North Sea and hugging the coast. We were usually given their position at briefing and told to keep well clear. In fact I rarely crossed the coast without a few thousand feet in hand just in case. The gunners on these convoys were trigger happy and 'pooped' off their guns at all and sundry. One night I watched wounded crewmen being off loaded from a Fiskerton Lanc, Someone said they had been hit by 'friendly' shells from a convoy.

Lancaster II DS842 JI-F *Fanny Ferkin II* on 514 Squadron at Waterbeach at Deenthorpe, Northamptonshire on 3 May 1944 during a visit to the GIs of the 401st Bomb Group. *Fanny Ferkin II* was the regular mount of Pilot Officer Bob Langley and crew for 18 ops February-June 1944. The aircraft was SOC in March 1945 when on 1668 HCU. (USAF)

Lancaster III ED593 *Admiral Prune II* on 106 Squadron with the CO, Wing Commander Guy Gibson in the foreground, centre. In 1943 the Squadron often dropped sea mines on 'Gardening' operations and naval officers were attached to the unit so several of the aircraft including *Admiral Airgoosk*, *Admiral Chattanooga* and *Admiral Foo Banc 5* displayed Admiral-prefixed nicknames. *Admiral Prune* was lost on the Turin raid on 4/5 February 1943. *Admiral Prune II* operated on 106 Squadron from then on until May 1944 and went to 5 LFS and finally 1656 CU.

Sergeant Edward Albert Bowman, flight engineer on Lancaster III ED885 on 156 Squadron at Warboys which was lost without trace with pilot officer John Adam Mason RNZAF and crew on the operation on Krefeld on 21/22 June 1943. Bowman had joined the RAF in mid-1941 after releasing himself from a reserved occupation after seven years' apprenticeship. His mother refused to believe that he was dead and when she received the telegram she suffered a nervous breakdown. (Essex Aviation Society)

What of the German fighters; the FW 190s and Me 110s? In the early stages of the Bomber Command offensive these were controlled from the ground with one fighter allocated to each radar 'box' with the information on the progress being passed from one 'box' to the next. But later, when we were operating, the fighters were allowed to roam free, each fitted with their own search and find radar equipment. At the time we were unaware of the methods adopted by the Germans - all we knew was that the fighters were there and if we didn't keep a constant look out we could be shot from the sky without knowing what had hit us.

I would be gently weaving our Lanc either side of course to give the crew, particularly the gunners, a greater field of vision. It was almost a hypnotic situation, staring fixedly at the instruments with the occasional glance ahead when suddenly I would be jolted from my reverie by a cry from Peto in the rear turret or Jock in the mid upper: 'Fighter on the starboard quarter' and instantly the whole crew was 100% wide awake and a little shiver ran down my spine. We waited to see if he had spotted us and if we were his next intended victim. Sometimes it was another Lancaster - we could not be too careful - but sometimes it was a German fighter. Peto said 'Standby by to corkscrew' and as the fighter closed in on us it would be 'Corkscrew port - go' and I would immediately jab the control column forward and the same time pulling the starboard wing up and over and in no time at all we would be entering a powered turning dive. As the speed built up I would wing over in the opposite direction expecting all the time to see the fighters' tracer bullets streaking past. As the airspeed built up to around the 260 mph mark I would start to ease the 'stick' back easing the plane over into an opposite turn and up we would go turning and twisting in this fixed pattern until that blessed shout from Peto, 'OK Skipper we have lost him, back onto course'. We have escaped this time, what about the next time? We have still a long way to go before the end of the tour. If we were attacked on the outward journey we would still have our full bomb load and most of our petrol. The Lanc would be heavy and it was desperately hard work and if the fighter was still there the whole procedure had to be repeated. The 'corkscrew' followed a fixed pattern - practised in training it enabled the gunners to sight their guns with reasonable accuracy. The exertion required in flying the Lancaster through this manoeuvre was intense and I always finished up bathed in sweat.

Fellow fliers used to say that once a determined fighter pilot was stuck on your tail it was usually 'curtains' for you and your crew. I didn't entirely agree with this conclusion. Maybe our attacks were not by a determined pilot or perhaps it was because I panicked after that first call of 'corkscrew go'. Some pilots may have eased their aircraft into the manoeuvre; I threw it into the corkscrew. But the panic could and did last only a few seconds and after that initial twisting plunge it became a determination to shake the bastard off at all costs. So the 'corkscrew' was a very important manoeuvre and undoubtedly saved many an airman's life.

What we did not know until after the war was the fact that as we were operating over Germany the enemy had introduced a new type of attack fighter code-named 'Schräge Musik' ['Oblique Music']. Realising the most vulnerable part of the Lancaster and all the 'heavies' was their bellies (none of the British heavies had underslung belly turrets) the Germans had installed in some of their fighters a fixed upward firing machine gun. The idea was for the fighter to fly up, unnoticed, from to a position under the bomber and open fire on a completely unsuspecting crew. This method, we were told after the war, had been highly successful and had accounted for many of our bomber losses. I wonder how this knowledge would have played on our nerves had we known of these specialised fighters?

We in the Lanc operated in a height bracket of between 20,000 and 24,000 feet except for that climb out of the target area. The height was always dependent on how cold the night was. The colder the night the higher we could fly, the engines developing more power from cold dense air. Sometimes the outside air temperatures could be as low as -500 Centigrade. Below us, until they were taken off bomber operations, were the Stirlings and these could only attain about 15,000 feet fully loaded and at this height they often took the brunt of the German attack and they, along with the Halifax I's operating 2/3,000 feet below us always ran the risk of being hit by our falling bombs when in the target area.

One night, homeward bound over Germany, I carried out my routine check of the crew positions. All OK except Peto in the rear turret. I called him again and still no response. I instructed Pat to go to the rear and see what the trouble was. As we were at height we were all on oxygen so this meant Pat had to take a small emergency oxygen bottle with a limited duration. I waited for a call over the intercom but it did not come so I instructed another crew member to go and see what was going on and this may have been Steve. He also would be relying on an emergency bottle. Once again no message from either of them. I now had three crew members in the tail of the aircraft without knowing what the problem was. Being unsure of their oxygen supply and being fully aware of the outside temperature and the lack of heating in the rear of the aircraft I had no option but to take the aircraft down to a level of warmer air where oxygen would not be required. By taking the power right off we were soon down to 10,000 feet. In our view a suicidal height but once again luck was with all the crew including Peto. Apparently the electrical supply to his heated suit had failed and at the same time his intercom plug had become disconnected. The other two had one hell of a job to get Peto out of the turret, he was no lightweight, in fact he was huge and I often wondered how he ever fitted into the confined space of the rear turret. In the excitement the two crewmen had forgotten to plug in and tell me what was going on, but I would have had to go down anyway. I didn't see Peto until we landed but they said he had icicles dangling from his eyebrows and was quite incapable of helping himself out of the turret. After some considerable time Pat and Steve (I believe it was Steve) were able to revive him and I don't think he suffered any after effects. But if my call to him had been delayed even by minutes he probably would not have made it.

Unfortunately both Peto and Pat did not complete their tour; they were both killed whilst endeavouring to complete their tour with another crew and are buried in the RAF section of the Military Cemetery at Kleve on the Dutch/German border. By coincidence my sister Peggy's husband, Ernest, is buried in the Army section of the same cemetery. He was killed when a land mine exploded under a jeep in which he was travelling.

At some stage during our tour both Pat and Peto were taken ill and missed out on some of our ops. This meant that when we had finished they both had a few trips to complete their tour. They were making up the crew of Flight Sergeant Reid when his aircraft was shot down. The records show that it was Peto's 26th trip of his tour and it was probably Pat's as well. It was terrible for their luck to desert them at the last fence. Initially, they were both listed as missing and we were sure that they would eventually turn up. The word 'missing' always seemed to soften the blow, there was a chance they would be OK and I could not believe otherwise. Some time later I received the news that they were dead and it was the end of all hope. Ken was also left with three trips to complete his tour. He did these, possibly with the help of Lupino Lane and we were to remain good friends right up to his death some ten years ago.

I can see Peto now, red faced with a balding head, coming back off leave one night and dumping himself on his bed, which was opposite mine and looking over the top of the tortoise slow-burning coke stove. He said 'I got married today'.

'You what? You blighter, why didn't you invite the crew?'

'What and have you drunken lot messing up my wedding'.

He had married a Land Army girl and she was to conceive and bear a son whom Peto was destined never to see. I did manage to contact his son John a few years ago and was able to write to him about his father and also to send him photographs taken at Fiskerton but I have since lost touch with him. Perhaps the intrusion into memories of a father he never saw caused him too much distress. Pat had no children, his English wife was called Mick but I never did succeed in contacting her.

I must apologise if I mentioned it before, but coke-burning stoves were the bane of my life. I think I said that if a strong wind was blowing and the fumes came back down the chimney they were always certain to set me wheezing for the night. Fortunately, a quick little tablet and a few puffs on the Potters Asthma fag and all was OK.

One night, 'stooging' out of Germany, I heard the chatter of our machine guns. I had received no call from Jock in the mid upper or Peto in the rear so it had to be Steve up front. There had been no call for a 'corkscrew'. There wouldn't be for a frontal attack. I couldn't see anything so assumed the attack was coming from below. It was all over in seconds. Looking out on my starboard quarter I saw a German fighter flying from left to right and trailing smoke. From his position in the nose of the aircraft Steve was able to follow the fighter all the way down and he claimed it as his very own. At de-briefing, on our return, I substantiated his claim. Steve was later awarded the Distinguished Flying Medal and although I never saw the citation I suspect that the German fighter had something to do with it.

On another occasion we were briefed to go to the Modane Tunnel. This tunnel carried one of the main railway lines from France through the mountains into Italy. We were told at briefing that the idea was to endeavour to close the tunnel and so prevent the movement of German troops into Italy. We were all very pleased with this arrangement, a nice quiet 'stooge' across France, an undefended target and back home. Another operation completed - no trouble at all. We were fourth in the line to take off and the squadron's operational effort was getting under way when there was a terrific explosion heard above the noise of the idling Merlin engines and a brilliant flash lit the sky. Some poor devil had crashed on takeoff and surely he and his crew must have 'bought it' (died). The runway must have been damaged, we could not see over that little rise in the centre of the runway. The trip was 'scrubbed' and back we went to dispersal cursing the character who had robbed us of that 'cushy' French trip. We were never again to get the chance of another French trip and it was to be Germany all the way.

I met that pilot, purely by chance, at a Bomber Command Association dinner many years ago and he was very much alive and well and for the first time I heard the full story. Even up to the time I left Fiskerton I had always assumed that the crew of that Lanc had 'bought it' and I had heard nothing to the contrary.

The pilot was building up speed and was halfway down the runway when the aircraft's undercarriage collapsed causing it to slew off the runway where it slowly slithered to a halt. The pilot shouted to his crew to get out as quickly as possible being very much aware of the 4,000lb 'cookie', a number of 1,000lb bombs and many cans of 4lb incendiaries stored in the bomb bay. A quick count told the pilot that the rear gunner was missing and back into the aircraft he went but could not find the missing man. They were all clear of the aircraft when the whole bomb load blew up. The missing rear gunner had managed to escape from his turret and had run off in the opposite direction, so the whole crew managed to walk away from the crash and counted themselves extremely fortunate to do so. Ernest Webb was the pilot. He was in 'B' Flight some distance from our own 'A' Flight and that's why the full story of that night did not emerge until that Bomber Command Dinner. We are now both good friends and regularly meet at 49 Squadron Association functions.

I am afraid I have been steering a fairly erratic course with these memories and will probably continue to do this, so, in this context, I would like to go back to the point when the crew had completed five operations. The date was now September 22nd and autumn and very soon winter were approaching. Long winter nights meant longer trips taking us deeper into the heart of Germany but winter also brought worsening weather.

Although I cannot recall the weather conditions on each op I do remember our tenth operation when we briefed to go to Leipzig. The official account, details of which are in my log book, records the weather as appalling and very difficult. We entered dense cloud early in the flight and continued to climb in cloud up to our operational height. When flying in cloud for a long period and relying completely on instruments most pilots start to imagine all kinds of peculiar things. At least they did fifty years ago when there was none of the sophisticated equipment of today. 'My left wing is low, the plane is flying left wing down'. 'My compass is giving an incorrect reading and we are getting more and more off track'. In fact, it took considerable concentration to avoid believing that all the instruments were incorrect. It needed the reassurance of the navigator to convince that everything was all right.

'Yes Skipper. Hold your course, we are on track, you are doing well'.

On this particular night our immersion pumps went unserviceable. Immersion pumps pumped petrol through to the engines when at height. We would be unable to get above 17,000 feet and we were still in dense cloud with no sign of it breaking. This was the only time I boomeranged', Royal Air Force jargon for an abortive sortie. We turned round and went back to Fiskerton. On our way home and by using H_2S we dropped our bomb load on the Dutch island of Texel. Some time previously we had been told that the Germans had evacuated all the civilian population from the area and filled it with coastal defence weaponry. Out of a force of 358 Lancasters, 271 got to the target area but the official report added that due to the atrocious weather it was unlikely that any damage was caused to Leipzig. After the war there was no report of damage from the city. There were many stories from aircrew returning from the raid relating to the severe icing conditions causing engines to seize up and only restarting when the aircraft had been brought down to lower and warmer levels. Old Man Luck was still pointing us in the correct direction.

Raid No. 13, which we were very pleased to put behind us, was to Kassel. We went there two nights after Leipzig and it was a completely different story. The city took the full force of the attack but 43 aircraft, 7.9% of the attacking force, failed to return.

The multiple German defences may have been the main hazard but as I have written before these were closely followed by the inclement weather of the 43/44 winter and the worst threat the weather could produce was fog. To have flown for hours over Germany with all the senses keyed to fever pitch only to return to base and to find it blotted out by an impenetrable blanket of thick mist was almost the last straw. When I say 'return to base' I really mean to say 'return to the vicinity of base'. Our navigational aid 'Gee' was very efficient and undoubtedly dramatically changed bombing procedures but it wasn't accurate to that last few miles. Fortunately with fog there is no low cloud base to worry about but the rest of the Squadron's 'effort' are returning to base at around the same time. On almost every raid over Germany there were considerable losses from aircraft colliding over or near their own base and not always in foggy conditions. Also many a badly damaged aircraft struggling back from a raid on maybe two engines only, would make it to its base only to crash on landing destroying the aircraft and its crew.

When base was eventually located, maybe with aid of a QDM, which was a course given by them in order for the aerodrome to be found (a very useful service on a foggy night), I would call up on R/T: 'Bandlaw K-King to Passout, how do you hear me' and back would come the reply 'Your turn to land is No. 5'. It would be a WAAF operator on the line and they often came in for some ribald comment from a weary pilot, particularly when he was told he was told he was No. 5. So our plane would circle at its stacking height slowly dropping down as each plane landed and all the time the crew peering out into the murk to keep the 'Drem' lighting in site, or at best the beacon flashing out the identification letters 'FK' for Fiskerton. The 'Drem' lighting was a circle of lights all round the airfield erected on poles on the local farmland. The lights roughly indicated the normal circuit and approach for landing and there were so many airfields around Fiskerton that the 'Drem' systems almost over-lapped. 'Passout' was the Fiskerton call sign and 'Bandlaw' the call sign of our own 'A' Flight. Navigation lights would have already been switched on when entering Fiskerton air space but on a few occasions we were told to extinguish them and all the 'Drem' lighting would also be turned off and we knew there was an 'intruder' in the vicinity. German long range fighters who, using bad weather as a cover were able to come in low over the Lincolnshire coast, possibly undetected by radar, hover around an airfield and then pounce on an unsuspecting aircrew who, tired and long since having forgotten the enemy, made an easy target.

So, we would continue to 'stooge' around the airfield hoping not to mislay it again. Our petrol load was always calculated to give us something in hand given reasonable weather conditions but on these occasions many a nervous glance was directed at the fuel gauges.

So the lights would go on again as soon as the 'all clear' was received and if the fog was still around we would grope our way down through the murk and land with Ron once again shouting out the airspeed so that all my attention could be directed in getting the Lanc down safely. Another operation complete, only another 'so many' to go and seven souls breathed a sigh of relief.

But very soon we were to be equipped with a new innovation - 'FIDO' (Fog Intensive Dispersal Operation) - a highly expensive way of dispersing fog. It was very simply a perforated pipe, one on each side of the main runway, for its full length. Raw fuel passing through the pipes was ignited and the resultant intense heat just burnt away the fog. Not many airfields were graced with this device so we were fortunate. When in use FIDO could be seen for miles. Not only by us, I always thought, but also by those damned intruders. Landing a Lancaster into the FIDO system seemed like a descent might be into Hades. It was only when the plane got reasonably close to the runway that a pilot realised there was indeed a space between the two strips of flame affording sufficient space to land. The process certainly kept pilots on their toes. No swinging off the runway in a crosswind unless they wanted to straddle those flames. Nevertheless it certainly got rid of the landing in fog problem. One operational night when the fog was very dense, we were the bolt hole for dozens of Lancs. Unable to get in at their bases they were diverted to Fiskerton. Lancasters were lined up on the runways not in use and on every available perimeter track. If 'Jerry' had got wind of this he could have enjoyed a 'Hey-day' or 'Hey-night'.

Normally, when flying on operations at around 22,000 feet we would be above the weather but in unstable air conditions the cloud tops could go up to 30,000 feet plus and inside these clouds flying conditions could be very unpleasant with the aircraft being buffeted around like a cork in an angry sea. It was usually possible to miss these clouds and fly around them making the necessary calculations to get back onto course. Only on the blackest nights did they remain invisible. But sometimes there may have been no way of flying around them or even through possible valleys created by the clouds. Clouds such as these were called cumulo-nimbus and they were almost always electrical thunderstorms. In their worst form they cause the hurricanes in the Caribbean and other tropical latitudes where the atmosphere really does warm up. We had experienced brushes with this weather situation on a few occasions but, one night, well into the homeward journey we encountered weather which I remember vividly, in more ways than one.

We ran into dense cloud and I tried to get above it but with no success. Initially, it was fairly smooth going and I was, by now, quite accustomed to such flying conditions. But the going got rougher with the aircraft becoming difficult to hold on a steady course and we were flying into the heart of an electrical storm. I knew that the cloud tops would be well above the capacity of the Lanc and that the cloud base could be as low as 600 feet. We didn't know whether it thinned out to the right or to the left so the only thing to do was to keep going until we flew out of it. We then experienced St. Elmo's Fire and this occurs when the whole aircraft becomes charged with static electricity. The propellers become giant Catherine wheels and every bit of Perspex in the plane (all the windows) are framed in a blue flashing light. A scaring but fantastic experience. I had never seen anything like it before. In these conditions it was nothing for the plane suddenly to lose a few hundred feet and regain them just as quickly. We must have passed through a series of these storms without realising it; we were in cloud for what seemed like 'forever'. Ken eventually said that we were over the North Sea and should start dropping off height. This was a relief because I don't recall any icing up and to get to lower levels would help eliminate this further hazard. Once again there was no time for ration eating and smoking over the North Sea - it was going to take all my concentration to get us all safely back to Fiskerton. I was well aware that the safety height over Lincolnshire was 1,500 feet (the height to which one could safely descend in cloud) and to break cloud below this height without knowing one's exact position was asking for trouble. So I was back with Ken and his 'Gee' fixes and when he said we were over the coast I continued to lose height below 1,500 feet. I was very conscious that Lincoln Cathedral must be at least 500 feet above sea level so I was putting implicit faith, once again, in Ken's navigational skills. Suddenly, we were out of the cloud and very low with perfect visibility and the 'Drem' systems of Lincolnshire's airfields, for miles around, formed a very welcoming scene. One operational night and sometime after de-briefing, we heard of reports coming in of engines freezing up and only restarting when the aircraft reached the warmer air levels at lower altitudes. If these incidents did occur on the same night as our experience then, once again luck had been with us. Perhaps I should have mentioned that on 18 October we acquired a brand spanking new mount. Yes, a new Lancaster straight from the factory and she was called 'K-King'. We were to do 19 operations in this aircraft and she never let us down once. The whole crew and indeed the ground crew all became very fond of this plane. Somewhat like 'Friday afternoon' cars there were also planes of the same ilk. Although the Lancaster was a superb aircraft one could sometimes hear a pilot saying that his aircraft flew left wing low or perhaps some other similar problem and although he had told his ground crew somehow they just couldn't get right. No such trouble with 'K-King'; she flew like a bird and with such a plane the confidence of the crew must have been at a high level when we took off in her on that same day for our 11th operation, this time to the city of Hanover. Our fourth visit to Hanover, the previous had been ten days earlier. On this fourth visit it was all Lancasters,

360 in number of which 18 were lost, 5% of the force. One of the Lancs lost was the 5,000th Bomber Command aircraft lost on operations since the beginning of the war.

Before leaving 'K-King' it's worth mentioning that she would almost certainly have been delivered to the Squadron by an ATA pilot. Although largely comprising of men, this special organisation also had a considerable number of lady pilots on its strength and their main task was to ferry planes of all makes and sizes all over the country. It's quite possible that 'K King' was delivered by some slip of girl and possibly without any assistance. We finished our tour at the end of February 1944 and left 'K-King' for another pilot and crew. She survived until the night of 7/8th May 1944 when she crashed at Salbris in the centre of France having flown a total of 399 hours. Our crew had accounted for about 250 of these hours. Not bad when the average life of a Lancaster was nearer 50 hours. What she was doing over Salbris I don't know, but there were a few raids in the Bordeaux area about this time and she might have been on one of these.

After a raid de-briefing was always a tiring business. Each member of the crew had to give his own account of events to his own specialist officer and I had to give a report which was usually shortened and placed on record for perpetuity. I have some of these, photocopied from the originals at the Public Records Office at Kew, Richmond. After de-briefing they would let you get away to the traditional eggs and bacon meal and then to a much earned sleep. And if it was a cold night and most of them were, we did not bother to take off our silk 'long johns', they were just as warm in bed as they were in the air. One night, on entering the de-briefing room there was a gentleman sitting at our table with rings all the way up his arm. It was Air Chief Marshal Sir Ludlow-Hewitt, an ex Commander in Chief of Bomber Command. Taking an extreme interest in our stories he was a very pleasant old gentleman. We didn't get round to seeing Bomber Harris until after the war but at least we met one of his predecessors.

In the winter of 43/44 Fiskerton villagers, noticing an unusual amount of aerial activity disturbing their afternoon peace might well have thought 'There's something big on tonight' and they would probably have assumed correctly. It was the practice before most operations for the pilot to carry out an air test on his aircraft, certainly with his engineer but not necessarily with his whole crew. If any minor defects were discovered these could be rectified by the ground crew before the evening's take-off time. There are many Night Flying Tests (NFT's) recorded in my Log Book, each taking approximately ten minutes.

If someone in the village had been looking skywards on 20 October (the night we boomeranged from the Leipzig raid) sometime in the afternoon they might have spotted 'K-King'. Officially she was on a night flying test but also she was engaged on an unauthorised flight. On a few occasions Ron, my flight engineer, had expressed a wish to see his home town of Droitwich from the air. It was not all that far from Fiskerton and I thought we stood a good chance of getting back before anyone noticed anything untoward. Weather conditions were good that day and we duly arrived at Droitwich and flew around a little, perhaps a little lower than we should and I thought 'We have got this far so why not fly on to

JO-*S Nifter* on 463 Squadron
RAAF at Waddington in 1944

'The Vibrant Virgin noseart was very
much in the style of *Esquire Magazines*
Alberto Vargas

Lancaster X KB910 VICKY THE
VICIOUS VIRGIN which served on
428 'Ghost' and 420 'Snowy Owl'
Squadrons RCAF in April 1945 and
was returned to Canada in June that
year.

Virgin Vickie. Note the cherry as
in 'keep her cherry'.

Right: Sergeant Fred Charles Edwards, flight engineer, on 50 Squadron at Skellingthorpe who was killed on the raid on the V1 site at Prouville on 24/25 June 1944 when Lancaster III JA899 was shot down with the loss of six members on Pilot Officer l. G. Peters RCAF (PoW) crew. An eighth crewmember evaded capture.

Below: Bomber Command's last Victoria Cross was gained on the night of 23/24 February 1945, the posthumous award going to Captain Edwin Swales DFC SAAF on 582 Squadron, operating as Master Bomber for the attack on Pforzheim. Edwin Swales' crew, L-R: Pilot Officer N. 'Al' Bourne DFC RCAF, air gunner; Flight Sergeant Gerald Walter Bennington DFM RAF, flight engineer; Flight Sergeant Bryn Leach DFM RAF, air gunner; Flight Lieutenant Clive Dodson DSO DFC RAF, bomb aimer; Captain Edwin Swales DFC SAAF, pilot; Flight Lieutenant Dudley Archer DFC* DFM RAF, navigator; Pilot Officer R. A. 'Whisky' Wheaton DFC RAAF, 2nd navigator; Pilot Officer A. V. 'Bert' Goodacre DFC RAAF, wireless operator.

Newent and show the crew my home town'. Here, at just a small country town I felt I could really get down low, so we proceeded to give Newent the works, roaring down the High Street at roof height and just missing a large crane sited at the saw mills. We landed after being 14.5 minutes in the air ready to take any 'flak' they would sling at us but incredibly, nothing happened. The ground crew must have kept quiet about the petrol consumption and our Flight Office must have been too busy preparing the night's op.

After the Leipzig raid we went on that highly successful raid on Kassel. Then the squadron experienced a long operation free period of three weeks. This would almost certainly have been due to inclement weather coupled with a moon period. Every night from the 11th. November to the 17th. We were on night training exercises with some of the them taking 2½ hours, so there was little time to get to the Saracen's Head in Lincoln or the White Hart, both recognised as the most favoured pubs in the 5 Group area. They used to say that if you wanted to find where the target was for the night go along to the Saracen's about lunch time, ask the bar maid and she would tell you. By the way, if you went to Lincoln to find the Saracen's today you wouldn't be successful. It was demolished a few years ago. We used to force Ken to play the piano at the White Hart, at least he liked to think that we were forcing him and the appreciative pints placed on top of the piano saved the crew many a 'bob'.

On the 18th November the target for the night was Berlin - 'The Big City' - and I hadn't been there since my '2nd dickie' in August and the crew hadn't been there at all. The very mention of the name Berlin created a certain tension and apprehension amongst all those present at briefing, but this was to be the first in the Battle of Berlin which would eventually comprise 19 major raids on that city. Martin Middlebrook in his book *'The Berlin Raids'* maintains that the 'Battle' commenced with that raid back in August. 'K-King' was to take a very active role in the 'Battle' taking part in eleven of the raids. With my '2nd' I took part in 12. Not many pilots exceeded this total. To date I have met one who did 13 and one who did 15. To do that number he must have missed out on some of his leave periods. Did I mention about aircrew leaves? Because we flew, or at least were on duty seven days a week we would get a week's leave every six weeks (presumably for the Sundays we flew). This reminds me. Quite recently my sister Peggy told me that I was at home at Newent for my 21st birthday. So it must have been a leave period when I went to Newent instead of elsewhere. This would account for the gap in my Log Book between the end of October and the 10th November. For the life of me I cannot remember my 21st. but we must have celebrated in some way or another. This raid on Berlin was my 14th and the crew's 12th, so we were almost half way through our tour. It was also the raid in which we encountered those strong head winds and had to land at the American base in Norfolk.

600 aircraft from Bomber Command were lost over Berlin in the 'Battle' and the controversy over whether it was a success or failure has continued ever since.

There were to be a further three raids on Berlin in that week and we participated in all of them. Then Berlin again in the following week and the next night to Leipzig again and this time we got there.

This was a hectic two weeks and I suspect that the leisure time we did have would have been spent in the Sergeants' Mess. We used to get off the airfield whenever we possibly could but the comforts of the Mess were very much appreciated and these sometimes included impromptu parties which did tend to get a little hectic. High Cockaloram was one of the favourite games or perhaps one ought to call it a sport. Two teams, each with the main contestants riding on someone else's back and the idea was to knock the rider to the floor with whatever weapon was available. The side left with the most mounted riders won the game. Also *'The Muffin Man'* played to the tune of *'Do you know the Muffin Man?'* It involved doing something with pints of beer balanced on one's head but for the life of me I can't remember what. The mind boggles. Whatever it was the rules usually went out of the window and a general free-for-all ensued.

You may be wondering and if you weren't I will tell you anyway; how did we cope with the calls of nature? I have already told you about the funnelled tube available to the pilot but, also, at the rear of the Lanc was an Elsan toilet. Available to all the crew I would always tell them to be quick about it and get back to their post as quickly as possible. No reading of the weekly magazine, especially over enemy territory. If my needs were very urgent then Pat would come up to cockpit and take over. Mind you, I was very reluctant to do this and usually tried to 'hang on' until we were over the North Sea and on the way home.

We also had a rest bed at the rear of the aircraft and this is where they put Peto when they pulled him out of the rear turret.

There was one occasion when such an arrangement would just not have been used. On one operation we were routed to return just as dawn was breaking. This was achieved by a very late take off and on the return journey we were scheduled to be crossing the Dutch coast at daybreak. The whole attacking force flew back over the North Sea at sea level. I have forgotten the target for that night but I will never forget the sight of Lancasters as far as the eye could see all at wave-top height. There was precious little authorised low flying at this stage of the war so this was an occasion to be relished and I doubt if there was a pilot in that returning force who did not enjoy that helter-skelter dash for home.

Interspersed with these raids to Berlin were raids to other cities. We went to Leipzig (for the second time), Frankfurt and Brunswick. When we were expecting a lull over the Christmas period we were sent to Berlin again on the night before Christmas Eve. I can't remember where I was Christmas '43.

On the 5th January we went to Stettin in Poland on the Baltic coast. It was my 23rd op and the crew's 21st and we were slowly approaching the end of our tour. This was to be our longest penetration into enemy territory and we were to land nine hours and ten minutes after take-off (with a full fuel load of 2,155 Imperial gallons the Lancaster could stay airborne for just over ten hours so this trip was pushing things to the limit). Each Merlin engine burned about 50 gallons an hour and a considerable amount could be added to this for take-off and climb.

This was a 'Gardening' operation. In plain language a mine laying exercise in enemy waters and the water in question this time was the harbour approach into Stettin, one of Poland's major ports overrun by the Germans at the start of the war. Mines were dropped on parachutes to minimise the impact when they hit the water and it also meant going in quite low to drop them. We were routed in over the most northerly cape of Denmark (occupied by the Germans) right up to the Swedish coast and then we turned due south for about a 200 mile run up to the target. At some point we must have crossed over into Swedish territory because, suddenly, all hell was let loose with the Swedes shooting off with everything they had, but only up to about 10,000 feet. It was quite a sight, quite like flying over a bright red carpet with nothing coming anywhere near us. We learned later and I don't know how true it was, that they did exactly the same for the Germans. They were a neutral country of course and they were telling us to stay up there. Come any lower at your peril.

I wonder what the crew would have thought if we had known at the time that we were one of only six Lancasters engaged on minelaying that night and that the main force of 348 Lancasters were bombing the city of Stettin. Not much 'protection in numbers' that night. 16 aircraft - 14 Lancasters and two Halifaxes were lost that night, 4.9% of the attacking force but we had a tiring but uneventful trip. Unless this was the night we witnessed the Aurora Borealis (The Northern Lights), way to the north shafts of light like searchlights piercing the night sky. We only saw it on one occasion and I really must find out what causes this phenomenon, some say it's the reflection of the sun's rays off the polar ice, but how can that be in winter when there is so little sun in the Polar Regions.

One other natural happening and this one did give us some problems, was condensation trails. Today, they are part of everyday jet travel and maybe the Americans in their Flying Fortresses used them to bring the German fighters into battle. But when Peto called up and said' Skipper we are forming con trails', I always endeavoured to fly at a different level where they were not forming. Even a few hundred feet would sometimes be sufficient. There just couldn't be a worse indication of position in the night sky.

After Stettin we went to Brunswick nine nights later and then there were four more Berlin raids which took us up to the end January 1944. I had now completed 28 operations and the crew 26 (except for those members who had been sick). Almost half our tour had been taken up with raids on Berlin and it was incredible that we had survived. Going into breakfast one saw but tried not to notice that a certain table was empty, maybe sometimes two but these would soon be filled with crews straight from training. The crews of Hodgkinson, Brunt, Cottingham, Petty and countless others had all gone missing. I knew these four pilots; they were all from 'A' Flight and as I said before I trained with Hodgkinson and Brunt. But it was never going to be us, not the crew of 'K-King', not after we had come so far.

My turn came for taking a 2nd Dickie and it must have been to Berlin. I can't remember who it was. Some five or six years ago a fellow called Tudor-Jones approached me and said I had taken him on his 2nd Dickie. I couldn't remember him. But I did congratulate him on his survival and told him it must have something to do with guidance I gave him on that night. Also there's a rear gunner in Bristol, chairman of his ACA Branch, as a matter of fact and he says he flew as my rear gunner one night. I couldn't remember him either. But with Peto, Pat and Ken all missing trips with me due to illness, someone had to fill their places.

All through my training and operational tour my promotion had progressed smoothly and rapidly. Aircraftman No. 2 when I joined up. Leading Aircraftman at EFTS and SFTS. Sergeant when I received my wings in Canada and then, whilst on the Squadron at Fiskerton I was promoted to Flight Sergeant then to Warrant Officer and then in January 1944 I received my Commission. I did not apply for a King's Commission, I was informed, possibly by my Squadron Commander, that my name had been put forward and that I was to attend an interview at our parent airfield at Scampton. Contrary to other non-commissioned pilots' efforts to gain a commission, I didn't want one. We were still a non-commissioned crew, we all slept in the same billet, shared the same mess and enjoyed our off duty time together and what was more there were only a few more ops to do to complete our tour. I just didn't want anything to disrupt our crew harmony. It was with this in mind that I journeyed to Scampton and I believe it was the eminent Air Vice Marshal 'Cocky' Cochrane who interviewed me. The Air Officer Commanding 5 Group, none other. Although I did express my wish, it fell on deaf ears. When I saw the rank of my interviewer I didn't expect much else. I was told it was the practice to commission all pilots approaching the end of their tour. This was 5 Group policy and I must abide by it or words to that effect. So, on the 10th January 1944 I became Pilot Officer Jones and was given a short leave to get myself kitted out with the uniform. I was no longer paid in cash at a pay parade but became the proud possessor of a bank account in the Glyn Mills Bank. Into this account was paid the princely sum of about £50 for the purchase of the uniform. Today the overcoat alone would cost at least three times as much. One of the first operations with this new gear was to make the hat look 'operational'. Take out the wire stiffener from the hat and then sit on it, throw it around and generally misuse it until slowly it began to look the part. Sylvia and all at home were particularly pleased with my change in direction and in the event things did not change very much as far as the crew were concerned. We were still united, commission or no commission and I was still just 'Skipper'. I was now resident in the Officers' Mess and that was the only real change which took place.

Unbeknown to me, whilst I was still a Warrant Officer and had completed 19 operations (five on Berlin), Wing Commander Adams our Squadron Commanding Officer had recommended me for the award of the Distinguished Flying Cross with the citation as follows:

'This Warrant Officer has completed 19 sorties of 120.05 hours operational flying as Captain of a Lancaster in 49 Squadron. All of these sorties have been against the most heavily defended targets in Germany, five of them having been on BERLIN during the past month. Often in difficult weather conditions and against sharp opposition from the enemy, he has always carried out his work in the air with quiet efficiency and grim determination. He has proved his intention of taking his aircraft to the correct target exactly and precisely and of bringing it back to this country without fuss or ugly incident.

I recommend that Warrant Officer Jones be awarded the DFC.'

Signed by W/Cdr. Adams 6th Dec 1943.

It was mid February 1944 and I was on leave in Newent at my parents' home when the news of my award broke. It appeared in the 'London Gazette' on the 15th. February 1944 and it must have been from this source that the local press got the news. The Gloucester 'Citizen' had, somehow, managed to locate me and before I knew where I was I was on the roof of the Citizen office in

Gloucester being photographed and interviewed. For a very, very short time I was famous. My one regret was that I did not go to Buckingham Palace to receive the award. Up until a few months previously King George VIth had awarded all DFC's but his health was failing and at the time was only awarding the higher decorations.

But I did receive a letter of congratulations from His Majesty bearing his signature. This I still have.

One further item of interest regarding the above. Officers obtained no financial reward for this decoration but a Warrant Officer did. On the 11th May 1945 my bank account was credited with sum of £20.00. It had taken a long time to come through and it provided the financial back-up for a great binge in the Officers' Mess for yours truly and friends.

Retracing my steps, I remember buying the blue and white striped ribbon of the DFC, taking it back to Ashridge Crescent in Woolwich and Sylvia sewing it onto my 'best blue' and also my battledress blouse.

Ken was to receive his commission a few months later and also was awarded the DFC. Later his navigational ability took him to the rank of Squadron Leader, a thoroughly deserved reward. His private life was a different matter, but that's another story. As I have said before we were good

Essen at the end of the war devastated by repeated bombing.

friends right up to his death about ten years ago. Steve's DFM (a Medal not a Cross for non-Commissioned Officers) made up the number of 'gongs' received by the crew. It should have been seven, one for each member of the crew. I was grateful and always will be for such a competent crew. There was never any major dissention and they accepted me as their 'Skipper' from the start. We were good friends on the ground and a good team in the air.

Schweinfurt, the ball-bearing manufacturing centre of Germany. Knock out the ball-bearing factories and the whole German war machinery will be out of action. Everything ran on ball-bearings. This is what they told us at briefing on the 24th February 1944. This was to be my penultimate sortie and hopefully this applied to most of the crew as well. The Americans were bombing it by day and we were to bomb it by night. And here I must say how much we all admired the Yanks in their B-17s (Flying Fortresses). They flew in daylight and their losses were horrendous. The Americans, even if they had wished to switch their bombing activities to night time, as the Royal Air Force had been forced to do, would have been unable to do so because their crews had never received extensive night flying training. They were wholly committed to day time bombing. The general belief in those days was that the Yanks, as they were universally known, carried out precision bombing whereas the RAF method was pattern bombing. This belief indicates that there was a considerable difference between the two methods but this is only true up to a point. Most people are familiar with photographs of Fortresses going into the attack and these photographs show the formations of Fortresses spread over a considerable area of sky. As they approached their target they did not break away and attack the target in line astern, they maintained their heading and as they arrived at the target so they released their bombs. Inevitably they would fall over a considerable area.

Bomber Harris, more affectionately known to 'his old lags' as 'Butch', in the early days of taking over Bomber Command, wanted to achieve a force of 4,000 bombers and with a force of this strength he was utterly convinced he could defeat Germany and eliminate the necessity of invasion. He was never able to achieve this number of aircraft. There was the 1,000 bomber raid on Cologne in 1942, achieved by draining the bottom of the barrel (including Training Command aircraft) and a small number of raids immediately after Cologne with a similar number of aircraft achieved in the same manner but his raiding forces never achieved that number again. Losses on every operational night of between 4% and 9% were only just sustained by an all-out production line. Yet Harris was never shaken from his belief that bombing would save the lives of thousands of invasion soldiers and sailors and this was the resolve he successfully implanted in all his aircrews.

So my 29th operation and four members of the crew's 27th operation took us with the main force to Schweinfurt. I had high hopes of at least Ron, Steve and Jock finishing their tour along with me but I wasn't too sure about Ken, Pat and Peto, they had missed out on quite a few trips. I suspect that we were all apprehensive about the approaching end of our tour and at even this late stage our luck could still run out so when a piece of spent shrapnel managed to find its way through the underside of our Lanc and into the cockpit between my legs it was a good indication the anti aircraft guns had got our range. We had completed our bombing run and we were on our way home so with one thought in mind 'get out of the guns' range' I stuck the nose of K-.King right down and sped post-haste towards the ground. This incident I clearly remember - the speed built up very quickly and we were well over 300 mph when I started to pull out of the dive. The controls were as heavy as lead and only lightened as the speed fell away. The maximum permissible speed for the Lanc was around 350 mph and I must have been pretty close to it. Anyway the wings didn't drop off and we were out of range of those guns and we eventually landed safely at Fiskerton.

734 bombers attacked Schweinfurt, the attack being split into two raids with a two hour gap between each raid. The first time a major attack had a two hour gap between waves. The raid was considered a success. 33 bombers were lost, 4.5% of the force.

Reporting to the Flight Office the next morning I was told that our tour was completed. I just couldn't believe our luck. I always understood that the commitment was 30 operations. For the four of us it was the end of nightly journeys over Germany. There was no explanation given but later I was to learn that a pilot, completing 200 hours of operational flying constituted a tour. Actually I had completed 190 hrs. 35 minutes including that 'boomerang' to Leipzig so, somewhere, someone, had got their sums wrong and I could have done the full 30 ops within the 200 hours. Perhaps they thought that with twelve trips to the 'Big City' included in the tour it was sufficient to call it a day. I was not asked to volunteer for a second tour which would have meant a further 20 ops, possibly with the Pathfinder Force. I was informed, as were Ron, Steve and Jock, that we would be 'screened' which meant being posted to training unit to instruct future bomber crews. Ken, Pat and Peto were to stay behind and complete their tours with other crews. I could have volunteered to continue with a second tour with all the crew sticking together but in spite of the additional skills we had acquired in the last six months I was firmly convinced that luck had been the biggest factor in our survival (I felt I owed it to Ron, Steve, Jock and myself to call it a day and seek fresh fields). If we could have foreseen the fate of Peto and Pat perhaps other decisions would have been made.

As you will see from this narrative we never had to return with our aircraft shot to ribbons and we never had to return on two or even three engines but every raid in which we participated was a battle. Some were more intense than others and this was dependent on the weather conditions and the state of readiness of the German defences. When we thought back about those nights over Germany we must have considered how lucky we were and how fortunate we were to have got through the tour unscathed.

During the 29 ops I completed, 798 bombers were destroyed over enemy territory. Of the 5,586 crew members in these aircraft statistics show that only one-eighth could expect to become prisoners of war. These figures did not include aircraft lost over Britain due to bad weather, enemy intruders etc.

On the night of 26/27th November after a raid on Berlin, 14 Lancasters crashed on return. On 16/17th December, another Berlin raid, 29 Lancasters and one Stirling crashed due to very low cloud, some crews abandoning their aircraft and parachuting to safety. Although 5 Group were not greatly affected on this occasion it might well have been the night we returned in that very bad storm and experienced very low cloud conditions in the Lincoln area. So we turned our backs on Fiskerton leaving Ken, Peto and Pat to complete their tours and it was to be some weeks before I heard that Pat and Peto had gone missing and that Ken had completed his tour.

I had been in the Royal Air Force for almost exactly 2½ years and there was still another three years and nine months to serve. I felt I had come a long way from those early days in Newent. I now had confidence, an essential ingredient as I was 'screened' to teach trainee pilots how to fly bomber aircraft. After a short leave I was told to report to No. 5 Lancaster Finishing School at Syerston. I arrived on the 26th February 1944 after having left Ron, Steve and Jock to journey to their own units where they also were detailed to take up instructional duties.

I was only based at Syerston for a few weeks but during that time Sylvia arrived unannounced at Newark just a few miles down the road from Syerston. She had travelled without her parents' permission. Understandably, they were against us getting married, Sylvia was still only eighteen but early marriages were not uncommon in wartime. We had discussed getting married for many months and had decided that if and when I completed my operational tour we would then press for Sylvia's parents' permission. When Sylvia travelled north and stayed overnight they may have suspected the worst but the fact was that Sylvia and I spent the night sitting on a park bench discussing at great length our plans for the future. Morals in those days were a little bit tighter than they are these days. A few days after Sylvia returned home she telephoned me with the good news that her parents had consented to her marriage and that the date was fixed for 28th. April. I had already acquired a very soft spot for my future mother-in-law and I hoped that the sequence of events had not caused her too much distress. The wedding was to take place at a small church half way up Shooters Hill (Christchurch) and the reception in Welling just down the road in Kent.

The 31st March saw me moving south to No.11 Operational Training Unit at RAF Westcott. My posting was as a Staff Pilot which indicated I was scheduled for instructional duties. Westcott was just a few miles from Aylesbury in Buckinghamshire and it was the unit through which all trainee New Zealand bomber pilots were funnelled. Although there were many British personnel amongst the ground staff and many British and Commonwealth aircrew trained on the unit the station always maintained a very definite New Zealand atmosphere. Cullinane and Kelly were two Kiwi instructors in our Flight and they used to receive delicious parcels of food from their homes. These, they always spread liberally amongst their fellow instructors and I particularly remember their Dundee cakes which used to arrive in vacuum packed tins. A luxury indeed with rationing as it was.

It would be many years before I returned to Fiskerton and by then the runways had all been broken up and the resultant hardcore heaped in piles. There was and still is little traffic on the roads around Fiskerton. They connect destinations only; there are no through roads. Just as well because the multitude of right-angled bends, probably following the boundaries of ancient farming

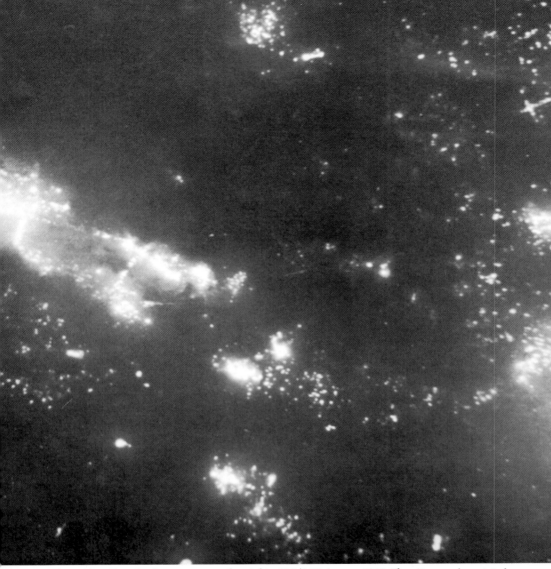

The raid on Dresden in progress on the night of 13/14 February 1945. The city was devastated by 796 Lancasters and by 311 bombers of the 8th Air Force the following day. (IWM)

plots, makes driving hazardous. Water filled dykes exist on either side of the roads. I still return with our Squadron Association every two years. One hangar would be standing but the place was almost unrecognisable but I was shown where 'K-King' used to park in dispersal. Now all is quiet again but the village still remember us and have commemorated our presence with a plaque in their little church and a glass case containing some of the Squadron's history. I am happy to say my crew are named on a copy of the Squadron Battle Order for the first major raid on Berlin.

Chapter 9

Three Passions and a Lucky Penny

Eric Stephenson

Eric Stephenson was a Geordie, from Tyneside born in his maternal grandmother's house in the riverside town of Jarrow on 22 July 1922. He had washed out of pilot training and became a navigator. During training he had escaped death on the flip of penny coin. For nearly 30 years Dr Eric Stephenson was a medical officer in the RAAF, rising to be Director General of Air Force Health Services with the rank of Air Vice Marshal.

'Our crew' recalls Pilot Officer Eric Hay Stephenson, a navigator, 'was just about ready to set off from 1661 Lancaster Conversion Unit at Morton Hall for Langar near Nottingham in mid-October 1943 when a message came through telling us that 207 Squadron was on the move. There was now no point to going to Langar and instead we might as well head for the unit's new location at Spilsby. This was a brand new airfield built on farmland a short distance west of Skegness in Lincolnshire. The airfield was originally intended to go three kilometres to the north-east, at Steeping, on the site of Gunby Park owned by retired Field Marshal Sir Archibald Montgomery-Massingberd. The Field Marshal objected strenuously to the planned construction, supposedly making a personal appeal to the King, with the result that the airfield was relocated. Even winning his point did not mollify the old gentleman, who still found living close to a busy wartime bomber base was more than he could willingly accept. He was always complaining that we were very noisy fliers and getting terribly upset whenever guns were being tested. Although the range was nowhere near his house, the guns used to make a hell of a racket. Apart from that situation, our relationship with the local population of the district was pretty variable. We were three miles from town, roughly and at that time of year it got dark by four o'clock in the afternoon, so if we went to somewhere like a pub we met a lot of people but did not see much else.

At the aerodrome there were no permanent buildings, just Nissen huts and, of course, hangars. My sleeping quarters were in one of the Nissen huts, which I shared with my pilot Ralph Allen and Flight Lieutenant Derrick Reay and Flying Officer Bob Mair. We each had a bed and mattress, a locker and a little hanging wardrobe and there was the usual large potbelly stove in the middle of the room, for heating, with a few chairs around it. We were not exactly impressed by this accommodation when we saw it, but it was pretty standard fare for the RAF during the war. The best of the arrangement was that we could get our laundry done through a local contractor and the cost was put on our mess bill. The Officers' Mess was also in a Nissen hut, which had an extension housing the anteroom. We got very good food there and excellent service provided by members of the Women's Auxiliary Air Force. They were truly wonderful to us and even when we came back from a raid in the middle of the night they always had a fine breakfast waiting.

The base commander was Group Captain Walter Cheshire[8] and he used to make a point of coming into breakfast and sitting down with officers who had recently joined the squadron. One morning he joined Ralph and me at our table. While Ralph was off at the bain-marie getting his bacon and eggs, the Group Captain said to me, 'Stephenson, I understand you're the officer in charge of Hut 33'. It impressed me that he knew that, since I had only been given the responsibility a couple of days before. After I confirmed his information, he said, 'Well look, the NCOs in that hut are all aircrew and many of them are from overseas and may not know all the English ways of the RAF, so you must be sure that everything's in good order. Make sure the water's hot and get the barracks people to fix any broken windows, faulty lights or leaking ceilings, anything like that. Remember, war or no war, don't let your standards slip.' I have always remembered that advice and tried to live up to it.

My own comfort was largely taken care of by my cousin Audrey, the daughter of Uncle Will who originally sparked my interest in becoming a doctor. She was living at Boston with her doctor husband, John Pankhurst and their three children. A phone call to her drew an enthusiastic welcome, 'Come anytime, Eric and stay as long as you can'. Spilsby was actually pretty isolated and I cannot remember how I made it to Boston for the first time, but John drove me back to the base for 8.30 the next morning with a bicycle strapped to the back of the car for my future use. I went to Boston as often as I could after that and I still remember the comfortable home with central heating and full of the joy of family life. It was wonderfully relaxing and a

On leave in London Back row, left to right: Sergeant Takle, Sergeant Stone, Sergeant Vowles. Front: Left to right Sergeant Millward, Pilot Officer Stelphenson, Flight Lieutenant Allen, Flight Sergeant Brindle.

restorative balance to the somewhat pressured life on the base.

It is a point worth making that the members of the squadron were of various nationalities. Apart from Englishmen, Irishmen, Scotsmen and Welshmen, there were Australians, Canadians and New Zealanders. I think we had at least one Rhodesian crew and there were even two Americans. One was a pilot from the Bronx and the other was a navigator from Atlanta, Georgia. They had joined the Royal Canadian Air Force because they just wanted to fight in the war. When America came into the conflict they transferred to the Army Air Corps and wore American uniforms, but remained flying members on 207 Squadron. They were both damn good people, very respected and popular with everybody, but sadly both were killed.[9] The point is that the squadron was incredibly mixed. In the mess the insults would fly, but the acid test came whenever the chips were down because there was never any hesitation about cooperation then.

Before we did our first operation as a crew, the pilot and the navigator had to do what was called a 'dickie trip' to test our ability to cope. On 18 October, about a week after we joined the unit, the squadron undertook a raid on Hannover as its first operation from Spilsby. This provided the opportunity for me to make my dickie trip flying with Squadron Leader David Balme, the commander of 'A' Flight, while my pilot flew with Flight Lieutenant Ken Letford. Now, Letford was a quite extraordinary man. He was just about to finish his tour and Balme finished his a couple of months later.[10] Letford chiefly became famous during the civil war in China in 1949 when he landed a Sunderland flying boat alongside the British frigate *Amethyst* which the communists trapped on the Yangtze River and rescued some of the crew.

The other interesting thing about Letford was that he had a warrant officer navigator named Langton Connelly, an Australian who could 'smell' his way around Germany. Connelly had learnt by heart the configurations of the searchlight patterns over certain cities and with the Germans being like they are he could distinguish between places 50 miles away. He taught us as best he could the patterns at Essen and the Ruhr, Hamburg and so on; generally, he did not worry about Berlin, because that was obvious and we had track markers to help us out.

On my dickie trip, my job mostly involved sitting in the flight engineer's seat (when he was not needing it or busy doing things) and keeping a lookout to make sure that nothing bumped into us. Occasionally I had a look up in the astrodome. Squadron Leader Balme kept drawing my attention to things, saying, 'Look, look, see that over there, that's a so and so'. Once he said, 'See that explosion? That's a scarecrow flare.' These were just great globs of fireworks that the Germans sent up to make a big bang and give the impression of an aircraft exploding. Knowing how to tell the difference was very useful skill to have. We had one brush with a night fighter, but the gunners fired at him and scared him off. The flak was fairly intense near Hannover but never really worried us. We found the target well marked by the Pathfinder Force, so we dropped our bombs and quickly headed for home. I was left with the strangest feeling, thinking that it could not be this easy. Then I remembered the dictum that bombing enemy territory in wartime is 99 per cent sheer boredom and one per cent sheer terror.

Our first trip as a crew on operations was on 23 October 1943. We went off to bomb Kassel and the skipper just said, 'Okay fellows, here we go. We're in it.'

Although we might have had a few quivers at that point, I think we all felt qualified and ready for operations and confident we would do alright. A couple of factors had, by this stage of the war, changed what it was like to be on operations in Bomber Command. The first was some highly successful attacks that had contributed to boosting the confidence of the force. The raid on the Möhne and Eder Dams was one such turning point and the raid on Peenemünde against the Germans' secret V-weapons program was another. I would include, too, the battle of El Alamein; even though that had been an important land victory, it had a huge impact because undoubtedly the Air Force had contributed quite considerably to the outcome.

The second factor was the collective perception within Bomber Command that improvements in our technology were allowing us to hit back effectively at the Germans, for a change and that was putting us in front. With more and more units converting to the Lancaster, the less successful types like the Halifax and Stirling were being taken out of operations and put to use merely as trainers. It was not only that things seemed to be improving all the time in Bomber Command either. Following its wonderful victory in the Battle of Britain, Fighter Command was moving from strength to strength in terms of the aircraft it had to provide escort protection to the bombers. When the Merlin engine was fitted to the P-51 Mustang, it turned a moderate fighter into a world-beater and put a hell of a dent into the Luftwaffe. That gave a tremendous boost to the bombers' morale, especially among the Americans.

We did alright on our first trip, even though we 'boomeranged' - that is, came back before reaching our target. The Gee direction-finding system[11] that we carried on board was a very good indicator of our ground position, providing it was not jammed, but it was jammed out of existence by the Germans before we got to the Dutch coast, so then I was on dead reckoning. As we crossed the coast I remembered a warning we had been given to avoid all large cities, because flying at only 20,000 feet there was a high risk of getting caught by predicted flak. When a certain town, which I expected to see appear slightly to our starboard side, suddenly came up in front of us, I thought, 'That's funny, my navigation can't be that hopelessly off because the met winds had all seemed correct up until then! I asked the skipper what course he was flying, according to the indicator and he looked down and said, 'The compass says I'm on so and so', which was about 15 degrees out. I asked the flight engineer to check the 02 compass and as he did that something wet came off on his hand. The alcohol liquid had leaked out and the gimbal rings were jamming, so the compass was actually useless.

The skipper said, 'Well, it's up to you. What do you want to do?' I answered, 'The 08 [hand-held magnetic compass] is notoriously unreliable and I don't know how good the DR is - that could be out as well! 'Okay! he said, 'are you happy to navigate this kite?' When I said that I was not, he just said, 'Right, then we'll boomerang. Look for a reasonable site.' A few moments later he said, 'There's one just over there, a few miles away. Those German searchlights, we'll drop our load on them.' We did that and headed for home. I got a bit of a kick up the backside when we got back. The operation had been an all-Lancaster attack involving 320 aircraft. These would have been in three waves spread out over 18 minutes flying time, all travelling at the same height (give or take 500 feet above or below) and at something like 200 mph. Packed in a box like that there was not much room to be doing gigs around the place and when I gave the turn I had done so directly over Rotterdam. Luckily, the Germans below us held their fire - I imagine they were sensible enough to realise that a single aircraft was not going to do much damage. Mind you, if we had dropped our bombs there, we would certainly have copped it.

Flying in crowded formation like that could be incredibly dangerous and we spent a lot of our time in the air just making sure there was nothing headed in our direction. On one of our later night trips Sergeant Maxwell Millward, our engineer, shouted out a warning, 'Skipper, dive port! The skipper did as told and we were not conscious of anything at all until we landed and got out to find there was a gash in the top of the fuselage. It turned out that we had been hit by somebody's SBA aerial,[12] which hung just a few feet beneath an aircraft - that showed how close we were to collision on that occasion.

Warrant Officer Connelly taught us another thing to watch for while keeping place in formation. He said, 'Remember, when you're behind planes with four large

Wing Commander David M. Balme DSO DFC who flew a tour on 207 Squadron. He took command of 227 Squadron in March 1945.

Pilot Officer Fred Whitton Gallagher (left) and crew on Lancaster III EE197 EM-M on 207 Squadron which crashed at Spilsby on return from the raid on Brunswick on 14/15 January 1944. Outbound the port outer failed and was feathered. After jettisoning part of the bomb load, the crew continued to the target where they came under sustained attack from a FW 190. After a difficult return flight, the Lancaster touched down at 2254 and broke up, injuring Flight Sergeant C. E. D. Stewart the flight engineer. Gallagher was awarded an immediate DSO and Stewart, a DFM.

motors, they've got a huge slipstream. As you go along, you'll find that every once in a while you'll get a jolt and then perhaps another one a minute or so later and you'll know that you're in the bomber stream. But if a jolt is so rough that it throws you out of your seat and knocks all your maps on the floor, it means you're too damned close!'

As we returned to base from that first trip, the starboard inner engine burst into flames just as we got on the circuit. The engine had to be feathered, but we landed safely. Afterwards we worked out that if we had gone on, instead of turning back in the Rotterdam area, that engine would have burst into flames just about the time we were over the target. We would have been in deep trouble then. During our debriefing for this trip, we were told that if we had been a more experienced crew we would have been expected to press on.

Our next operation was to Düsseldorf on 3 November. The operation was uneventful for our crew, although we later learned that Flight Lieutenant Jock Reid (who had been one of our instructors at OTU) earned a Victoria Cross on that trip, for pressing on with the operation after being injured. After that second operation, Ralph Allen and I were sent to RAF Scampton to do an administration course for junior officers. When we returned to Spilsby towards the end of November, we found that the squadron was now involved in the Battle of Berlin; in fact, Bomber Command had made an initial raid on Berlin while we were on course. During our first operation to Berlin on 22 November, we were towards the front of the bomber force, the target was well marked and we were fortunate not to be attacked. We returned to base without incident and were the first aircraft home. Using Gee, I directed the pilot when to call up base and as the aerodrome lights came on we found that we were flying straight down the main runway. The crew were very impressed by that.

I recall that there was an NCO named Powell - a flight sergeant, I think he was, although we all called him 'Chiefie'. I used to chat to him occasionally about little technicalities regarding the plane, especially as a navigator and he always gave me advice. He taught me that when you speak to a senior NCO who has been at the game for probably 20 years and you are a sprog pilot officer with barely six months under your belt, you ought to listen to what he says. I have held Air Force NCOs, both RAF and RAAF, in high regard ever since.

There was the time I got into a plane about half an hour before takeoff for Berlin and found I did not have an astrocompass. When I went looking for assistance, the only person I could find was Chiefie Powell. I told him what I needed and he got hold of a bicycle and went rushing about the base. Inside 20 minutes he was back with the astrocompass and he was sweating like anything in spite of the fact it was a cold November night. I realised that I had put him to an awful lot of trouble and thanked him for his efforts. He said, 'That's alright, sir. You mustn't forget I've got nearly 40 blokes working on this bloody kite and they work all hours and in all weathers. They all want you to bring the damned thing back.' I realised that was the other side of the coin.

Some of the better navigational aids, like H$_2$S radar, were just being introduced or were yet to come at that stage, but we still had a few good techniques that we employed. One involved the Pathfinders dropping special track markers at designated spots on the ground to aid our navigation. These were not even on the flight path, but might be up to six miles off track. We would be told before take-off, 'Look for a green marker on spot X', so we knew we had this as a check on where we were at particular points in the operation. Usually there would be one after about an hour's flying into enemy territory and a second hour or two before the target. These were a great help on a long trip to somewhere like Berlin. The Pathfinders ran huge risks to place the markers, often having to go down to virtually treetop height to do it. Of course, once they had Mosquito aircraft it was a piece of cake, because nothing could stop a 'Mossie'.

I also had a particular dodge or gimmick that I worked with the flight engineer, which I do not imagine would have been approved of by people at the time. It stemmed from the fact that Lincoln lay almost exactly due west of Berlin and there was no point to juggling our route on the return leg of an operation. Since we knew the enemy's fighters would be chasing us anyway, the thing to do was to head for home in the most direct line possible. I knew that taking a shot on the Pole Star and applying what was called declination gave me our latitude, approximately. One night I used a lipstick that Freda had given to me to draw a circle of about five centimetres diameter up on the flight engineer's perspex bubble and I told him, 'That's the Pole Star. If it gets outside that circle, call me ... loudly!' Not a very sophisticated piece of navigation, I realise, but it was fairly reliable and effective. (We were never as bad as the American B-17 that landed at Gatow airfield in Berlin, with the crew thinking they had made it back to England.) Of course, once we made it to the Dutch coast we could start using Gee again, because German jamming was not a problem. We did another sortie to Berlin on 23 November and returned safely. Ralph and I were not too worried when we got back to our hut and found that Bob and Derrick were not there, because they could have been further back in the bombing raid or they could just be late or were forced to land somewhere else. In the morning, however, we learnt that their aircraft was missing. Later it was confirmed that they were killed in action and that was a bit shattering. [13] It probably influenced my action a day or so later.

After our operation to Berlin on the 24th was cancelled, I decided to do a quick trip to London to see Freda. I wanted to see her again as I was going to ask her to marry me. I had a nasty feeling I might not see her again if I did not get there quickly. With hindsight it was probably not a very sensible thing to do, as Spilsby was so isolated. On that morning we were in the crew room at about 10.30 awaiting operation instructions, when we were told that the operation was cancelled. I dashed back to our hut, changed my battle dress into walking out uniform and got to Boston somehow, before going onto Peterborough for a train to London.

Freda was now in the WRNS, the Women's Royal Naval Service and stationed at a place called Crosby Hall in Chelsea, a magnificent old building on the embankment, so I hotfooted it down there as soon as I got to London. I was overjoyed to be with her again. I calculated that I had not seen her since 17 August when we left OTU, which was the last period of leave that we had. I was sure we were due for some more leave now that we were on operations, so I asked her to marry me. She accepted my proposal and we decided to wed on 1 January 1944 at the Holy Trinity Church on Brompton Road, Chelsea, followed by a reception at the Blue Cockatoo, a restaurant we both liked quite near the 'Wrenery' not too far from the church.

Lancaster III JB138 JUST JANE which operated on 61 Squadron from August 1943 until February 1945, flying 113 operations. It finished its operational career on 5 LFS.

Lancaster B.I W4964 WS-J Johnnie Walker/*Still Going Strong!* on 9 Squadron at Bardney. Johnnie flew 106 ops April 1943 to October 1944 when it became an instructional airframe and was finally SOC in November 1949.

We agreed that Freda would invite all her pals and our mutual friends, including Miss Sawyer who had taught us botany and zoology and I would ask my crew also. I spoke to Canon Brian Green about marrying us and he agreed to do so. Freda was going to contact the bridal hire service set up by J. Arthur Rank, the movie mogul. He had adopted the wonderful idea of allowing servicewomen who were marrying servicemen to rent any costume from his studio wardrobe and providing the garment was cleaned when returned it only cost about a quid. Freda being Freda and it being in the middle of winter, she chose a most elegant white velvet gown trimmed with swan's down (so she told me). After we had made this arrangement I dashed back to the squadron, having first spent the night at Peterborough railway station waiting for a train to Spilsby. Trains from London to Peterborough were reasonably frequent, but not from Peterborough to Boston. I cannot remember how I got to Boston in the end, but I did. I arrived somewhat jaded, but my personal mission was accomplished,

Fortunately, the Berlin sortie scheduled for that night was cancelled. I spoke to Squadron Leader Dudley Pike, who commanded 'B' Flight (to which we had been transferred a day or so before), to tell him of my marriage plans and desire for leave on 1 January. He assured me it would be okay. All aircrew were due to fly another operation against Berlin that night - Friday 26 November 1943 - after which the squadron could expect to get some more leave. We used to do a night flying test every day that operations were scheduled, to test all the instruments that might be used. The operation on the 26th went without incident and on the Monday we proceeded on leave after completing the seven-hour trip to Berlin.

We initially headed for London because everybody except Ralph Allen (who lived at Weston-super-Mare in Somerset) and Bob Stone, a good-natured Canadian and most popular member of the crew lived in or around that area. Bob usually stayed with some 'friends'; we never asked who the friends were. While we were together, we decided to have a picture taken of the whole crew. Freda and I completed arrangements for our marriage. My parents were still against the idea, but I did not worry about that. Later on, I got a letter saying that they would not be coming to the wedding. We all met up again at Spilsby on 9 December and did night flying checks on the 9th, 10th, 12th and 16th. On 16 December we were due to make another sortie to Berlin.

On the night of 16 December 1943 our flight engineer, Maxwell Millward was not able to fly with us. 'Mike' as he was always called, was the oldest member of the crew and we had all clicked with him straight away. He had been a fitter before graduating to aircrew and really knew his stuff and was very good. Instead we had a substitute, Derick Peppal. The trip had a fateful feel to it from fairly early on because the route we were ordered to fly went directly to Berlin across Holland and northern Germany, without any significant diversions. I read later that the German controllers were able to plot our course with great accuracy and so directed a lot of fighters up at us from the moment we crossed the Dutch coast. Our aircraft alone was attacked twice by German night fighters on the way to the target. In fact Joe Brindle the bomb-aimer said that the rear gunner, Bob Stone, had set one of our attackers on fire and caused it to blow up below our aircraft, but we never had this confirmed.

The target was in the south-west suburbs of Berlin, so we did not have any trouble getting to it. I forget what it was that we were supposed to be hitting, but we were always a bit cynical about this anyway. Bomber Command made no bones about the fact that we were doing area bombing, because there was no other way at night. Often we did not even see the ground, so inevitably we were doing area bombing rather than precision attacks. Berlin was covered by cloud but the Pathfinder Force had developed a technique called sky-marking, which involved dropping flares which burned above the clouds and we just had to bomb the flares. The Pathfinders had done their job pretty well and we got away our big 'cookie' bomb, as well as several hundred incendiaries, with reasonable accuracy. Bear in mind that a cookie was 4,000lbs of high explosive and when it went down it made a hell of a hole wherever it landed.

Because we were in the third stream for this operation, we had been tasked to photograph the pattern of explosions with an infra-red camera that we were using for the first time that night. We were under strict instructions to fly straight and level over the target for 29 seconds after we had released our load, in order to take pictures of the tail end of the raid. This meant we were highly vulnerable, because we could not corkscrew or take any of the usual evasive action meant to throw off enemy fighters. Moreover, the Germans had a trick of putting huge quantities of searchlights into thick cloud, because that lit up the cloud and made an aircraft passing through it as obvious as a fly walking across a sheet of white paper. Of course, the fighters would have no trouble at all in seeing us either.

We were still completing our photographic task when all of a sudden I heard the voice of Derick Peppal the flight engineer say on the intercom, 'Christ, predicted ...' There was also a 'beep, beep, beep' sounding over the intercom as he shouted, which came from a device called Fishpond warning there was an aircraft underneath us. This warning came too late because right at that moment all hell broke loose around me. My instrument panel disintegrated and I got a gash on the forehead from a flying piece of metal that left me momentarily dazed. I then realised that everything was very bright for what was supposed to be a dark midwinter night over Berlin. When I pulled back the curtain that separated me

Seven of the eight crew on Lancaster I ME827 EM-I on 207 squadron at Spilsby which crashed in Holland at Bergen-op-Zoom (Noord Brabant) on the raid on Wesseling on 21/22 June 1944. Flight Lieutenant Fred Whitton Gallagher DSO, pilot (KIA); 33-year old Sergeant Maxwell Benjamin 'Grandpop' Millward, flight engineer (KIA) (2nd from right); Warrant Officer A. Young, navigator (PoW) (behind Gallagher); Sergeant Raymond William Lloyd (KIA); Flight Sergeant Ronald Parson Scott (KIA): Flying Officer Peter William Ball (KIA); Sergeant Kenneth Waddington (KIA). Flight Sergeant Murray Sherman RCAF, who was also killed, is missing from this photo. In total, 36 other Lancasters, including four others on 207 Squadron, one Mosquito and two Fortress IIs were lost. Sergeant Millward's original crew led by Flight Lieutenant Ralph J. Allen was lost on Berlin on the night of 16/17 December 1943 when he was sick. Five of the crew survived to be taken prisoner. The two gunners were killed. (Terry Millward).

from the front part of the flight deck I saw the port wing was on fire. Having several hundred gallons of 90-octane petrol burning just a few feet away from me seemed to be an occasion requiring rapid action, although I am not a person normally given to that.

It was then that I saw the skipper and the engineer, had their chutes on and were heading forward down the small stairs into the bomb-aimer's compartment. The skipper waved to me, indicating that I should follow them; he told me afterwards that the intercom had all been wrecked.

The controls were wobbling backwards and forwards in a crazy fashion and the aircraft was in a flat spiral dive, probably in what was known as a 'falling leaf'. So I went back to the navigator position and clipped my parachute pack onto my harness. Just then the rear gunner called the skipper on his intercom to say his turret was jammed. I realised I was still in contact with him because I was wearing my helmet and headset and before disconnecting it I told the gunner to use the turning handle and to bail out quickly. It was then that I noticed that the wireless operator was still sitting calmly at his radio. I thumped him on the shoulder, pointing to my chute and indicating for him to go forward as I called 'Bail out!' over the noise of the engines. He told me afterwards that he had no idea of what was going on and probably would not have got out if I had not told him.

All of this took a few seconds only. Then I nipped towards the nose of the aircraft, leapt down the small steps and dived headfirst through the open escape hatch and into the cold night air. I rolled on my back as I had done so many times in diving from the edge of swimming pools, counting to five before pulling on the ripcord. It was a chest type chute and because I had always placed it on my chest in such a way that the D ring was on the right I knew exactly where to find the ripcord. When I felt the opening shock of the parachute between my legs I looked up and initially I was horrified that the canopy seemed so small. I thought it had been ripped off until I realised that it was so far above my head because the shrouds were about 30 feet long. We had never done a jump before, just practised landings by swinging down on harnesses hanging from a beam, so I did not even know how to steer a parachute properly. After I pulled on the risers and the chute responded, I felt much better.

The complete and utter quiet that I experienced at that point was astonishing. Of our burning Lancaster there was no sign and because we had been at the end of the raid the other bombers were now gone too. The only reminder of the war going on was little puffs of reddish light coming up from the ground, which I took to be light ack-ack shells or something. What they were aiming at, I had no idea. Of course, if I turned around in my harness there was a very vivid reminder behind me in the form of the burning city, but even so it was all terribly silent and quite extraordinary. Some distance below me I could see one or two parachutes of other members going down. They seemed a long way off and I appeared to be drifting even further from them. Luckily the prevailing winds were taking us all away from fires in the target area. I guessed we were going to come down in one of the outer suburbs a good distance from central Berlin.

Even in my slightly dazed state, I was engrossed in the picture laid out in front of me, which was so beautiful in a bizarre sort of way. I also found myself wondering how I was going to explain all this to Freda. I thought, 'Just two weeks before our wedding, she'll be livid! Gradually I became conscious of snow-covered ground coming up at me, but I did not even see the church steeple that snagged my parachute and sent me crashing into the wall of the building, giving me another crack on the head and knocking me unconscious. When I came to sometime later, I found I was hanging alongside a clock face about 30 or 40 feet above the ground. I could not see what time the clock was showing, because I was hard up against the wall, but my wrist watch was stopped at 8.21 probably from the force of impact. I could hear the mechanism grinding away inside the tower and every now and again there was a loud clunk as the clock tried to chime. The Germans had obviously taken the clappers out, just as had been done back in England with clocks. It made a lot of noise and it bothered me. It occurred to me what a thorough mess I had made of our wedding plans by turning up at the wrong church on the wrong day and in the wrong town.

There were now people on the ground shining torches up at me, including a tall man wearing a strange orange helmet who called, 'Are you English or American?' I think I replied to the effect that of course I was English; Americans did not fly at night. I have no idea how I was lifted down from the steeple because by then I had lapsed back into unconsciousness again. I came to lying on my back on a table looking up at my skipper, Ralph Allen, while a man whom I later found was a German doctor stitched up my head. I heard from Ralph that his chute had also got snagged, in a tree in the backyard of a German house. Joe Brindle was also there, after landing on the edge of a lake.

We were then taken to a hospital in Berlin, or certainly near Berlin and put into what had been a maternity wing, presumably until the raids got so bad that the patients were evacuated elsewhere. Over the next two days I slept a lot, so much that the next day when I got up to use the toilet I could scarcely walk. Looking at my right leg I found it was bruised and swollen and very painful. We patients were being looked after by two British Army medical orderlies who had been captured three years earlier at Dunkirk, of course with German guards on the outside of the ward. One of the orderlies took me to the X-ray department where it was found that I had a Pott's fracture of the right ankle, which had to be put in plaster. I went back to bed and had something to eat and then fell asleep again. When I awoke the next day my right arm felt sore and stiff and the elbow was swollen and badly bruised and would not move very well, nor comfortably. So it was off to the X-ray room again, where another fracture was found and another plaster applied.

While at the hospital we also met up with the other survivors from our crew. Five of us had managed to escape using our Irving parachutes: Flight Lieutenant Allen, Flight Sergeant Joe Brindle, Sergeant Peppal, Sergeant W. J. Vowles and myself. Sadly, neither of our two gunners, Sergeant Bob Stone and Sergeant Ernie 'Taff' Takle, a lad from the South Wales with a dry sense of humour had got out. It appeared that the latter had most likely been killed when our bomber was attacked from below, probably by a Messerschmitt 110 or 210 armed with upward-firing cannon. Years and years later I met up with Wing Commander Bob Tuck, one of Britain's leading aces and he recounted being told by Adolf Galland, the German ace he befriended after the war that the night fighters used to wait for our bombers to finish dropping their bombs. This was because when attacking from underneath with upward-firing guns they had to get within 150-180 metres to be really effective and if a bomber still had its cookie on board the resulting explosion would take out the fighter too. The day after the second X-ray, with me sporting two scarcely-dry plasters on a bitterly cold day, we were taken to the bahnhof, the railway station and put on a train to Frankfurt am Main, a trip which took two days and many stops. At Frankfurt we were sent to Dulag Luft at Oberursel, about eight miles away, which was the Luftwaffe's main reception and processing centre for captured allied airmen. There we were put straight into solitary confinement cells, which the Germans did not heat. With my damp plasters in the middle of a German winter, I did not sleep very well that night. Next day we were fingerprinted, photographed and interrogated.

During briefing before each operation we had been reminded that, if captured, we should give only our number, rank and name. My interrogator, however, spoke perfect English and tried to get more information by being friendly and sympathetic. Immediately he saw my plasters and head bandage, he said, 'Oh, what jolly bad luck. Well, how are things at Spilsby?' That was a bit shattering. After offering me a cigarette, he began to ask a lot more questions, but I kept

Lancaster KB941 PT-U PASSION WAGON which operated on 420 Squadron RCAF from April 1945 and was returned to Canada in June that same year. It was disposed of in 1947-48.

'B-Baker' was an equally colourful Lancaster on one of the Canadian squadrons showing a dragon releasing a bomb.

pointing to my head and saying, 'Don't remember, lost some memory! I knew a little bit about post-traumatic amnesia. He wanted to know who was the station commander; that sort of thing, but after getting nowhere he went out and I was put back in the cells for the rest of the day. The next day the interrogator came back and tried again. He was a member of the Luftwaffe, not Gestapo and really quite pleasant and not threatening in any way. 'Well, have you remembered the name of the station commander?' he said. Realising that he would obviously keep on at me, I made a vague comment like, 'He had a name like a cheese! That misled him completely, because he immediately began thinking of Camembert and Rockforth and Gouda and so on. He had no idea of any of the English cheeses, fortunately for me and eventually he gave up.

We were taken out of our cells and put into a general part of Dulag Luft where there were a lot of other prisoners with whom we were allowed to mix. I had my watch taken by the Germans, but we were given a postcard to send to our next of kin. The cards had to go via neutral Switzerland and took about six to eight weeks to arrive, but at least our families then knew we were okay. We even received quite reasonable food for Christmas and the New Year. Certainly, we could have been much worse off.

Early in January 1944, 48 of us PoWs, or as our Luftwaffe jailers called us Kriegsgefangener (which we soon shortened to 'Kriegies'), were put into cattle trucks for a railway trip. The wagons had a sign on the side in French that read '8 horses or 40 men' and could not have been less comfortable. We sat on the floor all the way to a place called Sagan in Upper Silesia, located about 100 miles south-east of Berlin. (These days Sagan is known as Zagari and lies in south-west Poland not far north of the border of the Czech Republic.) The journey took two days, none of us had greatcoats; just the battledress we had been wearing when shot down and we were forced to huddle together for warmth.

Footnotes for Chapter 9

8   Later Chief Marshal Sir Walter Cheshire and Air Member for Personnel for the Royal Air Force.

9   1st Lieutenant Frank B. Solomon and his navigator Flying Officer Willis A. DeBardeleben, who were killed on the night of 1/2 January 1944 on the operation on Berlin. All seven crewmembers on Lancaster I W4892 which crashed in the vicinity of the Daimler Benz works at Genehagen were killed.

10   Wing Commander David M. Balme DSO DFC flew a tour on 207 Squadron whom he joined as a Flying Officer in March 1943, reaching the rank of Squadron Leader ten months later. He took command of 227 Squadron in March 1945. After the war he became a professor.

11   Gee was a radio navigation system that allowed aircraft to determine their location by timing synchronised pulses sent from three transmitters in the United Kingdom. It did not extend over the horizon, and the Germans could jam it, but it was very effective over England and the North Sea.

12   Standard Beam Approach equipment. SBA was used by the pilot on return to base and enabled him to home onto the runway in bad weather.

13   Flight Lieutenant Derrick Reay was the skipper of Lancaster I EM-S W4959 and Flying Officer Bob Mair was on his crew. All seven men were killed.

Chapter 10

A Lancaster Pilot's Impression on Germany

'Dick' Starkey

Dick Starkey was a 21-year-old pilot on 106 Squadron. At the end of January 1944 he made three raids on the Reich capital in four nights. 'I did nine Berlin trips and after you'd been briefed you often got a couple of hours rest. We'd lie on our beds and not a word would be spoken. When the time came, we were like men going to the gallows. In the locker room there might be 100 of us putting on our kit and it was as quiet as anything. We had 'wakey-wakey' tablets and some people used to take them before they got to the flights but it started to wear off then when they needed it. I didn't take mine until I was in the air, so they wouldn't wear off.

'The sight of a Berlin raid had to be seen to be believed. The Pathfinders used to drop flares two minutes before the raid was to begin. There were hundreds of searchlights and the red flashes of guns. You had to hold it steady for up to two minutes after your bombs went to take a photograph. Immediately afterwards you put on full power to get out of that arena and often you'd be followed into the darkness. There would be 600 miles to go before you got home. The German defences were fantastic. On March 24 the bomber stream had become a gaggle spread across 50 miles of sky and stretching back another 150 miles. Most of the aircraft were well south of track and many wandered over the defences of the Ruhr, Germany's industrial heartland, where the flak gunners were plentiful and deadly efficient.'

'That winter was the lowest point for Bomber Command. I remember gathering round the stove in the officers' hut on cold evenings with the two pilots, a navigator and a bomb aimer discussing what we would do if we were shot down. It was an obsession with the bomb aimer. He was frightened of it and it was always in your mind. We pilots knew there wasn't much chance of us getting out. I came back to sleep after one raid and the navigator and bomb aimer hadn't returned. By the time I woke up all their equipment had been moved out. I met them in Stalag Luft III.

At the beginning of October 1943 we were ready to join an Operational Squadron and were posted to 106 Squadron 5 Group stationed at Syerston between Newark and Nottingham. We were placed in 'B' Flight which flew twelve aircraft the same as 'A' Flight. The Squadron originally operated against enemy shipping but its main task in 1943 was the bombing of Germany; however there was always a Naval Liaison Officer attached to it. 'Our first two weeks were taken up with cross countries, practice bombing and 'circuits and bumps'.'

One night we were despatched with another crew to Bottesford to do circuits and bumps; we were the only two aircraft on the circuit so everything went smoothly, as one aircraft took off the other would be on the downwind leg.

However after one landing, I was taxiing round for the next take off but could not see the lights of the other aircraft, which should have been on a downwind leg. I soon found out what had happened as we proceeded round the perimeter track; I saw the tail light of the other Lancaster in front of me and knew it was stood. I stopped the aircraft and waited, but the other one didn't move forward. After a short time one of my crew left the aircraft and went forward to see what had happened. When he returned he said that a NAAFI wagon had stopped on the perimeter track to supply the night duty ground crew and the other pilot of the Lancaster had not seen it, because it did not have any lights and he continued taxiing. The van had become fast under the Lancaster's belly and of course it could not move; this left the pilot mystified why his aircraft wasn't moving. Evidently when the ladies in the van, who were serving food to the ground crew, saw the huge machine bearing down on their little van, they fled. Who could blame them?

On 20 October 1943 I received my commission two hours before taking off on the operation after the crew were put on the Squadron Battle Order for our first trip - target Leipzig - and what a trip it turned out to be. We took off in Lancaster DV297 and climbed to 20,000 feet. We had no trouble on the first part of the trip but the weather over Germany was appalling, with cumulus clouds reaching over 20,000 feet and we were frequently flying in and out of the tops in icing conditions. About half way to the target, the airspeed indicator suddenly dropped off the 'clock'; this left us in an awkward situation and I had to fly on instruments to maintain the aircraft in a normal flying position, It reminded me of the Air Force adage - 'There I was at 20,000 feet with sweet **** on the clock'. This is where I needed my instrument flying training, because the airspeed indicator was very important during corkscrewing which was our main evasive action against fighters.

At this point of the operation 'Monica' pips (advanced warning of aircraft approaching - either friendly or enemy) were recorded and the mid upper gunner instructed me to dive port. He had sighted a twin-engined aircraft which appeared out of the clouds as we also emerged. He quickly gave the evasion order and then fired a burst at the enemy aircraft before it disappeared into the clouds.

It must have been a shock to the night fighter pilot when tracer bullets flashed past his aircraft, but under the conditions he could not do much about it.

On route the searchlights were ineffective because of cloud thickness and still without the airspeed indicator we bombed on ETA at a large glow on the clouds which we took to be the target. The return journey was uneventful but the appalling weather conditions did not improve until we descended over the North Sea and air temperature increased; the airspeed came back on the 'clock' much to my relief.

All aircrew were allowed nine days leave every six weeks. During the six weeks they might fly twelve operations and during the winter of 1943-44 the bad weather was the main reason for 'stand downs'; also we did not operate during the 'moon' period which ran from four days before to four days after full moon; so eight operations was a good average. Several crews took leave during the moon period, leaving a few crews to operate, if required, on specific targets, probably in unoccupied countries.

On 11th November 1943 106 Squadron moved to Metheringham in East Lincolnshire, about fifteen miles south east of Lincoln. At that time a few stations in 5 Group were situated around Newark and Nottingham and it was decided to move Squadrons east near the East Coast and The Wash. Metheringham formed a base with Woodhall Spa (617 Squadron) and Coningsby (619 and one other Squadron).

The Squadron arrived at Metheringham just as the 'Berlin Season' was about to start and over the next four months several crews would be lost. However small things occurred which go beyond belief and I will describe such a situation at Metheringham. Although the flying personnel and ground crew on 106 at Syerston were transferred to Metheringham, the administrative staff, including the station commander, a Group Captain, came from Bottesford. In the Officers' Mess Squadrons' aircrew outnumbered the Administrative Staff and as both parties had used different methods for settling mess bills at their previous stations, a meeting was held to decide by majority which method to adopt. Naturally as there were more aircrew, our method of paying for drinks as they were ordered was adopted against the Administrative Staffs' practice of putting everything on a Mess bill and settling at the end of the month. This would have meant relatives of missing aircrew settling their bills. The only reason I am writing this is because the Station Commander said afterwards he would hold both Flight Commanders responsible if the practice didn't work. A childish thing to say when the aircrew by majority preferred the system and had seen it operate satisfactorily. What an attitude on a front line Bomber Station. As it was the Station Commander was never enthusiastic about the Squadron and vetoed any immediate recommendations for decorations to aircrew.

Conditions at Metheringham were far different to Syerston, which was a peace time station with permanent buildings and fixtures, whereas Metheringham was a wartime aerodrome with many Nissen huts, situated on the edge of the Fens and in November could be foggy and cold. There were six officers to one Nissen hut on the officer aircrew site; the other occupants were two other pilots from my flight, a bomb aimer and navigator from the same crew and an Administrative Officer from Station Headquarters. I remember on nights when we were stood down the five aircrew occupants would sit round a stove and discuss their reaction if shot down by a fighter. Although all of us had seen many bombers meeting that fate we could only surmise the conditions in the aircraft as they dived helplessly out of control to the ground. The bomb aimer said that as he was more or less lying on the escape hatch in the nose of the aircraft he would abandon it without difficulty, he hoped, when the pilot gave the order. The three pilots more or less accepted what would be their fate because of extreme odds against their survival, having to try and control the aircraft whilst the crew bailed out. The navigator just hoped he could get to an escape hatch. This then was the topic of conversation on those nights in the middle of the Battle of Berlin when the odds were very much against survival. The bomb aimer and navigator would later be shot down and I and my crew would also be lost on a later raid.

If the Squadron wasn't operating various exercises were flown during the day including navigating and blind bombing by H_2S which were fitted to all aircraft between January and March 1944. Blind bombing targets from 10,000 feet were made on various cities in England with the navigator and wireless operator working together on H_2S and instructing the bomb aimer when to operate the camera on a 'bomb run'. The photographs indicated successful attacks on the majority of runs.

On some days I would take the opportunity to 'beat up' my home town of Barnsley and the Lancaster became a familiar sight as I flew low level, about 300 feet above the ground making a pass over my home where there would be many tablecloths waving in the vicinity. On one occasion, 9th February 1944, I did a low level across the town passing over the Town Hall at about 200 feet. As I flew over I noticed quite a crowd in front of the building and my rear gunner confirmed this as we left the town behind. Later that night I telephoned home and my dad asked me if it was my aircraft that had flown low over the Town Hall. I said yes and asked him why there was a crowd. He said the King and Queen had been visiting and had just come out of the Town Hall as the Lancaster passed over; everyone thought it was a salute to their Majesties. In those days there was no publicity if they were to make a visit to a locality.

My crew made friends with some of the Land Army girls who lived in a hostel in the village of Martin on the outskirts of the airfield. Our first meeting with them was on the first Sunday after we moved to Metheringham. The Squadron was not operating that night and the weather was typical November Fen weather, foggy and drizzly. We were not aware there was a Land Army hostel nearby and rang telephone enquiries to ask if there was one in the district. We were told it was right next to the telephone kiosk we were using and gave us the number. We rang them and from that moment our social life, when we were not operating, was taken care of, with some of the nicest girls (several from Yorkshire) I had met. There could be no serious relationships because of our work, crews were regularly going missing and a lot of them had boyfriends in the Services.

Cookies including one inscribed 'A Gift from Down Under' waiting to be loaded on Lancasters on 467 Squadron RAAF.

I shall always remember the dances in the Village Hall at Timberlands, a nearby village, on Saturday nights, when we could make it. The Station Dance Band would play and before walking to the dance from Martin we would meet in the local pub in the village and have a few drinks in the 'Nook'. These girls were very kind and if their work started at around the same time as we landed from a raid some of them would be waiting near the dispersal over the boundary to see if we had returned safely and when I came on leave there was always something to bring with me, i.e. eggs.

In June 1997 I returned to Timberlands and met Mr. and Mrs. P. Mason who were teenagers at that time. The Village Hall is still the same and they told me some of the girls had met and married local boys and were living in the area. My Flight Commander on 106 completed two tours early in 1944 and was waiting to be posted, when one day he sent for me and said 'you think you can fly these Lancasters, well I'm going to show you how one should be flown, so let us go out to your aircraft'. I said I would get the crew together but was told not to bother there would just be the two of us flying it. When we arrived at dispersal and entered the aircraft he sat in the pilot's seat and I stood by his side to do the flight engineers duties. After taxiing to the end of the runway he looked at his watch and opened the throttles, the aircraft quickly picked up speed and he was soon airborne, immediately starting a climbing turn which brought him to the downwind leg at 500 feet where he levelled out.

As the runway disappeared under the wing he turned and dived to port; since taking off he had lifted the flaps only when required but not fully because he was soon ready to lower them again; he had raised the wheels during the climbing turn and put them down again just before he dived towards the runway. He lowered the rest of the flaps on the short run in and touched down 45 seconds after becoming airborne, it was some flying with marvellous control. As we taxied off the runway he told me to change seats and do exactly as he did in the same time - if I could. Our crew had completed around eighteen operations at the time and I was a competent pilot of a Lancaster, especially our own, which we were flying. I knew I could do a 'split harse' circuit but wasn't sure I could beat his time; the result of my endeavour was a 60 seconds circuit, with which I was satisfied, but he said laughingly 'I would never be as good as him'. However I could then side slip a Lancaster to lose height and this helped my time.

This Flight Commander when the Squadron operated from Syerston, where there was a valley at the end of one runway through which the River Trent ran, took off on that runway with a full load of bombs and petrol, but lost an engine just after takeoff and disappeared into the valley at the end of the runway whilst trying to maintain height. I am told that everyone watching expected one big explosion as he hit the valley floor, but the aircraft came into view, staggering to climb to sufficient height, to complete a circuit and landing. He struggled to maintain height on the downwind leg and managed to turn on the approach to land with the bombs, (he never had sufficient height to jettison). The landing was made successfully on what was a great feat of flying.

During February we had a Squadron photograph taken in front of a Lancaster one afternoon, after which our crew was to carry out an H_2S exercise taking photographs of Peterborough railway station, lasting two hours. I knew there was not enough time to complete the exercise before dark if the Squadron photo session was a long one. It turned out that we were left insufficient time to complete our flying exercise in daylight and advised our new Flight Commander from Training Command of the situation. He ordered me to take off and do the exercise, this was typical of Training Command attitude, especially someone who had just been transferred to a Squadron; there was no flexibility. Another crew captained by an Australian were detailed to do an H_2S exercise, similar to ours, over Derby, but we agreed to report 10/10ths cloud over the cities and return immediately. We arrived over Peterborough with clear skies but would have had no chance to complete twelve photo runs before dark. The light wasn't very good but I decided to do some low flying as there was little chance of being identified. The bomb aimer and navigator took up positions in the nose of the aircraft to enjoy the ride and we were soon down to 50 feet over the flat countryside when I noticed a railway bridge in front of us with a policeman riding a bicycle across it. We roared over him and when we had passed the rear gunner, who could not see the bridge until we passed it, said a policeman was picking himself up from his bicycle which had fallen over. It was a case of letting off steam, first of all for the Flight Commander's attitude and secondly we operated over Germany at 20-25,000 feet and any opportunity to get away with a bit of low flying, we took it. Incidentally many years after the war I learned that the Australian pilot was killed in a car accident in New South Wales where he was Head of the Horseracing Board in that State.

Another practice which was popular with the crew was air to sea firing off Skegness, when a lead marker was dropped in the sea and all gun turrets were used to fire at it. I do not know if it benefited the gunners but it gave us all a lot of fun because I flew the aircraft just above the waves which left four lanes of disrupted water as the propellers spun just above the tops. We finished the exercise by continuing low level towards the Clock Tower on the sea front, climbing quickly about 400 yards from the shore. On one occasion when we did the exercise I chose an area of the sea two miles North of Skegness and when the manoeuvre ended turned the aircraft toward land at wave top height. As we quickly approached the shore I realised we were heading straight for Butlins' Holiday Camp which was taken over for training by the Royal Navy for the duration of the war. I could see the sailors queuing for dinner and decided to give them an 'appetiser' so flew the Lancaster at around 100 feet over their heads. Unfortunately a high ranking Naval Officer was visiting the establishment and took a dim view; someone identified the aircraft letters and next day I was on the carpet before the Squadron Commander, for dangerous flying. When I told him we were air to sea firing at low level and came towards land, I started my climb just off shore but was still at a low altitude when I passed over the Camp. I remember he smiled and ordered me not to repeat the practice again, but as I was already climbing over the Camp would take no further action.

Our third operation was to Frankfurt on the 20th December 1943, the second had been to Berlin at the commencement of the Battle of Berlin, which opened in November. We took off for Frankfurt in JB534. My mid-upper gunner had been granted compassionate leave and his replacement was a sergeant, whose crew had already completed their first tour and he had to complete his last trip by flying with other crews. We had no trouble on the outward journey and flew at 21,000 feet. The target was covered by a lot of cloud so the ground markers were hidden and I also remember that the Germans had lit a decoy fire south of the city. About ten miles north of the Target on our return journey, we were fired upon by cannons and machine gun fire from what we presumed was a night fighter, the rear gunner immediately instructed me to corkscrew as enemy tracer came from the port quarter. I did so and after one complete corkscrew resumed normal course. I could tell we had been hit around the port main plane and prayed we would not catch fire. However after breaking off the first attack the fighter attacked again almost immediately and the aircraft was hit again. I corkscrewed but no fighter was sighted by either gunner so we resumed course. The fighter was never seen and although the rear gunner attempted to open fire on three occasions, his guns failed to function. When we resumed course it was evident that the aircraft had been severely damaged because it started to shudder violently and I had great difficulty controlling it. The vibration transferred to my body as I fought to maintain control. The rear gunner reported that the port fin and tail plane rudder was extensively damaged and a large part had disappeared. As for the main plane we could not see any damage but knew there was some.

Soon after the attack the navigator instructed me to change course, but on applying rudder and aileron the aircraft began to bank steeply and I had to put her back on an even keel by using automatic pilot - manual controls were ineffective. The shuddering continued over the North Sea and I gave instructions to prepare for any eventuality. However we managed to remain airborne and after approximately two and three quarter hours we approached Base.

The wireless operator informed the Control Tower of the condition of the aircraft and that it was essential to make a right hand circuit and also that we must land immediately. Permission was given to circuit at a height of 800 feet and other aircraft were ordered to maintain their height until we landed. On our approach down the funnel of the Drem system we began to drift to starboard and I dare not counteract this because to make a turning to port would have been a disaster. After an anxious couple of minutes we touched down on the grass in darkness fifty yards to the right of the flare path and as the mid upper gunner left the aircraft he knelt down and kissed the ground, having completed a memorable 30th operation.

When the aircraft was examined next morning, the full extent of the damage was revealed. There was severe damage to the port fin and rudder, more than fifty percent was missing, the port side of the fuselage had been riddled with bullets which stopped just before the wireless operator's position but had gone through the mid upper gunner's legs. Material covering the port aileron had been ripped off and most frightening of all a cannon shell had exploded on the underside of the port mainplane creating a jagged hole approximately one foot in diameter. If the shell had exploded further forward it would have hit the fuel tanks and the aircraft would have 'gone up'. Repairs had to be carried out on the airfield by workmen from Avro's and took approximately six weeks to complete. Unfortunately he was not able to enlighten me as to which parts had been replaced because records were no longer available. However he did tell me that 1,171 man hours were employed on the aircraft in order to bring it back to operational standard. JB534 was transferred to 'A' flight after the repairs were completed, only to crash on Timberlands Fell near the airfield when returning

'Tally Ho! Here We Come!'

from its first operation after repairs.[14]

Our Squadron was a Path Finder support Squadron which meant on certain raids a couple of crews were selected to take off before the rest of the Squadron and fly ahead of the Path Finders dropping 'Window' (small strips of material) from the aircraft to fuzz the enemies radar, where following aircraft could fly. One other crew besides ours was detailed for a supporting role on another raid to Frankfurt. We took off in broad daylight; darkness was due to fall about the time we were due over the South Coast, (we were taking a Southerly route) on the way to France before altering course for Frankfurt; but when we approached our point of departure from England although the light was fading it was still too bright for our operation. However daylight soon faded as we crossed the Channel and as we arrived over the French Coast darkness had fallen. We had no window protection because the two of us were ahead of the Path Finders and had to be very alert for fighters, anti aircraft fire and searchlights. Our trip went smoothly but it was strange to be the first aircraft over a city before a raid. After flying through heavy flak we dropped the bombs by H_2S, took photographs and returned to Base thankful we had not suffered any damage. The other crew had more excitement because after they dropped their bombs there was a massive explosion on the ground, they said they had never seen anything like it. When their photographs were developed back at Base, these were done on an overlapping basis, whatever they had hit showed as a white flash about 3 feet square and Intelligence thought they may have scored a direct hit on an ammunition factory situated on an island in the river.

I flew to Frankfurt in 1998 and as we approached the airport saw an island in the River Main which had a chemical installation. This island was the one my colleague hit.

One of our pilots, an Australian, returned from an operation one night saying his Lancaster had been turned over by a near miss from an anti aircraft shell. He was over Holland on the way to the target with his bomb load when the incident happened. None of the other pilots in the Flight had been affected by such an incident and we asked him how he got out of it. He evidently pulled the control column back, this was because it reversed its role as the aircraft was upside down and it dropped nose heavy like a stone; the pressure on the aircraft must have been terrific and it took him and the Flight Engineer all their strength to pull it out of the dive. It certainly proved the Lancaster was a great aircraft because no structural damage occurred.

Most wartime Bomber airfields had three runways; two of 2,000 yards in length and one of 1,600 yards, the latter was only used when the wind was in line with it. One of the 2,000 yard runways at Metheringham was generally used because of the prevailing wind. For dark take offs at night a line of lights, like cats eyes, had been installed across the runway 800 yards from the end to give pilots a guide to the distance remaining for takeoff; these were very important because getting a Lancaster off the ground, fully loaded with bombs and petrol was a mouth drying experience as the end of the runway rushed toward you, the last thing you would want or remember was an engine failure. The take off after straightening the Lancaster on the runway was started by holding the aircraft tightly on the brakes and pushing all four throttles fully open. The aircraft would start moving forward and you gradually released the brakes, at the same time pushing the control column fully forward in order to get the tail up as quickly as possible and build up speed. At that point the flight engineer would operate the throttles by pushing them through 'the gate' to get extra boost, this could only be maintained for two minutes before he brought them back to normal maximum revs. The two minutes would give us time to get into the air as I concentrated on lifting her off the ground, meanwhile the Engineer would call the speed out as it slowly built up - 90 ... 100 ... 110 mph, at which point I started easing it off the ground, which sometimes it was reluctant to leave and by that time we had left the 800yds marker well behind and were thundering towards the end of the flarepath. You were then fully committed and had no chance if you had to cancel take off, it would be the aircraft and the crew.

I remember waiting to take off one night when two bright flashes lit up the sky as two Lancasters exploded at nearby airfields - no doubt crashing due to engine failure. At 120 mph the wheels came off the ground and as the speed built up I would start a flatish climbing turn out of the Drem system with the inner wing barely 50 feet off the ground. Sometimes I left our Drem system with insufficient speed to turn and would approach another airfield's system nearby who were also dispatching aircraft, so we had to be very alert and keep clear of their aircraft. As the altitude increased very slowly I brought the aircraft round to fly over the Airfield and set course given to me by the navigator. We would leave the coast at Skegness, if we were flying straight to Berlin and then the bomb aimer would fuse the bombs and I would turn off the navigation lights. The first part of the flight was over the North Sea and, apart from flashes on the water as some crews jettisoned their bombs; it was hard to believe there were 800 bombers all closely flying in a stream approximately ten miles long and five miles wide. 'Monica' was continually picking up approaching aircraft which alerted the crew to locate them visually and it was usually another Lancaster which would slide across the sky above us, probably 50 feet higher silhouetted against the stars with exhaust emitting blue flame from under the cowlings.

When the Bomber stream approached Texel Island the Germans put up their usual flak barrage with some success. No Bomber Command story would be complete without a reference to Texel Island near the German Coast in the North Sea. In the winter of 1943/44 the route to Berlin and other cities sometimes took us near the Island, with its many anti aircraft gun emplacements firing heavily at the Bomber stream. As we neared the Island, crews knew a few would not survive the onslaught and waited for the inevitable; this happened when four or five aircraft exploded as they were hit with full bomb loads and flaming parts of aircraft spun down to hit the ground and spread a trail of fire. Any ex Bomber Command aircrew operating at that time would agree that a special raid ought to have been made on the Island to take out as many guns as possible.

Bomber Command suffered its heaviest losses during the Battle of Berlin on the night of 24 March 1944 when seventy four aircraft were lost. Our crew operated that night and the following is my description of the raid. The outward route was over the North Sea to Denmark then south-east over the Baltic Sea crossing the German Coast and continuing south-east before turning south through the target. The trip was to be one of the worst we encountered because of the strong winds. On the way out over the North Sea the navigator was finding winds with speeds far in excess of those in his flight plan and coming from a more northerly direction than predicted at briefing. We were 'wind finders' that night and I remember the navigator advising me that the wind speed was unbelievable - approaching 100mph and should he broadcast his findings back to Bomber Command. I said if he was satisfied with his calculations he must transmit them back to England.

A number of aircraft were detailed as windfinders on every raid and when the navigators had calculated the actual wind speed and velocity they were transmitted back where an average wind speed was calculated from those sent back by aircraft and then relayed to the Bomber Force to use on their journey. I ordered my navigator to work from his own calculations and ignore the wind speeds being sent back to us because they were far too low. By the time the Danish Coast was crossed we were many miles south of track as a result of the high wind speed from the north. At that time nobody had heard of the Jet Stream, but many years after the raid and on reflection, Bomber Command met this phenomenon on that night. The Force was scattered over a very wide front as we approached Berlin well before zero hour. Some Captains ordered their navigators to work to the winds broadcast from England and found themselves hopelessly off track; others navigated on their own findings and were reaching points well in advance of ETA but they were not as far off course as the others. We arrived over the target early and I decided to risk going round the city on the eastern side, by which time the PFF markers would be going down and we could start our bombing run.

The activity in the sky over the city was awesome and frightening, as were all raids on Berlin. The sky was full of sparkling flashes as anti-aircraft shells from twelve hundred guns burst in a box barrage which was sent up every two minutes, containing the equivalent of an ammunition dump. I estimated that anyone getting through that would be very lucky indeed especially as the aircraft had to be flown straight and level with bomb doors open during the bombing run and take photographs after dropping the bombs. There were also hundreds of searchlights, making two cones over the city which the bombers had to try and evade. The fighters no longer waited outside the perimeter of the target where they were in little danger from their own flak, because we were now severely damaging their cities. They flew amongst us in this area of death ignoring their own safety, meeting the anti-aircraft fire in order to get amongst us and many a bomber was shot down when most vulnerable with bomb doors open. When we were on our bombing run with two other Lancasters, whose bomb aimers had chosen the same markers as my bomb aimer, a twin engined fighter flew past our nose with cannon and machine guns firing at one of the Lancasters; there were tracers flying all over the sky as my gunners and the others in the third aircraft joined the targeted Lancaster to return the fire. However we lost another aircraft that night as the stricken Lancaster turned over on its back and went down in flames; we did not see anyone escaping because we were concentrating on the bombing run.

The Luftwaffe were now using single-engined fighters in the battle, generally over the target and as I took a quick glance down at the fires I saw twelve of them circling up line astern towards the bombers whose bellies were red from the reflection of the flames below. The searchlight cones held two bombers like moths round a candle; the pilots were tossing their aircraft all over the sky but they were held like stage artists in a spot light. The next move was from the fighters who came in and inflicted the coup de grace, the bombers plunging down in flames before exploding and cascading in balls of fire to splash among the inferno below.

A pilot had to take whatever action he could to get across the target area and one practice was to fly near a coned aircraft and hope the action against it would help him get across. This wasn't always possible because although the brightness was less intense they could be seen. When a raid was at its peak with eight hundred aircraft bombing in a twenty minute period, the illuminations had to be seen to be believed. The Target Indicators red and green chandeliers two hundred feet in length cascaded down with a shimmering brightness, flak was bursting, filling every part of the sky with twinkling bursts and as you tlew towards them there was no escape; you thought you would never get through it. Many years afterwards I read in a book that a bomb aimer who flew on the raid was so awed by the experience, he just repeated: 'Jesus Skipper - look at that flak - just look at it. We'll never get through it - just look at it'. That summed it up perfectly. After bombing the target I gained height to 25,000 feet and with relief at surviving the anti aircraft, searchlights and night fighter defences, but we had another fight on our hands before we reached England. The strong head winds and night fighters who had not finished with us.

It soon became apparent that our ground speed was very slow and we did not appear to be making much progress. As we crawled our way west to the next change of course which was to take us north-west between Hanover and Osnabrück, the navigator was continuously amending his air plot to try and keep us on course, but we were being blown south of our intended track. The conditions were getting worse and because of the effect of the wind on navigation found ourselves further west than the point where we should have turned north-west to fly between Hanover and Osnabrück. Instead we amended our course to fly between Osnabrück and the Ruhr, making sure we kept well clear of the latter area. We had seen many aircraft shot down since we left Berlin, proof that the force was well scattered and aircraft were being picked off. As we looked over towards the Ruhr we saw many more, who had wandered over that area, shot down so they had flown into the two heaviest defended areas in Germany; Berlin and Ruhr in one night. I was concentrating our efforts to get to the coast without further trouble when a radar controlled searchlight was suddenly switched on just below the aircraft; these searchlights had a blue-white beam and more often than not hit the aircraft at the first attempt.

The searchlight crew knew they were near us because the beam started creeping up in front of the aircraft. I put more power on and raised the nose to maintain our position above the beam, but it still continued creeping towards us. I was just on the point of putting the nose down and diving through it when it was switched off - talk about a dry mouth. If the searchlight had found us it would have been joined by others and as was the customary practice a night fighter in the vicinity would have attacked us as we were caught in the beam.

Our last turning point was near the Dutch Border and although our ground speed was very slow the intensity of the defences had slackened off and for the first time in the raid, fighter activity had ceased. Maybe they had landed to refuel because we were approaching their airfields in Holland. We did not have any further trouble and eventually reached the North Sea Coast where I pushed down the nose of the aircraft and did a very fast descent to 2,000 feet, to the relief of the crew who were thankful to have the raid almost behind us. As we flew towards the English Coast, the wireless operator received a signal ordering us to divert to Wing, an OTU near Luton. It was a dark night and normally as you approached the coast you saw the odd searchlight but we did not see one light and I was surprised when the navigator told me, that according to his calculations, we had already crossed the coast; and gave me a course to Wing. We were by then well inland with navigation lights on flying at 2,000 feet but could not see a thing. Suddenly a searchlight switched on to us followed by two more; they could not have been practising because they could see the lights of our aircraft. I cursed as they held us, thinking back to the hundreds we had evaded over Germany only to be caught in the beams of a searchlight battery in England. I was told afterwards that the lights were operated by a crew of ATS girls.

We eventually landed at Wing, after a flight of seven and a half hours on the last big raid to Berlin; it had been the worst because of the strong winds encountered, which led to the scattering of the Bomber Force assisting enemy night fighters and anti-aircraft batteries to shoot down seventy four bombers. Many bombers were diverted to Wing that night and at breakfast before returning to Metheringham I met the Wing Commander who had given me a Wings Test in Canada. He had been transferred from Training Command and was assembling a crew on Wellingtons at Wing before being converted on to Lancasters. It made me feel quite a veteran with twenty operations completed and he who had been the Officer in Charge of Training at Swift Current had yet to start.

One little story I can relate occurred during the time of the Battle of Berlin. When I came home on operational leave I would often visit the local where some of the customers would ask me to take small items back with me to drop on the city. One of these was an ancient pair of pantaloons belonging to a lady named Pally Kirk who was over eighty years of age. She wrote a message on them for Adolf; I am sure she thought if someone picked them up they would be taken to the Fuhrer; and as she wrote something less than complimentary she told everyone she had given Hitler a piece of her mind. Anyhow they landed on the 'Big City' so for an old lady the operation was successful.

I have already explained how 'Gee' worked by sending radio waves out which could be picked up as far as West Belgium to give a reliable ground position. These signals were eagerly awaited on the return journey to show our true position.

On this particular night when we came into 'Gee' range the navigator took a fix which put us many miles north of track whereas we should have been approaching Northern France. I looked at the heading I was flying on my compass and passed this to the navigator; whereupon he said I was flying on a heading 10° more than his plotted one. I asked him to look again and he had mistakenly given me the wrong heading at the last turning point. I had to make a decision, because I knew we could not reach the right track by turning towards it; this would mean flying over enemy territory as a solitary aircraft, well out of the Bomber Stream. We had already left the Main Force some way back; and on enemy radar our aircraft would be shown as gradually edging towards west North West. I decided that as we had been lucky not to have been intercepted and as we had only fifty miles to fly to the coast, to continue the heading and hope our luck held.

After crossing the coast and when we were over the North Sea, I instructed the navigator to give me a course to come in over the East Coast. The effect would be that all Bomber Command, except one aircraft, arriving over the South Coast and our aircraft would fly in over the East Coast. We would have to identify ourselves by means of IFF (Identification of Friend or Foe) which had to be used if an aircraft was fifty miles or more off track, so the wireless operator switched it on immediately; also when we were well away from the enemy coast I switched on the navigation lights and hoped we did not meet a 'trigger happy friendly night fighter'. However we did not see another aircraft and arrived safely at Base. As Captain I was held responsible for the navigator's error but under operational pressure these could be made and fortunately we got away with it.

There was also another R/T system which operated for aircraft who were lost between dusk and dawn. It was called 'Darky' and helped the pilot by giving him his position. He had to call 'Hello Darky' three times and give his identification, only then would the nearest airfield reply to his call; but if he did not give an identification, no matter how many times he called, he would not receive a reply. It was also pointless in calling 'Darky' between dawn and dusk. There was a case in 1943 of an American pilot who had recently arrived in England and was on a map reading exercise over the country which was different to America where roads ran east and west and north and south, which was a great help in navigation and he became hopelessly lost.

Although he was flying during daytime, he called 'Hello Darky' several times but got no reply. He became very exasperated and after calling 'Darky' again with

Lancaster I R5868 'S-Sugar' on 467 Squadron RAAF at Ridgewell, Essex, home to the Flying Fortre
equipped 381st Bomb Group in the USAAF, on 18 February 1945. (USAF)

The Duke of Gloucester visited RAAF bomber squadrons at Waddington after an attack
Gelsenkirchen on 12/13 June 1943 and saw the veteran bomber 'S for Sugar'. Left to right: Gro
Captain Bonham Carter, the Station CO and the Duke of Gloucester, with Wing Commander Willi
'Bill' Brill DSO DFC of New South Wales, who was CO of 467 Squadron in 1943-44, looking over Sug
107 of whose 135 operations are shown by the bombs painted on her fuselage above Goering's famo
boast. Also shown are one DSO and three DFC ribbons. At the extreme left is the AOC RA
Headquarters, London, AVM H. N. Wrigley CBE DFC AFC.

Lancaster 1 R5/29 / KM-A of 44 Squadron at D[?], Dunholme Lodge, Lincolnshire before setting out for Berlin on 2 January 1944. This aircraft was a veteran of more than 70 raids over enemy territory, the first being to Duisburg in July 1942.

the same result, he finally shouted into his microphone, 'Hello Darky, Hello Darky, Hello Darky, where are you, you little black bastard?'

Another incident occurred one night when we were again over Belgium returning from Berlin. Our position was somewhere near Liège and things were quiet, when predicted flak suddenly burst too close for comfort and rocked the aircraft but didn't damage it. My immediate reaction was to shove the nose down and put the aircraft into a steep dive, because the next burst would have been in the same area and would most certainly have 'got us'. There was also another incident when the 'cookie' (4,000lb bomb) did a 'hang up' and the bomb aimer couldn't release it over the target. If this happened the practice was to look for an alternative target on the return journey and release it by hand. We eventually saw a searchlight battery with three beams, so we made a bomb run and although the bomb aimer could not use his bomb site, he released it by hand and as it dropped the light went out; we could picture everybody running for shelter. It wasn't a bad attack because the bomb burst close to where the lights were operating.

There were many operations to Berlin between November 1943 and March 1944 which were carried out by all Lancaster Forces from Nos. 1 and 5 Groups; other aircraft being deployed over occupied countries on some of those nights. At the end of the Battle of Berlin our crew had flown on nine operations to the city; three of them out of four nights at the end of January when we were in the air for twenty four hours out of ninety six. It was also a period of changing situations; you could be watching *Alexander's Ragtime Band* featuring Tyrone Power, Don Ameche and Alice Fay in a cinema in Lincoln at eight o'clock one night and the next night at eight o'clock be over Berlin. I think the following story sums up a Bomber Crew's chance of survival. The Squadron was briefed for a raid during the Battle of Berlin; take off to be at 6pm. The crews reported at the normal time before the raid but on this occasion takeoff was put back for two hours.

To fill the time in two other Lancaster pilots and myself cycled back in the blackout to the mess and played table tennis to fill time in before the revised take off time. We returned to the crew room only to be told it would be 12 o'clock midnight; so we returned to the mess and continued our game again. The Squadron finally got off the ground at midnight and we landed back after another harrowing raid at 6am. As the crews came into the Interrogation Room our main question was 'Is everybody back?' If not the flare-path was left on for a time until news was received that missing aircraft had been forced to land elsewhere, or no further communication was received from them when the lights of the flare-path would be turned off. No further news was received from the aircraft of my table tennis partners who had failed to return and as I cycled from the airfield to the mess the flare-path was turned off. After I had breakfast I looked in the Ante room and there on the table were the bats and balls as we had left them before they flew off into Eternity (both were killed). The Battle of Berlin which lasted from November 1943 to March 1944 cost Bomber Command over 500 aircraft and approximately 3,500 aircrew; either killed or taken prisoner.

I always made a practice when we reached the enemy coast on a return journey to put the nose of the aircraft down and dive steeply to about 2,000 feet before levelling out and skating back over the North Sea. My engineer always drew my attention to the fuel consumption during this practice but as long as we had sufficient to get us back, the cost in fuel was worth it. This practice also brought me into a forecast which the staff of the control tower back at the airfield would make between themselves as to which aircraft would be the first back from a raid, ours or one piloted by 'Bunny Lee' an Australian pilot with roughly the same number of operations as our crew up to our being shot down and honours were about even. I always thought that Bunny survived a tour of operations but at a recent Squadron reunion dinner I was told that he and his crew failed to return from their last operation.

There were other operations apart from those to Berlin during late 1943-44 and on looking at my log book the names of some of the towns or cities were Stuttgart, Augsburg, Munich, Leipzig, Stettin and Essen etc. The operation to Stettin was made on the 5th January 1944 and took nine hours flying time and even though it was in the middle of winter, the return journey over the North Sea was flown partly in daylight. We were told at the briefing for the raid that dawn would break over the sea North of Holland and it was a possibility the Germans would despatch fighters to intercept us, so it was necessary to fly as low as possible. At daybreak, we had already been in the air for seven hours and were looking forward to landing, this was an incentive to drop as low as we could and I flew the remainder of the trip at fifty feet above the waves until we reached the East Coast. No enemy action materialised.

Our crew flew on the operation to Leipzig on 19th February 1944 which cost Bomber Command seventy eight aircraft. It was another raid when the forecast winds were wrong, they were much stronger than expected and resulted in the bomber stream arriving over the target early. The raid was made during the Battle of Berlin and as the two cities are fairly close to each other the German night fighter command expected another raid on Berlin, to which city we appeared to be heading and for the first time I can remember Dornier bombers flew above the bomber stream on either side dropping flares to suspend in the air and form a 'lane' towards Berlin. They were also helpful to the night fighters. The turning point to fly south to Leipzig was ignored by several crews who for some unknown reason decided to take up the time by flying towards Berlin where they were caught in the 'lane' of flares which never seemed to go out and hung there for what seemed like ages. We saw all this happening as we flew towards Leipzig, I had decided to risk flying over the city and go round again on the East side by which time path finders would be dropping markers on zero hour. We could bomb on them and hopefully be away. On the return journey we saw many combats but were not troubled ourselves.

In March 1944 there was talk of an invasion which many thought would come in the summer and we were called to a briefing one day for a raid different to all the others. The raid was to be made against a factory making powered gliders for the Germans at a factory at Chateauroux in unoccupied France. This attack was to be nothing like the high altitude bombing of German cities; it was to be made by twenty two aircraft bombing individually between 7,000 feet to approximately 11,000 feet flying in full moonlight. The raid would be controlled by a Master of Ceremonies flying a Lancaster who would open the attack by placing a red spot fire on top of a large hangar and then call in the attacking force with the first wave carrying 4,000lb and nine 500lb bombs. The first and last bomb fitted with delayed action fuses to explode several hours later. The second wave of Bombers would carry incendiaries to set the factory alight. We were to fly from our base, another Squadron from Coningsby would also be on the raid and both Squadrons had to rendezvous at a crossroads two miles north of the target which would be marked by a Master of Ceremonies five minutes before zero hour. The first wave of attackers was called 'Apples' and the second wave 'Pears' with the Master of Ceremonies called 'Big Stiff'.

The met forecast was for cloud cover at fairly low level on route over France, clearing well north of the target to give us visibility to identify land marks such as rivers. However the cloud-cover extended a lot further south than Paris and we did not clear it until a few minutes before 'Big Stiff' was due to mark the cross-roads. As ETA approached we waited for him to call up, which he did on time saying he had found the rendezvous and would be dropping the marker. We waited for him to do this because our ETA had not come up with a corresponding identification of the cross-roads. To our relief when the marker dropped we were only three miles from it and by that time we were down to our bombing height - 7,200 feet; I commenced circling the cross-roads and could see the factory a couple of miles down the road. The planes continued to circle as the MC ordered; and this gave the night shift at the factory sufficient time to evacuate before we commenced our attack.

The first aircraft bombed on time in perfect conditions without any opposition, except for one gun which was firing near the town of Châteauroux a few miles south. I was surprised when the first aircraft dropped its 4,000lb bomb on the airfield adjacent to the factory with the other bombs also bursting on the field. We were the second aircraft to attack and as the target was only 250 yards wide and half a mile long running by the side of a road, we came in on a diagonal run across it. It was perfect for the bomb aimer who could see where he had placed his bombs; the 4,000lb bomb exploded on a workshop and destroyed it as the photograph

A Lancaster on 431 'Iroquois' Squadron landing at Croft.

proved and the 500lb bombs straddled all the buildings ; it was a perfect bomb run. After bombing we turned 1800 and ran up the side of the road observing the result of the rest of the attack; after the first wave had done their job the target looked gutted with smoke and flames, but the second wave went into fire it with their incendiaries. One crew on the return journey talked continuously with their R/T switched on and although they were ordered to be quiet they kept on for some time. One aircraft was lost on the raid and we wondered if it was the crew who 'broadcast'.

Many years after in the 1980s, I visited Puerto Pollensa in Majorca several times and made friends with quite a number of French people. One lady in particular, who spoke English, was very friendly with my wife and I and on one occasion we were talking about the war. The French were evidently very appreciative of the RAF; I mentioned the Châteauroux raid and the time given for the night shift to evacuate the factory before the attack commenced. There were a number of French people stood around and she turned to them and talked to them for about a minute. I noticed their faces showed a look of appreciation at what she was saying because I was suddenly embraced, kissed on both cheeks and patted on the back; our friend had told them about the raid which had given them great pleasure to hear and of the time given to workers to evacuate the factory, otherwise many would have been killed.

On one occasion in the Mess I was talking to our Flight Commander who had finished his second tour and was waiting for a posting, he was giving me his views on what would be happening on German night fighter aerodromes at that particular time as they were preparing for the nights operations. I was later going to a briefing for the night's operation and it was his usual way of testing your reaction to dangers you might meet. At that time the Battle of Berlin was in full swing and he already knew the target, so my aim was to persuade him to divulge it; would it be the Big City? or I hoped, one where the defences were not as heavy and concentrated. We were standing next to a rustic fireplace in the mess which was part of a large Nissen hut; and he went on about the German defences getting better, as he did so he started scratching the mantelpiece with a pen knife.

At first I did not take much notice but when he scratched the letter 'S' followed by 'T' I began to take notice. Was he identifying the target? If so, it certainly wasn't Berlin. All the time he was talking he was scratching letters; the ST was followed by UTTGART, STUTTGART- what a relief when he looked at me and nodded, it wasn't Berlin after all thank goodness but Southern Germany. The reason I am writing of this conversation is that ten years after the war I made a nostalgic visit to Metheringham; and in the old mess which was partly in ruins with half the corrugated roof missing, stood the same fireplace, which had been protected from the weather by the roof, part of which covered it. At the time I remembered the conversation with the Flight Commander and his spelling out of the target on the mantelpiece with a knife. Naturally I looked to see if there was any evidence of his work and there were the same letters which were in the brickwork after all those years - remarkable.

A few weeks before we were shot down I was told that a mine laying operation was planned during the April moon period and our crew would be involved. Mines were to be laid around the Gdynia canal on the far side of the Baltic and three or four aircraft from 106 Squadron would fly at low level to drop the mines. Anti aircraft fire was expected and would probably be firing at us horizontally. We practised for the operation by flying low level exercises around the central part of England. However before our crew could participate in the raid we were shot down on the way to Nuremberg, but at a Squadron Reunion dinner in 1997 I met an ex flight engineer from a crew who operated about the same time as ours, who told me they had taken our place and the operation was a success. It was a long flight mostly low level apart from over Denmark where they had to gain height, before descending over the Baltic and running into the drop zone at 100 feet with heavy flak to contend with; they all returned having successfully laid the mines.

Reference must be made to two anti aircraft weapons met during the winter of 1943/44. One was named 'Scarecrow' and the other was a rocket which flew horizontally at a certain height and changed course, then increased speed by further propulsion, like a meteor. The scarecrow would be put up by the Germans usually in a dark part of the sky on the route where no other defence was in use. The idea was to scare aircrew because it would suddenly burst and resemble an aircraft being hit, bursting into flames, exploding and bits descending to the ground. The only difference was that an aircraft plunging down in flames and exploding would hit the ground and splash along it whereas the scarecrow would burn out and never reach the ground. There is some controversy about whether scarecrows existed, but I can say, without any doubt, in my mind they did. The rocket projectile did not cause much trouble apart from keeping an eye on it until it burnt out; as you watched it change course and regain speed with a burst from its tail it looked dangerous but I never saw one collide with an aircraft.

As heavy raids continued the night fighters took an increasing toll of bombers and they were guided on to their targets by radar operators on the ground. This was countered by German speaking radio operators in England instructing the night fighter pilots to cancel the previous order and fly elsewhere. In turn the Germans got over this by using coded music to let their pilots know the intended target. For instance marches were played if the target was Berlin and on many occasions I remember my wireless operator saying they were playing nothing but marches on the German radio.

To continue with the Battle of Berlin, on one of the operations our 4,000lb cookie exploded near the Reichstag; this was confirmed by the photo of the burst which must have damaged the building.

Although we were losing a lot of bombers on the Berlin operations, aircrew were alerted to the possibility of German suicide troops landing in the vicinity of airfields to kill them on the ground and plans were ready to disperse crews away from their quarters to other sites on the airfield. At the time we thought the Germans must have been desperate to mount such an operation but maybe our raids were inflicting unacceptable damage to property and morale. However the attacks never materialised but our losses continued to rise.

Our ground crew at Metheringham who looked after 'Q for Queenie' were of the best. They did their job magnificently and nothing was too much trouble. I remember asking them if they could find a leather cushion for the pilot's position and the next time I flew it was in place; I think they took it from the flight commander's aircraft. They also named the aircraft *Queen Of Sheba*' and painted a picture of a nude lady just under the pilot's window. When we returned from an operation the crew shot a line to them saying the flak over the target was so hot she came back tanned. We had a drink with them once a week at the local village pub when operations permitted; I remember one of the lads came from Leeds and another from Liverpool.

After I was repatriated from Germany at the end of the war the RAF sent me on a refresher course flying Oxfords at Coleby Grange near Lincoln. I was waiting in the bus station at Lincoln for a bus to the airfield one night when a voice shouted 'Dick' and on turning saw one of them running towards me. The last time I saw him was at dispersal on the night we were shot down and as he shook my hand he said 'All the ground crew had been relieved and happy when they heard I had survived, but were grieved over the other lads who lost their lives'.

Before I leave this part of the story on our operation experiences I will relate what happened on a raid to Augsburg in February 1944 when the main target was the Daimler Benz factory where engines were assembled for Messerschmitt aircraft. It was the first time an operation was planned with two waves of aircraft bombing two hours apart. We were in the first wave and the weather over Germany was clear with a starlit sky, no cloud and snow on the ground. It was our second visit to Bavaria, having bombed Munich on a previous operation; and as you gained experience it was possible to identify cities by the position of searchlights and anti aircraft guns. Augsburg and Munich are both in Bavaria and as we flew east towards them both defences were in action, especially the searchlights. We identified one cluster of searchlights ahead of us as Augsburg and confirmed with the navigator's H_2S that this was the target. However as we approached the two minutes before zero hour when markers were dropped by the Path Finder Force nothing happened which was strange; a point I conveyed to the crew. The mid upper gunner immediately came on the R/T and said the markers were being dropped on the beam of the port side. I looked over my left shoulder and there they were dropping on the other city which of course was Augsburg; we had mistakenly identified Munich for Augsburg. I turned towards the target which was several minutes flying away and knew we should be over the city when the first wave was already on the return journey.

I thought about all the defences concentrating on one aircraft - ours - at the same time we would be on our own on enemy radar. Should we drop the bombs straight away and skirt the city to get on the return track or risk it and bomb the fires in the city which were now well alight. I decided to carry out the operation and approached the target. Fortunately the flak was not very accurate although some of it too close for comfort; I managed to evade the searchlights and the bomb aimer dropped the bombs from our solitary aircraft twenty minutes after the Main Force had gone. It was an uncomfortable few minutes as we flew over the city and were relieved to get to the other side.

The day before Nuremberg on 30th/31st March 1944 Bomber Command was set for a raid on Brunswick. Four crews were on the last ten trips of their tours and it looked as though they would complete the thirty operations (a complete tour) at about the same time, so it was decided to stagger the remaining trips. Following this decision we were to stand down for the Brunswick raid. My crew were keen to do a second tour of twenty trips with 617 Squadron who were stationed a few miles away at Woodhall Spa; as mentioned before this station, Metheringham and Coningsby formed a Base and there would have been no difficulty with the transfer. However the operation to Brunswick was cancelled because the Met Forecast was not good.

On the 30th March Nuremberg was the target and I was told by the flight commander that my crew would be stood down again. I informed the lads of the orders but as one man said; that as we had been a stand down crew for a cancelled operation one of the other crews should do so for the Nuremberg raid; and asked me to see the Flight Commander again. Although I had to decide whether or not to let the order stand I agreed that we should be put on the Battle Order and gave my views to the flight commander. At first he said the order would not be reversed but after some thought to our request changed his decision. It was our last trip. With only three weeks to go to the end of our tour (the raid was to be the crew's 22nd trip). I remember that after the afternoon briefing, some of the crews had reservations about the operation. The attack was planned for what would normally have been the middle of the stand down period, when a near full moon would be visible. The forecast was for high cloud on the outward route with the target clear. However in the early afternoon a reconnaissance aircraft reported that the route would be clear of cloud but the target would probably be covered. This was after the crews had been briefed for the operation, but it was not cancelled. We took off in Lancaster ND535 'Q' and climbed on course over the Norfolk Coast towards Belgium. The moon was bright and almost full, making near daylight conditions.

At our cruising height of 21,000 feet the air temperature was very low and the Bomber stream began to make condensation trails as we flew on route, over Belgium towards the long leg which ran from South of the Ruhr East to a turning point North West of Nuremberg. It was this long leg that crews were apprehensive about because it ran for over two hundred miles. We did not know at the time that the route took us over two night fighter beacons; and the German Controller, ignoring diversionary operations over Germany and the North Sea, transferred most of his fighter force to those beacons to await the Bombers. Flying conditions over Germany were ideal for fighter aircraft against slow bombers who had inferior armament; and the sky was absolutely clear with a near full moon and four-engined bombers making condensation trails which could be seen for miles.

The fighters began their attack and from the number of tracers being fired, it appeared there were combats everywhere; I saw around thirty aircraft go down in a short period and as we continued to the target the ground became covered with burning aircraft. We continuously operated the 'banking search' looking for enemy aircraft coming up from below. This was achieved by turning steeply to port for 15° to see if fighters were preparing to attack and then banking to return to the original course. I made reference to 'Monica' on the Leipzig raid which was a much more reliable aircraft detector with its audio system than 'Fishpond' (visual aid) attached to H_2S which more often than not failed to work, as ours did on the Nuremberg raid.

We had been flying the long leg for many miles and when we were in a position sixty miles North West of Nuremberg our luck changed; a fighter attacked with tracer and cannon fire which rut the port mainplane and outer engine, flashed past outside the perspex covering of the cockpit and between my legs. I remembered when we were attacked north of Frankfurt in December and prayed we would not go up in flames. However within three or four seconds the port outer engine and mainplane were alight.

It was always the one you didn't see that shot you down as in our case and if 'Monica' had been available we would have been aware of the fighters approach. There was only one action to take - I gave the order to abandon aircraft. The engineer feathered the port engine as he helped me with the controls because we were going down at a very fast rate; and the next few seconds I remember vividly. The bomb aimer acknowledged my order to bail out and said he was leaving the aircraft. The navigator came to the cockpit to escape through the front hatch. The rear gunner also acknowledged the order but said he could not get out of his turret;

Pforzheim on the night of 23/24 February 1945.

this was because the port outer engine powered the turret; the alternative way was to turn the turret by hand controls in order to fall out backwards. There was no reply from the mid upper gunner and the wireless operator; I assumed they must have been killed by the burst of fire which ran along the side of the aircraft. The flight engineer handed me a parachute from one of two in the rack at his side. I managed to connect one of the hooks on the chute to the harness I was wearing, (we did not wear seat type chutes) at the same time trying to control a blazing aircraft which was diving at well over 300mph. I gave up all hope of survival and waited for the impact; a terrifying experience. That is the last thing I remember because the aircraft exploded with a full bomb load (we had no time to jettison) and 1,500 gallons of high octane fuel, which must have ignited and caused the explosion. As I lost consciousness I did have a feeling of being lifted out of the cockpit and must have been propelled through the perspex canopy. When the petrol tanks exploded in the port wing outside my window a fire ball must have been created in the aircraft which would incinerate anything in its path and I must have been just ahead of it as I was blown from the aircraft.

Many years later I was told an unopened parachute was found next to the body of the flight engineer who had landed in a wood four miles from the wreckage of the aircraft. He must have been blown out like me, but I was lucky my parachute had opened probably by the force of the explosion; also as he could have taken the parachutes out of the rack in any order I might have had the one that didn't open. There is also the possibility that he was unconscious or killed by the explosion, but as we were only two feet apart in the cockpit when the aircraft went up and I did not operate my parachute, because I was unconscious; something did, I was extremely lucky. When I regained consciousness and realised what had happened my first thought was 'where am I?' then I heard the sound of aircraft engines as the main force passed overhead and I was suspended somewhere over Germany by parachute. I expected to feel the parachute supports in front of my face but could not find them - I thought I was coming down without a parachute! I desperately groped around and located the one hook attachment and hung on, this attachment was well above my head, evidently the pad of the parachute once it has opened rises up to a position over your head and I wasn't aware of this. By this time I did not know how quickly I was descending, I was coming down without flying boots and as I looked up saw the canopy of the parachute quite clearly in the bright moonlight, riddled in parts with a number of burnt small holes, some half an inch in diameter; and it was terrifying because I was afraid that my descent might be too fast for a safe landing. Although the moon was bright I could not see the ground, but there were several fires burning which I took to be from our aircraft. The fires did not help me to judge my altitude because I did not know the size of them. I also had facial injuries including a nose bleed, these must have occurred when I was blown out of the aircraft.

As my thoughts dwelt on landing, I hit the ground with an almighty wallop and rolled backwards down a small hill. When I reached the bottom I regained my wind and could see hills silhouetted against the night sky. My neck and back were very painful and when I attempted to stand, my right leg collapsed. It was out of line just above the ankle and I knew it was broken. I must have then lost consciousness again and when I came to the moon was low in the sky behind the hills. I could not walk and waited for someone to arrive. I soon heard shouting in German and realised I had left Metheringham an hour and a half to two hours before where everyone spoke English and here I was for the first time listening to a German voice. I saw a torch light about two hundred yards away so I shouted back and the torch came towards me. A number of people arrived and the torch was shone in my face. I could make out both young and elderly men; one of the younger men started shouting and was about to hit me in the face with a rifle when he was stopped by one of the older men. One or two of them went off to search the wreckage and the others wrapped me in the parachute placed me on a stretcher and carried me to a horse drawn cart which took me to a small village called Königsberg about one thousand metres away.

When we arrived I was carried up some steps on the outside of a building and placed on the floor of what was the Burgomeister's Office. After the war I was informed the German pilot who shot us down was Oberleutnant Martin Becker their night fighter ace who received a very high decoration when he was sent for by Adolf Hitler the day after the raid, having been credited with eight victims on the night. I

Oberleutnant Martin 'Tino' Becker of Stab I./NJG 6 scored his first victory on 23/24 September 1943 when he destroyed a Lancaster (possibly DV174 of 460 Squadron RAAF) near Speyer during a raid on Mannheim. He would fly in all weathers and in the weeks following he scored a further five Abschüsse against RAF Viermots before the year was out. On 19/20 February 1944 Becker reached double figures and on the night of 22/23 March he claimed six Lancasters and Halifaxes shot down. Becker ended the war with 58 night kills (all four-engined bombers) and the Ritterkreuz and Eichenlaub.
(Karl-Ludwig Johanssen)

was also told that he shot down over fifty allied aircraft during the bombing of Germany and was one of their night fighter aces. There have been several reasons put forward for the unacceptable loss of 97 bombers and their aircrew. One of them is 'They knew we were coming'; the other one is the weather, not bad weather but clear weather and temperatures so low they created condensation trails. As one who participated in the raid I accept the latter reason; and as the route happened to pass over two night fighter beacons, it made it easier for their pilots to get amongst us and shoot us down with their armament, 20mm and .50 calibre cannon and machine guns compared to our pea shooters .303 calibre machine guns. What grieves me even after fifty years is why we were allowed to go. The weather reports on the day of the raid which were obtained by PR.V aircraft changed from one which would give some protection to the bombers to a later one which completely changed the picture and should have influenced a decision to call it off.

In 1988 I met the navigator/radio operator in Martin Becker's Me 110 night fighter. It was at a reunion of Luftwaffe Night Fighter Crews and members of the Doncaster Air Gunners Association at Laage near Rostock to which I was invited and Carl who had been informed of my visit knew I was interested in tactics used by Martin Becker when he shot down our Lancaster on the Nuremberg raid. The first point was to compare our records with those of the Luftwaffe for 30th/31st March 1944, to ascertain the position where we were shot down, and according to the log he had of British bombers destroyed the entry made for 'Q-Queenie' was 12 miles North West of Wetzlar, a difference of 2 kilometres only from our calculations. Although Carl could not especially remember the destruction of our aircraft; Becker shot down eight aircraft that night, he said they generally used the same tactic when a bomber was visually identified. Most of what he then told me confirmed my impression of the attack and answered questions which I had on my mind. I always thought a night fighter attack was made from port quarter down, i.e. on the left hand rear of the aircraft to fire upwards in to the wing to hit the petrol tanks and engines and set the aircraft on fire, also to line up the cockpit to disable the pilot; this action was carried out only if the gunners in the bomber had not seen the fighter and given the pilot a corkscrew evasive action.

Becker, however, used a different method; if his aircraft had not been 'picked up' as he stalked the bomber, he approached it on the starboard rear side at a lower altitude, pulled up the nose of the aircraft and commenced a skidding movement from right to left by applying rudder, at the same time firing with all his armament into the bomber. Becker's attack on the Lancaster fits my impression of the way he destroyed 'Q-Queenie' and killed two of my crew; George Walker - wireless operator and Jock Jameson - mid upper gunner.

Fifty years later when I made the visit to the site of the crash I was taken to the crash site by Herr Lepper who was fourteen years of age in 1944 and carried the torch by which they found me near the wreckage. The Lancaster had certainly made a mess of the wood and no doubt the same to the field where it crashed and exploded.

Footnotes for Chapter 10

14   JB534 was piloted by Flying Officer Reginald William Dickerson who was killed along with three other members of his crew on return to base when he avoided another Lancaster. Sergeant Walter Charles Hills died of his injuries that same day. The three other members of the crew were injured.

Chapter 11

Mailly

The posting came through telling us to report to RAF Waddington, just outside of Lincoln. This was a pre-war station, so we were billeted in barrack blocks. None of your Nissen huts and pot-bellied stoves. The table service in the mess was very nice and the bar excellent. We expected to get straight onto ops, but not just yet. Instead we had a few more cross-countries and other exercises, which took another week or so. I told Liz, one of our WAAF drivers, that I felt like an impostor; here were all these aircrew types we were rubbing shoulders with going on ops every night and us not yet 'baptised'. Of course, eventually we were put on Battle Orders and had to report for briefing. All the crews assembled in the briefing room at the appointed time and all stood up when the CO entered the room. A large covered map of Europe was on the wall. The CO then started to address us and on saying the target's name removed the cover to show the location. Tonight it was a German Army base at Mailly le Camp, in France. The Germans had thousands of troops there, with tanks, lorries and workshops.

As we taxied around the perimeter to the main runway, the WAAFs, airmen and others were there waving us off and wishing us good luck. Off we went, thundering down the runway and away into the night. All of a sudden it seemed lonely and quiet, apart from the droning of the engines.

It was 3 May 1944 and a clear moonlit night - so clear, in fact, the moon cast shadows of the trees and hedgerows below. We arrived at the target at 0005, only to find there was a mess-up and the Master Bomber couldn't contact the other aircraft. We were ordered to orbit 8 miles north of the target. This created complete chaos, with dozens of aircraft flying round in circles. While all this was going on, Cheshire [Wing Commander Leonard Cheshire, Marker Leader for the raid] was going down to ground level ensuring the TIs [Target Indicators - brightly coloured pyrotechnics dropped by the marker aircraft for the main force to bomb on] were within the target area, minimising the risk of harming any French people. We were carrying a bomb load of 10,000lbs - one 4,000lb 'cookie' and twelve 500lb high explosives.

'We were ordered back to the target at 00.13 and bombed at 6,750 feet, which is low for a Lancaster. Minute by minute, Mac the rear gunner was reporting to the navigator 'Aircraft going down on the port quarter'...

'Aircraft going down dead astern, Nav'... At each report the navigator would enter it in his log. These reports were so numerous that Frank, the navigator, asked us not to bother any more as he maintained they were special shells the Germans were sending up to try and demoralise us by looking like aircraft going down in flames. In actual fact they had no such things. It was incredible to see so many aircraft go down. As I watched, I thought 'God, I've got another twenty-nine of these to do'. The 8 minutes we were orbiting north of the target gave all the night fighters in that part of France time to get airborne and they had *a field day; we lost forty-two aircraft that night. Such loss rates were by no means unusual. Few crews made it through a full tour of thirty operations unscathed.*

Charles Sleigh, 463 Squadron RAAF. **16 Mosquito and 346 Lancaster bombers took part in the raid on Mailly and 42 of the latter fell victim to flak or fighters. One of the other Australian squadrons, 460 at Binbrook, lost five of its seventeen Lancasters. Charles Sleigh flew his final operation, Tuesday 15 August 1944.**

On the night of 14/15 July 1944 a civilian airliner from Lisbon airport landed at Whitchurch airport near Bristol and a twenty-year old man called 'John White', a civilian escaper from the internment camp at Vittel, France presented his bogus British Emergency Certificate 1398 to the security control officer. He told officials that his real name was Nicholas John Stockford and he had been shot down on Wednesday 3 May when over 360 Lancasters bombed a Panzer depot and training centre at Mailly-le-Camp almost halfway between Troyes and Châlons-sur-Marne, about 50 miles south of Rheims. Stockford was a former boy apprentice engine fitter at a training school in South Africa before he remustered as a RAF flight engineer. His story that he had been shot down when Lancaster III ND556 'F-Freddie' on 207 Squadron piloted by 26-year old Flight Sergeant Leslie Harry 'Lizzie' Lissette RNZAF had been attacked by a FW 190 was checked and it was confirmed. The pilot was on his fourth operation. His girlfriend had been a nurse on a hospital ship bombed off Crete and was believed lost but 'Lizzie' a tough, powerfully built New Zealander, who had been a teamster with four horses hauling logs out of the mountains near Napier, never spoke much about it. A third attack soon finished off the bomber. Tracer hit the port wing, blowing off the dinghy hatch. The dinghy began to inflate and then shot back over the tail plane like a big hoopla ring. Lissette could see down through the wing to the ground. The port undercarriage was partially down. A little later Sergeant Ronald Ellis the 25-year old rear gunner reported a fighter coming in port quarter down. They were hit again in the bomb bay and a small fire started. 'F-Freddie' went down at Chaintreaux in Seine-et-Marne, twelve kilometres SE of Namours. Lissette, who remained at the controls to the end, was critically injured and he died later in a French hospital. He and Sergeant Ronald Ellis the 25-year old rear gunner from Doncaster shared a joint grave in Chaintreaux Communal Cemetery. The bomb aimer, Sergeant L. Wesley, from West Bromwich was taken prisoner. Stockford, who was from Chipping Norton in Oxfordshire, Sergeant Ron T. 'Curly' Emeny the 20-year old mid-upper gunner, 18-year old Sergeant Philip N. King the WOp/AG from Birmingham and the navigator, Flight Sergeant John Pittwood from Warley, Birmingham, evaded capture. Pittwood was taken along the Burgundy Line and he reached Gibraltar via Spain. He landed at Lyneham on 24 June. Twenty year old Ron Emeny, the mid-upper gunner, who was from Bow in London, had suffered serious burns to his head but he also made it safely to Gibraltar and arrived back in England at Whitchurch the following day.

Nicholas Stockford had landed near the village of Ferrières, sixteen miles north of Montargis and he hid in a wood. Believing that he was heading due

Crew of Lancaster ND556 on 207 Squadron flown by Flight Sergeant Lissette RNZAF (centre, holding the mascot) which were shot down on 3/4 May 1944 on Mailly. Back Row L-R: Sergeant Ron Emeny, mid-upper gunner (Evaded); Sergeant Laurie Wesley, bomb aimer (PoW); Flight Sergeant Jack Pittwood, navigator (Evaded); Sergeant Nick Stockford, flight engineer (Evaded). Front: Sergeant Ron Ellis, rear gunner (KIA); Lissette and Sergeant Philip King, wireless operator (Evd). Lissette was critically injured and died soon after in a French Hospital. (via Phil King)

south Stockford was in fact walking north-west. He continued west and then south-west for the next four days. On 8 May a man whom he met in the village of Boiscommun contacted the abbé of St Loup-des-Vignes. The abbé in turn contacted the schoolteacher in the village, Yvette Jublot, and on 10 May she hid him above the school. Having found him a set of civilian clothes, Stockford was escorted by 'Jean' to Paris at the end of May. On 13 June he was taken to Lyon and, after an evening meal, moved on to Toulouse and to Bordeaux, where he was again hidden. Two days later a guide called Benito arrived and Stockford was given false Organisation Todt papers to state that he was going on leave. They made their way to St Jean-de-Luz, each with a bicycle and pushed on to the Spanish border on 21 June until they were within four kilometres of Hendaye. From there they went on to a farm-house 200 yards from the Franco-Spanish frontier. They went down to the River Bidassoa and Benito forded Stockford over on his back. Once in Spain they went to Irún and San Sebastián, where they stayed the night before continuing on to Bilbao. Stockford remained there for a week while his false papers were prepared in the name of John White. On about 2 July, having been provided with a safe-conduct pass and an identity card, Stockford was taken to León. There a Spanish guide took him to the Portuguese border and handed him over to two Portuguese guides, one called Manuel, who took him to Murça, a little over 100 kilometres down the road to Oporto. On 7 July he was contacted by a Frenchman named Guerche and a Portuguese named Mirandella, who told him that the line had been broken owing to the arrest of an organisation member in Oporto. Even so, Stockford was taken to Oporto on 12 July and after dinner with the assistant British Consul there, Mr Connolly, took the Lisbon train with no identity papers. In Lisbon, he went to the embassy and was seen by a man named 'Terry' aged about twenty-one, who took him to 37c, Rua de Buenos Aires and 'John White' was given a place on the aircraft returning to Bristol.

Sergeant Philip King came down at 0130 hours on 4 May a few yards from a barn to which he immediately went to hide his parachute and Mae West. 'Having done this, I took out my compass and started out in a Westerly direction. Soon I found myself on the main road from Dordive to Chateau Laundon. I kept walking until 0500 hours when I lay down by the side of a small river. After thinking it over, I decided I could be seen too easily so I moved over to a grain stack nearby, falling asleep. I was awakened, by a very old Frenchman with a pitchfork, who immediately began jabbering in French. When I had finally indicated to him that I was English and showing him my identity discs, he took me to a nearby farm owned by Monsieur Mois Bretanue. On 13 May two chaps came in a small van, taking me to a small house in the village of Souppes, where I spent the night. Next day I was taken to a farm near Dordive called 'La Carabinierie' and was owned by Madame Sonya who was married but separated from, a collaborator called Petit. At the farm was a French escaped conscripted worker. I left the farm about 15 July to help the French operate a dropped radio and also to help them in parachute operations. While helping the French I met a chap codenamed 'Andre' who had been dropped from England. He took me to Chambon and from there to Ste-Loup-Des-Vignes where I spent the night in a priest's house. I was introduced to

Major Ian Fenwick, who was in charge of a detachment from the SAS Brigade.'

A week or so after the Normandy landings 'D' Squadron, 1 SAS, was given the job of harassing the enemy in the area to the south of Paris known as the Orleans Gap, between the Forêt de Fontainebleau and the River Loire. The whole operation, codenamed 'Gain', was under the command of Major Ian Fenwick. With him were ten officers and fifty men.

I had been with them but a week in the forest when word came that the German commander at Orléans had asked for three divisions to clear the Forêt d'Orléans of Maquis and the British which were believed to be there. While in the forest I met Pilot Officer H. O'Neil O'Neill RAAF, Staff Sergeant Frank Hines[15] and Flying Officer E. F. D. Vidler.[16] 'I went to Ladon with Vidler and stayed for two days at a house owned by Dr. Prudence Huoy where Vidler had stayed before. A Gestapo scare sent us back to the forest and I arrived there, (5 August) to find Major Fenwick getting ready to clear his unit out. We spent the night in camp and at 1530 hours Sunday, 6 August, we heard sounds of firing coming from a water hole 200 yards from the camp. I developed that 600 Germans with mortar and light artillery had entered the camp from the NE and West. At the advice of one of Major Fenwick's sergeants we headed South on our own toward Nancrey-Sur-Rimarde. The airmen left the SAS on 4 August but were back on the following day, rejoining them in a small wood a kilometre south-east of Nancray-sur-Rimarde.

On 6 August Major Fenwick took a party of five in a jeep to collect supplies from the main camp in a wood south-west of Chambon-la-Foret (Loiret). They were on their way back when they ran into 600 Germans at Chambon. Major Fenwick, Lance-Corporal Menginou (known to the airmen as 'Maginot') and a sergeant in the FFI were killed in the ensuing skirmish. Corporal Bill Duffy was wounded and taken as a prisoner to a hospital, from which he later escaped. Sergeant F.W Dunkley, also taken prisoner, was never seen again.

'We struck out on our own, finally coming onto the SE side of the forest. Walking down the road we came to two houses standing close together. We had hardly washed up and eaten when the Maquis began to arrive from the forest. They had just begun to tell us what had happened when a car raced in, taking cover in the garden. This turned out to be 'Agripa', a White Russian dropped from England. He confirmed the desperateness of the situation, so we decided to strike out for Nancray on our own. It was getting dark - 2200 hours. Sunday night. We spent the night in a small wood and as we were setting out again in the morning, we encountered a lad who said Major Fenwick was in a little wood nearby and wanted us to follow; six SAS men remaining with us. A half an hour had hardly passed when we heard gun and mortar fire from Chambon. A few minutes later the same lad who had taken us to the Major earlier in the day rushed in to say that the Major had been killed and his jeep wrecked.

We struck out immediately on our own for the house in which we had been helped at St Loup. Our helper allowed us to remain three or four days, sending us to Courcelles, where we were directed to a farm, the 'Mona Lisa' run by Monsieur Le Grand, two kilometres NE of the town. Here we spent but one night, pushing on to Escrennes where we stayed at the house of Monsieur

Grossier, a wine merchant. The following night we went to Grigneville and stayed at the house of Marie Jeanne Beauballet, finding on our arrival there three of Major Fenwick's men, troopers Curran, Philips and Hunt. The next night was spent at the house of Yvonne Bruneau at Chantillon-Le-Roi, as were the next few days, Monday 14 August-Sunday 20 August. On Saturday afternoon a Lieutenant Williams from the XII Corps came by and on Sunday we returned to Allied hands.

While Vidler and King went off together and to eventual liberation, O'Neill, Hines and three SAS (Corporal Curran and Troopers Hunt and Phillips) went to a barn on the outskirts of Nancray. After the SAS left a couple of days later to rejoin their unit, the two airmen stayed put until liberation on 22 August.

While awaiting the order to bomb Flight Sergeant John A. Sanderson RNZAF on 166 Squadron at Kirmington called the crew on intercom that their Lancaster had been hit by flak and that the port inner engine was on fire. The New Zealander feathered the engine and Sergeant W. T. Viollet the wireless operator went to the astrodome and peered out, his face illuminated by the flames coming from the engine. Then the fire went out. The Lancaster completed its bombing run and 30 minutes after midnight, Sanderson set course for home. Ten minutes later they were attacked by a night-fighter. Sanderson corkscrewed violently but cannon shells tore into the fuselage and set the hydraulic system on fire. Sergeant John Thomas Cockburn the 21-year old mid-upper gunner left his turret and was trapped by fire which stretched right across the fuselage immediately behind the turret. One by one the crew began bailing out. Viollet landed in a small ploughed field surrounded by woods north of Troyes. As he made his escape through the woods he saw the wrecks of three Lancasters. He could not distinguish any identity marks but in one he saw the dead body of the rear gunner. Viollet was able to evade capture and return to England. Sanderson was badly burnt but was found and helped by local people and taken to Madame Duquesne at Troyes where he stayed for a short while before being taken to Loines aux Bois where he was sheltered by Madame Patris. Sanderson was discovered by the Germans and both he and Madame Patris were arrested. She was sent to a concentration camp but died on the train en route for the camp on 2 July. Sanderson and three of the crew were taken into captivity. Cockburn was killed and 27-year old Sergeant Jack Arthur Bodsworth the rear gunner who had bailed out with his parachute on fire, died also.

Lancaster ND733 on 550 Squadron at North Killingholme was on the homeward leg, just south of Paris, when it was attacked by a night-fighter. With the trimming tabs shot away the pilot, Flight Sergeant T. A. Lloyd, struggled to keep control of the aircraft but managed to shake off the enemy fighter. Five minutes later a second attack set fire to the aircraft's bomb bay and fuselage. The order to bail out was obeyed by the mid-upper gunner, rear gunner and bomb aimer. Before anyone else had the chance to bail out ND733 went into a dive, which helped to extinguish the fires and Lloyd managed to put the stricken bomber down at RAF Ford on the south coast of England. Bomb aimer Flying Officer E. Yaternick RCAF and rear-gunner, Sergeant A. C. Crilly were captured, but Sergeant J. G. Pearce the thirty-year-old mid-upper gunner managed to evade, despite his parachute catching in some telegraph wires. By late evening on 4 May he was in the hands of the Resistance and, helped on his way to Gibraltar, was flown back to the UK on 23 June.

Twenty-three year old Pilot Officer Colin Dickson RAAF and the crew of *Naughty Nan* on 467 Squadron included four fellow Aussies - Flight Sergeants' Stanley D. Jolly, bomb aimer; Robert Isaiah Hunter, WOp; 22-year old Oscar Skelton Furniss, navigator and 20-year old Hilton Hardcastle Forden, rear gunner. Thirty-three-year old Sergeant Philip Joseph Weaver, flight engineer and 19-year old Flight Sergeant Horace Skellorn, mid-upper-gunner, were the two English members on the crew. Nan was shot down shortly after bombing and crashed 25 kilometres NNW of Troyes. Only two of the crew survived. Stanley Jolly managed to bail out safely and Robert Hunter having tried to bail out via the forward escape hatch was forced to go back to the rear door with the aircraft well ablaze. He then fell through the floor but was suspended by his parachute on his back, completely surrounded by flames. After considerable effort he was able to open the door in the rear and jump. By this time he was badly burned on his face and different parts of his body. He managed to land without further injury though nearly unconscious and was unable to remember much of what happened thereafter. Jolly owed his initial freedom to Mme Berque who risked her life getting him onto a train for Paris where he was assisted by Bernard Monin. Robert Hunter made his way to les Grandes-Chapelles (Aube) and asked for help. Most people were too frightened and turned him away but one woman took him in. Despite his burns and his dizzy state a member of the FFI arrived and took him to their camp about two hours away. Moved to Troyes later that day, 4 May, Hunter received the first medical treatment for his burns. The French doctor who attended him said that he would have to go to 'the Hôpital de Dieu (l'hôtel-Dieu Saint-Nicolas) and have his hands amputated as gangrene had set in and the blood had practically stopped circulating. That evening a Frenchman and his wife took him to the hospital and the Germans were notified. Operated on, on 5 May, Hunter remained unconscious for the next two weeks but the good news was that doctors had managed to save his hands. The Gestapo tried to get him to talk but using his burnt and badly swollen lips as an excuse, he pretended he was unable to do so. When the time to evacuate the hospital came on 22 August, the Australian was ignored and left in isolation. Just in case, the French doctor injected him to raise his temperature and he was sent to another hospital as a 'scarlet fever case'. He was liberated on 27/28 August by the US 3rd Army.

'R-Robert' on 460 Squadron RAAF flown by 29-year old Flight Sergeant George Kenneth Gritty RAAF crashed at Châlons-sur-Marne in a garden between the streets Porte Murée and Mélinet causing a fire in the home of Mademoiselle Potlet. Several people were injured by falling wreckage. The bodies of the dead airmen were found in the debris in Rue Mélinet. Flight Sergeant Bryan Morgan the 20-year old rear gunner recalls. 'I could see aircraft going down all around me. We were shot down about midnight. Suddenly our fuel tanks were hit and I could see a mass of flames, Sergeant Joseph Chandler my mid-upper gunner in his turret in flames, there was no chance for him. I knew our communications had failed though the aircraft was still flying but losing height. There was no point waiting for an order to bail out so I opened the door, got my parachute and clipped it on. I turned the turret manually and jumped out. I pulled the cord and remember looking back at the aircraft and seeing it disintegrate. I later discovered we had been shot down by a Focke Wulf 190. Four of our crew died; three got out. My pilot died along with my wireless operator, Sergeant Stanley Russell, the mid-upper gunner and the engineer, 19-year old Sergeant Lionel Vale. I later met up with the bomb aimer, Sergeant Léonard Henri Williams. The navigator, Sergeant Joseph Orbin, got out and was hidden in a nearby village but we never met up.

'I landed in Châlons-sur-Marne on a bridge. There were Germans in the distance walking away, watching the sky and they didn't see me. I jumped into the Marne and came up near a barge which was low in the water. I spent a few hours on it under a tarpaulin then in the early hours I walked down the river bank and hid for the day. I could see a farm in the distance and remembered from the Escape & Evasion lectures that we should look for an arable farm, as the Germans regularly visited dairy farms for supplies. My hands were swollen, especially the knuckles, but I knocked on the door late in the evening. There was a party taking place inside but immediately there was silence then the door opened slightly by a Madame Castagne. I managed to say *Je suis aviator Anglais.* Apparently I then fainted and the next thing I remember is sitting in a chair in a dressing gown. A girl was breastfeeding her baby. I was 19 and had never seen such a thing before and must have looked surprised as they all laughed at me! I had a bandage on my burnt face and I'd also torn the skin on one leg. I hadn't adjusted the parachute harness as you never think anything will happen, so my shoulders were in a bad way. I must have been in shock as I don't remember feeling any pain. They put me to bed where I stayed for two days. A man who spoke English visited me but said there was nothing he could do for my shoulder but it looked OK. After about a week I could move it more easily. There was always a cauldron full of chicken and rabbit cooking on the stove because if it was being cooked it couldn't be stolen by the Germans! The farm belonged to Monsieur Champenois who was wounded in WWI and had contacts with the local Maquis. He contacted a local Basque man, André Etchegoimbery, who ran a 'safe house' in a small village.

'After about a week I was taken by car and joined the *Maquis* Group *Melpomène* which was led by Jacques Degrandcourt. Others in the group were Jacques Songy, Roger Romagny and Gino Zappola. As an air gunner I was made very welcome, as they needed help with their armaments. I slept either in the woods or in a barn on a farm owned by the Jeanson family in Le Fresne, not far from Châlons. 'The Maquis group had hand grenades, guns and ammunition, much of which had been dropped by the British but some of the instructions were in English and some of the explosives had not been stored properly. They had opened the metal containers, resealed some of them and buried them in a line several feet apart. The plastic explosive had been buried separately and had become damp and some exploded later. It made a large hole and the Germans had come and investigated but didn't return. The Germans didn't like going into the woods, they probably suspected the Maquis were there but didn't know how many. We were a very big group but never all together at the same time. Several of them were charcoal burners and woodsmen and we would have got lost without them. There was also a Russian, Maxime (known as le petit Russe) who had been captured at the Russian Front but escaped and managed to walk across Germany. He was our expert in trapping and shooting hare, rabbit and deer. He also knew all the edible plants in the forest. He dug with wooden tools and found all sorts of root vegetables we never knew were there. We had a car equipped with a machine gun and the post of machine gunner was occupied by Maxime. I wasn't allowed to go with them on active patrols but was told their most common target was German vehicles, which used to be accompanied by out-riders. I used to check the villages and try to ascertain where the Germans were, as no-one would recognise me. I had been given an identity card as Marcel Julien Bernad, which said I was *sourd-muet,* a deaf mute. I stayed with the partisans from May until August by which time I was very weak and malnourished so they took me back to the Jeanson's farm to be looked after. General Patton's 3rd Army was coming through and, aided by the Maquis, I managed to get a note to them. They came to get me in a Red Cross jeep driven by Private Clura H. Long and carried me back through the front line to a field hospital where I stayed a few weeks and I'm sure the Americans saved my life. I was flown back to England on 3rd September. I later discovered that Jacques Songy and Roger Romagny had been sent to Natzweiler-Struthof and then transferred to Dachau where they both survived. Jacques Degrandcourt was caught in July 1944 and deported to Germany where he perished in 1945 in Vaihingen, a sub-camp of Natzweiler. I owe my life to those brave people in the Resistance. If they had been caught they would undoubtedly have been shot whereas I would have ended up in a PoW camp.'

Sergeant Philip King, wireless operator on Flight Sergeant Lissette'screw. (via Phil King)

Flight Lieutenant Thomas H. Blackham DFC on 50 Squadron was unable to shake off a fighter, which followed them soon after leaving the target area and shot the Lancaster down. The Lancaster exploded and crashed at St-Mesmin, west of the RN19. Six crew died but Blackham, who was wearing a seat type parachute when the aircraft exploded, survived, along with Flight Sergeant Stewart James Godfrey the bomb aimer. Both men evA Lancaster Pilot's Impression on Germanyaded capture but Blackham was picked up and later incarcerated in Buchenwald concentration camp. Godfrey was assisted by Madame Deguilly of Romilly-sur-Seine before being passed to a Resistance group but on 24 June he was killed when the Wehrmacht attacked their camp. Flight Sergeant Godfrey has no known grave.

Also shot down on the Mailly-le-Camp raid was Lancaster 'A-Apple' on 625 Squadron flown by Squadron Leader R. W. H. Gray. On the way back to the coast a night fighter set the Lancaster on fire and the fuselage aft of the flare-chute became an inferno. Sergeant Benjamin Escritt, the 23-year old rear gunner could have jumped at once but he stayed in the turret giving his captain instructions for evasive action. 'It's burning in the turret; the flames are all around my arms' were his last words. 'A-Apple' exploded north-west of Sens killing the heroic rear gunner and four other members of the crew. Gray and Sergeant P. J. Evans, the wireless operator were flung into the night by the explosion and 'A-Apple' crashed at St-Agnan (Yonne), 25 kilometres south-east of the Forest of Fontainebleau. Gray was taken prisoner. Evans, who landed safely near Villethierry, five kilometres south of St-Agnan evaded capture. Helped at first by the baker and his wife and by the local schoolteacher, he then asked to be put in touch with the local priest, as he had been instructed to do during his escape and evasion lecture in England. He was and he was taken away to Nevers (Nievre) some distance to the south. After four days there a young woman escorted him north to Paris by train, where he was hidden in two safe houses, firstly in the home of two women doctors and, next, with Monsieur and Madame Olga Christol (who would shelter a total of thirty-nine airmen in their house). Evans arrived back in England on 24 June.

In all, forty-two Lancasters of the main force were shot down, as were a Mosquito and a Halifax of 100 Group. Just fifty-eight of the 315 men lost in these forty-four aircraft survived, twenty-four were taken prisoner of war and thirty-four evaded.

Footnotes for Chapter 11

15   The top turret gunner on a B-24 Liberator in the 801st 'Carpetbagger' Group in the USAAF which had been shot down on 4 July 1944.

16   O'Neill and Vidler, who were on Flight Lieutenant George McGowan Doolan RAAF's crew of Stirling III LJ448 HA-D on 218 Squadron at Woolfox Lodge that was shot down on 20/21 April 1944 on Chambly, crashing at Asnceres-sur-Oisne by this time had been on the run for over three months. Doolan and one other crewmember were killed; one man was taken prisoner. Vidler, O'Neil and two others evaded capture.

Chapter 12

One Hell of a Story

We remember our Helpers, those people, from every walk of life who rose up in the middle of oppression and tyranny and exhibited enormous compassion and fellow feeling for us, the lost and stranded...How fortunate we were to have been able to so enrich our understanding of human values in time of danger.
RAF Escaping Society toast to helpers in occupied countries.

On Wednesday 21 June 1944 the weather, as with previous days, remained dull and the slight northerly wind kept temperatures a little chilly. On this, the shortest night of the year, at the Lancaster stations in 5 Group Bomber Command, their date with destiny was a synthetic oil plant at Wesseling nine miles south of Cologne. At Dunholme Lodge, four miles north of Lincoln the two Lancaster squadrons - 44 'Rhodesia' and 619 trooped into the briefing rooms where the tape on the wall map showed a route ending just below the Ruhr near Gelsenkirchen - Germany for a change. Crews were immediately aware that this meant only one thing; fighters! One hundred and thirty Lancasters would be accompanied by five crews in 1 Group and six Mosquitoes would mark the target using the 'Newhaven' method. Another 123 Lancasters and nine Mosquitoes of 1, 5 and 8 Groups would attack a synthetic oil plant at Scholven/Buer. Plans were to bomb both targets simultaneously. Clear weather conditions were expected at both target areas.

619 Squadron had been flying Lancasters for just over a year. ME846, better known as 'C-Charlie' was captained by 20-year old Pilot Officer Mark Anthony Hamilton 'Dave' Davis RAFVR from Birmingham. The fifth and youngest child of John and Martha Davis, his brother, Dudley Hamilton Davis had been shot down four years before flying a Hampden and had parachuted out at 50 feet and survived to be taken prisoner. 'Dave's bomb aimer was Flight Sergeant Peter Edmund Knox RAAF, 20 years old, from Sydney, Australia. The only son of Brigadier Sir Errol and Lady Knox, his father managed the Melbourne *Argus*. Educated at Xavier College at Melbourne University he then studied art at Newman College before applying to join aircrew. 'There was I suppose a certain middle-class appeal about it' he wrote later. Knox trained at No.2 Air Observers School at Mount Gambier and at Port Pirie in South Australia and Nhill, Victoria before sailing for San Francisco on the Matson liner on 5 May 1943. After further training at Camp Myles Standish, Massachusetts, he sailed to the UK on the *Queen Mary* troop ship on 30 June-1 July and completed further training at Penrhos in north Wales, Turweston, Silverstone, Scampton, Winthorpe and Syderstone. One of ten bomb aimers crewing-up at Silverstone in early 1943, they were the only Australians there and so knew that they were going to be lone

Aussies in their crews. When his crew finally came together they were all sergeants aged between 18 and 21.

With the exception of Sergeant Thomas Alfred Newberry, 21-years old from Chadwell Heath, Dagenham, their Brylcreemed wireless operator, they 'tended towards the quieter side of life in the mess'. Newberry's father was a railway line keeper. Having joined the RAF Tom Newberry was part of a crew that trained on Short Stirlings on 1661 Heavy Conversion Unit at Winthorpe before being posted to 619 Squadron. Eighteen-year old Pilot Officer John Ernest Ralph 'Porky' Bowering RCAF from Kingston, Ontario was the mid upper gunner on the crew. 'Before we were posted to our Squadron' recalled Peter Knox 'we enjoyed one of those experiences which enriched our lives. One day towards the end of April the day dawned without a cloud in the sky - a perfect day for flying. With that wonderful perversity of the nameless authorities on high, some commander with a soul decreed that our station should be closed for the day so that we could all enjoy the sunshine. Porky Bowering and I went for a memorable walk along the Trent to Newark. It was pleasantly warm, still, clear day which lingered on late into the evening. He was to die within two months along with many others on the course. I have always thought that the officer who freed us from duties so that we could breathe in some true English country air in pure peace had true humanity.'

Sergeant George Harry Moggridge RAFVR from Mile End in London manned the rear gun turret. His father worked in the London Docks. As a boy he loved anything to do with aircraft and flying. It was said that 'He always had a model aeroplane in his hands'. He was also a keen member of the Boy Scouts. At family

An hour before midnight on 7/8 August 1944 1,019 heavy bombers set out to blast the Normandy battle area again. Five aiming points on German defences protecting the approaches to Falaise were marked for air bombardment, which was joined by 720 artillery pieces delivering high explosive and flares. The targets were in front of Allied ground troops 16 miles from Falaise so bombing was carefully controlled and only 660 aircraft bombed before 600 Canadian tanks attacked, followed by infantry in armoured personnel carriers. By dawn of 8 August the Canadians had penetrated the German defences for three miles. Ten aircraft - all Lancasters - were victims of Nachtjäger and one to flak.

'sing songs' around the piano the scouting song *Riding Along on the Crest of a Wave* was his favourite. Not surprisingly as a much-loved son, his parents George Percy and Clara called him 'Sonny'.

Flight Sergeant Leslie Edwin James 'Tag' Taylor the 21-year old navigator was from Cheltenham, Gloucestershire. He joined the RAF as a volunteer after his elder brother, Norman, was killed in a Blenheim on 114 Squadron returning from a shipping patrol in the North Sea on 28 April 1941. Sergeant W. Dennis 'Geordie' Belshaw the 20-year old flight engineer was born and brought up in Ladysmith Terrace, Ushaw Moor, Durham, the only son of Dorothy and Arthur Belshaw. 'Geordie' had an older sister, Dorothy, who sadly died at the age of eight when he was six, and a younger sister, Vera, who was born not long after Dorothy's death. His father died when he was eight years old and the family moved to Bearpark. 'Geordie' left school at 14 and was a delivery boy for a local shop, until starting work in the store at 16 with a view to eventually training as a manager but he joined the RAF in 1941 at the age of 18 and passed out in 1943.

Normally new pilots on a squadron were given the 'second dickie' seat to fly with an experienced crew before flying the first op. After being posted to Dunholme Lodge Peter Knox found that it was 619 Squadron policy to send only the bomb aimer on a raid with another crew and he flew as second bomb aimer on a raid to destroy a railway junction in Belgium in May. He saw a lot of loud, no flak, no searchlights and no fighters and dropped his bombs in the Channel. 'We soon learnt all the jargon' he wrote. 'Going on operations meant 'dicing with death' or 'juggling with Jesus'. Difficult targets were 'the arse-hole of death'. Crews that did not return had 'bought it', 'Gone for a Burton (a beer)' or more commonly 'gone for a shit'. Much of the talk was about the number of operations a crew had done... After a night of operations by Five Group a report was circulated on the Group's activities and posted on the squadron bulletin board. Missing crews were identified. There was full disclosure of casualties. No one was under any illusion... [we knew] the odds of completing a tour of operations were poor.'

The clear weather conditions that had been predicted on 21 June deteriorated as the midnight hour approached and both targets were covered by 10/10ths cloud so at Wesseling H$_2$S was used. More than fifty Abschüsse were claimed by Nachtjagd as the result of an effective Tame Boar operation against the Wesseling force, I./NJG1 being credited with 16 victories by eight He 219 Uhu ('Owl') crews. In fact 37 Lancasters were lost on the Wesseling operation. At Dunholme Lodge 44 and 619 Squadrons each lost six Lancasters. Among the missing was 'C-Charlie', which at 01.20 BST was hit by ground fire over Bladel Woods near Postel in Belgium and the starboard engine was set on fire. Davis said in a calm, clipped voice, 'Abandon aircraft - emergency jump jump'. He must have known his fate. In the face of death he made the greatest of all sacrifices; he kept the Lancaster steady so that his crew could bail out. His body was never recovered. 'Porky' Bowering and George Moggridge also died. Peter Knox wrote: 'We each had to confirm over the intercom that we were jumping. As I had to lift up the escape hatch I responded first. 'Air-bomber jumping'. There was no shouting, no calls for help. In a numbed state, I moved into the escape routine. All this time the pilot was holding the plane steady. This was an environment for which there had been no rehearsal. I was no longer responding like a robot to in-built commands.

The disaster which had hit us struck me. Then I recollect thanking God I had escaped and rather desperately willing that my mother and father should somehow know I was alive. Within a very short space of time I saw the explosion as our plane plummeted into the ground. I wondered if the others had got out and I shouted out the name of 'George' (Moggridge). My voice seemed to be lost in the vast dark space around me and I realised there was no possibility of making any form of human contact. It took 15 minutes to reach the ground. I passed through some clouds and hit the ground on the fringe of a pine forest. My parachute was snagged on a small tree. Luck was on my side. I was unhurt. The weather was fine. It was dark and I was in an isolated area.'

After initially receiving help from the Resistance, 'Geordie' Belshaw was captured and became a prisoner in Stalag Luft III where he was joined by 'Tag' Taylor and Tom Newberry, who is believed to have been the last person to bail out of the crashing aircraft. He landed in a tree possibly damaging his arm before he was captured by the Germans.

From the moment Peter Knox landed by parachute he followed the instructions he had been given. He got out his emergency pack, compass, knife, iron rations and water purification tablets. He then hid his parachute and any identifying clothing in a small hollow and piled pine needles on top. As instructed, he headed west following a track, there were houses nearby. He wrote: 'After an hour or two I came to a canal. There was a lock and barges tied up to the bank. Since this was the shortest night of the year, it was getting close to dawn and I was tired. I found a deep hollow on a hillock overlooking the lock and decided to make that my hiding place for the day. Only one person - a young schoolboy out for a ramble - saw me. He gave me a friendly smile and fled. He obviously did not report me because no one else came remotely close. There was no telling the most likely spot to fall into friendly hands. I knew that I only had rations for two or three days. I stuck to my plan of walking west; crossing the canal became a challenge and besides, I needed water. As dusk settled I summed up courage and walked to the lock. I watched until the keeper was well away from the little foot bridge on the rim of the lock and moved quickly across it. Once clear of the lock I scrambled down the bank.

'When it was completely dark, I set off along a track which looked reasonably deserted and kept walking away from the canal. All was quiet and I was able to skirt any houses that I saw. At the first light of dawn I came to a main road with fields on the other side. As I crossed it a group of cyclists came into sight. They looked like workers heading for a factory. When they passed me, one of them wheeled his bicycle around, stared and then re-joined the others. I just put my head down and kept walking.

'I realised that I had to find a hiding place for the day now that people were up and about. The lane I was in forked left and right and I remember thinking that this could be a decisive choice. I went left and after a few minutes saw a hedgerow bisecting a field. Because it was midsummer the hedgerow was in full leaf. I found a place with a little hollow, well hidden from view. I still had some of my rations left and do not recollect feeling hungry. It was still dry and warm. The shoes made from the cut down flying boots were fleece lined and my feet were sweating. I took my shoes off and hung up my socks on an inside branch to give them some air. I felt reasonably secure for the day and snatched some sleep.

'At some time in the middle of the day I heard a dog barking and within a few minutes it had unearthed me. A man, presumably the farmer, pushed aside the leaves. He was clearly not a German and I knew that the moment had come to identify myself. I said in French that I was aviateur anglais and he and the dog very quickly disappeared. There was nothing I could do except wait, hope and pray that he was a Dutch or Belgian patriot. I still did not know on which side of the border I had landed. It was close to evening when I heard voices and two men approached me [most likely the Cools brothers, who were members of the Balen-Resistance. They went to the Vermierdt family home in Reysberg to look after Knox, who then moved him to a stable in the meadows on the other side of the village - Schoorheide-Malou, where he stayed for 24 hours]. 'I again used my schoolboy French to explain who I was. This was a tense moment for them as well as for me. If they were going to hand me over to the Germans I would lose my freedom. If I was a German posing as an English airman to infiltrate the underground movement they stood to lose their lives. They said they were friends and told me to follow them at a distance of 50 yards or so. There was no other conversation. I obeyed their instructions and we wandered through more lanes to a farm. They pointed to a barn with a hay loft and told me to wait there. I went up a ladder and lay down in the hay. Before long another man came back with some food. He spoke some English and now the interrogation began. We

Lancaster X KB832 WL-F on 434 'Bluenose' Squadron RCAF blows up shortly after take-off from Croft on 22 March 1945 for the daylight operation to Hildesheim. Flying Officer Horace Payne RCAF took off at 1055 but the Lancaster was caught by a sudden blast of wind, which took the bomber onto the grass. Payne tried to bring the aircraft back onto the runway but he over corrected and he then closed the throttles but he was unable to avoid racing across the airfield. A tyre burst and a collision occurred involving Lancaster X KB811 SE-T on 431 'Iroquois' Squadron RCAF before KB832 came to a halt near East Vince Moor Farm. A fire started in the port engine and this spread rapidly. The crew managed to get clear and a general evacuation order was broadcast. At 11.27 hours the bomb load exploded and the force of the blast removed the roof of the farmhouse and set fire to hay and nearby buildings. Incredibly, no one was injured but it was late afternoon before the airfield was declared fit for use. (George Kercher).

were both nervous. In the event of being captured, our instructions were to tell the German interrogators nothing except our 'name, rank and number.' On the other hand we had been told that if we were lucky enough to be picked up by the Resistance movement they would have to establish our credentials and ask very direct questions to verify we were genuinely from an RAF plane. They would also want this type of information so that they could compare it to replies received from any other members of the crew they might pick up. This would help them confirm they were dealing with genuine airmen. I was asked for the number of the squadron, the airport from which we had left, the name of the pilot, the target, the type of plane and its engines, when and how we had been shot down. I was plied with questions about England and asked to name the latest popular songs. I accepted that I truly was in the hands of the underground movement and provided answers to all the questions.

'I was grateful for one thing; the interrogator did not ask to see my 'dog tags', the metal discs we wore around our necks with such basic information as name and blood group. I had taken a shower before getting into my flying gear and had left these identification markers back in a squadron bathroom.

'I slept well that night in the hay. The human contact had been reassuring and I felt that there was nothing I could do except to follow the instructions I received from the people who had found me. They brought me more food in the morning - both meals were of omelettes and fried potatoes as I recall and some form of warm drink. They tasted good. I think that I must have relaxed after the tension of the previous three days because I have only a hazy memory of my movements in the next day or two.

'I saw only the person bringing me food and rested and slept. I imagine, in retrospect, that someone was vetting my answers and planning what to do with me. I was moved away from the farm and taken to the middle of a small pine forest to be held in isolation for two or three more days. My minder [Colonel Victor Neels] was a youngish man who spoke some English. I knew now that I was in the Flemish speaking part of Belgium close to the border with Holland but little else. I was given a blanket and a waterproof sheet and food was brought to me a couple of times a day. I used the waterproof sheeting to make a type of tent under some branches and must have spent most of the time keeping out of sight. Not that I recall seeing any strangers. I do remember that there was a tremendous thunderstorm. The rain took a long time to penetrate the pines. I thought that I was lucky until I found that the water kept dripping off the lower branches for hours after the storm had passed on its way. [17]

'Within a week of being shot down I was accepted as a valid RAF escaper and on 26 June 1944. I was brought into direct contact with the Resistance movement. I was provided with a bicycle, the prime means of transport in this part of petrol starved occupied Europe and escorted to a house in a nearby town. It was strange and not a little frightening to be back among people. I think I expected to see German soldiers lurking behind every doorway. It was all very humdrum, at least on the surface. People were walking about the streets, talking on corners. I saw no one in uniform. Inside the house I met a middle-aged woman who was a central figure in the underground movement [Mrs. Jeanne (Leemans)-Schlesser - born in Dinant, Belgium - She was arrested in the summer of 1944 and sent to prisoner of war camp]. She told me I was to be held on a nearby farm before being taken south to Brussels. I learned that I was now in Geel. She said that travel had become very difficult since the invasion of Europe and because of the allied bombings of all forms of transport. Then I was introduced to the two people who were to accompany me to the farm. They were in fact the farmer's son and daughter, Jules and Dimpna Sterckx. It was all very efficient and brisk. I was to learn after the war that, tragically, this good woman (Mrs. Leemans) who helped over 100 airmen to escape was denounced to the Germans and taken to one of the prison camps. For the Belgians it was very high risk work.

'Jules, who was about my age, and his younger sister were the children of Flemish farmers. They had to escort me through streets where they were known. It was the first time they had undertaken such a mission and it was a feat of great courage on their part as I was obviously a foreigner to this region. Many dangers existed for them.

'As I came up to the farm building. I was taken inside and introduced to the farmer, Frans Sterckx, his wife, Maria Clementina Sterckx-Heyns and Marcel Maes, Dimpna's fiancé. I was also delighted to find out that there was another RAF man being held on the farm. [18]

'The farm was to be our base for the whole month of July and the first part of August. We were held there while the great battles around Normandy were being waged. The escape route for airmen through France was blocked and there was little the underground movement could do except to put us in a safe haven until the Allied forces liberated the occupied territories. This was a dangerous enough exercise for those involved. We were told that the Germans made repeated sweeps of the Belgian countryside looking for young Belgians to draft into labour gangs. If allied airmen had been found on a farm the results would have been disastrous for the farmer and his family. We not only had to be kept hidden from the Germans, it was also essential that we be kept out of sight of other farmers. This was an area of small-holdings and it was a major problem to keep two tallish men out of sight of prying eyes.

'A small recess had been built inside a pile of bricks stacked against the rear of the farm building. We had to crawl through a small opening into this recess. It was then bricked up again. Inside was a mattress and little else. Reg and I spent our nights there sleeping head to toe. Ventilation came from spaces left between the unevenly heaped bricks. It was an effective hiding place and occasionally - presumably if there was fear of a German raid - we were joined in it by Jules. That made it a tight squeeze.

'During the day we had two hiding places. One was in a broad hedgerow. There was space in the centre for quite a cosy little nook. We had room to lie down, sit up or crawl around. I cannot recall feeling cramped. The second hiding place was in the centre of one of the fields of corn. The farmer had cut out a small square and there we had more freedom to move around since the corn was at its full height and we were reasonably out of sight if we stood up with a stoop. Both Reg and I were fit and of fairly even temperament. There was no friction between us even in such close proximity.

'In the dark of the evening we were able to take some exercise, walking up and down in the vicinity of the farm house. Clearly we had to follow the advice

Lancasters at rest at East Kirkby.

of the farmer and his family as to where we spent the day and when we could approach the house in the evening. Then we could talk with them, have the occasional wash and use their lavatory. The house was blacked out and the farm dogs would bark if any strangers were approaching. We also had meals with the family at night. They were most generous in the food they gave us. Because it was a farm there were a lot of eggs and I recall a pig being killed for meat, this had to be done in secret because the Germans kept a tight grip on all food and requisitioned grain and animals to supply their forces and home markets.

'Fortunately the Germans did not approach the farm house while we were there. We were, however, very close to an airfield and we used to see German planes taking off and landing. Sometimes they flew directly over us as we squatted in the patch in the corn field and we would have to take cover in the crops. We could not identify the planes which were small but not frontline fighters. They looked to be military observation aircraft. Whatever they were, they looked sinister to us and we dived out of sight.

'We passed the day talking, sleeping and playing endless games of cards. The family had some 52-card packs and we taught one another the games we knew. 'Chinese' and 'Miss Milligan' were favourites. We discussed our families and our upbringing and what we planned to do after the war. We tried to learn a little Flemish from a grammar book but not very seriously. We did, however, pick up the words of *Lillie Marlene* which was the popular song of the moment. Our main contact was with Jules. He gave us news about the progress of the war. Generally we were in a state of limbo and one day drifted into another. The weather remained mainly fine and warm but one night there was a tremendous thunder storm. We all gathered in the main room of the farm house. I sensed that as farmers living close to nature there was genuine fear of the lightning and thunder which seemed to be all around us. No damage was done and the crops survived.

'As the summer progressed the corn had to be harvested. We were gradually losing our most secure cover. Somewhere in the Resistance movement the decision was taken that we would have to be moved. The family must have been relieved but they did not in any sense hustle us out. We were taken in to their main room and given a drink when one of the underground workers came to tell us the plans. When the day came for us to go, they all gathered bravely outside the house to bid us farewell.

'Our move was from the countryside to Turnhout and we had to make the journey of several miles on bicycles. Our guide was a young priest. Fortunately the country through which we passed was flat. The muscles in our legs were in poor condition after the six weeks of inactivity and pedalling the bikes was hard work. We were taken by back routes and had to cross a canal using a footbridge by a lock. A few minutes before we arrived at the lock we saw RAF fighter planes diving down to attack barge traffic on the canal. We could see people gathering by the lock and the priest decided it was too dangerous to proceed. We turned back and took a different route feeling rather relieved that we had not been at the lock a few minutes earlier and shot at by our own planes.

Turnhout was a fair sized town and it was a strange experience to be riding through streets with people shopping and going about their business. The priest took us to 80 Kwakkelstraat where we were to be held for a few days before being taken to Brussels. Care was taken about our entry. The woman who was to look after us had a flat on the second or third floor of the house. We had to get rid of the bikes and get through the front door as quickly and as casually as possible. Our new minder was in her late 30s or early 40s. She was quite tall and on the thin side. [Mrs. Zosine Emilienne Verstraeten]. Her husband [François Verstraeten] was a soldier in the Belgian army and had been made a prisoner of war. A city woman, she was intelligent, kind and had a good sense of humour. She was a fluent French speaker, although Turnout was very much a Flemish town. Reg and I were told that our stay was to be short and that we would be moved to Brussels as soon as the necessary arrangements could be made. We never ventured out into the street but could move freely around the flat which had two bedrooms and a sitting room.

'It was decided that we should move singly to Brussels and after a very few days Reg left. I followed a couple of days later. During that time two US airmen were brought into the town by the underground. They knew no French and I had to translate a message to them prepared by one of the Resistance people. I cannot recall much of the text but I do recall that it urged them to be patient and explained what was being done for them. Subsequently I met them for a few minutes. They were gunners from a Flying Fortress which had been shot down a few days previously and were having trouble in coming to terms with their predicament because of communication difficulties. I was able to reassure them that they were in good hands but could do little for one of the pair who said that 'my dawgs (feet) are killing me.' He had been given a pair of shoes that were far too small for him. (Probably Captain Griffith and Sgt Daniel Cargill shown as having stayed at Kwakkelstraat at same time as Peter Knox).

'The trip to Brussels via Antwerp was my first contact with people outside the narrow circle of the Resistance friends. A middle aged man escorted me by train. I huddled by the window and he sat beside me so that no one could talk to me - we were in one of those trains with little compartments with long interfacing benches each holding five or six people. The train became quite crowded but the journey was uneventful. There were no searches, no inspectors and no talkative neighbours. At one point we halted in the countryside close to a German military camp and I could see the soldiers moving around. It was my first real sighting of Germans in person, other than the pilots we used to see in their planes when they flew over the farm.

'In Brussels I was taken from the station to a cafe and there I was handed over to another man to be taken by bus to the house in the heart of the city where we were to be held. There I was reunited with Reg who had also made the transfer safely. This did not always happen. After Brussels was liberated and we were freed I spoke to an RAF man who had travelled like me to Brussels from Antwerp. His escort, a middle aged man, had handed him over to the Germans. Fortunately for him the Germans left him behind when the Allied armies entered Brussels. The escort must have been a spy who worked for both sides. I have often wondered if we had shared the same escort and I had been one of those he passed along the underground chain to sustain his credibility as a Resistance fighter. Certainly the description fitted.

'On the morning of 4 September it was clear that the Germans had withdrawn and the city was about to be liberated. The streets were thronged with people and Reg and I joined them early on. We stood in the main avenue as the tanks and armoured cars of a Guards Regiment drove in. It was a wonderfully happy scene and we joined in the chorus of welcome, cheering and waving at the soldiers. When they stopped and took up positions by the roadside we had a word with them. It was all very disciplined. At one point a rumour swept the town that there had been an armistice and the war was over. People danced and sang. The Guards officers ordered their men to stay by their vehicles and not to join in the celebrations. Soon the rumour subsided and we had the reassuring sight of the troops 'brewing up'.

'Reg and I were anxious to find someone to report to. We were directed to an area on the outskirts of the town which the RAF had taken over. Light planes were using it as a landing strip. We trailed out there hoping to hitch a lift back to

England. The sentries told us this was forbidden and that the Army would look after us. It had a section detailed to round up people like ourselves. Clearly they had to be careful. We were dressed in civilian clothes and could have been spies or saboteurs. The city, though jubilant, was tense. There were many frightened people who had collaborated with the Germans.

'By the next day the British Army was in full command of the city and had requisitioned the main hotels. It was not long before we were directed to a reception centre and made contact with the military personnel with responsibility for looking after escaping prisoners of war. Airmen like Reg and I who had been shot down and evaded capture and, presumably, agents and spies and others with a call on Allied protection. After some form of preliminary vetting we were accepted as genuine and given a room in a leading hotel [the Metropole in Brussels]. We were fed and one of the officers kindly gave us champagne taken from German stores. Other airmen straggled in but none that I knew. In the lobby of the hotel late in the evening I saw a war correspondent with Australian flashes on his shoulder. I asked him if he knew whether there was anybody from my father's paper, the Melbourne *Argus*. The next morning I managed to find Geoff Hutton, an old friend. It was quite an emotional moment because I thought that now I could let my parents know that I was alive and well. In fact, it was not as easy as it seemed. There were strict rules on the release of information about anyone who was officially a 'casualty'. The news that I was alive would eventually arrive on the desk of the Melbourne *Argus* early on Saturday morning 9 September. My mother and father were at their Woodend weekend home 50 miles outside Melbourne. The sub-editor on duty woke them up with the news. I don't think there was much sleep in Woodend that night.

'For Reg and I and the other airmen in the hotel there was a wait of a day or two before arrangements could be made to get us back to England. The RAF would not fly us back from Brussels and we had to be transported by Army trucks to Paris. We joined a long convoy of vehicles on a rather wearisome journey. We were all, I think, suffering a reaction from the euphoria of the preceding days. We spent a night in Paris and then we were flown in a Dakota of RAF Transport Command to an airport somewhere on the outskirts of south London. The pilot had a nervous bunch of passengers. For all 30 or so of us our previous flight had ended with a parachute jump. For the RAF men it was a homecoming. For me it was a stop on the way back to Australia.

'I spent several days in London going through the process of being re-incorporated into the RAAF. It was all very matter of fact and routine. There was no such thing as counselling. I had to have a basic medical, collect my mail and recover my own effects. It was an eerie experience going out to Uxbridge, to a building where all the possessions of missing airmen were held. It was a soulless, depressing place with row after row of cubicles holding kitbags, uniforms and the few personal belongings we carted around with us. In London, I was briefed on the fate of the crew. I also learned that our squadron had been decimated on the night we were shot down. Half the planes had not come back. The official records show that it was a disastrous operation for the RAF as a whole. A total of 127 Lancasters were sent on the raid and 41 were lost, about a third. It was the highest percentage loss suffered by Lancasters in one night during the three years

Escape photos of Peter Knox.

in which they operated (March 1942 to May 1945). Equally sadly the RAAF records showed that by September, eight of the nine other Australian bomb-aimers I had trained with had been shot down. Some were prisoners of war. Others had disappeared with their crews. During my time in England I visited the families of the British crew members and later the relatives of 'Porky' Bowering on my return trip to Australia.

'Immediately the war was over, I established contact with Jules, the son of the Belgian farmer who had harboured me, and with the lady from Turnhout. Jules was interested in emigrating to Australia and my father offered to help him. He never came. He went to the Belgian Congo and was tragically killed in a motor car accident in Kenya in 1957. His sister Dimpna and Marcel married. Mrs. Verstraeten, our kind friend from Turnhout, was reunited with her husband and her letters indicated she had settled back into normal domestic life.'

On 17 November 1945 Peter Knox married Monica Newcombe an English WREN who had been sent to Australia on troop ship on active duty with the Women's Royal Navy, at Newman College Chapel, Melbourne University. They later had nine children. Peter Knox died on 21 May 1998 in Kent.

Footnotes for Chapter 12

17 Victor Neels had taken Peter Knox to Iemert - to the home of Neel's aunt Mrs. Josephine Gombeer who married Leo Timmermans where Knox was hidden in the woods, in a place where there were also escaped Russian PoWs. Four days later Neels took Peter Knox to Mrs. Jeanne Leemans-Schlesser in Geel.

18 Flight Sergeant Reg Brookes, the navigator on Lancaster I LL887 HW-H 100 Squadron, also aged about 20, had been shot down on 22/23 April returning from a raid on Düsseldorf.

Chapter 13

J-Johnny

Do not despair
for Johnny head in the air
He sleeps as sound
as Johnny underground.
Cast out no shroud
for Johnny head in the cloud
And keep your tears
for him in after years
Better by far
Johnny the bright star
To keep his head
and see his children fed
John Pudney

It snowed on Sunday 2 January 1944. At Metheringham 26-year old Flying Officer Harold 'Johnny' Johnson, air bomber on Flying Officer Vic Cole's crew on 106 Squadron learned that having just returned from an eight-hour round trip to the Big City when Berlin was raided by 421 Lancasters and 29 Lancasters were lost that they were 'on' again that night. They were one of the 'gen crews' at Metheringham, having flown 25 trips since their first on 9 July 1943. Vic Cole, who came from Farnham in Surrey, had been employed by Shell before the war. 'Johnny' Johnson had been born in Stepney where his father was a cycle maker and plumber for the London County Council and had joined the Metropolitan Police in 1937. PC Johnson and another constable tried to enlist as pilot trainees and fight in the Spanish Civil War, which they thought would be over by the time they had completed training, but news of their proposed venture reached Sir Philip Game the Police Commissioner and they were summoned to Scotland Yard where they were suitably admonished. Game was ready to discharge them from the Police Force but they remained in the force. When war was declared in September 1939 'Johnny' was stationed at Rochester Row Police station. He could not volunteer for the RAF because policemen were 'reserved occupation' and on Saturday 24 August 1940 he was on duty in Downing Street when the first raid on London took place. He saw many things during the Blitz. In Hyde Park one night he came across Morag a prostitute who he had arrested once before. She was screaming. 'She lay there with a dead body beside her. When she appeared at the inquest the Coroner asked her if the deceased had given her any indication that he was dying. Morag said that he grunted once or twice. 'I thought he was coming but he was going' she said.'

Finally, in 1942, when policemen could be considered for aircrew, Johnny was selected for pilot training. The medical was at the Recruiting Centre at Lord's Cricket ground in the famous Long Bar with its trophies. All the recruits stood in line and were ordered 'shirts up - trousers down' as the MO stood ready with a stick. Suddenly a Cockney voice bawled out, 'Arry, if he gives you that bloody cup, you've won!'

'Johnny' was posted to St. Andrews in Scotland. Vendla, to whom he was engaged, came to visit him with the intention of arranging their wedding but on her return to London she broke off their engagement and returned her ring. 'Johnny' was sent to Canada and to RAF De Winton just outside Calgary for pilot training, where on a clear day the snow capped peaks of the Canadian Rockies are visible about a hundred miles away. 'The lovely family's who with other farming families, arrived each Saturday at the station's main gates inviting us to spend the weekend with them. I was invited to stay with a family. They were wonderful. So was the daughter! Enough said! It turned out that they were the aunt and uncle of my ex girlfriend Vendla, who they said, had married! In Toronto I traced my mother's sister and her family. One night, after celebrating with my cousins the car we were travelling in went over a cliff and landed upside down. We all got out unhurt but the car was a write off. My flying career was almost over before it had begun!'

'Johnny' completed just over eleven hours dual at 15 EFTS (Elementary Flying School) on the Miles Magister and in March, a further 41.10 hours on the de Havilland Tiger Moth and PT Stearman at 31 EFTS De Winton near Calgary - a one-horse town - before flying 30.35 hours solo. At 35 EFTS Estevan, Saskatchewan in May 'Johnny' completed a further 26.20 hours dual but he

Lancasters on 106 Squadron at Metheringham setting out for Frankfurt on 22 March 1944 when 816 aircraft including 620 Lancasters were dispatched. 106 lost one crew from the 26 Lancasters that failed to return from the operation.

'washed out' because he could not judge height during landings. On 1 July he returned to the Reception Centre at Moncton in New Brunswick for regrading as an air bomber. His training began at No.7 Bombing and Gunnery School at Paulson, Manitoba, eight miles from Dauphin the nearest town and this was followed by further training at No.7 Air Observer School at Portage La Prairie just outside Winnipeg. 'Johnny' passed out and in November promotion to Sergeant and then Pilot Officer followed within a week of each other.

'The journey home in the *Queen Elizabeth* was not as comfortable as one would expect from a luxury liner. The sleeping accommodation was in three tier bunks erected in the 'state rooms'. We had two meals per day; breakfast and dinner. Here we scored. As officers, stewards waited on us. Our steward came from Ramsgate, my home town. He looked after us by providing me with a large bag full of bacon rolls each morning because our very next meal was in the evening. There were no seating arrangements. You used your life jacket to sit on. Officers were utilised on aircraft recognition which helped to break up a rather boring day. Our speedy, zigzag course saw us home without incident and we landed safely at Greenock. We, the officers, were all sent on leave. I went home to Ramsgate, where, during my school days I used to sneak down to the River Stour and swim naked. Sometimes I would borrow a master's bike and cycle to Reculver Towers and swim in the sea. Just before I left school I was placed in Isolation hospital at Eastry in Kent for four weeks suffering from diphtheria. I was the only patient in the ward with a smashing nurse in charge! My brother was a publican and I was in his pub one evening when there was an explosion in the restaurant next door. All the contents of the downstairs seemed to now be in the street. I got through to the kitchen where I found the owner injured and unconscious. He was a big man and I was able to get him out on to the road. The ambulance staff took over, the fire brigade attended and I slipped off for a pint! The local newspaper made a bit if a meal of it but I refused to let them take it any further. I'd seen a lot worse than this and had done more in the way of rescue duty during the London Blitz.'

On 28 January 1943 at 19 OTU Kinloss in Scotland 'Johnny' crewed up on Whitleys on 'F' Flight. On 28 April his crew was posted to 10 OTU at St Eval where they performed six operational sweeps in the Atlantic on Whitleys armed with mines, searching for elusive U-boats. Each flight had a duration of nine plus hours but they did not count as operations, merely 'training flights'! On 2 June the crew was posted to 1654 Conversion Unit and four days later they joined 106 Squadron at Syerston six miles North-West of Newark, Nottinghamshire. 'Johnny' had soon formed the opinion that there was not a better pilot anywhere than Vic Cole. 'Vic always went in as high as he could and would then glide the Lancaster home. Nine times out of ten we would be first back.' The rest of the crew included Alfie Bristow the navigator, Bill Haig the WOp/AG, Eddie McColn, the 'excellent' flight engineer and Malcolm 'Parky' Parkinson the always alert rear gunner.

Fatigue mixed with anger caused severe rumblings and ructions at briefings on many stations in Bomber Command. Once again the target on the night of 2/3 January 1944 was Berlin again. And there were to be no diversions. A long, evasive route was originally planned but this was changed to an almost straight

Johnny' Johnson married WAAF Enid Thorpe who was from Norwich, on 28 March 1944. Enid was in charge of the Officers' Mess at Syerston and 'Johnny' always received large helpings of eggs and bacon! However, he had not asked his Station Commander's permission to marry and he threatened 'Johnny' with a Court Martial. Apparently an officer marrying a corporal was not the 'done thing'. 'Johnny' fought his corner and said that he could give him his discharge papers because the Met Police would welcome him back with open arms. Instead, having completing 28 ops and his first tour he was posted south to Skellingthorpe where he flew further ops on 61 Squadron. Enid was posted north.

in, straight out route with just a small 'dog leg' at the end of it to allow the bombers to fly into Berlin from the north-west, to take advantage of a strong following wind from that direction. It would be another midnight take-off and runways would have to be cleared of snow to allow 383 Lancasters, Mosquitoes and Halifaxes to take off. At Metheringham, where 106 Squadron had moved to in November 1943, Vic Cole's crew climbed aboard 'G-George' for the trip to the 'Big City'. The weather was foul throughout and cloud contained icing and static electricity up to 28,000 feet but clearer conditions were expected at the target.

'On approaching Hannover' recalls 'Johnny' Johnson 'with the cloud we were in thinning, 'Parky' Parkinson ordered Vic to 'corkscrew starboard'. Without hesitation he carried out this operation but not before all hell broke out. We were under attack by a Me 110, which had come out of the cloud with us and was underneath us. We were an easy target and he opened fire with his Schräge Musik guns. He missed the bombs but we were holed everywhere and one or more shells must have hit the No.2 tank in the port wing. The jettison toggle dropped out and so did all the petrol but there was no fire. Next Vic called out 'Prepare to abandon aircraft - I can't get this bastard out of the dive.' I jettisoned the escape hatch but the 'G' force took over and I could not move. I knew that I was going to die and in that terrifying moment I had a vision of my Mum and Dad together with my fiancée Enid. We were circling to such a degree that we were more or less transfixed but as a last resort Vic put the auto pilot in and it pulled the aircraft out and his corkscrew tactics lost the Me 110. We slowly levelled out at 6,000 feet before beginning a slow climb and Vic ordered the bombs to be jettisoned. I said 'No' - we've got a 4,000lb 'cookie' on board and we were too low. I would take a chance on 8,000 feet but I was not about to do so at 6,000 feet. We finally dropped the 'cookie' and the rest of the bombs at 10,000 feet and I had remembered to fuse them.

'Next 'Parky' Parkinson called out, 'Skipper we're on fire at the back.' The WOp/AG was belting out 'Mayday', 'Mayday'. I got a fire extinguisher and climbed over the main spar but there was no smoke and the interior light was on. I could see that the rear door was open. John Harding the mid-upper gunner had bailed out! We found out much later that he broke his ankle on landing and was captured. Eddie McColn estimated that we had less than an even chance of making it back to base but Vic decided to try and get us home. Alfie Bristow quickly assessed a heading for base and I went up into the mid upper turret as Vic knew we would probably be attacked on the way home. We came back fairly low over the North Sea. We couldn't afford to ditch because the back door was open, all the hatches were gone and we were full of holes. Everything was wide open for water to come in. We were very fortunate that we were not attacked again. Vic flew very carefully, hit the Lincolnshire coast and flew straight to Syerston. We landed and as we taxied off the runway all four engines stopped! The first to get to us were our overworked, underpaid, seldom mentioned ground crew - God bless them - with the blood wagon not far behind. But we didn't need him.

'Next day the station commander sent for Vic and he wanted to know why he hadn't continued to the target! At that moment the engineering officer came in and told the Group Captain that our Lancaster had been SOC - it had a broken back.'

The operation on Berlin - the 'Big City' on the night of Friday/Saturday 24th March 1944 was 'the scariest time' recalls 'Johnny' Johnson. We were on our way back from Berlin when the bomb aimer said he could see a light in the sky and there was a Me 110 crossing in front of us. I went into the front turret and the mid-upper turned his turret round that way. Obviously the fighter saw us and soon got onto our tail. 'Parky' took over control of the aircraft - once the rear gunner is shooting at an aircraft he directs the pilot. All we heard from 'Parky' was: 'Keep her straight and level, skipper.'

'The gunners wanted an even platform. It was all right for him, but just sitting there was scary. It was like waiting to be shot down. I thought 'This is it!' On went my parachute and it seemed ages before I heard, 'Keep her like that.'

'As soon as it was in range, there was the noise of six machine guns in unison followed by, 'It's on fire, dive starboard.'

'When we levelled out, we saw the two bail out and the skipper waved to them as they were going down. Because there were no other witnesses we were only given a 'possible' and not 'aircraft destroyed'. More or less we attacked it, rather than it attacked us - very lucky. In all, we would go to Berlin twelve times, dodging the massive banks of searchlights, the AA shells and night fighters, the latter paying more attention to us than was healthy - usually on the way home.'

On 28 March 'Johnny' Johnson married WAAF Enid Thorpe who was from Norwich. Enid was in charge of the Officers' Mess at Syerston and 'Johnny' always received large helpings of eggs and bacon! However, he had not asked his Station Commander's permission to marry and the Group Captain threatened 'Johnny' with a Court Martial. Apparently an officer marrying a corporal was not the 'done thing'. 'Johnny' fought his corner and said that the Wing Commander could give him his discharge papers because the Met Police would welcome him back with open arms. Johnny had completed 28 ops and his first tour with the award of the DFC. On 5 April the Group Captain posted 'Johnny' south to Skellingthorpe where he flew further ops on 61 Squadron with Flight Lieutenant Hamilton. Enid, meanwhile, was posted north!

On 4 June 'Johnny' joined 83 Squadron at Coningsby for training for 'Tiger Force', the planned aerial assault on Japan which never took place after USAAF B-29 Superfortresses dropped the atomic bombs on Hiroshima and Nagasaki and Japan surrendered unconditionally.

On 6 May 1946 'Johnny' was released from the RAF at Uxbridge and he returned to the Police Force. He and Enid eventually settled in Norwich where he retired with the rank of Sergeant in November 1967.

Chapter 14

'Bill'

Terry Owen

On Wednesday 5 July 1944 HM King George VI, Queen Elizabeth and the Princess Elizabeth toured RAF Mildenhall before holding an investiture. The occasion made a big impression on 22-year old Sergeant 'Bill' Matthews, flight engineer on Pilot Officer Matthew Michael Golub RCAF's crew on 15 Squadron. The young man from Bow, Mile End had been an enthusiastic cyclist and often cycled to Newmarket to take part in 25 mile cycle races and then cycled home to Mile End again afterwards. At the age of 15, he cycled on his own to the Isle of Wight for a week's camping holiday! After leaving school with a glowing school report he had joined a company in Finsbury Square in the City as a trainee book keeper and accountant. He was called up by the RAF and served initially as a flight mechanic but though he had promised his mother that he would not volunteer for air crew, after a time he did just that! Late that Wednesday evening Bill wrote a letter to his parents about the Royal visit and that all being well, he would be home on leave on the following Tuesday. At 22:59 hours Bill joined the other members of Golub's crew and they took off in T-Tommy. The night was clear and there was a bright moon when the Main Force left England. Golub's crew were part of a force of 542 aircraft of four groups - 321 of them Lancasters - detailed to bomb two flying-bomb sites and two storage sites at Wizernes in Northern France. Another 154 Lancasters of 1 Group hit the main railway area at Dijon and all aircraft returned safely. The V-1 sites were hit and at Wizernes 81 Lancasters dropped mixed loads of 11 1,000lb American-made semi-armour piercing bombs and four 500 pounders from 8,000 feet after marking by five Mosquitoes but three Lancasters were lost without trace and another was brought down by flak. At Mildenhall there was no word from T-Tommy. Another crew saw LL890 get caught in searchlights as it went out across the Channel near Dunkirk after dropping its bombs on the site at Wizernes. All seven of the crew, including Bill Matthews, 'who would not change his job for the world', were dead.

When my grandmother was about 17 years old (so that would be around 1911), she visited a fortune teller. The fortune teller told her that there would be two very bad years in her life: 1944 and 1976 and both would be bad in connection with the initial 'W'. At the time she joked about this as 1976 would mean that she would still be alive aged 82, which in 1911 was a very good age! She later married my grandfather, William and then also named their son, William, my mother's brother. In July 1976, my grandfather, William, died. 1976 had also been a terrible year for my grandmother, as she was knocked down by a car in December 1975, sustaining broken bones in both legs, above and below each knee and a broken arm. So she spent much of the year in hospital until the summer when she returned home, only for my grandfather to then die in his sleep on the night of Wednesday/Thursday 7th/8th July 1976.

Sergeant William Victor Matthews was killed on the night of Wednesday/Thursday 5th/6th July 1944 on Lancaster LL890 on 15 Squadron at Mildenhall, after attacking the V1 rocket sites at Wizernes in northern France. Bill was reported 'Missing' and no body or wreckage was ever found. After he went missing, my grandmother became interested in spiritualist church mediums. A neighbour called Mrs Presland had also lost her son and had started going to a medium, which gave my grandmother the idea. So she booked a meeting with one at the Marylebone spiritualist church in the Russell Square area of London. Her first visit was alone and she deliberately did not give away any clues as to who she had lost. For example, she did not wear her RAF broach. The medium warned that her face would change as the session started as her spiritual guide would take over and sure enough it did change to a distorted appearance unlike that of the medium's normal expression. The medium immediately said that there is was a terrible roar, like engines. As the session progressed, she went on to say there was a lot of heat and at this point the medium began to physically sweat! She concluded by describing how the person (Bill) had been hit twice, once in the head and once in the thigh and that his final thoughts had been with my grandmother.

Subsequently, my mother decided to go to a group spiritualist session with my grandmother, but they decided to go in separately to see if the medium would realise that they were together. Again both witnessed the medium's face show a distorted change and then after some other messages to others within the assembled group, the medium said to my mother that there was an airman standing behind her with his hand on her shoulder. The airman was smiling broadly and revealing a missing tooth on the side. The medium also said that the airman was holding his other arm out across the circle of people present, towards where my grandmother was sitting! At this point the medium asked if she and my mother were together. It was also true that in life, Bill did have one tooth missing on the side, which was only visible when he smiled broadly!

At another visit to a medium, my grandmother was told that she must stop praying for his return, because he could not return and that it was only stopping him from moving on.

For the birthday of my mother, Irene Owen, in July 2010, we had been thinking of taking my parents somewhere for the weekend, since we often find that it is near impossible to think of anything that she wants or needs, as a birthday present. But the question was where to take her? But then my colleague, Stewart Jenkinson, mentioned the Lancaster bomber taxi runs at the Lincolnshire Aviation Heritage Centre at RAF East Kirkby in Lincolnshire. Stewart is ex-Army Air Corps, now in his sixties, with a strong interest in the history of the RAF and of World War II. We thought this was a superb idea, since my mother had lost her brother Bill in 1944 on a Lancaster bomber. Also it tied in nicely with another idea we'd had, namely to stay at the Petwood Hotel nearby, which had been the home of 617 Dam Busters' Squadron during WWII. So we booked both as a surprise weekend away. Right up until moments before we arrived at East Kirkby, my mother still had no idea when we were going and was guessing it might have something to do with a horticultural event!

We all found RAF East Kirkby a fascinating place with great atmosphere. Watching the Lancaster taxi run and subsequent guided tour inside the plane was a superb birthday treat for my mother and thoroughly interesting for my father, Conrad and my wife, Natalya and I. But little did we know at this point that the best was yet to come.

Stewart had recommended that we visit the control tower museum and this we did after we had watched the first taxi run and completed the tour of the plane. We wandered the rooms packed with models and information and found ourselves a little split up. And then behind me out near the top of the stairs I heard my mother's voice shriek 'Conrad! Conrad! ... it's my brother!'

As my mother had waited for us all to appear from various rooms, she had loitered at the top of the museum stairs. And there on the wall above the stairs was a life size blow up of a photo of King George VI and Queen Elizabeth and Princess Elizabeth, meeting the air crew at RAF Mildenhall on 5th July 1944. And at the right hand end of the photo was a full length image of Bill! She had not known of the existence of this picture in 66 years.

Shortly after this photo had been taken, Bill wrote his last letter home and then went out on a night raid to bomb the V1 rocket launching site at Wizernes in north France, on the night of 5th/6th July 1944. He never returned from this mission and neither his body, nor wreckage of his flight, were ever found.

A Royal visit to Mildenhall on 5 July 1944 when crews in 15 and 622 Squadrons operated from the station. Far right is Sergeant Bill Matthews and next left, 37-year old Sergeant C. A. Canday, both of whom were KIA that night when Flying Officer Matthew Michael Golub RCAF and his crew on 15 Squadron were shot down and lost without trace. (via Fred Coney)

Obviously my mother was shocked at seeing this photo and indeed we all were. She commented on how tired Bill looked. It was such a shame that my grandmother, Jayne 'Jennie' Matthews, who died in 1997 aged 103 years, had never known of the photo's existence.

But it had certainly been a special weekend away for my mother, to have discovered it at this point. However, despite taking many photos of the picture on the wall, the hunt was now on to discover where on earth this photo had come from. We asked the team at RAF East Kirkby about it, but nobody could remember where it had come from and that included the two elderly Panton brothers, owners of the base and their Lancaster bomber itself. So on return, I started contacting many archive sites, including the Imperial War Museum, the RAF Museum Hendon, Getty Images and Pathé News etc. But unfortunately we drew a blank. The most promising moment was viewing some archive Pathe News footage of the Royal visit to RAF Mildenhall, which must have been filmed at the same moment as the photo was taken. The rolling newsreel panned along the same set of faces as in the photo and got to the chap standing beside where we knew Bill would have been standing, but then cut! Such a shame.

So as Christmas 2010 approached we had still not traced the origin of the photo and had virtually given up the search. And that was where my colleague Stewart Jenkinson once again came to the rescue and in rather spooky circumstances.

Stewart had a day off to go Christmas shopping with his wife and daughters in Basingstoke and he found himself waiting outside a woman's clothes shop for his wife and daughters to finish inside. Opposite was Waterstones bookshop and so he wandered in to kill some time. Before him was a display of books and being interested in military books, a book on Lancaster bombers immediately caught his eye. The book was 'Legend of the Lancasters' by Martin W Bowman.

He picked up the book and let it flop open at random and to his (and my) amazement it fell open at the Royal visit to Mildenhall photo with Bill that we had found at East Kirkby! It was an extraordinary coincidence. And now we had a reference, as the photo was credited to a man named Fred Coney.

Stewart was familiar with Martin Bowman's books, several of which he already owned. So at that moment, he phoned the office to get hold of me and gave me details of the book, which I immediately ordered (my mother's Christmas present instantly sorted).

A little internet searching on Fred Coney told me that he was from Mildenhall and had served on 15 Squadron during the war. Sadly, it also told me that Fred had died aged 94 on 2nd August 2010, just after our visit to East Kirkby.

But I decided to contact Pen & Sword publishers, to ask them to pass my request for information on the photo of Bill, on to the author Martin Bowman, which they were happy to do. And very shortly thereafter I received a phone call from Martin. We had several long chats and I was able to gratefully obtain a good resolution copy of the photo, which my mother now has framed in 15 Squadron RAF colours, on her hall wall (another present thereby sorted!).

I was also happy to assist Martin with further material of interest to him, such as a copy of Bill's last letter, a copy of his log book and some other photos etc.'

Chapter 15

What The Stars Foretell

Where are the Aussies, the sports and the cobbers,
Talking of cricket and sheilas and grog,
Flying their Lancs over Hamburg and Stettin
And back to the Lincolnshire wintertime bog?
Lancasters **Audrey Grealy**

'The imponderables are legend, the mystery inscrutable. It is never likely to be solved'
wrote Ralph Barker in the *Daily Express,* 1983. The mysterious survival of 19-
year-old air gunner Jack Cannon had its origins not in the flak-infested skies of
Nazi Germany but in the picturesque Sussex village of Hellingly near Hailsham
on an October night in 1944. There, in a 17th century house alongside the
churchyard which the villagers and Cannon himself, had reason to believe was
haunted, his future was dramatically foretold.

Cannon and two other members of his crew, Australians like himself, had
spent a hectic leave in war-torn buzz-bombed, blacked-out, intensely exciting
London. They had stayed at the Waldorf, eaten at the brassiere off Piccadilly
Circus and met old mates at the 'Codgers' off Fleet Street and the 'Coal Hole'
in the Strand. When it came to theatres the inevitable favourites were the girls
at the Windmill. Giving scant thought to tomorrows that might never be, they
lived far beyond their means as an NCO aircrew and before their leave was
over they ran out of money.

'I know what we'll do.' said Cannon... We'll go down and see Evadne.'

'Evadne who?'

'Evadne Price.'

It was a name to conjure with. She was a remarkable woman. Then 48, but
as dark-eyed, black-haired, gipsy-looking and vivacious as ever she was actress,
playwright, novelist, columnist, mystic, astrologer, spiritualist and seer. She
had recently had a play running in the West End. But the majority of her public
knew her for her *What the Stars Foretell* feature in a national newspaper.

Jack Cannon had been a cub reporter on the Melbourne *Argus* before joining
up and his news editor Keith Attiwill had asked him to look up Evadne when
he got to England and see how she was. She had married Attiwill's brother, but
he had been reported missing killed at Singapore. Evadne though had never
believed he was dead. 'I can see him in a small room on an island,' she had
said. This had proved to be true. He was indeed on an island, kept in solitary
confinement for two years.

Evadne was living at Church Path, Hellingly in the old house alongside the
churchyard known as Prior's Grange once said to have been inhabited by

The 'Coal Hole' in the Strand. (Author)

monks. Cannon was convinced they inhabited it still. Church Path, with its cottages fronting on the churchyard was an intimate, tranquil place but Cannon found it creepy in a *déjà vu* sort of way. Evadne Price however, obviously loved it. He had visited her first during training. When he arrived he had looked so youthful to Evadne and his dark blue Royal Australian Air Force uniform was so unfamiliar to her that she thought he was some sort of Boy Scout. From then on she appointed herself as his English aunt.

Now, with their pockets virtually empty, the three improvident Australians took the train from Victoria to Hailsham and made their way out to Prior's Grange. Hellingly was close to buzz-bomb alley and several bombs had fallen prematurely nearby. As a stimulus to morale, Evadne Price was putting on one of her plays that night in the church hall and the three Australians went along to see it. The play opened with a bang. The bang was a buzz- bomb, which fell a mile away, just after the curtain went up. Evadne Price, who was playing the housemaid, entered, ostensibly to answer the telephone, but the effects man missed his cue. At that moment the bomb exploded. 'Was that the telephone?' asked Evadne. After that the play never looked back.

A party at Prior's Grange wound up the evening. When the other guests left Evadne asked Cannon to stay and help with the dishes. His fellow Australians were packed off to bed. It seemed that Evadne had something to tell him. But there was a long silence before she spoke. 'In a fortnight's time,' she said at length, those two boys upstairs are going to be killed. I can see you coming out of a wood with your face bleeding and with an injured leg, walking with the aid of a stick.'

'That's great,' said Cannon dully. 'Thanks very much.' Within 48 hours they would be back on ops over Germany.

'I'm so certain of it,' continued Evadne, 'that I've written to your adjutant naming myself as your English next of kin.'

Bomb-aimer, Flight Sergeant Wren Stobo would always kiss one at the WAAFs before take-off. They always lined up to see the crews off, treating them like heroes.

A disturbed night, which he blamed on the monks, left Cannon a bit hazy next morning. He must have been having nightmares. Then he remembered the shock of Evadne's flash of clairvoyance. It had not been a dream. Later he rationalised it. They were all a bit high after the show. Tongues had been loosened. Evadne had been right about her husband, but professional stargazers and psychics were wrong as often as they were right. By the time they got back to 460 Squadron RAAF at Binbrook in Lincolnshire he had almost forgotten about it. Better forget about it altogether.

Cannon's had been an exclusively NCO crew until the previous month, when his pilot Dennis Richens had been commissioned. On the night of October 23 the main force of Bomber Command was detailed for an attack on the Krupps works at Essen. The target would be marked by the Path Finder Force. Among the many hundreds of bombers in the main force were 26 Lancasters on 460 Squadron. Selected crews were briefed to aim at a specific wing of the factory. Richens' crew was among them. His bomb-aimer, Flight Sergeant Wren Stobo (named after Sir Christopher) had earned a reputation for accuracy. Of Richens' seven-man crew, all were Australians except the flight engineer, Sergeant Eric Sutherland. He was a Yorkshireman. Ken Frankish, the navigator and John Treloar the radio operator had been Cannon's companions on leave.

Both were 21. Frankish, from Western Australia, was a talented cricketer who would certainly play one day for Western Australia if he survived the war. Treloar, whose father had fought with the Anzacs at Gallipoli, came from the same town as Richens. Jack Cannon occupied the mid-upper turret. The tail gunner was Dick Bergelin. Cannon was the baby of the crew, Stobo at 26 the eldest. Teased as the grandpa of the crew, he seemed old to Cannon. Stobo was a likeable eccentric, with a fund of superstitions. One of them was that he must always kiss one at the WAAFs before take-off. They always lined up to see the crews off, treating them like heroes. Sometimes, as this evening, they boarded the aircrew trucks in a flurry of banter and accompanied them out to dispersal. This didn't inhibit Stobo from performing his second superstitious rite of wetting the Lancaster's tail-wheel. Everyone watched for it and cheered as he did it.

It was a blustery autumn evening, scattering the leaves and bringing a thin, driving rain. They took off in daylight, at about half past five. Darkness would overtake them as they crossed the North Sea, providing cover when they reached enemy territory. Once clear of the English coast, Cannon and Bergelin tested their guns. On his first trip, a daylight raid on Walcheren Island, Cannon had fired at what he was warned was a FW 190 diving in to attack them. His fire was accurate and he thought he was going to start his operational career with a victory. Then he noticed the aircraft's markings. He had nearly shot down a Yankee Thunderbolt.

At night it was even more difficult. Gunners tended to shoot at anything that didn't have four engines. Cannon was always scared of blasting away at a Mosquito in mistake for a Junkers 88.

As Richens' Lancaster, 'H-Harry Two', climbed to its bombing height of 18,000 feet. Cannon switched on his electrically-heated clothing, but the temperatures in his turret was well below freezing and he couldn't get warm.

Lancaster III JA686 'K-King' on 83 Squadron blew up at Wyton on 26 November 1943 killing eight personnel and injuring four. The Lancaster had been bombed up ready for the Berlin operation that night; an electrician entered the aircraft to make final adjustments to the flare chute mechanism which contained a live and highly sensitive, magnesium flare - commonly referred to as the photo-flash, which was released with the bomb load to record the point of impact of the bombs. It was said afterwards that the photo flash slipped from the launching tube and exploded immediately, setting off the 4,000lb bomb which atomised everything within range. Included in those missing was Corporal Marion White McDowell, a popular WAAF corporal who drove the tractor (like the WAAF pictured) which pulled the bomb trolleys. John Searby recalled that he saw her quite often 'as I made my rounds, hauling the string of five or six big bombs, each onits separate trolley - turning into the hardstandings one by one where the armourers unhitched a trolley and wheeled it under the waiting bomb bay. Then off she would go to the next hardstanding to repeat the process. A pleasant girl with a cheery word for everyone and we were all very sad at her death. Her contribution and that of the ground airmen killed with her should not be forgotten. It provided an example of men and a woman killed on active service doing a vital job which everyone took for granted.

It was easy enough in these conditions, to lose concentration, but he forced himself to keep on the alert. Over the French coast they ran into a cold front, giving thick cloud up to 18,000 feet and beyond. They continued in cloud to the bomb-line. The route had been well chosen to avoid the enemy defences, and not until they were approaching Essen after two hours' flying did they meet intense flak.

The Pathfinders were less punctual than usual, but they saw the first marker, a single red flare, at 1935. This was followed by a single green flare, but no other markers appeared for seven anxious minutes. Then a red target indicator cascaded down but was soon lost in cloud. Groups of red and green flares followed, but the greens were too scattered to be of much help. The Pathfinders were having a bad night. Fixing their position as best he could, Frankish gave Richens a change of course and they left the main force and steered for their target. Even now the flak was no more than moderate and there was no sign of enemy fighters. Searchlights, too, were absent. They were carrying one 4,000lb bomb, five 1,000-pounders and six 500-pounders, plus about a thousand 4lb incendiaries. Entrusted with a special task they were determined to fulfil it.

Getting what guidance they could from the markers, they began their bombing run. Cannon, from his station on top of the fuselage, peered down and watched the black and red puffs or the flak come eddying up towards the m in deceptive slow-motion. He could smell the sulphurous stench of the flak-bursts, but there was nothing he could do about it.

They had just dropped their bombs when he saw something that looked like a red hot coal climbing into the sky towards them, lazily but inexorably. This one was going to be close. They said that when you could smell the flak you were for it. He knew now that this one had their name on it. He could still see the fiery, incandescent orb soaring towards him when oblivion came.

* * *

The rain falling through the trees dripped incessantly on the body of a man dressed in flying kit who was either unconscious or dead. The question was not resolved for many hours. Then at last the body stirred into involuntary movement. It was still some minutes before the first glimmer of consciousness. Then, reaching out into the impenetrable darkness, fingers scrabbled for the watch that was normally kept by the bedside. But there was no watch, only the dankness of rain-soaked undergrowth. Cannon had no idea where he was, but at least he knew he wasn't in bed. He was lying in a patch of damp bracken under a canopy of trees. He was not really sure whether he was dead or alive. It was all too much for his bemused brain and he slipped back into unconsciousness.

Then the raindrops, accumulating in the foliage above him before being released in larger globules, became so persistent that he stirred again. Where was he? Where did he go last night? Was he suffering from a massive hangover?

Lingering in his nostrils was the same sulphurous stench he had sniffed in his last moments of consciousness. That was the key. Memory, still blank round the edges, was coming to life at the centre. They had been sent to bomb Essen. That was it. A section of the Krupps works. Vaguely he recalled their bombing run, and that lambent ascending flame. It must have destroyed them. But where was the wreck of the Lancaster? 'What had happened to the rest of his crew? How had he escaped? At first he thought he must have bailed out, but he had no recollection of doing so. He couldn't even remember collecting his parachute pack from its stowage. He felt for his parachute harness and was puzzled to find that he didn't seem to be wearing it. Yet he had had it on in the turret. He was quite sure or that. Without it he certainly couldn't have bailed out. But why had he taken it off? Every thought that came to him only intensified his bewilderment. But one thing seemed certain. They had been shot down over, the target, and he was lying in a forest somewhere on the edge of the Ruhr. They had been due over Essen at 1930. They must have crashed soon after that. His watch, which was still on his wrist, disclosed that it was now after midnight.

Dimly he remembered from his subconscious that during his hours of oblivion he had heard shots. German guards would have seen the Lancaster come down and would be out searching for survivors. Very probably they had captured some of the crew already. Or shot them. He had to get moving. Richens had always made his crew take the escape and evasion lectures seriously, but it was an effort now to remember what they'd been told. A single phrase drummed on the membrane of his mind. Travel by night, hide by day.

Before dawn he had to put some distance between himself and the crashed Lancaster. He had no doubt that their plane must have crashed. That was just about the only thing that made sense. But which was should he head? He remembered the scarf in his escape kit, stuffed into a capacious pocket in his flying suit. Printed on the scarf was a man. The forest was now silent and there was no traffic noise in the distance. He would try to get started. He removed his collar-stud and unscrewed it; the base was a miniature compass. Then he risked striking a match. Supposing he was still somewhere near Essen? He had two choices: to go west... for Holland or south-west for Belgium. Eventually he decided to head west-south-west to try to reach the British front line.

It was an optimistic plan; rendered still more so by his instant collapse when he tried to stand up. His left leg crumpled beneath him and a head-wound which had stopped bleeding earlier reopened, oozing blood down his face. He still had to get away from his pursuers and he began, slowly and painfully to crawl like a crab through the forest. He had no clear idea whether he was scrambling away from the shots or towards them. He just had to keep moving.

The autumn was not yet sufficiently advanced to have denuded the trees and the branches above him shut out the sky. It was like dragging about in a dungeon, with orientation constantly in peril. When he lit a match and checked with his compass he found he'd been going round in circles. But for hours he kept on.

Suddenly ahead of him the tree-trunks acquired definition. Beyond them, he was sure; was an open space, where some degree of reflected light seeped through. He would be careful to keep within the sanctuary of the forest, but he might get a chance to reconnoitre the route ahead. Once or twice he still fancied he could hear the occasional rapid burst of shot, as though someone was firing a machine-gun, but he thought it was getting further away.

Reaching the edge of the forest, he was disappointed to find that dawn was being presaged by a seasonal ground-mist. There was certainly open ground ahead, but otherwise he could discern nothing. Then, rising like wraiths above the mist, the dome-like turrets of a castle stood strangely suspended in mid-air. Nothing could have looked more menacingly Teutonic and he floundered back into the forest. A place like that would be heavily guarded and he half-expected to hear the barking of guard-dogs.

Exhausted by his efforts and sick with nausea, he sank back to rest. Only one thing, he felt, could restore him: a cigarette. He inhaled the smoke avidly, hiding the glow of the cigarette under his jacket. Then he ate a malted milk tablet from his emergency food pack and felt better.

The morning fog might be a blessing. Instead of waiting for nightfall, he might get safely clear of the wood in daylight, putting a useful distance between him and the crashed plane. As first light seeped under the horizon the mists expanded, rolling around him as in some fanciful film. He almost wondered if he was in another world already. But a light drizzle; reassuringly earthy, was still falling. Now was the time to work his way into the open. Somehow he had to evolve a more practical method of propulsion. Choosing a stout piece of wood from the forest floor as a staff, he found that with its support he could just about hobble along. Thus he emerged from the forest just as Evadne Price had predicted. Keeping a hedge at his shoulder for safely, he advanced laboriously across the field. He was half-way across when, not 20 yards distant, he saw something move. He dived at once for cover into the base of the hedge. It could be some species of cattle. But he knew in his heart it was not. It was a man, mercifully facing away from him, hoeing the ground. If he waited for the man to move on, he might crouch here all day. But his cover was flimsy. When the sun came up and the mist cleared, his hiding-place would be easily revealed. He recalled another phrase from the escapers' guide. 'A man alone in a field is the best person to help you.'

Could it be true? So far as he could see the man wasn't armed. It might be worth a try. He had nothing to lose. He pulled out the card in his escape-gear which listed simple foreign expressions. He looked for 'Where am I?' and found it in German, Dutch, Flemish and French. He would try it first in German. Peering through the fog, he could still make out the ghostly outline of the farmer, as he supposed him to be. The man, intent on his hoeing, was still presenting his back to the hedge. There could be no half-measures now. If things went wrong he would try to escape through the fog. But what would he do if the man proved aggressive?

Tucked into his suede-leather flying boots was another item of escape equipment - a long-bladed sheath knife. He drew it, and then crept like a predator close to the ground. Dropping his staff and seizing the man from behind, he stubbed the tip or the knife gently but firmly into his neck. *'Wo bin ich?'* he demanded. He judged that the man was in his middle forties, about his own height. His colouring was Aryan enough, but he also had the ruddy complexion of the countryman. The man looked round in utter amazement. In doing so he caught a sidelong glimpse of an apparition. His attacker was a mixture of the madman and the macabre. His face was badly contused and blood was dripping from a wound in his head. Momentarily shocked, the man was weighing up his assailant, wondering how easily he might be overcome.

But feeling cold steel on his neck, he bided his time. Meanwhile he made no attempt to answer. Cannon tried him In French. *'Comment s'appelle ce place ici?'* When this, too, brought no response Cannon increased the pressure of his knife on the man's neck. Desperately, his voice rising to a hoarse crescendo, he reverted to his native Australian. *'Where am I, you silly old bastard?'*

Slowly, the man began to smile. His dialect was strange to Cannon, but the words he uttered were the most incredible he had ever heard.

'You be in Norfolk, lad. Over there be King's Lynn.'

For a moment Cannon stood dumbfounded. Then he reeled with stupefaction and fatigue. The man grabbed his arm and helped him across what he now saw was a lawn. The man was the estate gardener: he had been hoeing an onion bed.

Cannon was taken into the turreted castle, which he now learned was Houghton Hall, home of the Cholmondeley family. The gardener; his name was Fred Dye - sat him down before a log fire and went off to call an ambulance and fetch his wife Soon Daisy Dye was cleaning the blood off his face and examining the wound, making him tea, and cooking him a breakfast of bacon and eggs. They did not tell him they had been up half the night, trying to rescue his comrades.

He was taken to hospital at the nearby RAF station at Bircham Newton. There he was given sedatives which silenced him for the next two days. Then came the questions. All he was able to learn was that after he was knocked unconscious his crew had somehow managed to fly the crippled Lancaster back across Holland and the North Sea. Staggering under a weight or ice they were unable to avoid because they could not climb above it, they had sent an SOS and tried to reach the airfield at Bircham Newton; crashing within sight of their goal. Of the seven men on board, Jack Cannon, already unconscious, was the one whose chances seemed slimmest. In fact he was the only one to survive.

The Squadron Diary recorded the tragedy briefly. 'One aircraft, 'H-Harry

Cannon increased the pressure of his knife on the man's neck. Desperately, his voice rising to a hoarse crescendo, he reverted to his native Australian. 'Where am I, you silly old bastard?'

Two', Flying Officer D. R. G. Richens, crashed at 2156 in a field adjacent to Bircham Newton. Six men were killed and one bailed out.'

So he had bailed out after all. He had no recollection of doing so and could scarcely believe it, but he did not ask any more questions. The shock of losing his mates shut all else from his mind. It was a mystery that one day he might try to solve. Meanwhile he was grateful for the message, when he was ready to leave hospital that he was to report to Mrs K. Attiwill at Hellingly in Sussex. There, sitting in the churchyard in the late autumn sunshine he began his rehabilitation.

Twenty years later, when working as London representative of an Australian newspaper, he went back to Houghton Hall and renewed his brief wartime friendship with Fred and Daisy Dye. His visit was intended to clear up the mystery. Instead, what he was told only complicated the riddle. The Lancaster, ploughing into the wood, had hit a huge beech tree head-on. Fred Dye showed him the tree. Savaged in its upper branches by violent amputation, it still had a lopsided look that the multi-coloured autumn foliage could not hide. After the plane hit the tree there was a terrific explosion followed by a sheet of flame which spread over a large area. The flames were so brilliant that they lit up the whole picture gallery,' remembered Daisy Dye. She had one there to adjust the blackout curtains, thinking there was an air raid. 'Then came a series of smaller explosions.

'My husband and young Lord John Cholmondeley, who was on leave from the Navy raced towards the burning bomber but they were driven back by the heat. Within minutes dozens of men were on the scene, but we all knew that nobody could have survived that first explosion. For hours ammunition was

Houghton Hall (Author)

bursting and zinging out in all directions.' These were the 'shots' Cannon had heard. 'By 3 am the last of the men had gone. We went to bed worrying about the men who had died and thinking about their families.'

Again the only conclusion Cannon could come to was that he must have bailed out. But when Fred Dye took him further into the wood, he changed his mind about this once and for all. First Dye pointed to where his parachute harness had been found - high in a tree 400 yards from the wreck. Next he took him to another tree, 500 yards in a different direction, where his parachute pack, still unopened, had turned up some days later. Neither the harness nor the pack were anywhere near the spot where Dye estimated Cannon had found himself when he came to Cannon had to agree.

What about the record in the Squadron Diary? According to Dye, this must have been no more than an assumption. How else, the squadron had argued could anyone have survived? Cannon could understand his harness being torn off. But if he hadn't bailed out - and he obviously couldn't have done - why was his pack not still strapped in its rack at the time of the crash and incinerated with the rest of the plane?

'I still cannot answer these questions,' says Jack Cannon today. He can only conclude that he was either blown high through the air by the first explosion, which he believes might have been caused by a bomb - presumably one or the smaller ones - which hung up, or catapulted through the cupola of the mid-upper turret on impact with the beech tree. This would account for his head injuries.

In either case, he must have been propelled through the air for hundreds of yards before ending up, perhaps, in the arms of a leaf-laden tree which cushioned his fall. Could the parachute pack possibly have belonged to someone else in the crew? Could he, in a state of amnesia, have buried his parachute after baling out, as the escape-guide recommended them to do? It sounded plausible, but where was the parachute? In his weakened state he could not have hidden it properly. It seems possible that the injuries Cannon sustained over the target were what ultimately saved his life. Surely no living projectile could be catapulted for such a distance without mortal injury unless it was already unconscious. But this too is speculation.

Since his visit to Houghton Hall in 1964 Jack Cannon has simply accepted that his survival, in some inexplicable way, was miraculous.

Severely iced-up and unable to climb above cloud, a SOS message was received from the aircraft and PB351 was diverted to Bircham Newton, Norfolk, on return. It is believed that while the Lancaster was making a very low circuit over Bircham Newton prior to landing, it struck a tree near Houghton Hall and blew up on impact at 21.56 hours. Eric Sutherland was later buried at Shipley (Nab Wood) Cemetery, Yorkshire. The five Australians were buried at Cambridge City cemetery. Ken Frankish's headstone records, 'Farewell Ken. A good innings. Well Played.' Stobo's says, 'Loved Husband of Flo and Daddy of Frances'. Treloar has the Latin inscription, Tradidit Lampada Vitai. ('I hand on the light of life')

In May 2004 in a million to one chance the Jack Cannon story surfaced again. It was during the prelude to the celebrations for the 60th Anniversary of D-Day. Martin Bowman was invited to accompany a Channel 9 Australian TV crew and two D-Day veterans to France to film a segment for the *60 Minutes* programme. One of the D-Day veterans was 84-year old 'Bluey' Arthurs from Claremont, West Australia. He had been a Sub Lieutenant Watchkeeping officer/gunnery officer on LST 420 off Sword Beach on 6 June 1944. In all, Bluey took part in five landings - 'Husky' (Sicily), Salerno, Anzio, Normandy and Tarakan, Borneo in May 1945. In the hotel in Bayeux one night Bluey was telling some war stories and when they dried up Bowman began to relate the story of the RAAF Lancaster crew that crashed on the estate of an old Norfolk mansion. When he got to the bit about Jack Cannon being blown out of the aircraft in his turret Bluey, startled, asked, 'Who was the pilot?

From memory Bowman said, 'Ken [sic] something'.

'Bluey' leaped out of his seat and completely astonished, said, 'Ken Frankish'?

Bowman said, Yes I think it was, why?'

'Bluey' said that when his tour in Europe was up and he was waiting to return home to Australia he had gone to Kodak House (RAAF HQ) in London, where he was given a warrant to visit to an Australian squadron at RAF Binbrook. He was there on the night of 23/24 October where on the ops board the Lancaster Ken Frankish was on was rubbed out. 'Bluey' lived at 18 Walcott Street Mount Lawley, Perth. Ken Frankish lived at No.22!

'Bluey', who attended the funeral of the crew at Cambridge City Cemetery, explained that Frankish was a talented cricketer who would certainly have played for Western Australia if he had survived the war; hence the inscription on the 20 year old navigator's headstone.

After seeing action in the Med in LST's 430 and 420 I returned to the UK in late March 1944 and was able to spend a week's leave at the 10 Squadron RAAF Sunderland base in Coastal Command at Plymouth. In October 1944 I was on leave waiting for passage back to Oz and went to Kodak House and arranged to spend a week on RAAF Bomber Squadron at Binbrook. I was accompanied by another RANVR officer Fred Woolley from Brisbane.

Fred and I went to the briefing of the night's operation to Essen and after dinner went up into the control tower and watched the planes taking off on their mission. I was particularly interested because on the squadron I had met a pilot - Bill Utting with whom I had worked in Perth in civvy-street. I did not meet Ken Frankish as he had not graduated to the officers' mess. Later that evening Fred and I again went up into the control tower and watched as the planes returned and were marked off on the operations blackboard. I well remember the tension as it became apparent that two planes were very much overdue and the tower was reluctantly closed down. The next morning Mark Dray - another West Australian who was the Adjutant on the squadron - came to the cabin where Fred and I were quartered and said - 'Bluey', you come from Perth - you might know a Perth boy Ken Frankish who was killed in one of those missing planes last night' - 'Good God he lived two doors from me'.

There was another incredible coincidence in September 2004. Martin Bowman took a telephone call out of the blue from Rex Barker who was ringing after being put in touch by the Mosquito Aircrew Association. Barker wanted information about a pilot called Richens who had been killed on Mosquitoes.

Right: The headstone marking the grave of Ken Frankish (Author)

Below: The crew of Harry Two are buried at Cambridge City Cemetery. (via 'Bluey' Arthurs)

The animated conversation between two aviation authors led to a scratching of heads and it turned out that the Richins killed on Mosquitoes was Dennis Richins' brother! Bowman then related the story of Bluey Arthurs and the gravestones in Cambridge. Barker, who had never seen the graves of the crew, said that he had Stobo's watch, which has inscribed on the reverse *'from Flo and Frances'*. Sadly, Barker tearfully related that Stobo never saw his daughter before he died.

Chapter 16

An Australian in Bomber Command

David Scholes

On 26 May 1943 twenty-year-old David Scholes left Australia for the war in Europe. Scholes was born in Melbourne in 1923 and educated at Scotch College. In 1940 he quit his medical studies at Melbourne University to join the RAAR. Selected for pilot training he learnt to fly at Western Junction in Tasmania where he met his future wife Pat, gaining his wings at Deniliquin, NSW. In 1944 he was posted to England travelling via New Zealand and across America, arriving in Scotland. Then, attached to the RAF, he flew single and twin-engined aircraft day and night before beginning a tour of operations on 61 Squadron in 5 Group Bomber Command in July 1944.

'Wolverhampton is a nice little township' wrote Sergeant David Scholes on 7 July 1944 'although built all higgledy-piggledy, up and down hill. The shops are quite clean also the streets and the people seem quite nice types. I like it far better than its large neighbour, Birmingham. The pubs are quite decent as we find out tonight and the beer quite good. During the morning of Saturday 8 July rain falls and we spend our time looking through the shops. After lunch we catch the bus back to Birmingham, a very interesting drive, where we go looking for cherries and tomatoes in the market square and eventually succeed. We have tea at Darkie's place - very good too, although I get up feeling as though I could eat more! Now this sort of Darkies. To me she appears to be a very quiet innocent and plain girl. I should say she would be very old-fashioned in the things that are most modern today. However, although not striking to look at I am sure she is very good natured and decent. Obviously she doesn't know the score, but as Darkie hasn't that many more clues, they should make a fine Birmingham city couple. We catch our train to Nottingham via Derby where we find we are stranded due to our train being late and missing the connection. We sleep on the seats! A slashing little piece in green from the Services Canteen makes us some tomato sandwiches with those we bought at Birmingham.

'On Sunday, 9th July we finally set off for Syerston after the usual amount of messing about. The station we found 'bang on' just as we had been told. Our quarters were champion and the food good. Next day numerous boring talks filled the day. We went to see *Dive Bomber* in the evening at the station cinema. A bloke came home, pissed as a newt, having fallen in the Trent out of a boat! For the next few days we all did extensive study and were full of gen and itching to get cracking. We did circuits and twitches at Woodhall Spa. The Lancaster is a fine A/C (but still I think there are 3 too many engines). Then it was three engined work and corkscrews at Waddington. It appeared a wizard

David Scholes RAAF. (Scholes)

station and I hoped to go there. I found the Lancaster a very easy aeroplane to fly and already had full confidence in it.

'On Saturday 22 July we got up and dashed about getting clearances and packing our stuff. We were posted to 61 Squadron, Skellingthorpe. I was of course furious about it all; because I was almost certain that we would go to either 463 RAAF or 467 RAAF at Waddington. However, all the bitching that I could do could not change the situation and off we went in the bus. We arrived at Skelly in the early afternoon. Soon we were organised in our billet and we were taken down to the flights. B Flight was the flight we were in. The Squadron Commander was Wing Commander Arthur Doubleday DSO DFC and Spam [Bar]. He was an Australian; coming from somewhere near Wagga - farm people I believed. He was a wizard fellow and I liked him very much straight away, when he had a little yarn with us all in his office. I was sure we would not be too badly off here. It was not far to Lincoln and 61 was better off than 50, the other squadron, as convenience in position went. We were quite near our messes and not far from the flights. This was not a peacetime station, but we were quite comfortable and there was no bull to put up with. The Squadron letters were QR (50 being VN). Well, 35 trips to do and I guess I'll know a good deal more about the game and in general, everything!

'Next day I got around the place looking out all the different things and places that would be of interest to me. I was down to do a 2nd Dicky that night with the Wing Commander. This was a good show, because I wanted to get it done and finished with. However, later on it is scrubbed so we went on a 6½ hour X-country instead finishing off with a little bombing. Des Murray, the navigator's oxygen went for a Burton at 20 thou' so we went round at 12,000 which turned out OK. Des came from Queensland and was a very quiet and nice fellow very keen and a gen man. All the crew were Australian except for the bomb aimer, Ron Mayall or 'Darkie', who was from Birmingham and the flight engineer, 19-year old Jack 'Spanner' Foreman, from King's Lynn in Norfolk. His 'better half' lived in Goole in Yorkshire. The WOp/AG, Jock Gardner, was from Melbourne; Geoff Allen, rear gunner from Launceston, Tasmania and Bill Jackman, mid-upper from Melbourne. We got on well together.

'On Monday 24 July Geoff and I were down to go to war. However, after the Ops Meal Geoff's trip was scrubbed. I was to go with Flying Officer Watkins, a very nice fellow who had nine trips so far, which on the face of it didn't sound so good because I'd rather have gone with the Wing Commander or someone with a few more trips in. The feeling at briefing was so queer. I expected I would get used to it though. There were two targets that night - Stuttgart and Donges. I was going to Donges to bomb oil storage tanks, not far from St Nazaire.

'Eventually we got out to the crate - 'Y-Yoke' and did a run up. The waiting before T/O I found most trying. At length we got in for the last time and started the engines again. We taxied away. All round the perimeter track aircraft were taxiing slowly down towards the caravan, where crates were turning onto the runway at about 1 per minute. We got down there after a long taxi. All the people from the station were here to see them off. I saw my crew there amidst them all. The feeling was somewhat like that feeling when one leaves dear old Australia on a troopship. We turned into wind and took off, climbed and circled the airfield before setting course for the first TP - down near Reading somewhere. 'Well this is it'.

David Scholes wrote up the op in his diary: 'On course we climb slowly. Up through a thin sheet of st. cu. cloud and all is clear above except for the odd wisp of cirrus. The sun has set and the sky is a weird blue-grey as we climb on. By the English coast we are almost at height and far below I see the Sussex coast slide slowly from sight behind me. That funny feeling comes into ones middle again and a lump comes in the throat. On we go out across the channel. Then quite suddenly all the nav lights that have been burning steadily around us, go out one by one. We are alone now - just a lot of bodies in a great whirling machine. Darkness comes suddenly. We cross the French coast near St Malo. All is quiet. On we go; nothing happens. Then, far ahead and to starboard I see some flak bursts and several searchlights flick on and weave about in the blackness. We begin to window and weave slightly as we approach the scene, but we are well to port. The place is Lorient so we are more or less on track. We are not fired at for we are well beyond range. Other aircraft however are in range and we are being continually engaged. We run on down SW and go out across into 'the Bay' to turn further port, running to the coastline. Past St Nazaire we turn inland S of the target to the last turning point before running in. The feeling of excitement becomes more intense as I look at the watch - 15 minutes before H hour. At H-11 the fun begins and we are near the turning point. Great strings of yellow cascading illuminating flares go down as PFF locate the target. Over the VHS the Controller and Deputies can be heard. A red TI goes down as a proximity marker. We turn towards the target. Other Lancs are all round us, their four silver exhausts showing up. The marking is not going well. The pilot begins to weave more violently as flak becomes more intense and the risk of fighters is now greater. Another Red TI goes down. We are almost there and still no marking down. There is nothing that can be done but orbit. This is an awful business - hundreds of A/C circling waiting to bomb and no one can see anyone else. The collision risk is very great. Another A/C narrowly misses us and passes overhead.

'The greens are down at last. The Controller calls them away with 'Tally Ho' and calls us in to bomb the greens. Here we go on the run up, the sight is terrific. Searchlights come from nowhere. We are at 9,000 feet. We weave violently towards the markings. Flak is coming up more now. I see a PFF A/C coned below and to port and they are giving him merry hell, however he escapes - good show! Now we are almost there. Never have I ever experienced such a feeling of tense excitement as this. The whole sky is lit up with weird lights - just like a ten times glorified Henley Night. Bombs burst with vivid white flashes. Flak is all around, and light flak, like snakes, conies up to meet us in long red streams. We steady up for the bombing run. It seems ages. One feels like a sitting pigeon, so exposed or like a man walking across Piccadilly with no trousers on would feel. At length the bombs go and the crate shudders as they leave the carriers. Away we go again weaving violently with much power on. We narrowly miss being caught in the fork of two probing searchlights, as we run out of the target. On we go straight up to 11,000 to the coast inland. 'Well, we are OK so far', is the way I feel. Eventually we reach the French coast again after what seem hours and hours. Away over on the starboard side I can see gun flashes from the front line and I wonder how they're going down there really; after all the papers are full of the better side of the picture. I also see V-1 in action.

'Out across the Channel we go heading for England. There it is. How relieved I feel when I see those friendly searchlights of London and Bristol. We cross the coast near Portsmouth and come up country to the right of Bristol. Some forty minutes later we arrive over base and soon our turn to land comes and we slip down to earth safe and sound - another Lancaster back home again, home again to go again. The crew-bus takes us back to the briefing rooms where we are interrogated. We give the intelligence types all the gen we can about the trip - the weather, the marking, defences on route and over the target, height, time, heading and speed when bombs went - indeed, everything. Off we go for our bacon and egg meal before bed. Everyone talks about the trip. Well, if I have 34 more trips like this to do I must set about learning and learning more about my job. I must keep the crew up to scratch and keep out any tendency of over confidence. Every trip must be the first trip. With constant work, keenness, alertness and a little luck I think we shall be alright.'

On Tuesday 25 July David Scholes' target was St Cyr, where wireless parts were stored also much military equipment. He wrote in his diary: 'Load 1 x 4000 HE 'Cookie' and 6 x 500 HE. We attack in daylight. A small piece of flak hits the B/A's compartment. We see one crate go in, but 5 chutes open. Spitfires escort us and I only see 2 ME 109s which do not attack. I have now got my own A/C, 'W-Willie', a Lanc III. She doesn't seem a bad old crate. Once we cross the enemy coast on the way home the trip becomes most enjoyable indeed for it is a lovely day and England looks so pretty in the sunshine - so does France for that matter, but the ugly black puffs specking the sky are very disconcerting and I am afraid I saw little of the French countryside in detail. Wing Commander Doubleday leads us.

'Wednesday 26 July: War. Target Givores Baden, a marshalling yard 12 miles south of Lyons in France. 9 x 1000 HE. Attack at night. It's an awful long way on paper. Off we go. Soon after crossing the French coast I see an A/C shot down. Poor chaps. We have to fly in atrocious weather to reach the target with lightning, hail, rain and terrific bumpiness. We have to orbit in this weather. The boys put on their nav lights. I see two collide and another hits a mountain. As we cannot see the TIs we turn for home planning to bring our load home again. Eventually after what seems an age of ups and downs cloud, lightning and odd flak we cross the enemy coast almost at dawn. We find it necessary to jettison our load to reach England, where we land, through fuel shortage, at an American airfield called Merryfield. After a meal and refuelling we fly back to base. This has been a dreadful trip and I never wish to do another like it. We sleep soundly until tea time. After tea we go down the road to the WVS hostel for supper. On the way home Geoff and I get some drops in our eyes at SSQ.

'Friday 28 July: NFT in morning - low flying. War. Target Stuttgart. 'Cookie' and clusters. Attack at night. All the way from the enemy coast to the target I see A/C going down. Just a fine, glowing yellow light slowly falling earthwards with occasional spurts of orange flame. Down and down for what seems ages, then a terrific flash which lights the whole sky momentarily as it hits the earth - a horrible but fascinating sight. Just before we drop our bombs a 109 attacks, but a violent dive to port succeeds in shaking him off. Geoff doesn't fire either, but due to his alertness we live on. We turn for home, and, instead of returning home low, as briefed, I climb to 23 thousand and stay there. All the way home more crates go down. Two are missing from here. 62 are lost from Group out of 195.

David Scholes' original crew at OTU : L-R: Bill Jackman, mid-upper gunner; Des Murray, navigator; Ron 'Darkie' Mayall, bomb aimer; u/k flight engineer; Jock Gardner, radio operator and Geoff Allen, rear gunner. (David Scholes)

Saturday 29 July: Up at 1400. Lecture by visiting padre. After tea we go into Lincoln per bike and see *This Happy Breed*. On the way home we pause awhile on a seat beside a park to eat some fish and chips. There is an early morning 'do' on in the morning, so we go straight to bed. This operational life is fine in a way - so exciting, every minute of life seems so important. I think a lot of home and Pat. I must get through it all.

'Sunday 30 July: War. Target Cahagnes (between St Lô and Caen). 700 A/C taking part. 13 x 1000 bomb load. Over target about 8/10ths cloud and we are ordered down below the cloud base. However the mission is abandoned and the Hun gun positions, which are worrying our troops, go untouched. We have a good look at Cherbourg on the way home. We are ordered to proceed home via Pershore and Squire's Gate, in order to use sufficient fuel to lower the AUW to maximum landing!! Waste of petrol? By mistake I join Fiskerton circuit and land there with a full bomb load! However I take straight off again and return to base. Damned shame we couldn't bomb.

'I have received my commission and so I battle off down to London to get all my stuff fixed up. I stay at the Strand Palace as usual. This step, although really important, seems to be an every-day occurrence to me. I am interested in but one thing - the completion of this tour of operations. And so I arrive back at the Squadron - a different uniform, a different mess, but not a different fellow. The new mess I find wizard, such a change to my old mess in which I have eaten for so long. I cable home and Pat.'

David Scholes next operations were to more targets in France, Mont Candon, near Dieppe on Tuesday 1 August and Bois de Cassan that Wednesday: War. On Thursday it was Trossy. Scholes wrote: 'Over target one crate was hit by flak and crashed, flaming down to earth, with another one. Nobody got out.' When they got back the crew went to the Plough for a drink or two after tea and had 'a good old time together'. 'We got some fish and chips, took them home, and devoured them in a few moments!' After a little local flying on Friday afternoon they went into Lincoln for tea at the Saracen's Head (Snake-pit) after which they saw *Demobbed* - an English show, not too brilliant.

Saturday 5 August: Up at 0200 for meal and briefing. War. Target St Leu d'Esserent. 14 x 1000. Daylight. Again we have to take a spare gunner to fill Bill's place in the mid upper turret (Sergeant Jebb). Fires his guns in dispersal! W/C Doubleday leads the squadron. This is a V-1 store again like the other targets lately have been. We get hit by flak in the starboard wing. This is the closest that the damned stuff has been to us yet and I hope, the closest it will ever come to us. The attack goes well enough I suppose. Some small patches of cu. cloud make it difficult for the bomb aimers. We get ours away on the target area successfully however. Another lovely day. Big hole in wing.

'Sunday 6 August: Up at 0700 for ops meal. War. Target L'Isle d'Adam. 14 x 1000. V-l store. Bad weather just before target splits the force and the fighter escort and just as we drop our bombs some dozen or 18 ME 109s attack from the port quarter up out of the sun. The next few moments are unrememberable. I do remember seeing two Lancs go down and two Jerry pilots come floating past on the port side. I can see the black crosses on some of the 109s - too damned close. We formate with 7 other Lancs and at full power, climb to 20,000 into thin cirrus which affords sufficient protection. Not until in sight of the English coast do we break up. Good show, home again. Coombs is missing.[19] Damn this war business, I get cheesed writing about it. Afraid therefore that my notes about my ops are somewhat brief and in concise, however all my life I shall remember every minute of every one of them.'

During a period of leave to Scotland and London David Scholes took his rod and the gun and got 'farther away from war than anything in this world'. 'It's damned hard to say goodbye to all this' he wrote ' - in the back of my mind I cannot get the awful idea away that this could be my last leave!' David Scholes felt 'like an escaped prisoner or an animal let out into a new pasture'. 'Poor England' he wrote: 'so full of worry and trouble, bustle and noise, clouds and fog, laughter and joy, misery and sorrow - silly, wonderful, little, big Britain... In the summer time I love the countryside. In the winter it is too cold, foggy and miserable to love anything except a huge fire.' In London he would often stay at the Strand Palace were the rooms were 'absolutely wizard' and take tea at the Boomerang Club - usually 'bang on'. During a trip to the capital in February he had noted that 'one of the famous London pea-soup fogs was just closing down and vision was already limited to about 75 yards and all the lights were on. It was quite a brown, yellowy colour.' He and his crew would pass the time in the Savoy Tavern or the Codger's Club, off Fleet St, 'for a few more'; and 'Hardy's and the 'Boomer' and lunch at the Milton's Head; once he saw *Phantom of the Opera* starring Nelson Eddy, at the Odeon and had tea at 'The Black Boy Grill'. Another time, after lunch he went to see *Thirty Seconds Over Tokyo* - 'a damned good film'. He ordered his new uniform from Carr Son and Woor. In Nottingham there was the Victoria while the rest of the crew stayed at the YMCA. They would all eat in the Overseas Club, drink in the 'Black Boy' and round off the evening at the Palais de Dance.

Early on the morning of Wednesday 16 August he caught 'the local puffing-billy to Edinburgh which only just got him there in time for the 1000 hours' fast train to London. They stopped at Newcastle, York and at Grantham before getting out and catching the 'very slow, slow train' back to Lincoln. 'We have tea at the Snake Pit' he wrote. 'Here I learn that Rod Mellowship is missing since a raid on Rüsselsheim. This shakes me to the core. Rod was such a wizard chap and Ron Hore the WOP was one of the best too. It seems that there were a lot of fighters about that night. This puts the finishing touches on my 'twitch' that has slowly been developing in me whenever I have thought of returning to camp.' Flying Officer Rod Mellowship and Flight Sergeant Ron Hore were among five Australians on the crew of 'X-X-ray' on 467 Squadron RAAF at Waddington and they were both killed.

The op to Hanover on the 17th was scrubbed, much to David Scholes' relief but on Friday the 18th ops were on again with a trip to Bois de Cassan V-1 Bomb dump. Next day, Saturday 19 August, he was up at 0200 for the op to La Pallice oil storage tanks for U-boats. 'A most tiring trip' he wrote. 'The gaggle has to climb through broken stratus over the channel to reach B/H. At target there is unexpected layer cloud and we orbit port losing height to bomb. Darkie again saves the day and we bomb on the first run up. Flak over the target is quite accurate and, after we bomb, becomes intense. We get through untouched. We are diverted to Little Snoring, in Norfolk. (Mosquito MK 2s.) We have a meal and a couple of hours sleep before returning to base in shocking weather. We go to bed completely fagged out, for we have had about 4 hours sleep in the last 48. Showery weather continues with occasional thunderstorms throughout the night.'

His next op was on Friday 25 August and the target was Darmstadt. The controller makes an early return and the No. 1 & 2 deputies are shot down' he wrote, 'so we orbit for 35 minutes while PFF try to mark. During this business I see a couple of rockets flying at terrific speed in the horizontal plane - most alarming things! Spanner is most alarmed. There are fighters about. We get through it all OK. Fortunately there is a break in the searchlight belt between Mainz and Mannheim, through which we belt with 270 on the clock. F/O Church is missing on his 28th trip.

'Saturday 26 August: War. Target Königsberg. 'Cookie' and clusters. Night. City, fire raid. (East Prussia.) This almost breaks my heart when we take off - we are diverted before we take off. There is the odd spot of flak over Denmark. Over Sweden, all lit up in a terrific blaze of lights and Neon signs, there is a magnificent display of 'friendly' flak, both heavy and light. Being briefed for two searchlights we arrive to find 190 of the bleeding things. We weave in, bomb and get out somehow, I don't know, that's quite certain. The return is the same. At the Denmark coast we a/c for Lossiemouth in NE Scotland, however, after hours of flying at 2000 we cross the coast in daylight near Peterhead where I land at once, tired out completely body, mind and soul, after 11 hrs 25 minutes flying and a mileage of approximately 2000.

'Tuesday 29 August: War. Target Königsberg - again, oh hell!! (This may be as far as this diary will go.) 'Cookie' and clusters. Off we go and, although the route is slightly different, the trip in not much different until we reach the south east coast of Sweden, where we run into severe electrical storms which continue out over the Baltic Sea. Eventually we arrive in the vicinity of the target. The controller brings us down below C/B [cloud base] and I find too late, that we are port of track and so after orbiting and evading S/Ls [searchlights], proceed as planned. It was found necessary to execute this second attack as the first failed to burn out the centre of the city and the dock area. The object is political as well as direct support of the Russian troops. We cross the Danish coast in dawn light and it is early morning with an accompanying mist when we reach base - too late for a diversion. I land early and after taxiing to dispersal at the end of the runway in use. Just as I am closing down I get the shock of my life - a 50 Squadron crate passes over us at 20 feet and crashes headlong into the wood not 50 yards from where we stand. This is surely fate, for we have all missed certain death by a hair's breath. How it misses us I really cannot ever tell. I shout to Darkie and Spanner to see if they can get anyone out of the steaming wreck - luckily it does not catch fire. I close down, but damned shakily and quickly! Everyone is OK except the nav is dead. Evidently the cause was the misty conditions, coupled with the loss of one outboard and inexperience.

'Well we're home again, thank God!!'

'Thursday 31 August: War. Target Rollencourt. 14 x 1000 at 12000' V-l Bomb dump. Daylight. It is a shambles getting into our gaggle and we do not eventually reach our station until we cross the French coast. We make a dummy run, but successfully bomb on the second run up. Flak is light on our A/P but on the other one south east of us it appears much more intense. We dive away across the coast very fast and arrive back at base at about 2000 hrs. (The bombing was very good with a good concentration.) After a chat in the hut we all turn in.

'Tuesday 5 September: War. Target Brest. 12 x 1000 Gun positions hindering naval and military operations. Daylight. We take off very late and don't see a crate until near the target where I see a couple going home. We therefore go across the target solo and have a good run up. Flak is negligible, but we are a piece of pie for any fighter. Everyone has landed when we get home!

'Sunday 10 September: War. Target Le Havre. 14 x 1000 German troop positions and strongposts. Daylight. A damned fine show. Never have I seen such vivid proof of the awful destruction caused by a concentrated HE attack. Columns of smoke billow up to a great height while the bomb flashes are quite distinct through it, the ground waves too are easily seen. Somehow I feel sorry for the poor blokes down there below as we turn away. Nothing could live through such a bombardment or, if one did survive one would be insane for life I am sure. Never shall I forget this. Flak slight, but accurate.

'Monday 11 September: War. Target Darmstadt. 'Cookie' and clusters. Operate at night. The first attack was not good enough. I have never seen more fighter activity than tonight. All about us in the target area there is green tracer, snaking about probing into the darkness. Here and there a crate explodes and plunges down. On the run up Bill sees a 'Mossie' after a Ju 88. Just after leaving the target we narrowly miss colliding with another Lanc on the starboard beam. Spanner is speechless but luckily points and I miss him somehow. The fighters are active all the way home and if I ever weaved and kept my eyes peeled, I do tonight. Flak is

David Scholes and his crew on 61 Squadron at with Lancaster III PB596 behind. L-R: Bill Jackman, mid-upper gunner; Geoff Allen, rear gunner; Ron 'Darkie' Mayall, bomb aimer; Jack 'Spanner' Foreman, flight engineer; David Scholes; Jock Gardner, radio operator; Des Murray the navigator is absent from this photograph. PB596 crashed on 12 August 1947.

troublesome en route in and out. The moon rises, big and yellow as we cross the beautiful English coast on the way home. At base I am surprised to find that no A/C are missing from 61. (50 lose some). (286,000 incendiaries + 210 'cookies' are dropped).

'Tuesday 12 September: Tonight there is a war on but F/O Collins, an Aussie, takes my crate. I spend some time giving him all the gen I can. This is his first night op. Target Stuttgart. ('Cookie' and clusters). We watch T/O from the 'wagon'. 'R-Roger' loses two engines (inners) on T/O and prangs at the end of the runway (070°) - the bombs do not explode, for I'm writing this!' Next morning he awoke early to see if 'Willie' was home. 'I find it came back on three, having had the starboard outer shot out over the target by flak. Although an old tub, I have learnt to have a kind of affection and trust in her. We are stood down about midday so after tea we go to Lincoln and see the show *Music While you Wait*, put over - not bad.'

It was back to the war again on Sunday 17 September: 'Target Boulogne. 14 x 1000 Germans! Operate in daylight. In the beautiful, sunny, clear morning we T/O and gaggle across over Ipswich to the target. Here I nearly have my time again. Flak, although not intense, is extremely accurate. The crates on my port bow are all hit on the run up. All I can do is sit and wait my turn. Sure enough up she comes

Bombing up 'S-Sugar' on 61 Squadron. Note the Australian Kangaroos denoting the bombing operations and 'Snifter' the dog; Snifter is Aussie slang for having a beer, or a dog having a pee against a post.

on our port, bang on predicted stuff. How we are missed I don't know. Someone is hit ahead and an outer engine complete comes rushing past just below us, the crate plunges into the fields and explodes. However, the famous 5 Group bombing of Le Havre is repeated. On return we do find a couple of small holes in the elevators and near Geoff's turret. F/O Boland, an Aussie, put up a magnificent show. Although wounded in the right leg and left arm, he returned on three and put down a wizard landing before collapsing. (The B/A, too, was wounded.) His chute-harness was cut away by shrapnel - one piece lodged in his cigarette case. Lucky lad!'

David Scholes and his crew were given another period of leave on Wednesday 27 September. On their return he discovered that 'W-Willie' had gone down. 'Well, I'm damned' he wrote. 'Flying Officer Hornibrook, an Aussie, took her to the Dortmund-Ems canal and is missing. [20] Flight Lieutenant Stone and Flying Officer Goodbrand,[21] both RAF, are also missing from 61. 50 Squadron also have lost some crews since we have been away. This is indeed a blow. I expect we shall have to take any old kite until another 'W' arrives for us and there are some crates about. Willie and the kangaroo I painted on her nose have gone for a Burton. The whole business shakes me rigid. W/C Pexton has taken over of the Squadron as W/C Doubleday DSO DFC is time and tour expired and is posted to 27 OTU Litchfield. I go to bed thinking a lot and in poor spirits.'

In the afternoon of Thursday 28 September the crew went in 'G-George' to pick up 'Y-Yoke' which landed on three engines at Oulton in Norfolk. They collected the aircraft and returned to Skellingthorpe, landing at about 1800. That night the crew did a little cooking in the hut and had a 'magnificent feed' from their home parcels before turning in.'

The crew's next op was on Thursday 5 October, to Wilhelmshaven, in daylight with a Mustang escort. 'Ops meal is at 0230. Eventually after one false start we get weaving. I am Deputy NO 2 to W/C Pexton. We pick up our Mustang escort at position X (Catfoss) and proceed. We stray to port and go very close to Heligoland where a heavy barrage greets us. Low strato cumulus about 6/10ths covers the target. H_2S A/C run up OK and I bomb when they do. Heavy, but inaccurate predicted flak comes up, but I see no fighters. Some A/C bomb farms and small villages on the way out across the coast. I wish I still had mine for there are wizard targets - even a small vessel lying close to the shore. Only one bomber is missing on return. We cook ourselves some supper.

'Friday 6 October: War. Target Bremen. 16 cans. Night fire raid. The new 'P-Peter' has arrived and we are to take it to war tonight. All goes OK until we are well out across the North Sea at about 2,000' when the rear turret becomes U/S. Geoff, Spanner and Bill work for half an hour to fix it, but their attempts are in vain. I therefore return to base, jettisoning down to 56, 65m NE of Skegness, much to the disappointment of our 2nd Dickie, Flying Officer Cadman. He seems a very nice chap indeed and I should like to have taken him along to break the duck. The risk is too great, however, to chance seven lives as well as my own. We land a little heavily due to an unexpected slow running on this A/C. Just as we pass F/C on the perimeter track, the port tyre blows out so we leave the old thing there. Well, we have joined the Boomerang Club. They say you never finish a tour without a boomerang in your log book, so this is something. This new A/C seems a wizard kite and the ground crew also appear to be good types. Those we had on 'W' were bang on chaps all round especially Jimmy Meuse. I still have that funny worried sort of feeling inside me. I'm damned if I want to die yet. Life is too much worthwhile to say goodbye to it early in the piece. I put a successful tour down to 80% good management and skill, and 20% luck. You must have the luck part of it though, that is certain. How you miss a load of incendiaries or odd cookies at night, I'm damned if I know. I'm going to be grey haired soon I reckon.

'Saturday 7 October: War. Target Flushing. 14 x 1000. ½ hour delay. Sea wall. Daylight operation. Spits escort. On T/O the front hatch blows up. It's a bit of a shaky do while Darkie tries to get it back on. I make him put on his chute in case he falls out, which he almost does, only Spanner is holding him. At length anyway they close it. We do two runs over the A/P [aiming point], 7 bombs at a time. Flak is not too bad. It seems a good prang. Tonight all of us except Darkie and Bill go down to the Fox and Hounds for a pint or two.

'Wednesday 11 October: War. Target Flushing. 14 x 1000 Gun positions in concrete emplacements. Daylight. 100 Group Spit and Typhoon escort. B/H [Bombing Height] 6,500'. We do a dummy run because of cloud, but on the second run we hit it smack on. The gunners see the bombs explode across the target. However we have two hang-ups and I get Darkie to aim at some slit trenches and M/T facilities at the NW tip of Walcheren Is. I do two runs for him here too. They overshoot slightly, but one lands on the road near Huns. The weather for return is poor, and makes flying unpleasant. Drift is bad on landing.

'Saturday 14 October: The boys go to Brunswick tonight, on a fire raid. F/O Hoad is missing on return. He had F/O Cadman with him as 2nd Dickie. I wish doubly now that I had taken him to Bremen successfully. He was such a decent sort of chap. The boys report many large fires on return - good show. F/O Collins lands at Woodbridge with no ASI.

'Thursday 19 October: War. Target Nuremburg. 'Cookie' and J type clusters. Night show, of course. Fire raid on city centre. All goes well on the way there. We see a raid going on at Stuttgart by 1 & 3 Groups as we pass it. A couple of crates go down while I look that way. We are a few minutes late in bombing (15,000') and are at the lowest height. Just after we drop our load - not more than 15 sees after either, we are predicted and hit by heavy flak. The A/C goes into a violent turn to starboard and loses height. This is the way we are supposed to turn anyway so I let it go. I find that the bomb doors will not close even by the emergency system and that the DR compass is U/S. By this time the A/C flies OK so I proceed to lose height down to 9 thou' into stratus cloud where I stay. Jock reports that hydraulic fluid and petrol is all over the place aft and there are many holes torn in the fuselage. Everyone is unhurt luckily. I cannot maintain a good speed with the bomb doors open and we become a straggler 25 minutes late at the second T/P. 'Window' coming in through the holes in the floor tends to short Jock's acks, so Spanner takes it off by hand although sparks and flame keep appearing. We begin to ice up and I cannot climb.

'Chunks of ice crash through the perspex off the airscrews and Spanner is struck in the face. We are losing fuel from the port No. 1 tank. Jock is so cold that he cannot move and remains huddled on the floor. I manage to gain a little height, almost stalling and stay in and out of cloud. Eventually I see the French coast and we a/c immediately for Woodbridge and I hope to God we make it. On arrival there I find the R/T is U/S so use the Aldis for permission to pancake. We pull the bottle and land with bomb doors open and half flap at 135 mph. I now find that the tail wheel is missing, but I don't give a damn because we're down and alive! (The old crate is full of holes, petrol is pouring out of her when we land and the fuselage is broken close to the mid upper turret, where there is a huge hole. Some pieces of flak went darned near some of the chaps - Darkie and Bill especially - very lucky). After interrogation, a meal and a medical check I go to bed.

'Friday 20 October: Eventually Air Crew Reception tell me that nobody is coming from base today to get us because of bad weather. So dammit, we are glad to be alive, so what? So we catch a transport to Woodbridge village and from there we catch a train to Ipswich (1/7½d ticket). We look like six penneth of God-help-us as we stop off the train in flying kit, just as we stepped out of the crate. I have a battle dress on and Pat's blue scarf and no hat - it's raining like hell too! We check

Lancaster ED860 on 61 Squadron being prepared for its 120th operation, to Bordeaux on 11 August 1944. Flying Officer Norman E. Hoad is in the cockpit. His crew are, left to right: Flying Officer K. C. W. 'Bill' Ball, navigator; Flying Officer W. H. Pullin, bomb aimer; Sergeant C. V. 'Moosh' Embury, rear gunner; Sergeant Norman England, MUG; Sergeant George Patrick 'Hoppy' Boyd, WOp; and Sergeant Cyril Stanley 'Lucky' Webb, flight engineer. Flying Officer Norman Hoad and the crew of QR-Y were shot down on the raid on Brunswick on 14/15 October. Webb and 'Hoppy' Boyd were killed; Hoad, Cadman, Ball, Pullin, England and Embury were taken prisoner.

in at the Great White Horse Hotel, with a little bit of trouble and have a clean-up and shave with a bare blade. Anyway I go to bed after a most amusing and happy night and I believe some cheese sandwiches washed down with brandy. We return to Woodbridge very shakily on Saturday morning. At about 1500 F/O Hill RCAF arrives to take us back to base. I travel as rear gunner and have some fun in the rear turret. I should hate to be one by trade, there is such a feeling of detachment about the whole affair. [On Monday] we get a brand new plane from the factory.

'Wednesday 25 October: War. Target Flushing. 14 x 1000 Gun positions that are worrying the Canadian troops on the mainland. Daylight operation from 4-5 thou. Things are unsatisfactory from the start with low cloud and rain. However we reach the target finally at about 4 thou. Flak is heavy and accurate. I see one A/C burning on the ground. On the run up my starboard aileron is shot away and the A/C holed in other places. It is very difficult to control and so I am forced to jettison the load. Another A/C goes down over the target and I narrowly miss collision with two other Lanes on a reciprocal heading. It is a shambles of an attack. Base is fit on return and we get in OK. Hugh Horsley has 179 holes in his crate! Old Si Borsht from Waddo is missing, plus 3 others from there. I learn later on down at the Plough. Bardney lost 4 crates too.

'Saturday 28 October: War. Target Bergen. U-Boat pens. 10 x 1000 HE/SAP [High Explosive/Semi-Armour-Piercing.] Night attack 11,000ft B/H. We have F/O

Wing Commanders W. L. Brill (right) and Arthur W. Doubleday, two farmers from Wagga, New South Wales, whose war careers marched almost in step, typifying many famous Australian air partnerships. After volunteering for the RAAF they were called up together in 1940 and thereafter their promotions were simultaneous. When they became wing commanders Brill commanded 463 Squadron RAAF and Doubleday 61 Squadron RAF. Each was awarded the DFC and DSO. Brill added a Bar to his DFC later. Both were original members of 460 Squadron RAAF.

Ainsworth as 2nd Dickie, a small fellow with a nice disposition. The target is cloud covered and we ice up heavily at 12,000'. I dive across the area at 300 through predicted flak. The collision risk is very grave so I turn out across the North Sea at 5,000ft still in cloud and hail. We are diverted to Leconfield so I jettison completely. On arrival at this station I find cloud below me at 600'. An A/C collides with a factory chimney on my starboard bow down so I climb quickly to 1,500 and proceed to some Sandra lights. This is Pocklington, where after an overshoot I land. Oodles more A/C come in here. After interrogation and a meal I go to sleep in the Officers' Mess beside a poor fire. A very shaky do this with plenty of panic attached to it - should have been scrubbed.

'Sunday 29 October: After refuelling, we T/O and return to base - first off and first back home. I am very tired having had little sleep, after a particularly nasty flight so I go straight to my bed quite done in and feeling a bit dizzy. Tomorrow we are due to go on leave so I have no worries, only pleasures to dream about. [On return] I discover that F/O McLaughton[22] is missing from a raid on Düsseldorf and that F/O McFarland shot down a Ju 88 and a jet A/C on the same attack. They have operated very little in our absence, due to bad weather. They have been briefed a lot though. They did a daylight to Homburg in the Ruhr.

Saturday 11 November: The boys go to Harburg, near Hamburg, to bash synthetic oil plants and the town. F/O Hill is attacked by a Ju 88 and is lucky to get back at all, due to extensive damage on all port surfaces. He is hit by flak too. 'S-Sugar' is therefore cat AC. He is a bit of a straight and level type. I go out and have a look at the A/C as soon as he has landed.

'Thursday 16 November: War. Target Duren. B/H 8000 ft force 1150. Daylight, but we are almost scrubbed from the battle order soon after briefing as the W/C has to go along. We see plenty of flak but no fighters, all 61 return. Some are lost from other bases. Target totally wiped out. Also Jülich.

'Tuesday 21 November: Flight Leut today. F/Lt! War. Target Ladbergen - Dortmund Ems Canal. 13 x 1000 Night time. H-Hour put back 3 hours. B/H 12 lowest 2! We have a darned good trip. All Belgium is lit up as we pass over it. We bomb from 5/5 after a drop from 12 because of cloud (st. cu.) over target. I can see the canal plainly on the run up. There is another attack by the Group further up towards Münster tonight. Both attacks go off OK. On the way home there are plenty of fighter flares and a rising moon. I see only one A/C shot down myself. The Cont. becomes coned!

'Wednesday 22 November: War. Target Trondheim U-Boat pens. 9 x 1000 SAP/HE and full tanks. 11 thou' B/H. We are early at target so dogleg. Hun is too clever and puts up a smoke screen with small M/Bs in the harbour. The Controller decides to A/M because of risk of damage to Norwegian people. I jettison just off the coast. The way home is as bad as the way out was with frontal cloud from 1,500' to 20,000', I fly back across the North Sea at about 800ft. Due to fuel shortage I a/c Peterhead and land at 0132. After interrogation and a wizard meal we go to bed. The six wind finding Mosquito XUs land here - or rather five, as one ditched through lack of fuel. The winds were extraordinarily strong tonight. We had a ground speed of only 158 tonight on return.

'Thursday 23 November: We try to get off at about noon today to return to base, but the SI is U/S. Spanner and I refuel to 1,200 gals however. This is a long range

Lancaster III LM630 PG-D 'Dumbo' on 619 Squadron at Strubby in the winter of 1944-45.

escort P-51 airfield with mostly Polish pilots. Am I ever green with envy! They are a lovely crate. In the evening we catch a bus into the town of Peterhead where we go to a picture. It is surprisingly warm up here in Scotland - the wind is a bit chilly at times though.

'Friday 24 November: We get off at about 1300. On the way down (after shooting the joint up) I find 'Monteviot' and circle it very low. The C/B is only 2,000 and I am not happy because of high ground so I climb to 4,000 to return. At base C/B is 400-500 ft so I do a split-oit circuit at about 200ft. On the deck I find a war on with 2,154 and 'Cookie' and clusters. I go to the W/C and tell him the crew is far to weary to fly so we are scrubbed. The target turns out to be Breslau! But after briefing it is scrubbed. I go to bed early. There was snow on the Border Hills. F/O James is missing from Trondheim. I thought he'd go. [23]

'Sunday 26 November: We have our first heavy frost this morning. Boy! is it cold. War. Target Munich. 'Cookie' and clusters. Full tanks. Attack at night. Route takes us over the Alps. All goes well until I am almost to the wagon for T/O when a fire develops in the rear turret due to fusing of gun-heaters. I taxi off port and await electricians. They say the A/Hs are U/S and there is a short up as far as the Elsan. They mess about trying to fix it until after last TOTA so I, as Captain, decide not to T/O late with a queer A/C on a 10½-hour trip. I don't know whether the crew are pleased with my action or not, but what I say goes in any case - never take more chances than necessary, that's me. There are 3 Boomerangs from 61 tonight.

'Monday 4 December: War. Target Heilbronn. 18 xj clusters. Rail junction and town, vital to the enemy. B/H 13,850'. Operate at night. This is a very fine war. We have a good trip all the way round. It is a little twitchy though - 1 & 3 Groups attack Karlsruhe at the same H-Hour. 17 A/C are lost from Command and 15 are on Heilbronn! 190s, 88s and 109s all up in strength. It is a wizard prang the entire target area is devastated by HE and fire bombs. Flak is light. Icing heavy. All 61 return. F/O Collins spends his 21st birthday over the target! He has 3 combats with an 88 in addition to a complete hang up. They manage to jettison the 'cookie' manually. Well, this leaves one trip to go. I shan't say any more. A man has got to be darned unlucky to go on his last trip - let's leave it at that just now.

'Wednesday 6 December: War. Target Giessen. 18 xj clusters. Rail junction. Night trip. B/H 10,850. Into the night fighter land. The weather is the worst thing on the way. Over England I fly at about 1,000ft I hold this across and into France. At about 3°E I climb to 3 soon after up to B/H getting iced up into the bargain. We bomb a bit late. (Jock puts on a show when the intercom goes haywire with his 'Ha ha hello' business). It appears a good prang. I see air to air firing and one A/C on fire. Also a load of incendiaries jettisoned on the way out of the target. Over Belgium on return we run into electrical storms with hail and sleet. I fly at about 1,000 again with nav lights on (not lower, because A/C have been shot down for V-1 because of them). Flying becomes very unpleasant. However, over the channel it breaks up

Lancaster III ED664 AR-A2 A-Aussie on 460 Squadron RAAF at Binbrook in 1943. This aircraft was lost on the operation on Berlin on 23/24 November 1943. There were no survivors on Flight Sergeant Maurice Joseph Freeman RAAF's crew.

Lancaster I PA177 HW-J2 JUG & BOTTLE which was flown by Squadron Leader Dave Robb RCAF and crew on 100 Squadron from 28 October 1944 before being SOC in December 1945. A pub of the same name now stands on approximately the spot at Holton-le-Clay where HW-J's dispersal was situated.

and England is clear.

'Back at base we are congratulated no end and told we are the first crew to finish on a P for 18 months! A public relations wodda asks me many questions for the Australian newspapers, especially Melbourne papers. Geoff pulls his chute to see if it would have worked! It does. Darkie tells me how the B/S went U/S and he used his fingers! - Crafty lad, the old Dark. Everybody is very happy. I myself feel a greater feeling of relief than I have ever felt. I may do another tour before I'm finished, against the Japanese, but let that come when it's due. Right now I feel bang on. I have a meal and go off to bed finding no trouble going to sleep.

'Thursday 7 December: Tonight we take the ground staff out for a big party across to the Bridge Hotel, Saxilby. Sixteen of us go altogether (five going in my little car). It is awfully cold, but we soon get warmed up with a couple under the belt. Certainly without these fellows we could never have dropped 420,000lbs odd of stuff on the Hun. The meal is magnificent and the boys thoroughly enjoy themselves. There are speeches all round. (I explain how I consider I have not given Darkie quite as fair a go as I might have.) At the end of the evening we all have on different tunics - I am an LAC! We are all quite happy. I drive home OK. Jock however, on his bike ends up in a canal and arrives back in a very wet state.

'Friday 8 December: I go to Waddo and collect some money in the morning and also wire the Strand Palace re a room. I hear that Don Smith is missing on Düsseldorf. Bill and Geoff set off to Leicester before lunch and I follow up after, having mended my trousers and arrive at the Grand Hotel at about 2000 hours. The others arrive (all except Darkie) and after booking in we drink in Simon's Bar until it closes when we go to The Swan with Two Necks to finish up. We're on leave again, but this is a special leave - it's finishing leave! Boy are we going to have a time. I get pretty tight tonight.'

Footnotes for Chapter 12

19 Pilot Officer Grahame Frederick Coombs and crew on 50 Squadron were shot down on the operation on Bois de Cassan. He and four crew were killed; two evaded capture.

20 On 23/24 September 1944 20-year Albert Keith Hornibrook was KIA on the operation to Münster. All except one of his crew died.

21 Flight Lieutenant Donald Edward Ross Stone was KIA. William Goodbrand was on 1652 HCU. Also lost on 61 Squadron that night were Squadron Leader H W Horsley and crew (four of whom including Horsley, evaded) and Flying Officer Ian Melville Campbell RNZAF (all except the rear gunner were killed).

22 Probably F/O William McGillivray on 61 Squadron who was KIA on the 2/3 November raid.

23 Thomas Cecil James and crew were all killed.

Chapter 17

The Night Ghost of St Trond

At about 00:35 hours I was directed on to an incoming enemy aircraft at an altitude of 3,500 meters. It was located on the airborne radar and after further instructions from Dr. Baro I made out a four-engined bomber at 00:45 hours, about 200 meters away above and to the right. I attacked the violently evading bomber from behind and below at a range of 80 meters, and my rounds started a bright fire in the left wing. The blazing enemy aircraft turned and dived away steeply, hitting the ground and exploding violently at 00:48 hours.

Heinz-Wolfgang Schnaufer's combat report, 29 May 1943

Wolfgang Schnaufer was born 16 February 1922 in Calw, Württemberg. He learned to fly gliders as a member of a National Political Institutes of Education in 1939 and he entered the Luftwaffe as a trainee pilot in November 1939. In April 1941 Leutnant Schnaufer was posted to Nachtjagdschule 1 to learn the rudiments of night-fighting. Unlike many of the German Experten, Schnaufer joined the Nachjagdflieger straight from training in November to fly Himmelbett sorties with II/NJG 1. His first operation came in February, when II./NJG 1 flew escort for the German navy's capital ships *Scharnhorst, Gneisenau* and *Prinz Eugen* when they broke out from Brest in the 'Channel Dash'. His first victory was claimed on the night 1/2 June 1942; a Handley Page Halifax over Belgium. However, while attacking a second enemy aircraft, his aircraft was hit by return fire and he was wounded in the leg. He successfully landed his damaged aircraft. By the end of the year his total stood at seven with three victories recorded on one night. Schnaufer was promoted to Oberleutnant in July 1943, when his total was 17.

By August Schnaufer's score had reached 23 and he became Staffelkapitän of 12/NJG.1 at about this time he teamed up with Bordfunker Leutnant Friedrich 'Fritz' Rumpelhardt with whom he developed an almost telepathic understanding and shared 100 victories. Prior to this Schnaufer had had two regular operators, Dr. Baro, with whom he shared twelve victories and Erich Handke, eight. The other member of the most successful crew in the Nachjagdflieger was Oberfeldwebel Wilhelm Gänsler, who shared in 115 victories including 98 after joining Schnaufer. Schnaufer's secret was superb aircraft handling combined with marksmanship (three victories were scored against violently corkscrewing bombers) and Rumpelhardt on the radar. Schnaufer flew only the Bf 110. At the end of 1943 Oberleutnant Schnaufer had reached 40 victories with four Lancasters being shot down on 16/17 December that year. He was awarded the Ritterkreuz des Eisernen Kreuzes. He recorded his 50th victory on the night of 24/25 February 1944. In March the 'Night Ghost of St. Trond', as Schnaufer had become known, was appointed Gruppenkommandeur IV./NJG 1. He claimed five enemy aircraft on the night of 24/25 May. Hauptmann Schnaufer was awarded the Eichenlaub on 24 June for 84 victories and the Schwerter on 30 July, with his total at 89. He was awarded the Brillanten personally by Adolf Hitler. Schnaufer was then appointed Geschwaderkommodore of NJG 4 on 4 November 1944; the youngest Geschwaderkommodore in the Luftwaffe at 22. His final fifteen victories came in 1945; nine of them in one 24 hour period on 21 February, to take his grand total to 121, in just 164 combat sorties.

The two consecutive nights, 20/21 and 21/22 February 1945 proved a profitable 24 hours for several German pilots. On the night of 20/21 February 514 Lancasters and fourteen Mosquitoes set out for Dortmund, another 173 bombers raided Düsseldorf, 128 aircraft attacked Monheim and 154 Lancasters and eleven Mosquitoes attacked the Mittelland Canal. Including diversionary and minor operations aircraft, 1,283 sorties were flown. Twenty-two aircraft failed to return. Worst hit was the Dortmund force, which lost 14 Lancasters. These raids were followed on the night of 21/22 February by 1,110 sorties against Duisburg, Worms and the Mittelland Canal and another 27 aircraft were lost plus seven Lancasters crashed in France and Holland. German ground control identified the course and height of the bomber stream heading for

.Oberleutnant Heinz-Wolfgang Schnaufer, Staffelkapitän, 12./NJG 1 at Leeuwarden points out his 47th Abschuss - he scored his 45th-47th victories on 15/16 February 1944 during a Bomber Command raid on Berlin when 43 aircraft were lost. Victory number 47 was Lancaster B.I W4272 of 622 Squadron, which he shot down into the Ijsselmeer 1 km south of Medemblik at 2333 hours. Flight Lieutenant Trevor Llewellyn Griffiths RAAF and his crew were killed. (Hans Bredewold via Ab A. Jansen)

Worms and before the heavies reached their target and succeeded in infiltrating 15 Spitzenbesatzungen of NJG 6 into the bomber stream in the area of Mannheim-Worms. No jamming of their SN-2 sets was experienced and neither were any Mosquitoes encountered. Eight Nachtjagd crews claimed 21 bombers destroyed in the target area. Oberfeldwebel Günther Bahr of 1./NJG 6 with Feldwebel Rehmer as Bordfunker and Unteroffizier Riediger as Bordschütze shot down seven Lancasters of the Worms force on their bombing run to the target in quick succession. Hauptmann Johannes Hager's six Viermots were his 40th-45th Abschüsse and he was awarded the Ritterkreuz. Hauptmann Heinz Rökker, Ritterkreuzträger and Staffelkapitän of 2./NJG 2 also destroyed six (his 56th-61st kills); five of his Abschüsse were of the Mittelland Canal force.

On 463 Squadron RAAF's battle order for the raid on the Mittelland Canal near Gravenhorst on 21/22 February by 165 Lancasters and twelve Mosquitoes was Lancaster B1 NG329 'Z-Zebra' captained by Flying Officer Graham H. Farrow RAAF. His crew was made up of Warrant Officer Russel Bermingham RAAF, bomb aimer; Sergeant Stan 'Lofty' Bridgman, flight engineer, Flying Officer Pete Harris, navigator; Flight Sergeant Jack Wiltshire RAAF, WOp; Sergeant Frank Bone, mid-upper gunner and Sergeant Stan Clay, rear gunner. This was to be their 15th op. Most of their operations had been flown on *Nick the Nazi Neutralizer* (officially 'N-Nan', but to the ground and aircrews 'Old Nick') but on this particular night, 'Nick' was in the hangar for a major inspection and service after completing 86 operational sorties.

Frank Bone the mid-upper gunner wrote: 'Take-off time was 17.07 hours. The bomb load was 14 x 1,000-pounders. Petrol load was 1,600 plus 50 gallons. H-hour was to be 20.30. It was quite a pleasant trip out and we bombed dead on time, 20.34 as we were in the last wave. After leaving the target the flak seemed to die down, but apparently the fighters were on the job. I counted seven kites going down in flames, so we knew there were fighters around, as by this time there was no flak at all. Stan, the rear gunner and I were reporting these to Pete the navigator so that he could log them. We were worried because we still had a 1,000lb bomb 'hung up' in the bomb bay. After Russ checked we were still over enemy occupied territory, he decided to see if we could get rid of the bloody thing, otherwise we would have to keep it until we were over the Channel.

'The skipper put the aircraft in level flight and the bomb doors were opened. It was a great relief to all of us when we heard Russ's voice over the intercom say 'Bomb gone'. We resumed our banking searches once again when suddenly we were hit in the starboard-inner engine from below. Cannon shells flashed past Jack, the wireless operator and also shattered the navigator's table. They seemed to come at an angle of about 60-80 degrees with the floor and from the starboard quarter down. Graham gave the order 'Put on parachutes', also telling Lofty, the engineer, to feather the starboard-inner engine, as it was, by this time, on fire. A couple of seconds later the skipper gave the order to jump as the whole wing was ablaze and the engines would not feather. (The accumulator had been hit.) The lights were going off and on, mainly off.'

Major Heinz-Wolfgang Schnaufer had taken off from Gütersloh at 0105 hours on 21 February in Bf 110C G9+MD. Employing Schräge Musik attacks delivered below the bombers in an Einsatz (sortie) lasting two hours nine

The most successful night-fighter crew ever. L-R: Oberfeldwebel Wilhelm Gänsler, bordschütze (gunner), Oberleutnant Heinz-Wolfgang Schnaufer and Leutnant Fritz Rumpelhardt, Bordfunker (radar operator). By August 1943 Schnaufer's score had reached 23 and by mid-December he had scored 40 victories. In 1944 he scored 64 victories, a feat unequalled by any other night-fighter pilot. In 1945 he scored 15 victories, including nine in one 24-hour period on 21 February, to reach a final score of 121. Schnaufer shared 100 victories with Fritz Rumpelhardt, 12 victories with Leutnant Baro and eight with Erich Handke. Wilhelm Gänsler shared in 98 of Schnaufer's victories. (Ab A. Jansen)

minutes he shot down two Lancasters at about 11,000 feet WSW of Mönchengladbach-SW of Roermond to take his score to 109. Returning to Gütersloh Schnaufer and his crew had a rest period until a Werkstattflug (air-test) was called at 1815 hours for Bf 110 G9+EF. The flight lasted 21 minutes and the Messerschmitt was declared 'serviceable.' Leutnant Fritz Rumpelhardt, Schnaufer's radar operator, recalls.

'The late night sortie on 21 February 1945 was to become Schnaufer's most outstanding achievement in two-and-a-half years' service as a night-fighter pilot. It was always a point of honour with him to be the first in the air after the order to scramble so that he could assess the situation and brief his squadron. Chance played quite an important part in the second operational sortie on 21 February. I was alone in the squadron mess having my supper, having missed the order 'Heightened Preparedness,' so when the order to scramble came the Major was ready but I was not. He did not mince his words about my apparent dilatoriness. In spite of the ensuing mad rush, the rest of the squadron was already airborne, on its way to Düsseldorf. By the time 'EF' lifted off from the aerodrome it was 2008 hours. Events now turned in-our favour. Following the instructions received from Ground Control we believed that the others had reached the engagement area but we were somewhat puzzled when we could see neither bombers, nor night-fighters nor in fact, any anti-aircraft fire ahead of us. Schnaufer was debating whether to follow our present track when we suddenly noticed over to the North, probably in the Münster area, a lot of light anti-aircraft fire. Again this puzzled us. Guns of that calibre were effective up to 2000 metres only, yet the British bombers usually flew between 3500 and 6000 metres over the Fatherland. Without further thought Schnaufer altered heading to the Northwest to cut off the bombers returning home.

'At 2500 metres we flew through a thin layer of cloud and our radar showed us several targets. Suddenly we were in a condition of 'Shroud;' above us a thin layer of stratus through which the moon shone giving us an opaque screen above which we could see clearly the black silhouettes of the bombers from quite a distance. Schnaufer closed upon a Lancaster flying along unsuspectingly slightly to our starboard at altitude 1700 metres. We had been airborne just over half-an-hour. The Major closed with the target, left to right, from below and delivered the first attack with the two vertically mounted 20mm cannons, just behind him, in the cabin. He aimed between the two engines on the right-hand side. The fuel tanks were located there and this method brings the quickest results. The time was 2044 hours. The right wing of the bomber was badly damaged; a huge flame illuminated the sky. The Lancaster held steady for a while, long enough to allow the crew to escape by parachute before it fell to earth and crashed.

'There followed attack after attack, the sky seemed to be full of bombers! Now the British crews knew we were there and began their violent manoeuvres, twisting and turning in an effort to escape us. Schnaufer had to follow all their corkscrew movements, to remain in a position under the bombers' wings where the return fire could not be brought to bear upon us yet ready to use the Schräge Musik. In one case we practically stood upon our wing tip whilst firing. Things became more difficult for us when we crossed the front line and the American anti-aircraft batteries opened up. Within a period of 19 hectic minutes we managed to shoot down seven bombers - without so much as a scratch - testimony to the Major's great skill and ability to get in quickly, line up his target and dive away quickly. Normally during this wild fighting I would hardly have had time to note the details thoroughly but because of the 'shroud effect' the pilot did not need my assistance at the radar to guide him on to each target and I had more time than usual to observe the effects. Oberfeldwebel Wilhelm Gänsler, our gunner, gave great support as usual but even he could not help when we attacked our eighth Lancaster bomber. Gänsler, an experienced Bordschütze who had formidable night-vision, had previously flown with Oberleutnant Ludwig Becker and had shared in 17 kills with him. He was awarded the Ritterkreuz. At the crucial moment we exhausted the ammunition to the upward-trained guns and as a result had the greatest difficulty in getting away from the concentrated fire from the bomber crew.

'We still had our four horizontally mounted cannons in the nose of our fighter but these too refused to function during our ninth attack and we had to stop chasing the bombers. On the way back to base we had to fly again over the American batteries and by now the major was thoroughly weary, almost spent. I called, therefore, upon Dortmund to give us all possible assistance to clear us back to Gütersloh with all expediency and with this help Schnaufer greased our faithful G9+EF on to the ground. The night's work was done, we were back at base and it was just short of 2200 hours. Once we had taxied in and shut down the engines, we sat in silence for a couple of minutes, thankful to have got through it and thought about the men who had gone down that night and hoped that they had managed to parachute to safety. Many years later I received a letter from an Englishman, Stanley Bridgeman. He had been a crewmember of Lancaster JO-Z of 463 Squadron RAAF shot down that night at 2102 hours above Holland. All his crew had managed to escape by parachute. My prayers had been answered in part.'

Frank Bone had left the rear turret of 'Z-Zebra' and sat on the step to put on his parachute. 'By this time, Stan had opened the rear door. I moved back towards the rear of the kite and stood on the step of the doorway. I could see the wing burning and before I knew what was happening, Stan pushed me, and out I went. (I had hold of my ripcord all the time.) I just glimpsed the tailplane rushing past and the next thing I knew, I was dangling in midair. I don't even remember pulling my ripcord. I looked up to see if my 'chute had opened as I didn't seem to be moving at all. I felt as if I was hanging in space. To my relief it was open, and I was just sailing smoothly down when I saw what appeared to be an Me 109 fly past me at about 200 yards distance. I thought, 'This is it' as I expected him to come in and have a crack at me. Luckily he flew right past me and headed in the direction of Germany.

'I was still a good way off the ground and could see our kite plunging earthwards in a ball of flame. Another was hit a little later and that met the same fate as our own and the other seven before us. By this time I could see the 'deck' quite clearly, and the roadways and haystacks in my vision were getting rapidly bigger. I had no sooner prepared myself for the impact when I landed and fell backwards. Surprisingly I didn't hurt myself at all.

'As I did not know where I had landed I released my parachute and was going to get rid of it when I saw two chaps coming towards me, as I had landed right by a lane. One came out of a farmhouse on the opposite side of the road and the other was running down the lane. I thought my time was up so all I could do was raise my hands and be taken prisoner. I was overjoyed when I heard one of them say: *Tommy, Tommy, dis is Ollande'*. They picked my 'chute up (they were after the silk) and took me to a farmhouse across the lane. I tried to explain that I wanted to get in touch with the Army authorities; I think they understood because they took me up the lane to another house, a big one. There, to my surprise, I found Russ. Boy; was I glad to see him! I put my arms round him and hugged him. The Dutch folk made us a cup of tea and gave us a cigarette, and did I enjoy it! Meanwhile, they had phoned through to Army headquarters and so a truck was sent for us. It was great to see and hear someone who could speak English again.

'The driver took us a little way along a road where we were overjoyed to find Pete who told us that the rest of the crew were in a farmhouse farther along and had all landed safely, but Lofty was wounded in both legs from fragments of cannon shell fired by the fighter. Lofty had had his trouser leg ripped off and was all bandaged up when we arrived. Still, we were all safe and alive, thank God.

'Pete told us we jumped 21.11 hours which was just over half an hour after leaving the target, and our height was 6,000 feet. We landed four miles inside our lines, so it's a good job we didn't get it a couple of minutes earlier, or else!!! Graham had lost one of his boots while descending, so he borrowed one of

Flying Officer Graham Farrow RAAF and crew pictured on 8 December 1944 after their diversion to Ford following a daylight to the Urft Dam. L-R: Flight Sergeant Stan Bridgeman; Warrant Officer Russ Bermingham RAAF; Flight Sergeant Jack Wiltshire RAAF; Flying Officer Pete Harris; Flying Officer Graham Farrow; Sergeant Frank Bone; Sergeant Stan Clay. (S. W. Bridgeman)

Lofty's. I lost the torch which I carried in my flying boot, but why worry? I could get another when I got back.'

Stan Bridgman recalled:

'I had left my seat to check the engineer's panel and was standing in front of it when the first and only burst of fire caused this panel literally to disappear. I felt two vicious punches in my legs, and fell over. On the pilot's instruction I endeavoured to feather the starboard engines, but the night-fighter's cannon shells had done their work, and it was not possible to do so. By this time both engines were on fire, and the pilot had started his fight to keep the aircraft level to enable his crew to obey his next order which was 'JUMP! JUMP!'

'It was at this moment the bomb aimer questioned the order by asking 'Did you say 'JUMP'?', and I remember thinking: 'This is a hell of a time to hold a debate'. However, the inrush of air from the opened hatch told me that No 1 had gone. As No 2 to exit I dragged myself to the bomb aimer's compartment, and then realised my chest-'chute was still in its stowage so I went back for it. Having obtained this somewhat necessary piece of equipment I looked through the hatch into the night; my next thought was to put my head through it and as I did so the slipsteam hit me and I made my exit in classic style, just as all the instructors had said we should - a head first somersault. I counted the '10' in very quick time and pulled on the ring, extending my left arm to its full extent then letting the ring drop. A hard jerk told me my 'chute had opened, and with the speed of my fall arrested, I became aware of our Lanc, poor old 'Z-Zebra', a blaze of fire from the starboard wing, heading away; and then the sound of the wind in the parachute cords was the best music I have ever heard.

I did not see 'JO-Z' crash. It was very dark and I kept loose limbed, and hit the ground quite reasonably.

'I could hear a dog barking nearby and due to the speed of events had no idea where I was, Holland or Germany. I gathered my 'chute, and started to push it into the nearby hedgerow. I heard movement nearby and a voice shouted 'There's one' in English. I shouted back: 'Are you a Limey?' and then out of the dark appeared two soldiers wearing the renowned 'Red Beret', part of a parachute division holding the line. I was unable to walk, so the soldiers carried me to a nearby farm and into the barn where the Dutch family Van Lipzig were forced to live due to their farmhouse having been destroyed by shell fire.

'First aid was given to me, and in the next few minutes other members of the crew were brought in. Transport arrived, and the Army lads took me to an advance aid post for further medical attention. After this I was taken to Helmond in Holland where a school had been converted to an army hospital. The following morning I was operated on for the removal of cannon shell splinters and attention to the damage done by the bullets which had passed through my thighs. It was painful, but when I thought that had the aircraft been three feet lower I probably would have been dead. I counted my blessings.'

Schnaufer's final 15 victories came in 1945, nine of them in one 24 hour period on 21 February, to take his grand total to 121. Schnaufer's final score was 121 bombers in 130 sorties (114 of his kills were four-engined Stirlings, Halifaxes and Lancasters) and he was decorated with the Ritterkreuz with Oak Leaves, Swords and Diamonds. Leutnant Fritz Rumpelhardt took part in 100 of these successful attacks and Oberfeldwebel Gänsler in 98. Rumpelhardt was the most successful Bordfunker in Nachtjagd being credited with 100 abschussbeteiligungen, or 'contributions to claims'. After the war their Bf 110 was evaluated by the RAF and was later included in a display of captured German aircraft in Hyde Park in London. It was eventually broken up, but one of its fins, showing Schnaufer's tally of 121 victories, is displayed at the Imperial War Museum in Lambeth, while the other is in the Australian War Memorial Museum in Canberra.

Schnaufer was taken prisoner by the British Army in Schleswig-Holstein in May 1945, but was released later that year when he took over the family wine business. He arranged for Wilhelm Gansler to move from East Germany and found employment for him in the family's business. Fritz Rumpelhardt became an administrative officer at an agricultural college in West Germany. Schnaufer was badly injured in an accident with a French lorry with faulty brakes while driving his open sports car near Bordeaux in France in July 1950. Heavy gas cylinders from the lorry fell on to Schnaufer's car and at least one of them hit him on the head. He died in a hospital on 15 July 1950.

Chapter 18

Day of the Jets

In order to avoid bombing attacks we transferred our machines during the day to the motorway Lübeck-Hamburg, near Reinfeld. But the night sorties were always flown from Lübeck, transferring our aircraft there at dusk, for the motorway had no airfield lighting. I remember with pride that I had flown the first operational jet aircraft of the world and to have been the only pilot of the Luftwaffe to have flown the two-seater version on night-fighting operations.

Leutnant Herbert Altner

German jet interceptors were among the last desperate attempts to prevent an inevitable collapse of Hitler's Thousand Year Reich. By early 1945 almost all Allied bombing raids were flown by day, such was the aerial superiority enjoyed by American and RAF aircrews. Oberfeldwebel Hermann Buchner, a bomber pilot who had been retrained on the Messerschmitt Me 262 at Lechfeld by the Thierfelder Kommando joined 10th Staffel, JG 7 at Oranienburg near Berlin. Major Rudi Sinner, commodore of III/JG 7, had been displeased to see so that few recruits were from the fighter arm; they were almost exclusively naval air arm, bomber and transport pilots. Buchner, who had recently married, was born in Salzburg and had joined the Austrian Air Force in 1937 and after the annexation of his country, had joined the Luftwaffe. He had been awarded the Knight's Cross for over 600 operational missions and had transferred to III/JG 7 as a Me 262 pilot. In March 1945 JG 7 relocated to Parchim airfield in Mecklenburg east of Hamburg for operations against US bombers. Railway connections between Cologne and Dortmund no longer existed because of

Lancaster B.X KB721 *Linden Rose* operated with A&AEE from April 1944 before joining 419 'Moose' Squadron RCAF in August 1944. It returned to Canada in June 1945.

An Me 262 of JG.7 carrying the 'Running Fox' emblem and a pair of launching tubes for 210mm rockets on the bomb racks under the nose.

Allied bombing and strafing attacks and it took two days by crowded troop train for Buchner to travel from Cologne to Parchim.

JG 7 had about ten operational Me 262s. Normally they were armed with four 30mm Rheinmetall Borsig MK 108 cannon and R4M 55 mm high explosive rockets mounted in twelves on wooden racks under the wings for attacking bomber formations. The rockets which had eight fins in the tail which extended after launch, had about the same trajectory as the rounds from the cannon, so both could be aimed using the Revi gun sight without adjustment. At Parchim the days were hectic and Buchner and his fellow pilots were really in demand. JG 7's mechanics were loyal and they worked tirelessly to keep the troublesome jets airworthy. The Junkers Jumo 004B-2 axial-flow turbojet unit fitted to the Me 262 was supposed to last from 25 to 35 hours but in practice they lasted only about ten hours' flying time. The prescribed time for changing and checking a unit was three hours but in actual practice it took eight to nine hours because of poorly fitting parts and the lack of trained staff. Despite its speed and performance at altitude, the Germans recognized that the Me 262 was not invincible. Its fuel consumption was enormous and that limited its range and endurance. It was particularly vulnerable during takeoff and landing. Allied fighter pilots made full use of this.

On 31 March there was something new for JG 7 - an early scramble. 'We were still at breakfast in the dining room and the weather was not very good' Buchner said. 'The cloud base was 150-200 metres above the ground. We flew with seven 262s led by Oberleutnant Franz Schall, an Austrian from Graz, one Schwarm and one Kette. Schall was an old pilot from JG 54 with aerial victories. He had guts and a hand for a good formation. Our mission was against US units in the Hannover region, take-off was at 0900 hours. We climbed in tight formation into the clouds, heading westwards. The clouds just weren't coming to an end and Schall asked the ground station guiding us whether we should make 'Luzi-Anton'. A brusque answer came back over the radio, 'First of all make Pauke-Pauke'.[24] At 7500 metres above ground, we had just come out of the clouds, when Schall got the order: 'Assume course 180, Dicke Autos [25] course 180!' At the same moment, someone from our unit cried, 'To the right of us, nothing but bombers, to the right of us!' Schall, as well as the rest of us, saw the bombers, flying north in a formation that was new to us. They flew, staggered, about 1000 metres deep and 2000 metres wide. They were not US bombers, however, but Tommies in night flight formation, doing a day-time attack on Hamburg. Schall ordered us to take up attack formation, already having long forgotten the order 'assume 180'. We were lucky to reach the band without fighter protection and Schall, a fighter with real heart, was not going to pass up a chance like this. As we got closer, we could clearly see what kind of bombers they were - RAF Lancasters - on their way to attack Hamburg, but still 50 kilometres away over the Lüneberg Heath.'

For some weeks 419 'Moose' Squadron RCAF gunners had been sniffing jet exhaust in the air trails over Germany. One pair had skirmished briefly with Me 262s. It was not until 31 March however that the all-Canadian 6 Group RCAF squadrons were drawn into anything like a large-scale battle when the Blohm & Voss ship-building yards at Hamburg; an important centre of U-boat construction, was the target for a force of 428 Lancasters and Halifaxes of Nos. 1, 6 and 8 Groups. Of these nearly half came from 6 Group, including Lancasters and Halifaxes representing every one of the Group's fourteen squadrons. It had been intended that the bombers should pick up their escorts - twelve squadrons of RAF Mustangs - over Holland but the third wave of bombers in 6 Group was late at the rendezvous point and missed the escorts. Over the target area the leading Pathfinder and other Lancaster formations became heavily engaged by at least 30 Me 262 jets, but had plentiful fighter escort protection and lost few bombers to the German jets. But there was no such protection for the third wave. At the rear of the stream, a gaggle of Canadian Lancasters ten minutes late over target found itself without the planned fighter cover and suffered heavily.

The jets materialized out of the overcast at 10,000 feet and with their great rate of climb, closed the remaining 10,000 feet vertical gap in a matter of seconds. In all, 28 crews on 419 battled with the Me 262s one or more times. 'H-How' flown by Flight Lieutenant Harry Alfred Metivier who had completed half a tour went down and he and his crew, most near the half-way mark of a tour were all killed. 'Q-Queenie', flown by Flying Officer Donald Stuart Maxwell Bowes and his crew, all of whom had reached or passed the half-way

Lancaster B.X KB872 NO! NOT NOW which operated on 431 'Iroquois' Squadron RCAF from February 1945. It returned to Canada in July that year and was disposed of in 1947.

mark of a tour, was the second missing aircraft. Flight Sergeants G. R. Berry, R. W. Rowlands and W. H. Milne survived to become prisoners-of-war but Bowes, Sergeant John Rea, Flying Officer John Joseph Gladish and Flight Sergeant Bruce MacLennan were killed. Gunners on the five crews that returned fired at the jets nine times, but on only three of these occasions were their aircraft actually being attacked. Their inability to lay-off and maintain correct deflection because of the jets' tremendous speed was therefore, not surprising and despite the 1,200 rounds that they fired, no claims were made by 419 Squadron.

Hermann Buchner recalled: 'On our first attack, there were seven Lancasters shot down with the R4M rockets. Now the large unit dissolved somewhat and the Rotten flew a renewed attack on the bombers. I made a right turn and lined up for another attack. This was made using the nose cannon. My Lancaster lay directly in my sights and I only had to get a bit closer. Now, I opened fire, the hits were good, but the pilot of the Lancaster must have been an old hand. He turned his Lancaster steeply over on its right wing, making a tight turn around the main axis. With my speed, I was unable to follow this tight manoeuvre and was also unable to see if my shots had had any effect, or to see how he flew on. I shot through the pile and had to think about returning home. The other pilots were also having the same problem. We had a shortage of fuel and had to get back to our own garden. At the same time, all called to the ground control, 'Autobahn', the course number for the direction back to our home airfield.

An Me 262 caught on camera gun film by an 8th Air Force P-51 Mustang pilot.

'Only one of us could be handled by 'Tornado' ground control, but all of us wanted to be given a course. We were still all in the tangle of RAF bombers, but none of us had visual contact with each other. We all had to go back down through the cloud layer. I thought to myself, 'Go back down alone!' At 7000 metres, I dived into the cloud layer, laying on a course of 090, 700 km/hour and the engines running at 6000 rpm. Over the radio, I could still hear my colleagues calling 'Autobahn' to Tornado, they were all still in the air. My altimeter showed that I was quickly losing height and at 1000 metres, it was already dark, I had to get out of the clouds soon.'

'My altitude was diminishing, the gauge showed 500, 400,300 metres - the ground must surely soon appear - yes, there it was. Doing 700 kilometres/hour, I shot out of the clouds and found myself over fields and clumps of trees. Unfortunately, I didn't know quite where I was. On my left side, I could make out the sea, was it the Baltic, or where was I? Anyhow, I flew eastwards with a normal turbine rpm and at 800 km/hr. In the distance, I could see the silhouette of a town. I quickly thought about it and then I was sure that the town had to be Lübeck. I had recently seen a film called 'Die Budenbrocks' in which the silhouette of the town had been shown. Flying over the harbour, I came under fire from light flak, but I was too fast, they had no chance of hitting me. Now I knew how I could get back.

My other comrades were also on their journey back to Parchim and now the traffic with Tornado was quieter, so I could also call up and ask for instructions, giving him my location. I was the last 262 to call in after the mission at 7000 metres. Now, he had his flock together. By the time I reached Ludwigslust, I had already been given permission to land, as well as the comforting news that there were 'no Indians on the airfield'. After 65 minutes flying, I landed without difficulty in Parchim, the last of the seven. My list of aircraft shot down was extended, one Lancaster confirmed and one definitely damaged. Altogether, we had certainly shot down ten Lancasters and five others had been damaged'. The seven 262s on the mission had landed without problems after 60-70 minutes flying time in bad weather conditions. The reported aerial victories were confirmed by Jagd Division and the bombers had off-loaded their cargoes over the heath, far from their target. Around 60 flying personnel were taken prisoner on the heath. During midday, another mission was flown against US units.'

Buchner survived the war. Schall was killed during an emergency landing on 7 April after attacking USAAF bombers in the Hannover-Magdeburg area.

Of the eight RCAF Lancaster squadrons, 433 'Porcupine' at Skipton-on-Swale was probably the most heavily engaged; with seven of its ten crews being attacked and fighting sixteen actual engagements. Two Me 262s attacked Squadron Leader P. D. Holmes' aircraft simultaneously from the rear and port quarters. Warrant Officer E. J. Ash in the rear turret opened up at the first jet and then was joined by his mid-upper, Warrant Officer V. M. Ruthig, in converging fire at the second. Their combined tracer hit the Me 262 in the wing, engines and nose and it broke away, scattering metal debris and pluming smoke as it plummeted downwards. Ruthig then coolly directed his skipper in necessary evasive action during five further attacks. He was later awarded the DFC. Another 'Porcupine' crew, captained by Flying Officer D. Pleiter, whose gunners were Flight Sergeants C. H. Stokes and M. A. Graham, claimed one jet as probably destroyed.

A Lancaster on 431 'Iroquois' Squadron at Croft, piloted by Flying Officer E. G. Heaven, was attacked by three Me 262s. In the rear turret Flight Sergeant Bill Kuchma lined his sights on the first at 700 yards and waited until it was a only 50 yards away before ceasing his fire; at which point the jet veered crazily to starboard, trailing smoke and debris and fell away. A second later its complete tail assembly tore away and the forward section tumbled over and over down into the clouds. Of the other two one was seen off with a thin trail of smoke pouring behind it. The Lancaster X captained by Flight Lieutenant P. J. Hurley was shot down and was believed to have crashed south of Hamburg. Hurley survived but all six crew were killed.

A Me 262 was claimed after it was sent down in flames by the combined firepower of a 428 'Ghost' Squadron Lancaster's gunners, Flight Sergeants R. C. Casey and A. E. Vardy; while Flight Sergeants C. K. Howes and S. J. Robinson, on a 424 'Tiger' Squadron Lancaster successfully countered two simultaneous attacks. Howes engaged one jet on the starboard quarter but had all four of his guns jam; while at the same time Robinson hammered a burst into the second German at dead astern. Its engines erupted in smoke and then the Me 262 fell away in a spiral dive obviously out of control and disappeared with blue flames rippling along the fuselage.

Seven 434 'Bluenose' Squadron crews reported ten combats, resulting in one Me 262 being probably destroyed and two others at least damaged. The Lancaster flown by Flying Officer Gilbert Paul Haliburton who was killed, crashed at Nettelnburg. Flight Sergeant Robert John Green also died but the rest of the crew survived and were taken prisoner.

For 429 'Bison' Squadron this was its first operation since converting from Halifaxes to Lancasters; with ten crews participating. Five were attacked, engaging in nine separate combats. 'V-for Victor' flown by Flying Officer R. R. Jones was shot down. He and Flight Sergeant Rancourt survived to be taken prisoner but the five other crewmembers were killed. Flight Sergeants D. H. Lockhart and R. Jones, rear and mid-upper gunners respectively in the Lancaster skippered by Flying Officer A. M. Humphries, both opened up at one Me 262, though all four of Lockhart's guns ceased firing after about 20 rounds. As the jet broke away however, Jones fired a fierce burst and the jet plummeted into the clouds apparently out of control and shedding metal from its starboard wing. On another 'Bison' Lancaster the mid-upper gunner, Flight Sergeant J. O. Leprich, was attacked directly over Hamburg. With his electrical firing circuit already out of commission, Leprich worked his guns with one hand, while hand-rotating the turret. He continued firing one gun after the other until the Me 262 was finally driven off by three escorting Mustangs which had returned to cover the Canadian 'straggler' formation. When last seen the Messerschmitt was spuming black smoke. Leprich was awarded a DFM for his cool courage and determination.

On a 427 'Lion' Squadron Lancaster Warrant Officer J. G. Jarvis was in the rear turret and he watched his tracers stitch along the belly of another jet as it rolled over and dived into cloud with dense black smoke trailing from its engines; though not before the Me 262's twin 30mm cannons had ripped chunks out of the Lancaster's fuselage, engines, elevators and rudders. Flight Lieutenant J. L. Storms on 427 Squadron piloted his aircraft back from Hamburg with one shattered aileron and a five feet chunk of one wing missing, but got the bomber down safely and earning for himself a DFC.

Five minutes of non-stop assaults cost five Lancasters (three other 6 Group aircraft had already fallen victims to fighter attacks); totalling 78 individual attacks, with 28 crews later reporting actual engagements. Canadian gunners claimed four Me 262s destroyed, three probables and four others damaged but no Me 262s were lost. The very speed of the jet fighter attacks was something entirely new to most of the RAF bomber crews and the official report on the action afterwards stated: 'The usual technique of the jet-propelled fighters appears to be an approach from astern or the fine quarters, possibly with a preference for slightly above, opening fire at 800-900 yards and closing rapidly to close range. In a few cases, however, fire was not opened until 300-400 yards. Combat reports stated that the closing speed of these fighters is so great that they frequently do not have time to fire more than one burst. More than one rear gunner reports that although he had opened fire at 900-1,000 yards he had only time to fire 200 rounds before the fighter broke away 3-4 seconds later at 30-50 yards and one stated he was unable to rotate his turret fast enough to obtain strikes on the fighter at this close range though he had opened fire at it at 900 yards...'

Altogether, eight Lancasters and three Halifaxes were lost on the raid. It was reported that three of the Lancasters and a 415 'Swordfish' Squadron Halifax at East Moor were shot down by the Me 262s. None of the returning Lancasters showed damage of any kind. The bombing results achieved on this raid can hardly be said to have justified the losses. Overcast conditions necessitated the exclusive use of sky-markers and though these were fairly well grouped, the

What is thought to be one of a pair of Messerschmitt Me 262 A-1a/U4s. This was intended to be a bomber destroyer version, fitted with an adapted 50 mm Mk 214 anti-tank gun in nose. It is seen here being inspected by American officers after being captured by the advancing armies.

bombing concentration was considered, at best, only moderate. The only visible results were puffs of grey smoke pushing through the cloud during the later stages. Common to every crew report were remarks concerning the gaggle leader's unnecessary time wasting on the final leg, an error which was no doubt the sine quanon of the gaggle's subsequent vulnerable position. Bomber Command commented that an officer of more senior rank should have led the gaggle (pilot of lead aircraft was a Flying Officer).

During a series of defensive operations against RAF and US heavy bombers on 31 March, JG 7 flew a total of 38 sorties with Me 262s and lost four aircraft. Allied records confirm that the jet fighters probably shot down 14 heavy bombers and two fighters, making this the most successful day ever for the Me 262.

It was not the last time that RAF Bomber Command encountered the German jets. On the afternoon of 9 April forty Lancasters of 5 Group attacked oil-storage tanks at Hamburg for the loss of two Lancasters, one piloted by Flight Lieutenant Albert Paulton Greenfield DFC RAAF on 61 Squadron at Skellingthorpe. At 1741 hours Lancaster QR-Y on 'B' Flight on 61 Squadron in the leading Vic of a formation had just released its bomb load when the German jets struck. Ted Beswick the mid-upper gunner, recalled:

'We had just left the target when suddenly the flak ceased and I saw several black specks in the sky behind us, growing larger every second and coming down on us at incredible speed. As I watched the Lancaster behind us, piloted by Flying Officer Greenfield, suddenly reared its nose up, burst into flames and then exploded. [Incredibly, two men on Greenfield's crew survived to be taken prisoner]. Out of this cloud of smoke and debris appeared a Messerschmitt 262 jet fighter, which continued its attack on us. Jimmy Huck, our rear gunner, immediately opened fire. I could not depress my guns low enough to add to his stream of bullets, but I yelled to the pilot over the intercom to corkscrew like hell to port! This brought the Me 262 up over the port fin and rudder and I could clearly see its pilot. I got him fair and square in my sight and kept the triggers down, following him as he overhauled us. Then, as he was abeam, I and the rest of the crew saw black smoke begin to belch back from the cockpit area and the Me's nose pitched over in a vertical dive down out of sight.

'Incidentally, this was not the end of our troubles, for we then discovered that we had a 1000lb bomb hung-up in the bomb bay. Over the sea we tried to get rid of it but could not dislodge it until we landed when the shock of landing did the trick. Unfortunately by this time we were on the ground and could clearly hear it rattling around, live, inside the bomb bay. We turned off the runway and held there while the armourers came running to us. They rigged a winch inside the aircraft and dropped cables through apertures in the fuselage floor. The bomb doors were then wedged open just enough for an armourer to get an arm through, make the bomb 'safe' and attach winch cables. Then they lowered it down. We may have had a 'shaky-do' that day but afterwards our hats went off to those armourers!'

Footnotes for Chapter 12

24　Literally 'kettle-drum - I am attacking'.
25　'Fat Cars' i.e. heavy bombers.

Lancaster B.I R5868 S-Sugar on 467 Squadron RAAF which completed its 137th and final bombing sortie on 23 April 1945 to Flensburg, is on permanent display at the RAF Museum, Hendon, London. (Author)

Lancaster I R5868 'S-Sugar' cockpit. (RAF Hendon)

Lancaster I PP687 on a test flight in March 1945 when the aircraft was supplied to 149 Squadron. PP687 was struck off charge in December 1946. (Charles E. Brown)

Leutnant Norbert Pietrek, who was awarded the Iron Cross 2nd Class. On 9/10 August 1943 he shot down Lancaster I W4236 'K-Kitty' on 61 Squadron. Three of Sergeant J. C. Whitley's crew were KIA. Pietrek received head injuries when he crashed at Kitzingen on 27/28 August 1943 and he suffered further head wounds when he crashed on 1 October. He never flew operationally again and in October 1945 he began most of the next ten years in captivity in the Soviet Union. (Norbert Pietrek via Theo Boiten)

Lancaster HA-P of 218 Squadron takes off on an 'op'.

'British Bombers now attack Germany a thousand at a time!' poster.

Sergeant Charles Brennan was the Canadian flight engineer on Flight Lieutenant John 'Hoppy' Hopgood's crew on the Dams raid, 16/17 May 1943.

Brennan's log book. The young Canadian was killed on the Dam's Raid when 'M-Mother' was shot down.

Date	Hour	Aircraft Type and No.	Pilot	Duty	Remarks (including results of bombing, gunnery, exercises, etc.)	Flying Time Day
					Time carried forward :—	131·55
15.5.43	1530	LANC 925	F/Lt Hopgood	Flt Engineer	Bombing + Tactical Practicks	1·25
15.5.43	2200	LANC 925	F/Lt Hopgood	1 "	X/C Moonlight Tactics	
16.5.43		LANC 925	F/Lt Hopgood	"	N.F.T. Formation Bombing	·50
16.5.43		LANC 925	F/Lt Hopgood	"	Formation Exercise	
16.5.43	2130	LANC 925	F/Lt Hopgood	Flt Engineer	OPERATIONS MÖHNE DAM	
					MISSING.—	
					Monthly Flying DAY NIGHT	12·25
					TOTAL	154·10
			S/C for W/Cdr OC 617 Sqdn.		F/Lt for OC B FLT	

THEY FLY WHERE NO ONE EVER FLEW BEFORE...
THEY FIGHT LIKE MEN FROM ANOTHER WORLD!

WARNER BROS. present

"THE DAM BUSTERS"

RICHARD **MICHAEL**
TODD · REDGRAVE

URSULA JEANS · BASIL SYDNEY   PATRICK BARR · ERNEST CLARK · DEREK FARR

PRESENTED BY

R. C. SHERRIFF   MICHAEL ANDERSON   WARNER BROS.

BBMF Lancaster B.I PA474 overflying the Derwent Dam in May 1993. (Author)

Lancaster VII WU-15 (NX611) of the French L'Aeronavale at Changi in 1965 during the flight from Australia to the UK where, after flying briefly in 1967-68 it became the gate guardian at RAF Scampton. Now known as *Just Jane,* NX611 is based at the Lincolnshire Aviation Heritage at East Kirkby where it is taxied regularly. (Jerry Cullum)

Lancaster B.X FM213 painted as KR726 VR-A in honour of Canadian VC recipient Andrew Mynarski is owned and flown by the Canadian Warplane Heritage. (Author)

BBMF Lancaster B.I PA474, Spitfire VB AB910 and Hurricane IIC PZ865 passing Lincoln Cathedral. (Author)

Lancaster B.I PA474 as 'Mickey The Moocher'. (Author)

PA474 with new nose art especially for 2013 to commemorate the 70th anniversary of the Dams' raid. B.I DV385 *Thumper Mk. III*, which joined 617 Squadron in November 1943 had bulged bomb bay doors to accommodate a 'Tallboy' bomb and took part in two attacks on the *Tirpitz*, was damaged four times and went to 46 MU before being scrapped in November 1946. (Bob Franklin)

BBMF Lancaster B.I PA474 in *Phantom of the Ruhr* scheme along with a Spitfire and Hurricane overfly Bardney. (Author)

BBMF Lancaster B.I PA474 in *Phantom of the Ruhr* scheme and Spitfire VB AB910 passing Bardney airfield, wartime home of 9 Squadron. (Author)

The superb Memorial to Bomber Command which was unveiled on 28 June 2012. Liam O'Connor designed the memorial, built of Portland stone, which features a bronze 9-foot sculpture of seven aircrew, designed by the sculptor Philip Jackson to look as though they have just returned from a bombing operation and left their aircraft. (Author)

Lest We Forget. (Author)

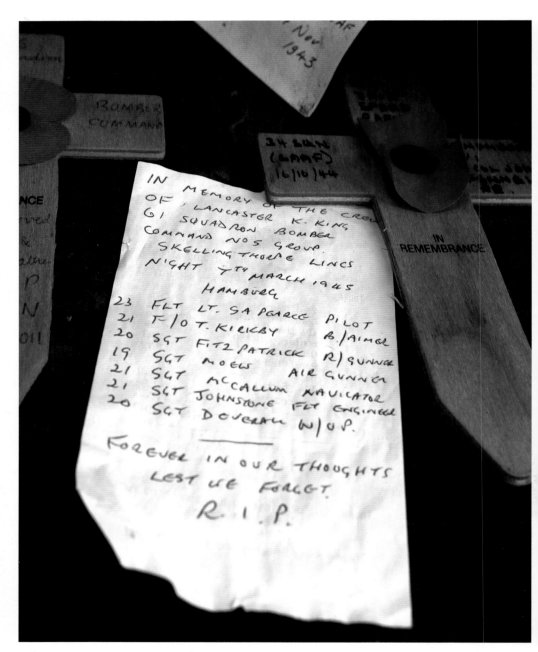

This poignant and sad note left at the Bomber Command Memorial lists Flying Officer S. P. Pearce and crew on Lancaster I NG182 on 61 Squadron at Skellingthorpe that were lost on the raid on Harburg on 7/8 March 1945 but Flying Officer Pearce and Sergeant W. K. MacCullum the navigator, survived and were taken into captivity. The men who died are Sergeant William Alexander Milne Johnstone, flight engineer; Flying Officer Thomas Hugh Burton Kirkby, bomb aimer; Sergeant Anthony John Deverell, WOp/AG; Sergeant Kenneth Leslie Mowl, air gunner and Sergeant John Fitzpatrick, rear gunner. (Author)

Opposite page: Australian tribute at the Bomber Command Memorial (Author)

The future. On a visit to the Imperial War Museum Lambeth in 2011 Arthur Burns' son Sean, on hearing that his gran's uncle flew in this type of aircraft he wanted to be photographed beside it. Arthur Burns is an associate member of 49 Squadron Association. Thirty year old Pilot Officer William Thomas Mathison flew 18 ops as a bomb aimer on 49 Squadron between 13 May and 5/6 September 1943 including two of the July Hamburg raids and Peenemünde in August. On 5 September Flight Sergeant B. W. Kirton's crew were shot down by a night fighter and ED416 'J-for Johnny' blew up. Kirton and Flying Officer B. N. Perry, navigator, survived. It is thought that more of the crew survived but were executed by the citizens of Mannheim. Mathison and the four other members of the crew are buried in Durnbach War Cemetery. (Arthur Burns)